WITHDRAWN

NARRATIVE AND DRAMATIC SOURCES OF SHAKESPEARE

Volume VIII

ROMANCES:
CYMBELINE
THE WINTER'S TALE
THE TEMPEST

NARRATIVE
AND DRAMATIC
SOURCES OF
SHAKESPEARE

Edited by
GEOFFREY BULLOUGH

Emeritus Professor of English Language and Literature,
King's College, London

Volume VIII
ROMANCES:
CYMBELINE
THE WINTER'S TALE
THE TEMPEST

LONDON: Routledge & Kegan Paul
NEW YORK: Columbia University Press

First published in 1975
by Routledge & Kegan Paul, Ltd
Broadway House, 68–74 Carter Lane
London EC4V 5EL
and Columbia University Press,
Columbia University, New York

Printed in the United States of America
10 9 8 7 6 5 4 3 2

RKP ISBN 0 7100 7895 1

CUP ISBN 0 231 08898 1

Library of Congress Catalog Card Number: 57–9969

To my wife
Margaret

PREFACE

WHEN many years ago I expressed a wish to make a large collection of Shakespeare sources and analogues I was reproved by two senior scholars of the highest repute. One said that it was supererogatory; the other that it must lead to what he called 'Teutonic pedantry'. Those were the days of textual 'revisionism', bibliographical discovery, psychoanalytic plumbing, and symbol-clashing, all useful as well as fashionable activities. 'Source-hunting' was disparaged as futile in the main, since Shakespeare's artistry did not 'abide our question'. With this I could not agree, and some excellent critics were already making new approaches to Shakespeare's reading and dramatic inheritance. So when the chance came, I seized it, though the task took much longer than, in my primal ignorance, I anticipated.

The aims of these volumes have been, not to discover new sources but to make those already known accessible to Shakespeare lovers, and in the introductory essays to indicate (however distantly) the imaginative process informing his dramatic structures. The method adopted was: to sketch the conditions in which each of the plays was written, to relate Shakespeare's treatment of plot and character to earlier versions of the same basic material, and to illustrate in some detail (more fully for the later, more complex plays) how he adapted, combined, and transcended his sources.

I confess, however, that a major driving force, besides delight in the plays themselves, has been the selfish impulse which the youthful Henry More admitted when his tutor at Christ's asked him: '"What is the Reason . . . that you so earnestly desire to know Things?" To which I instantly returned: "I desire, I say, so earnestly to know, That I may know."'

In the present volume I relate the last three comedies both to the major direct sources and, more broadly, to the romance

tradition as it survived in the Elizabethan period in such translated works as *The Mirrour of Knighthood* and *Amadis de Gaule*,
and their derivants both narrative and theatrical. All three
plays are shown to have had some topicality, not only by their
inclusion of masque-elements but also by the choice of material
bearing on events of interest to courtiers and citizens in 1609–
11.

As I worked I came to admire the detective insight and wide
reading of earlier editors and critics, whether Teutonic, Gallic,
or Anglo-Saxon, and I hope to write something on the history
of Shakespeare source-study to supplement the few remarks
on the subject in my concluding essay. This essay touches
mainly on problems such as Shakespeare's method of plot-
weaving, his 'thematic' choice of ancillary material, the
growth of his ethical interests, his discovery of the 'developing
hero', the influence of imagery from the sources.

My thanks go out to my predecessors in the field, including
Professors W. Clemen, F. Kermode, G. Wilson Knight, K.
Muir, J. M. Nosworthy, J. H. P. Pafford, F. Pyle, E. Schanzer,
V. K. Whitaker, and G. Wickham; also to Mrs M. Payne and
Mr N. H. MacMichael (Keeper of Monuments, Westminster
Abbey); to the Malone Society; and to the Trustees of the
Folger Shakespeare Library for permission to print a passage
from their copy of *Pandosto* (1592).

Finally I wish most cordially to thank the publishers and
printers of these volumes, the compositors who have had to
set some difficult texts, the editors, proof-readers, and others
involved in their production, and especially Mr Colin Frank-
lin (who planned the series), Mr Andrew Wheatcroft, and Mr
Tony Orme.

CONTENTS OF VOLUME VIII

LIST OF ABBREVIATIONS

1. Shakespeare's Works and Apocrypha

A&C	Antony and Cleopatra
Ado	Much Ado about Nothing
AFev	Arden of Feversham
AShrew	The Taming of A Shrew
AWW	All's Well That Ends Well
AYL	As You Like It
CE	Comedy of Errors
Cor	Coriolanus
Cym	Cymbeline
Ham	Hamlet
1H4	Henry the Fourth, Part I
2H4	Henry the Fourth, Part II
H5	Henry the Fifth
1H6	Henry the Sixth, Part I
2H6	Henry the Sixth, Part II
3H6	Henry the Sixth, Part III
H8	Henry the Eighth
JC	Julius Caesar
KJ	King John
LComp	Lover's Complaint
Lear	King Lear
LLL	Love's Labour's Lost
Luc	The Rape of Lucrece
Mac	Macbeth
MM	Measure for Measure
MND	A Midsummer Night's Dream
More	Sir Thomas More
MV	The Merchant of Venice
MWW	The Merry Wives of Windsor
NobKin	Two Noble Kinsmen
Oth	Othello
Per	Pericles
PhT	The Phoenix and the Turtle
PPil	The Passionate Pilgrim
R2	King Richard the Second
R3	King Richard the Third
RJ	Romeo and Juliet
Son	Sonnets
TA	Titus Andronicus
Tem	The Tempest
TGV	Two Gentlemen of Verona
Tim	Timon of Athens
TN	Twelfth Night
TrC	Troilus and Cressida
TSh	The Taming of the Shrew
VA	Venus and Adonis
WT	The Winter's Tale

2. Modern Editions and Other Works

Arden	The Arden Shakespeare (original)
Camb	The New Cambridge edition, edited by J. Dover Wilson, A. Quiller-Couch, etc.
Coll	Shakespeare's Library, ed. J. P. Collier
Conf	John Gower, Confessio Amantis
ELH	English Literary History (Johns Hopkins University, Baltimore)

List of Abbreviations

ElSt	E. K. Chambers, *The Elizabethan Stage*	*ShJb*	Jahrbuch der deutschen Shakespeare–Gesell-schaft
EngHist Soc	English Historical Society		
EngStud	*Englische Studien*	*ShLib*	*Shakespeare's Library*, 6 vols. 2nd Edn 1875, edited by J. P. Collier and W. C. Hazlitt
E Studie^r	*English Studies*		
FP	*Fratricide Punished*		
Hol.	Holinshed's *Chronicles*	*ShQ*	*Shakespeare Quarterly*
		Sh.Soc. Trans.	*Transactions of the New Shakespeare Society*
JEGP	*The Journal of English and Germanic Philology*	*SPhil*	*Studies in Philology*
Jest Books	*Shakespeare Jest Books*, edited by W. C. Hazlitt	*SpT*	*The Spanish Tragedy*
		Sh Survey	*Shakespeare Survey*
Lee	Sir Sidney Lee, *Life of Shakespeare*	*Texas*	*University of Texas Studies in English*
MalSoc	Malone Society Reprints	*TFT*	*Tudor Facsimile Texts*
MedSt	E. K. Chambers, *The Medieval Stage*	*TLS*	*The Times Literary Supplement* (London)
MLN	*Modern Language Notes*	*TR*	*The Troublesome Raigne of King John*
MLR	*The Modern Language Review*		
MPhil	*Modern Philology*	*Var.*	*The New Variorum edition*, ed. H. H. Furness, etc.
New Arden	The Arden Edition of Shakespeare (revised and reset)	*WSh*	E. K. Chambers, *William Shakespeare*
N & Q	*Notes & Queries*		
Oxf.	The Oxford Edition of Shakespeare, text by W. J. Craig; Introductory Studies by E. Dowden	**3. *Other Abbreviations***	
		Arg	Argument
		Chor	Chorus
		Prol	Prologue
PhilQ	*Philological Quarterly*	*Rev.*	Review
PMLA	Publications of the Modern Language Association of America	F	Folio edition
		n.d.	No date
		Q	Quarto edition
RES	*The Review of English Studies*	*S.R.*	The Stationers' Register
		STC	*A Short-Title Catalogue of Books printed . . . 1475–1640* (1950)
SEL	*Studies in English Literature* (Rice Institute)		

CYMBELINE

INTRODUCTION

THE date of *Cymbeline* is uncertain. It was not published until the first Folio, but it was seen by the ex-schoolmaster-magician Dr Simon Forman before 8 September 1611 when he was drowned in the Thames. Other references in Forman's journal (*Macbeth*, 20 April; *The Winter's Tale*, 15 May) were to plays seen at the Globe.[1] Probably he saw *Cymbeline* there too, but the Blackfriars Theatre, which the King's Men took over in 1609, cannot be ruled out, and some authorities have argued that the last comedies, with their ultra-romantic themes and masque-like features, were all written for the private theatre.

It seems likely that *Cymbeline* was written after *Pericles* and at about the same time as *The Winter's Tale* (1610–11), probably just before the latter, since there is a reminiscence of one of the sources of *Cymbeline* (Boccaccio) in Autolycus's threat that the old Shepherd's son should be 'flay'd alive, then 'nointed over with honey, set on the head of a wasps' nest' (IV. 4. 773–4). Noting that the name Belarius may come from Greene's Bellaria in *Pandosto*, J. M. Nosworthy concludes that perhaps 'the composition of the two plays was more or less simultaneous'.[2]

There are resemblances between *Cymbeline* and Beaumont and Fletcher's *Philaster*, performed by the King's Men before 8 October 1610, when John Davies of Hereford's *The Scourge of Folly* was entered in the Stationers' Register. An epigram in that collection compliments Fletcher on his *Love Lies Bleeding*—the sub-title of *Philaster*—apparently as a new venture. A. H. Thorndike's thesis that *Philaster* was written before *Cymbeline* and influenced Shakespeare's late manner has been much debated.[3] What evidence there is points either way. I suspect that

[1] His notes are given in *WSh*, ii, pp. 337–41.
[2] *New Arden*, p. xvi.
[3] *The Influence of Beaumont and Fletcher on Shakespeare*, Columbia U.P., New York, 1901; opposed by F. P. Wilson, *Elizabethan and Jacobean*, 1945, pp. 126–8.

3

Cymbeline came first, and that it was written for performance early in June 1610. This would leave little time for the composition of *Philaster* and for Davies to see it played before October, but that is not impossible. One must suspend judgment in the matter, failing more definite proof.

Shakespeare did not need to read or see *Philaster* before writing *Cymbeline*. He had been composing tragi-comedies for years (*Ado, AWW, MM*); he had used ingredients of the pastoral mode (*MND, AYL, TGV*), and in touching up *Pericles* (1608) had anticipated the free-flowing kind of romance he was now to write.[1] In striking out their own formula, Beaumont and Fletcher drew on Shakespeare's earlier successes, on Sidney's *Arcadia*, and on lessons learned in *The Faithful Shepherdess* (a theatrical failure).[2] There may have been mutual consultation, for in that age of collaboration, when acting-companies would gather in a tavern to read and discuss a new script,[3] there would be nothing extraordinary if the older and the younger playwrights working for the King's Men came together to exchange ideas.[4] The result is a certain resemblance in some features, with a general difference of handling. Both *Philaster* and *Cymbeline* mingle pseudo-history with romantic invention (but the politics is much more topical in the former); each contains allusions to hunting, the King's favourite sport; each has a girl disguised as a boy, a wicked mischief-making woman, a virtuous lady accused of unchastity, the contrast between a noble hero and an ignoble prince, the forbidden marriage of a princess with a commoner, movement from court to country, elements of the Masque.

A few specific parallels of detail have been noted. The names Belarius and Bellario are alike, but both may come from Bellaria in *Pandosto*, and how unlike the two characters are! There is a similar play on the meanings of 'strange', 'stranger' in *Cym* II. 1. 33–7 and *Phil.* I. 1. 77–9, both in contemptuous

---

[1] Cf. D. L. Frost, *The School of Shakespeare*, Cambridge, 1968, p. 212.
[2] Cf. E. M. Waith, *The Patterns of Tragicomedy in Beaumont and Fletcher*, Yale Studies in English, 120, New Haven, 1952, pp. 15–19; *Philaster*, ed. Andrew Gurr, 1969, xlv–lviii.
[3] Henslowe's *Diary* notes expenditure on such occasions.
[4] Cf. G. E. Bentley, 'Shakespeare and the Blackfriars Theatre', *Sh Survey 1*, 1948 pp. 38–50.

comment. Which came first we cannot tell.[1] Another resemblance occurs when Iachimo is defeated by the disguised Posthumus (V. 2. 2–6) and Philaster, having wounded Arethusa, is himself wounded by a Country Fellow.[2] The likeness of both situation and wording suggests influence, and since the Country Fellow is not otherwise involved in the plot but is invented to serve the needs of the moment, this suggests that *Philaster* was the imitation.

Another parallel comes in *Philaster* in the masque-like passage when Bellario introduces Arethusa and Philaster in wedding-garb and speaks of 'this blessed union' and calls them 'two fair cedar branches' who grew together until separated by Fortune but who are now united (V. 3. 20–44).[3] Compare this with the oracle in *Cymbeline* V. 4. 138–43, which is part of a masque-like episode. There is obviously a connection between the two.

It is of course possible that Shakespeare took over and adopted the cedar-image from *Philaster*, but the reverse is more likely. The basic idea of unity broken and regained in Bellario's speech is similar; his treatment of the cedars is different, yet he uses details which may have been suggested by the mountain-scenes in *Cymbeline*, and particularly by III. 3, where Belarius insists on their security and freedom in their cave, and Guiderius, while calling himself and his brother 'beastly', admits, 'Haply this life is best/If quiet life be best' (29–30). Compare 'O, there was none but silent quiet there'. Belarius soon afterwards likens himself to a tree stripped of fruit and leaves by 'A storm

---

[1] *Cym* II. 1. 33–7. *1st Lord.* Did you hear of a stranger that's come to court to-night? *Cloten.* A stranger, and I not know on't? *2nd Lord.* (aside) He's a strange fellow himself, and knows it not.
Philaster I. 1. 77–80. *Megra.* . . . there's a lady endures no stranger; and to me you appear a very strange fellow. *Lady.* Methinks he's not so strange; he would quickly be acquainted.
[2] *Cym* V. 2. 2–6. Iachimo says that the air of Britain enfeebles him because he has 'belied' its Princess: 'or could this carl/A very drudge of nature's have subdu'd me/ In my profession?'
Philaster IV. 5. 103–4. *Phil.* The gods take part against me, could this boor/ Have held me thus else?
[3] 'These two fair cedar branches,/The noblest of the mountain where they grew/ Straightest and tallest, under whose still shades/The worthiest beasts have made their lairs . . . O, there was none but silent quiet there! . . . /Till never-pleased Fortune shot up shrubs,/Base underbrambles to divorce these branches;/And for a while they did so and did reign/ Over the mountain and choke up his beauty/ . . . And now a gentler gale hath blown again,/That made these branches meet and twine together,/Never to be divided.'

or robbery, call it what you will'. Moreover for Bellario to
enter garlanded to play 'a more than human role',[1] though
'wanting a celestial harp', is an extraordinary turn which seems
more likely to have been a charming faraway emulation of the
divine intervention in *Cymbeline* than a source of inspiration for
the elder dramatist's conventional vision, whose origins we
shall find elsewhere. This episode points to Shakespeare as the
leader and Beaumont and Fletcher as his followers. But it is
not decisive.

A reading of the two plays soon shows that their differences
in aim, tone, and technique are more important than their
likenesses. As H. S. Wilson wrote, *Cymbeline* is 'more old-fashioned
in method, more complicated, and altogether more ambitious', dependent on dramatic irony, 'the gratification of
expectancy rather than of the shock of surprise';[2] and it uses
more traditional stage devices. *Philaster* is simpler in outline
and characterization, melodramatic, dependent on 'swift
emotional dialogue and clever plot', sudden turns of situation
and of motives not always consistent with what has gone before.
Obviously *Philaster*, if not a source, is an analogue of *Cymbeline*;
but I have not thought it necessary (even if there were space)
to give long excerpts from it here, since it is easily accessible
in a modern edition.

The theatres were closed because of plague from August
1608 to December 1609. The great event of 1610 at Court was
the investiture of Prince Henry as Prince of Wales, which
took place between 31 May and 6 June amid great rejoicings
and many entertainments, including Daniel's masque *Tethys'
Festival*, in which the royal family took part and the Queen as
Tethys said that she had visited Milford Haven,

> The happy Port of Union, which gave way
> To the great hero Henry and his fleete—

referring to Henry Richmond's landing there when he came to
dethrone Richard III. Shakespeare's use of Milford Haven as
the landing-place for Posthumus and the Roman army may be

---

[1] Cf. Gurr, *op. cit.*, V. 3. 41n.
[2] H. S. Wilson, '*Philaster* and *Cymbeline*', *English Inst. Essays, 1951*, New York, 1952,
pp. 162–3. Quoted by Gurr, p. xlix.

a reminiscence of this, as Professor Glynne Wickham has claimed, in pointing out that *Cymbeline*, 'with its British princess, its two British princes brought out of Wales, and the repeated references to Milford Haven', would be a very suitable subject for the festivities at the installation of the Prince of Wales.[1] He regards *The Winter's Tale* as even more suitable. I disagree with him here, but believe that *Cymbeline* may well have been composed, or adapted, for production at that time. Milford Haven may have been used by Shakespeare mainly to avoid having Dover again after *King Lear*, and in order to fit in with Imogen's adventures in the Welsh mountains, but the Welsh setting would be apt, and, as I shall indicate later, other evidence points to the installation-season.

That Shakespeare wrote most of this play has rarely been denied, but judges such as Pope, Dowden, Chambers, and Dover Wilson have rejected part or all of the vision in V. 4. because of its crudity and doggerel. Most of it is indeed poor stuff, in an obsolete style; but this may have been deliberate, and the speeches of Jupiter and Posthumus on waking are of higher quality. The vision has less dramatic function than that in *Pericles* V. 1, but the prophetic 'book' resembles the oracle in *The Winter's Tale*, and there are Shakespearian images here and there during the scene. Shakespeare's prophets and oracles often speak mediocre verse, and although the ghosts here are more banal than usual I see no reason to bring in another playwright.

Cymbeline belongs to a definite tradition of plays in which a faint historical flavour was given to romantic material by the use of names and incidents from the Chronicles.[2] Extant pieces of this kind included Dekker's *Old Fortunatus* and the anonymous *The Love-sick King*. Such plays had less historical basis than the old *King Leir* or *A Knack to Know a Knave*, where the chronicle material, though slight, was respected. Titles of lost plays in Henslowe's *Diary* suggest that there were many others.

According to Geoffrey of Monmouth and succeeding

[1] 'Shakespeare's Investiture Play', *TLS*, 18 Dec. 1969, 1456. See also his *Shakespeare's Dramatic Heritage*, 1969, pp. 249–65.
[2] See my essay, 'Pre-Conquest themes in Elizabethan Drama', in *Medieval Literature and Civilization*, ed. D. A. Pearsall and R. A. Waldron, 1969.

writers Cymbeline (Cunobellus) lived shortly after Julius
Caesar, becoming King in 33 B.C., and reigned for thirty-five
years. So he was King at the time of Christ's birth. Enough is
known about him to convince G. M. Trevelyan that, unlike
Lear, Shakespeare's Cymbeline 'was no myth . . . And so far
(ruled) in the south of the island, as to style himself, on his
silver coinage, "Rex Brittonum".'[1] These coins are of excellent
design and it may be that a tomb excavated at Lexden Park
near Colchester in 1926 was Cymbeline's. The objects dug up
included a small silver head of the Emperor Augustus, probably cut from a coin and mounted in silver in a circular frame.[2]
One recalls that Cymbeline had been 'nurtured in the household of Augustus Caesar'.

Apparently Augustus freed him from the requirement of
annual tribute, but, later, either in his reign or in that of his
son Guiderius, payment was demanded, and, when the Britons
refused, the Romans invaded Britain and were defeated twice
before the Britons agreed to obey [Text ID].

According to Spenser (*The Faerie Queene*, II. x. 50–1) Kimbe-
line succeeded Tenantius

> What time th'eternall Lord in fleshly slime
> Enwombed was, from wretched Adams line
> To purge away the guilt of sinfull crime.

Spenser asserted that Cymbeline refused tribute and was
attacked by the Emperor Claudius. He was slain in battle by a
traitor in disguise, but Arviragus (his brother) carried on the
struggle and

> Did drive the Romanes to the weaker side,
> That they to peace agreed. So all was pacifide.

Shakespeare set the play in the reign of Augustus.

The Mirror for Magistrates had two versions of the story,
with Guiderius as the hero. That by Thomas Blennerhasset in
the 1578 edition was written when, in Guernsey on military

[1] *History of England*, 1952 edn, p. 17.
[2] C. M. Matthews, 'The True Cymbeline', *History Today*, vii, 1957, 755–9. For the
legend as a whole see J. S. P. Tatlock, *The Legendary History of Britain*, Berkeley,
1950, pp. 381–3.

duties, he had no chronicles with him, so he used his invention more than his memory and made Guidericus defeat huge Roman armies and challenge Claudius to single combat.[1]

The 1587 *Mirror* had another poem, by Thomas Higgins, which followed Geoffrey of Monmouth's account. Higgins also wrote 'tragedies' of Nennius, Isenglas and Julius Caesar, which, like *Cymbeline*, insist on the difficulty found by the Romans in overcoming the British defences, both geographical and human. Thus in Higgins's *Julius Caesar* the Roman general was defied by Cassibellane 'Through counsaile . . . of all the nobles' when he had 'shew'd them what their auncestors had bene' (cf. III. 1. 17–18). As in Holinshed and other chroniclers, Caesar's ships were battered and in danger of being wrecked on the sands and rocks, and Caesar admitted:

> I have no cause of Britayne conquest for to boast,,
> Of all the regions first and last with whom I werd.

And in *Nennius* Higgins repeated that

> . . . Caesar he for all his bragge and boste
> Flew back to shippes.[2]

The council in *Cymbeline* III. 1, where the Queen and Cloten defy the Roman emissary, recalls the councils of Higgins's Cassibellane and Blennerhasset's Guidericus (Campbell, pp. 196, 387), and, as Prof. H. Brooks has shown,[3] the speeches contain echoes of *The Mirror*. The allusion to 'Our ancestor . . . that Mulmutius which/Ordain'd our laws' (III. 1. 56–7) need not come from *The Mirror*, for he was well known as the maker of the 'four great roads' of Britain, and the framer of laws which were later Englished by Alfred the Great. He was the son of Cloten, King of Cornwall, who ruled badly after the deaths of Ferrex and Porrex (Holinshed, I, Ch. XXII). The Admiral's Men had a play about him by William Rankine in 1598. They also had one on King Lud, founder of London, referred to at III. 1. 32 and V. 5. 481.

[1] L. B. Campbell, *Parts Added to the Mirror for Magistrates*, 1946, p. 386.
[2] *Op. cit.*, pp. 191, 290, 311. Nennius was Cassibellane's brother, and Higgins makes him (not Cassibellane, as the Queen says in III. 1. 31–2) fight hand-to-hand with Julius Caesar. Cf. Geoffrey, Bk IV, Ch. 3.
[3] *New Arden*, App. A(d).

In its historical aspect the play was intended to celebrate not only British defiance of Rome but also British friendship with Rome. Brut was a kinsman of Aeneas, so Romans and Britons were related. For Prince Edward in *Richard III*, Julius Caesar was the famous man who had built the Tower of London. Unlike his infamous Queen, Cymbeline sees no great shame in paying tribute and, having defeated the world-conquerors, he nobly submits (V. 5. 460–5).

Posthumus's disguise in battle had precedents in British history. According to Geoffrey of Monmouth Mulmutius Dunwallow made six hundred of his men don the armour of slain enemies in order to penetrate their ranks and charge the hostile leaders [Text IB]. Shakespeare's source was probably the story of the Roman Hamo who in a battle against Guiderius disguised himself as a Briton and pretended to fight on their side until he got near enough to Guiderius to kill him. The dramatist would read about this not only in Holinshed [Text ID], but also in Higgins's complaint of 'Guiderius'. Fabyan and Geoffrey asserted that Arviragus avenged his brother by killing Hamo beside a haven, and Grafton, followed by Higgins, wrote that his body was hewed into small pieces and thrown 'into the waters'. So Cloten's head is cast 'into the creek behind our rock'. The severing of his head is necessary so that Imogen may think his body to be that of her husband. In later English history Harold Harefoot, the unworthy bastard of Canute, had his head cut off by Hardicanute and thrown into the Thames.

Shakespeare picked up the name Cloten from reading about Mulmutius Dunwallow. Other names also came from the chronicles: Brut's grandfather was Silvius Posthumus; his wife was Innogen—and this may even be the name Shakespeare gave his heroine.[1] In *Much Ado*, another play in which the hero was turned against the heroine by false report, the first Quarto (1600) stage directions mentioned Innogen as the wife of Leonato, though she was given nothing to say. Coming again on the name Innogen may have brought Leonato to Shakespeare's mind and caused him to combine that name with Posthumus when he had to compose an honourable descent

---

[1] 'Innogen' became 'Imogen', 'Ymogen' in two versions of R. Higdon's *Polychronicon*. Cf. the edn by C. Babington, 1869, ii, pp. 444–5.

for his hero and to explain how he came to be living at the King's court and able to meet the Princess.

As Professor J. P. Brockbank points out,[1] when Brut and Innogen reached Logetia they consulted an oracle to find where they should go next. Brut fell asleep and in a vision the goddess Diana told him (in Latin verses) to seek an island beyond Gaul [Text IA]. This incident may have influenced Shakespeare when he decided to introduce divine intervention, as in *Pericles*.

The 'historic' material in *Cymbeline* is very slight; yet it is important. The romance tradition mingled royalty, nobles, commoners and peasants, combining heroic with erotic, idyllic and fantastic elements. Here the Romano-British setting was intended to add epic atmosphere to a plot of domestic intrigue, raising the rank of the principal characters and blending court-life, international politics and war with a tale of jealousy and feminine endurance. It enabled Posthumus to show courage and resource, and it made possible the introduction of ethical topics interesting to Shakespeare. More of this later.

In the battle in which Guiderius was killed, according to Geoffrey and later chroniclers, Arviragus dressed himself in his brother's armour and 'hurried here and there, cheering on his men to stand their ground as though he had been Guiderius himself. The Britons, taking fresh courage from his urging, stood firm and battled on, doing great slaughter upon the enemy until the latter broke and fled' (Geoffrey; cf. *infra*, p. 45). Seeking a substitute for this incident Shakespeare drew on his reading for *Macbeth*, and adapted the story of Hay and his two sons who, in a battle against the Danes, prevented the Scots from fleeing and so converted defeat into victory [Text II].

By including this incident, the dramatist was paying a tribute to one of the King's oldest friends, Sir James Hay, who had been made a life-baron in 1606 and became a Knight of the Bath on 4 June 1610, at the installation of the Prince of Wales.[2]

---

[1] 'History and Histrionics in *Cymbeline*', *Sh Survey 11*, 1958, 42–9.
[2] Hay had married Honora Denny on 6 January 1607 after several years' courtship owing to her father's disapproval. Hay was good-natured but extravagant. The King ennobled the prospective father-in-law and paid the bridegroom's debts. Hay became Earl of Carlisle in 1622. His cousin George was a Gentleman of the Bedchamber in Scotland (1596), and was knighted in 1609, becoming Earl

The Hays came of Anglo-Norman stock, but prided themselves on their descent from the yeoman hero of the Battle of Loncarty, and their armorial bearings testified to this.[1] The King and his courtiers would recognize the Hay ancestry in the feat of Belarius and the two boys. If *Cymbeline* were performed during the installation festivities, the allusion would be especially fitting. The play may have been written for that occasion.

Paul Reyher's suggestion that *Cymbeline* was written after July 1610, when Arabella Stuart and William Seymour were imprisoned when their long love-affair culminated in marriage, needs little rebuttal.[2] Here was a Princess marrying a commoner against the royal will—as in the play. But it would have been most unwise for any King's Company dramatist to touch on this affair, especially soon after its climax. As E. K. Chambers pointed out, this makes it likely that *Cymbeline* was written before July 1610 (*WSh*, i, p. 485).

The wager-story basic to *Cymbeline* is almost as widespread in folk-lore and literature as the 'terrible bargain' of *Measure for Measure*.[3] In Old French there were several variants. In the popular verse-romance *Le Comte de Poitiers* (thirteenth century), the Duke of Normandy wagers his lands against Poitou, who finds the wife entirely virtuous and so bribes her nurse to give him a ring and some of her mistress's hair. The jealous husband tries to kill his wife, but a lion saves her. The Count wanders disguised as a pilgrim until he discovers the trick played on him. He fights the villain, who confesses before dying. This gives the general pattern of the legend.

Roman de la Violette (also thirteenth century) is more chivalric in tone. Gerard's praise of his wife Oriant is challenged by

of Kinnoull in 1633. Another member of the family, Francis Hay, 9th Earl of Errol, was a papist and in 1608 was imprisoned at Dumbarton for religious contumacy.

[1] The Errol arms included a falcon, and had as supporters two uncouth men bearing on their shoulders two oxen yokes. Motto: *Serva jugum* (Sir Robert Douglas, *The Peerage of Scotland*, ed. J. P. Wood, 1813 edn, vol. i, p. 544). The Kinnoulls had as crest 'A countryman couped at the knees, vested grey, his waistcoat gules and bonnet azure, and bearing on his right shoulder an oxen-yoke proper. The supporters were two countrymen habited as in the crest, the dexter holding over his shoulder the coulter, and the sinister the paddle of a plough. Motto: *Renovate animos*' (Sir J. B. Paul, *The Scots Peerage*, Edinburgh, 1908, vol. v, pp. 216–39).

[2] P. Reyher, 'The Date of Cymbeline', *Rev. Anglo-Américaine*, June 1925.

[3] The theme has been discussed by Gaston Paris, *La Littérature française au moyen âge*, Paris, 1888, p. 83.

Liziart. She scorns Liziart's wooing, but her maid lets him see her in her bath, and he notes a birthmark like a violet on her right breast. Oriant is saved by a serpent from death at the hands of her husband.

In *Dou Roi Flore et de la Bielle Jehane*[1] the husband is a squire, Robin, who wagers on his wife's virtue with a knight, Sir Raoul. The latter sees her in her bath and convinces Robin by describing the marks on her body. Robin rejects her and wanders away. Jehane follows him disguised as a youth and serves him faithfully for seven years before he discovers her innocence. She reveals herself only after Robin has defeated Raoul. When Robin dies she marries King Florus.

A dramatic version appeared in one of the fourteenth-century Miracles de Notre Dame, *Comment Ostes, roy d'Espagne perdi sa terre par gager contre Berengier.*[2] The wife is Denise. Berengier bribes an attendant to drug her mistress so that he may see the secret token she carries—a bone from one of her husband's toes! The rejected Queen becomes a soldier; her husband, having lost his lands, goes over to the Saracens.

J. P. Collier noted parallels in this piece to Shakespeare's.[3] Berengier boasts that he could possess any woman living. 'If I could speak to her twice, at the third time I could have all my desire' (cf. *Cym*, I. 4. 108–9), and he tells Denise that in Rome her husband 'who does not rate you as highly as a cherry stone, has taken up with a girl whom he holds so dear that he does not know how to part from her' (cf. I. 7. 63–77, where Posthumus is said to mock at fidelity).[4]

The tale takes on a middle-class flavour in Boccaccio's *Decameron*, Day 2, Novella 9, where the protagonists are Italian merchants [Text III]. The villain, Ambrogiuolo, gets into Ginevra's bedchamber in a chest and steals a ring, a purse,

---

[1] Cf. R. Ohle, *Shakespeares Cymbeline und seine romanischen Vorläufer*, Leipzig, 1890.
[2] Given in L. L. N. Monmerqué and F. Michel, *Théâtre français au moyen âge*, Paris, 1842.
[3] *ShLib*, 2 vols, 1843.
[4] Iachimo's gambit was a commonplace. In G. Buchanan's *Franciscanus* (c. 1538), the speaker gives advice on seducing women whose husbands are away: 'If the first attack has failed to open the citadel, do not be defeated through timidity, but press the attack. Express your pity for the widowed woman, and enlarge on the fact that while she occupies a solitary bed the husband passes his night in company with a harlot.' Cf. W. Theobald, *The Classical Element in the Shakespearean Plays*, 1909, pp. 118–19.

a girdle and a gown. Bernabò, the husband, is convinced, not by these, but by the description of a mole with golden hairs under his wife's left breast. He orders a servant to kill Ginevra, but the servant helps her to escape in male clothes. Ginevra has adventures in the eastern Mediterranean, rising to high office under the Sultan of Alexandria. Discovering Ambrogiuolo's villainy, she brings him and her husband together. She is reunited to Bernabò, and Ambrogiuolo is punished by a cruel death.[1] From this version stemmed many others.[2]

In Spain Juan Timoneda's fifteenth story in his collection *El Patrañuelo* set the scene in Candia among merchants. The villain, Falacio, unable even to get a glimpse of Finea, bribes Crispina, an old woman who goes in and out of the house, to procure a description of Finea's bedchamber and the secret signs of her person. The woman cuts a few hairs from a mole on Finea's shoulder. Casiodoro, the husband, cannot bring himself to kill his wife outright, but maroons her on a desert island. She finds male clothing, is taken aboard a vessel to Cyprus, where, calling herself Pedro, she becomes the King's chief accountant before returning to Candy where she becomes the King's chancellor. Meanwhile her husband has ill-treated her father, whose plea comes before Pedro. By threat of torture she forces Casiodoro to tell his story; Falacio is tortured into confession. At a royal feast Finea dons woman's dress and reveals her identity, obtaining mercy for her husband. 'Of this story,' writes Timoneda, 'a comedy has been written called *Eufemia*.'

Lope de Rueda wrote this comedy, which Timoneda published in 1567.[3] In it de Rueda showed some individuality,

[1] For analogues see K. Mechel, *Die Historie von vier Kaufmännern*, Halle, 1914; also W. F. Thrall, '*Cymbeline*, Boccaccio and the Wager Story in England', *SPhil*, xxviii, 1931, 639–51.
[2] George Whetstone got from Bandello a version in which the offended lady turned the tables on her tempters. He told in long-drawn couplets of a Bohemian Lady Barbara whose husband, Ulrico, laid a wager on her virtue with two Hungarian nobles. The first comer she imprisoned and made him spin for his food; the second she made reel off the thread spun by his fellow-sinner. (*The Rocke of Regard* (1576), Bk 3, 'The Arbour of Vertue'.)
[3] *Las Primeras dos elegantes y graciosas Comedias del excellente Poeta y representante Lope de Rueda: sacadas a luz por Juan Timoneda*, Valencia, 1567. Cf. *Obras de Lope de Rueda*, 2 vols, Madrid, 1908.

substituting for the heroine's wanderings in male disguise a climax nearer to *All's Well* or *Measure for Measure*. The heroine (unmarried) has a brother, Leonardo, who goes off to seek his fortune and finds a noble and generous employer in Valiano. He so praises the beauty and virtue of his sister that Valiano resolves to send for her, with the intention of making her his wife. Paulo, the servant who goes for her, is so jealous of Leonardo's familiarity with his master that he returns without her, declaring that she is a loose woman, for he himself has slept with her and obtained a token, some hair from a mole on her shoulder. Actually he has never met Eufemia, but by pretending to be in love with her has persuaded her naïve maid Cristina to procure the trophy for him.

Enraged by Leonardo's apparent attempt to entrap him into a bad marriage, Valiano orders him to be imprisoned, and to be executed within a few weeks. Leonardo writes an impassioned letter to Eufemia accusing her of lewd behaviour with a stranger. Cristina confesses her folly and Eufemia hastens with her to Valencia, where they appeal to Valiano's justice and, confronting Paulo, prove that he has never even seen Eufemia. Paulo is condemned to death, Leonardo is restored to his post, and Valiano looks forward to marrying Eufemia.

This is a prose play in eight scenes with no sub-plot but several interpolated comic scenes to eke out a scanty story. Rueda does not show Paulo's attempts to get access to Eufemia or his persuading Cristina to get him a love-token. The weight of the action falls on three scenes: that in which Paulo returns and bears false witness; that in which Eufemia reads her brother's letter, and the excellent final scene in which she makes Paulo bear witness against himself. On the whole it is a clumsy play, much less effective than de Rueda's *Los Engañados*, which I have already referred to as a distant analogue of *Twelfth Night* (*supra*, II, p. 273). But its naturalistic approach is unusual. I give a translation of some scenes [Text V].

A version of the wager-story was made in Germany in the late fifteenth century, *Historie von vier Kaufmännern* (Tale of Four Merchants), in which the heroine takes the name Frederyke of Jennen (Genoa). Printed at Nuremberg in 1478 and four times again by 1510, the piece became well known in the Netherlands, Scandinavia and Britain. Hans Sachs used it and

Boccaccio's tale for a comedy in 1548. An English translation
of *Frederyke of Jennen* was printed in 1518 at Antwerp; soon an
edition appeared in England, and another in 1560.[1] It is a
verbose expansion of Boccaccio's succinct narrative, omitting
some of his details but adding new ones.[2]

Shakespeare, like Sachs, seems to have drawn on both
Boccaccio and *Frederyke of Jennen* for *Cymbeline*. Apparently,
however, there was no English translation of the *Decameron*
before that of 1620—which John Florio may have made.[3]
Shakespeare may have known enough Italian to read the
original, or have used the French version by Antoine le Macon,
(Lyons, 1558, etc.) as he probably did for *All's Well*.[3] I give
below the whole of Boccaccio's tale in the 1620 version, and all
of *Frederyke of Jennen* [Text IV].

It has often been stated that Shakespeare must have known
Boccaccio's story because in *The Winter's Tale* IV. 3. 794–802
he makes Autolycus threaten the Shepherd's son with the
punishment accorded to Boccaccio's villain, which is not found
in *Frederyke of Jennen*.

The likeness has been used to prove that *The Winter's Tale*
was written soon after *Cymbeline*. I believe this to be true, and
Boccaccio may have called up a distant memory in Shakespeare, but he had already used for the punishment of Aaron
in *Titus Andronicus* (V. 3. 179–83) a milder version of this
punishment, which he would find in the popular prose tale
on that theme. He would also find it in Apuleius's *The Golden
Asse* (trans. Adlington, 1566, Bk VII, Ch. 35).[4]

The play shares numerous other features with Boccaccio and
not with *Frederyke*. They include:

[1] Cf. W. F. Thrall, '*Cymbeline*, Boccaccio and the Wager Story in England', *SPhil*,
xxviii, 1931, 639–51. With later versions we are not concerned. A story in *Westward
for Smelts* was formerly thought to be Shakespeare's source; but the book was not
registered in *S. R.*, or published, till 1620.
[2] See Josef Raith's edn in *Aus Schrifttum und Sprache der Angel-Sachsen*, vol. iv, Leipzig, 1936. Raith used the 1560 edn, as I have done, with some alterations in
punctuation.
[3] H. G. Wright, 'How did Shakespeare come to know the *Decameron*?', *MLR*,
xlix, 1955, 45–8; and *Boccaccio in England from Chaucer to Tennyson*, 1957.
[4] 'The Master . . . tooke his servant . . . and . . . annointed his body with honey,
and then bound him sure to a fig-tree, where in a rotten stocke a great number of
Pismares had builded their neasts; the Pismares after they had felt the sweetness
of the honey came upon his body, and by little and little . . . devoured his flesh,
in such sort that there remained on the tree but his bare bones.'

(i) Talk about the wife as a special grace from God. Bernabò says that she was given to him 'di spezial gracia di Dio', and when Ambrogiuolo mockingly asks him if the Emperor had given him the special privilege of a virtuous wife, he answers that 'not the Emperor, but God, whose power is a little greater than the Emperor's had granted him this grace'.[1] In *Cymbeline* Posthumus calls Imogen 'the gift of the Gods . . . Which by their graces I will keep' (I. 4. 89–92).

(ii) The bedroom scene, with its taper by the bed, the pictures, arras, etc. (II. 2. 19–27) is closer to the Italian than to the German story.

(iii) In Boccaccio the other merchants 'earnestly laboured to break the wager' (cf. *Cym* I. 4. 104; 152, where Philario tries to avoid it).

(iv) In Boccaccio and the play there is some discussion about the terms of the wager (I. 4. 132–60), and the terms are formally set down in writing. In *Frederyke* the wager is made without discussion or written agreement. The host is stakeholder.

(v) Boccaccio's Ginevra has 'under her left breast a mole, round which were some soft hairs, fair as gold'.[2] At II. 2. 37 Iachimo sees it 'On her left breast', but later (II. 4. 133–8) he says, 'under her breast . . . lies a mole, right proud/Of that most delicate lodging', which comes nearer to the *Decameron*. *Frederyke* has: 'on that [left] arme she had a blacke wart.'

(vi) The hero is not alone when the villain claims the forfeit. In Boccaccio, Ambrogiuolo calls the merchants together, so that Bernabò is publicly humiliated. In *Cymbeline*, Philario is present. In *Frederyke* John calls Ambrosius aside 'that ye sholde not be a shamed'.

(vii) There is talk about servants being corrupted, though it is differently applied by Boccaccio and Shakespeare. In the former the husband says that Ambrogiuolo's description of Ginevra's room and his possession of her things might have been obtained by bribing a servant. He is convinced only by hearing of the mole and its golden hairs. Posthumus first

[1] Where the 1620 translation departs from Boccaccio I give a closer translation of the latter in these passages.
[2] Perhaps Boccaccio's description of the mole suggested the Shakespeare image of the cowslip, a yellow flower.

accepts, then rejects, Philario's suggestion that the bracelet
was stolen by a servant, 'being corrupted'. Her attendants are
(he says) 'all sworn and honourable' (II. 4. 113–26).

(viii) The husband sends a letter bidding his wife meet him
outside the city (cf. *Cym* III. 2).

There are, however, many details in common between
Cymbeline and *Frederyke of Jennen* which suggest that Shakespeare knew the latter as well as Boccaccio's tale:

(i) Men of different nations are present when the wager is
made. In *Frederyke* they are a Spaniard, a Frenchman, and two
Italians (a Florentine—the villain, and a Genoese—the hero).
In *Cymbeline* Shakespeare has a Roman (Philario), a Briton
(Posthumus), another Italian (Iachimo), a Frenchman, a
Dutchman and a Spaniard. The last two do not speak but
preserve the cosmopolitan nature of the gathering. In Boccaccio
the merchants are all Italians.

(ii) The villain suggests the wager. John in *Frederyke* does
so as soon as Ambrosius (because his wife is chaste) refuses to
'break his wedlock'. In *Cymbeline* a long discussion culminates
in Iachimo's challenge to Posthumus (I. 4. 50–118). Note too
that neither Ambrosius nor Posthumus starts by bragging of his
wife's fidelity, whereas in Boccaccio Bernabò expatiates on her
fine qualities and offers to wager his head against a thousand
ducats.

(iii) There is preliminary talk between the wife and her
would-be seducer. In *Frederyke* he quickly realizes by 'her swete
words and womanly behavioure' that he cannot win her.
Shakespeare invents a long and revealing interview.[1] In
Boccaccio her reputation is enough to convince Ambrogiuolo
that she is invincible.

(iv) In Boccaccio the wife has a little girl in bed with her.
No child is mentioned in *Frederyke* or *Cymbeline*.

(v) In *Frederyke* John says, 'Now have I sene a privy token
whereby he shall byleve me that I have had my pleasure of his
wyfe.' Cf. *Cym* II. 2. 40–2: 'this secret/ Will force him think I

---

[1] Iachimo here resembles the knight in *The Erle of Toulouse* who, when rebuked for
his treachery in trying to seduce her, replies, 'In me ye may full well trust ay. /I
did nothing but you to affray.'

have pick'd the lock and ta'en/ The treasure of her honour.'
His thoughts are not expressed by Boccaccio.

(vi) The husband requires his servant to produce proof of
his wife's death: in *Frederyke*, 'for a token your tongue and a
locke of your heere'. Cf. *Cym* III. 4. 125–7: 'some bloody sign
. . . for 'tis commanded/ I should do so'. In Boccaccio the
husband accepts her garments and the story that she has been
slain and then eaten by wolves.

(vii) The husband regrets that he has had his wife killed
hastily; in *Frederyke* 'that he spake not with her . . . to examine
her'; in *Cym* V. 1 so that she might repent, and because she did
not deserve death; he still loves her. Boccaccio's Bernabò
shows no remorse: 'his constant avouching of her treason' was
held by others to justify her punishment.

Some other resemblances noted between *Frederyke* and *Cymbeline* are trivial; but two seem significant:

(viii) In *Frederyke* the wife has 'a girdle of fyne golde set with
costly perles and stoones'. This may have suggested the bracelet
stolen by Iachimo (II. 2. 33). Her 'rynge with a point of
diamond' may have suggested the diamond ring which she
gives to Posthumus, of which much is made in the wager-
scene.

(ix) The wife in *Frederyke* 'came to Secant to an haven'.
The word 'haven' may have suggested 'Milford Haven' to
Shakespeare when he had decided to introduce Britons and
Wales into his plot. Boccaccio's Ginevra 'went to the sea-
coast' (*verso il mare*).

Since Shakespeare wished to place his Italian story of
feminine suffering and male folly in ancient Britain, he could
hardly utilize the Oriental and Moslem setting given by his
two main sources for the later adventures of his hero and
heroine. Moreover, the rise of Frederyke to be 'lorde and
defender of the Kynges realm' in Alcairo (Cairo), winner of
his battles and governor of his people for twelve years was not
in accordance with the idea of Imogen as a patient Griselda
or a sister of Marina in *Pericles*. He substituted the popular
medieval theme by which the ill-used woman wanders in
search of her man into a pastoral setting and there finds

solace and help until she can be reinstated. The theme was already in *Two Gentlemen of Verona* and *As You Like It*, and in the latter play it was already associated with a contrast between court and country, true and false nobility. Like Lear, Imogen will flee into the wilds, but whereas Lear found the elements in league against him, she will find some peace in the Welsh mountains.

Wales as a place for exiles was no novelty. In the romance *Sir Bevis of Hampton*[1] the child (like Hamlet) upbraided his mother for betraying his father, who had also been murdered by her paramour. She ordered his uncle to kill the boy. The uncle killed a pig and smeared his nephew's clothes with its blood as evidence of the murder. He clothed Bevis in mean attire and set him to tend sheep, promising to send him into Wales, where a relative would rear him up to avenge his father. Other misadventures, however, prevented the journey. The mountains were a natural refuge for fugitives but were regarded as terrible places. In *1 Henry IV* the King, in refusing to ransom Mortimer, showed the opinion held of Wales as a wild desolate region: 'No, on the barren mountains let him starve' (I. 3. 89); and this was thought to have been Glendower's fate after eluding English soldiers for years. In Fletcher's *Bonduca*, a play influenced by Shakespeare, the fleeing Caratacus and the boy Hergo are seen starving among the rocks. There were not many purely 'mountain pastorals', though goatherds from the hills traditionally debated with shepherds in the lusher valleys. But in Bandello's story of Don Diego, that knight, piqued by the cruelty of Ginevra, became a hermit in the Pyrenees.[2] There, although life was hard, the surroundings were not unpleasant, and Bandello gave a full account of how Don Diego and his servant made themselves comfortable in the wilderness [Text VI].

In *Cymbeline* Belarius and the two young princes have lived happily in the Welsh mountains for twenty years, climbing the heights and hunting the deer (III. 3). For a banished man to take children into the wilds was not uncommon in romances. The tale in *Decameron* preceding that of Bernabò (II. 8) tells

---

[1] Printed first by R. Pynson (*c.* 1503), later by W. Copland (*c.* 1565) and T. East (*c.* 1582). There was another edition in 1609–10.
[2] Translated by G. Fenton in *Certaine Tragicall Discourses*, 1567.

of the Count d'Angier who, accused by his overlord's wife of attempting to ravish her, took his son (aged nine) and his daughter (aged seven) as beggars to London, where the girl was adopted by a kind lady. D'Angier then travelled with his son to Wales, where the boy was taken in by a nobleman. This has been claimed as a source,[1] but with little cogency. The Spanish romance *The Knight of the Sun* has boy and girl twins (Floralisa and Celindo) who are reared like Guiderius and Arviragus. Floralisa says:

> What I think best of all is not to know who I am nor of what family, for I have been fed and brought up in a wood with my brother, without any converse or human society saving that of a wise man who has hitherto fed and reared us, and who taught us all that we could comprehend. We regarded him as our father until he told us the contrary. (Bk VIII, 17)[2]

This is unlikely to have influenced Shakespeare. In giving Imogen an unequal marriage and adventures in the wilds he may well have recalled an old play, *The Rare Triumphes of Love and Fortune* (1589),[3] which belongs to the same class of romantic drama as *Mucedorus*. Indeed, this play has so many minor points of resemblance to *Cymbeline* that it is tempting to regard it as an influence on Shakespeare, by contra-suggestion rather than by direct imitation.[4]

In *The Rare Triumphes*, Act I is taken up with a quarrel in heaven between the goddesses of Love and Fortune about their powers over men. Jupiter allows them to show their sovereignties over two lovers, Hermione (male) and Fidelia:

> Venus, for that they love thy sweet delight,
> Thou shalt endeavour to encrease their joy:
> And Fortune thou to manifest thy might,
> Their pleasures and their pastimes thou shalt destroye.

So this is a play of true affection crossed by circumstance, with divine intervention.

---

[1] By S. Levy, *Anglia*, vii, 1884, 120–7.
[2] Cf. J. de Perott, *ShJb*, xlv, 1909, 228–9.
[3] Ed. W. W. Greg, *MalSoc*, 1930. Also in Dodsley's *Old Plays*, vi.
[4] *New Arden*, xxiv–xxvi.

At the beginning of Act II Hermione and the Princess Fidelia discuss whether absence should excite doubts or jealousy in lovers' minds (cf. *Cym* I. 3. 25–30). Fidelia has a brutal brother Armenio (perhaps the original of Cloten) who upbraids Hermione, 'a foundling', for daring to love the Princess. Her father King Phyzantius banishes Hermione for the same reason. We learn that as a child Hermione was given to the King by a hermit, and has been brought up at court (cf. Posthumus). Fidelia is ordered to choose a husband from the other courtiers. There are obvious resemblances to the first Act of *Cymbeline* here, but they cease when the treacherous Penulo, after promising Hermione that he will bring Fidelia 'to the cave/ Where whilome lovers we were wont to meet', betrays him to Armenio.

Act II, however, may have a distant parallel to Belarius in the hermit Bomelio, who has been banished through the villainous plots of his 'fawning freendes' and has lived in the woods for five years. Unlike Belarius he hates his condition and laments dismally in poulter's measure before sending his servant Lentulo to market to buy the things they need. Fidelia comes into the wood mourning for Hermione, but is pursued by Armenio and (unlike Imogen) is forced to return home. Bomelio uses magic arts to strike Armenio dumb. When Hermione enters seeking Fidelia, Bomelio welcomes him to his 'darksome den' and tells him that he is his son, whom he gave to the King twelve years ago to ensure for him a noble's upbringing. Fantastic incidents follow. Bomelio goes mad when his interfering son destroys his magic books. At the beginning of Act V Jupiter sends word by Mercury to Venus and Fortune that since they have both proved their power they must now join to make the lovers happy. So when Phyzantius is led to where Hermione and Fidelia are together in the wood and exiles the young man on pain of death, 'Venus and Fortune show themselves' and command him to let them marry. Armenio's dumbness and Bomelio's madness are cured by a drop of blood from the tender breast of Fidelia, and Venus sums up:

> Now every thing united is by love:
> Now Gods and men are reconciled againe;

and Fortune moralizes:

> Thus, for amendes of this your late unrest,
> By Love and Fortune ye shall all be blest.
> And thus heerof this inward care I have,
> That wisdome ruleth Love and Fortune both.
> Though riches faile and beauty seeme to save,
> Yet wisdome forward still unconquered goeth.

This was the theme of all Shakespeare's romances from *Pericles* to *The Tempest*. It is difficult to resist the conclusion that he took some hints from a play which not only anticipated (however crudely in application) his general notion of dramatic romance, but also contained features of parts of the plot which he added to Boccaccio's story. These included: the unequal match between a Princess and a young orphan brought up at her father's court; the names Fidelia (Fidele in *Cymbeline*) and Hermione (transferred to the heroine of *The Winter's Tale*); the banishment of the young lover by an angry King and the latter's desire to marry his daughter to another courtier; the dweller in the wilds, exiled years before through a false accusation; his meeting with the King's daughter; the intervention of Jupiter to bring about happy discoveries and reunions [Text VII].

The sense of divine supervision is much more pervasive in *Love and Fortune*, but is given more ethical depth in *Cymbeline*. Shakespeare, indeed, seems to have used his memories of the old play merely as a starting-point for a very different treatment. He reversed the action of the exile-hermit: Bomelio sent his son to learn civility at court; Belarius vengefully kidnapped the king's two sons and taught them civility in the wilds. Shakespeare wished to give a different view of nature from that in *King Lear*, and to contrast the evils of the court with an idyllic country life; so he went to a different tradition for his account of Imogen in Wales, the tradition of pastoral romance.

Apart from her relationship with her husband, Imogen's adventures have much in common with the type of folk-story found in *Snow-White and the Seven Dwarfs*, where a wicked stepmother wishes to get rid of her young rival and tries to poison or enchant her; the girl flees and takes refuge with forest-dwellers for whom she acts as housekeeper until she (apparently) dies and is mourned in rural fashion; but she wakes and is

restored to her rightful position when her enemy is destroyed.[1]
Snow-White was probably not known in Elizabethan England;
but elements of the story appear in many ballads and romances.
The wicked stepmother is of course a commonplace, as is her
attempt to poison the heroine. The substitution of a sleeping-
potion for the poison occurs (cf. vol. 1, pp. 269ff.) in the
Ephesiaca of Xenophon, Masuccio's *Il Novellino*, and various
versions of the Romeo and Juliet story, including Shakespeare's
play.[2] Young ladies lost in the wilds sometimes sheltered with
hermits: thus in *The Second Part of Parismus* by Emmanuel Forde
(1599, 1609, Ch. 8), after Violetta and Sorana have foiled the
wicked Archas by substituting Sorana (his mistress) in Archas's
bed, Violetta, fleeing through 'a most desart and unfrequented
place', meets an aged man who takes her to his cell, then
accompanies her until he dies of exhaustion. Several of Spenser's
ladies in *The Faerie Queene* are found among rural folk. In
III. x Helenore, wife of Malbecco, is deserted by her seducer
Paridell:

> The gentle Lady, loose at randon left,
> The greene-wood long did walke, and wander wide,
> At wilde adventure, like a forlorne weft,
> Till on a day the *Satyres* her espide
> Straying alone withouten groome or guide;
> Her up they tooke, and with them home her led,
> With them as housewife ever to abide,
> To milke their gotes, and make them cheese and bred,
> And every one as commune good her handeled. (St. 36)

The last line removes any likeness to Imogen. Her graceless
husband finds her sleeping with 'a Satyre rough and rude' (48),
and she refuses to return home with him.

Nearer to *The Winter's Tale* than to *Cymbeline* is the incident
in VI. ix, where Sir Calidore finds the fair Pastorella among the
'lustie shepheard swaynes' (8), apparently the daughter of old

---

[1] Cf. B. Leonhardt, 'Über die Quellen *Cymbelines*', *Anglia*, vi, 1883, 1–45; K.
Schenkl, *Germania*, ix, Vienna, 1864, pp. 458ff.
[2] *The Most Pleasant History of Tom of Lincolne*, Anon., c. 1599, has a 'history which
Sir Lanucelot du Lake told to the Red Rose Knight, being on shipboard'. In it a
wicked Queen tries to prevent the maiden Dulcippa from marrying her son the
Prince, by giving her a poison which turns out to be a harmless drug. Cf. F. Brie,
ShJb, xliv, 1908, 167–70.

Meliboe, who sings the praises of the country life. Like Belarius he had been at court, but after ten years he had realized his folly and

> Tho back returning to my sheepe againe,
> I from thenceforth have learn'd to love more deare
> This lowly quiet life, which I inherite here. (25)

A closer parallel in verse to Imogen's adventures was in Tasso's *Jerusalem Delivered* which Edward Fairfax had translated in 1600. Erminia, daughter of the Moslem King of Antioch, loves Tancred, and when he is wounded she sets off in search of him, disguised as the Amazon Clorinda. Escaping from Christian pursuers she sleeps 'on Jordan's sandy banks', and next morning comes on an old man with his three sons making baskets (VII. St. 6). When she expresses surprise at seeing them there in the midst of war the old man praises their poverty and says that at one time he had been the Caliph's gardener but had returned to the country disillusioned with court life. He takes Erminia to his home, where she becomes for a while a shepherdess:

> Her little flocks to pasture would she guide,
> And milk her goats, and in their folds them place;
> Both cheese and butter could she make, and frame
> Herself to please the shepherd and his dame. (St. 18)

Another slight parallel may be seen in Bk VIII where Godfrey of Bulloigne is told that Rinaldo has been killed, for his headless body has been found in a hill-stream (St. 52–6). The body is not Rinaldo's however.

Another link occurs when Erminia, freed from bondage to Armida by Tancred's squire Vafrino, informs him of a plan (not unlike Posthumus's disguise) by which Emireno has ordered Ormondo and other fierce Muslims to assume the white and gold surcoats and crosses of Godfrey's bodyguard, so as to get near enough in the battle to kill him (Bk XIX, St. 86–9). Moreover Vafrino soon comes upon two bodies, one a pagan, the other a Christian. Erminia recognizes the latter as Tancred, and mourns over him. Fortunately he is not dead, and they are reunited (Bk XIX, St. 102–9) [Text VIII].

Shakespeare may well have read Fairfax, but, like most other partial analogues, these are inconclusive. They prove, however, that Shakespeare was consciously working in a tradition of folk-lore and literary romance when he added to what he found in Holinshed and Boccaccio. It remains to see how he handled his varied materials.

For Professor Wilson Knight *Cymbeline* is to be regarded mainly 'as a historical play' blending 'two primary historical interests, the Roman and the British'; it makes 'a national statement'.[1] For Mr J. M. Nosworthy, on the other hand, Shakespeare 'was no longer concerned with historical drama . . . but with the golden inconsequences of romance'.[2] These inconsequences have troubled other critics since Dr Johnson dismissed the whole conduct of the play as 'absurd and ridiculous to the last degree; and with all the liberties Shakespeare has taken with time, place and action, the story as he has managed it, is more improbable than a fairly tale'.[3] That the play is based on improbabilities is not to be gainsaid, rather admitted as essential to its nature as a romance combining ancient British history, modern Italian intrigue, mountain pastoral, the romance of lost children, in a fantasy where good would come out of evil and tragic motives would finally turn into a comedy of wish-fulfilment. In taking over the wandering tale of *Frederyke* and interweaving it with a legend of British resistance to ancient Rome, Shakespeare deliberately kept his action loose and episodic, as if to insist on the 'popular' ballad-like nature of the entertainment without introducing the alien scenes and irrelevant characters of *Mucedorous* and *The Rare Triumphes of Love and Fortune*.

It must be admitted that the self-conscious attempt to re-capture the spirit of such obsolete but recently revived romantic plays accords imperfectly with the linguistic concentration and the ethical emphasis of Shakespeare's late manner. There are alternations in style between a somewhat jejune awkwardness and a condensed and intricate presentation of thought and character. This was what especially led Furness and Granville Barker to conclude that 'a fair amount of the play is pretty

---

[1] *The Crown of Life*, 1948 edn, pp. 129–30.
[2] *New Arden*, p. xxvi.
[3] *Preface to Shakespeare*.

certainly not by Shakespeare.'[1] Yet Granville Baker also noted the 'sophisticated artlessness' of much of it; an apt phrase, in the light of which we may regard *Cymbeline* as a further experiment in a manner already tried out partially in *Pericles*, a manner which may be called 'ethical romance'. In this a loose structure, the result of adapting essentially narrative material for the theatre, is applied to stories of widely differing tones, and unity is sought by modulation from one to another and by using them to represent and reflect upon moral values. A brief analysis of the action will indicate how the dramatist succeeds in interweaving strands which at first sight seem incompatible.

At once (I. 1) we see that the social setting, bourgeois in Boccaccio and *Frederyke*, has been changed. Posthumus, though a commoner—and his birth and name (important much later) are lengthily expounded—has married the princess Imogen, sole heir to the throne of Britain since the kidnapping of her two brothers twenty years ago. This, the stepmother Queen's 'dissembling courtesy', Cymbeline's wrath, Posthumus's banishment, the exchange of ring and bracelet, and the (narrated) attack of Cloten on Posthumus, are all revealed to us in one swift scene. To contrast with Posthumus's gentility Cloten is next shown (I. 2) as a blustering fool, mocked by his own courtiers, and deservedly rejected by Imogen, whose sadness at her husband's departure for Italy is seen in I. 3.

So far we have been in the world of *The Rare Triumphes*, but now we broach Boccaccio, with Posthumus among the foreigners in Rome—not merchants, but gentlemen of several nations at the house of Philario, an old friend of Posthumus's father. There is no difficulty in modulating from the modernized world of ancient Britain to Renaissance Europe, where subtle dangers lurk for simple Britons, as Ascham and other Tudor moralists had pointed out. That Posthumus has already been rash in upholding the merits of Imogen is revealed by Shakespeare's invention of the 'contention in public' in France which nearly led to a duel; and it is not surprising that he rises to Iachimo's contemptuous teasing. The wager is suggested by Iachimo (cf. Boccaccio) but Posthumus is easily led to stake Imogen's ring (I. 4. 130–51) despite Philario's wish to declare it 'no lay'.

[1] H. Granville Barker, *Prefaces*, ii, 1963 edn, pp. 86–97.

Meanwhile in Britain the wicked Queen (like Medea an experimenter with poisons) tries to win over Pisanio, Posthumus's servant, and, failing, draws a bow at a venture when she gives him a box of poison which she hopes may kill him, if not Imogen (I. 5). But we know from Cornelius that, not trusting the Queen, he has provided only a soporific drug. So Imogen will not be in great danger from this. The real menace appears in I.6, with the arrival of Iachimo carrying a letter of introduction from her husband. Omitting the female go-between of the sources, Shakespeare brings the trickster and the virtuous lady together in a splendid scene. Unlike Ambrogiuolo and Johan, who quickly realize the folly of trying to seduce her, Iachimo goes to work at once, mingling flattery with the suggestion that Posthumus is false (I. 6. 32ff.) and transferring to him the libertine fancies of the other merchants in the sources (64–73). Suggesting that she should avenge herself by doing likewise (79–139), he is almost thrown out, but saves himself by pretending that he was testing Imogen's fidelity (139–88), and requests her to keep his precious trunk overnight, which she agrees to do ('In my bedchamber', 196).

No weakness of construction appears in this first Act, which is remarkable both for speed and range, as the action reaches out to Rome and then returns to Britain, with all set for the heroine's first great misadventure. Imogen's slight twinge of fear lest Posthumus be seduced by 'the shes of Italy' (I. 3. 29) has been cruelly intensified but then allayed; so she is quite unsuspicious of evil. One flaw may be noted, looking back from later events: there is no reference to the lapsed tribute and a possible quarrel between Britain and Rome, though these are going to be important. Family affairs in the royal palace and in Rome are alone of interest as yet. International politics will be mentioned almost casually at II. 3. 56–65 and II. 4. 10–39 and thereafter will loom large; but this is a romance, not a 'history' play.

The domestic danger to Imogen reappears briefly in II. 1 where Cloten is again proved a braggart and some of his unwilling companions sympathize with her and her banished husband. In II. 2. the major threat to Imogen's happiness grows when Iachimo emerges from his trunk, easily restrains himself from emulating Tarquin, and after coolly noting down the contents of the room, takes Posthumus's bracelet from her wrist and observes the mole on her left breast. The aesthetic appreciation shown by this Italian sensualist is contrasted with the oafishness of Cloten who next morning serenades Imogen with sweet music and song, but debases all with foul jests (II. 3. 1–32). Encouraged by his mother he plays the stock Ovidian lover ("'Tis gold/Which buys admittance.'), but Imogen gives him little chance to woo, and when he becomes abusive insults him by saying that Posthumus's 'meanest garment' is more to her than anything about him (II. 3. 134–8). 'I'll be reveng'd', he blusters, but he is still not very dangerous.

In Rome, however, her fortunes are thoroughly marred when Iachimo (II. 4) returns there and tells Posthumus of his 'conquest', quickly destroying the young Briton's complacency with his circumstantial evidence and the bracelet. Despite Philario's attempts to restrain him, the 'corporal sign' of the mole convinces Posthumus,[1] and he becomes just as sure of his wife's infidelity as he was previously of her faithfulness. He inveighs against all women (II. v).

In III. 1 the political theme comes into prominence when Lucius demands the unpaid tribute and the Queen and Cloten surpass Cymbeline in defiance of Rome. Cloten cuts a better figure here, as a sturdy (if crude) British patriot, than in his private brags; and the Queen is queenly for once. In III. 2 Posthumus has come over with the Romans to Milford Haven and written two letters, one to his wife telling her to come to him in Wales, the other to Pisanio, telling him to kill her near the end of the journey. The device is clumsy, but Imogen must meet her long-lost brothers in the mountains, and Posthumus must be able to take part in the battle between Romans and Britons. Irony and suspense are aroused when Pisanio at once tells us that he must murder Imogen, and by her pathetic eagerness to leave the palace and ride to her husband.

The scene is now set for her arrival in Wales, for we find Belarius (another banished man) living in a cave with two youths who prove to be Imogen's brothers. They enjoy their simple rustic pursuits but begin to long for wider experience

[1] Cf. Othello's 'ocular proof' III. 3. 361.

(III. 3. 10–44). Catastrophe strikes Imogen (III. 4) when the sympathetic Pisanio shows her Posthumus's cruel letter to him. He persuades her to disguise herself as a man and to take service with the Roman Lucius who 'comes to Milford-Haven tomorrow'. Thus she will at least be near her husband.

The timing here is erratic, for in III. 5, when Lucius leaves the British court with 'a conduct overland to Milford-Haven' (7), Pisanio, having shown Imogen that port 'from a mountain-top' (III. 6. 5), has got back from Wales, and her absence has yet to be discovered. Then Cloten goes after her, and will wear Posthumus's clothes, for, brooding still on that insulting phrase 'his meanest garment', he proposes to kill his rival and ravish Imogen while wearing them, before driving her home. This improbable twist is needed if Imogen is later to think her husband dead; but we are in a world of fantasy.

So now the disguised heroine, lost and famished in the wilds, comes to Belarius's cave, is discovered eating of their store, and is welcomed 'as a brother' by the two boys (III. 6). A brief scene in Rome (III. 7), where the invasion of Britain has been ordered and Lucius made commander of the army, indicates that some time may elapse before the hostile forces meet, and by its reference to the need to 'incite the gentry to this business' serves to explain (if we should ask) how Iachimo comes to Britain with the Roman army. He is in charge of the gentlemen volunteers (IV. 2. 337–41).

By IV. 1 Cloten is near the cave where (remarkable coincidence) Pisanio has told him that Imogen was to meet Posthumus. He rants in his grotesque vanity, unaware that Imogen is so near. But (IV. 2) she is sick in body and mind, and cannot go hunting; she has endeared herself by her charm and housewifery to the noble youths. She drinks of Pisanio's 'health-giving' drug, and in her drugged sleep knows nothing of Cloten's death at Guiderius's hands and the casting of his head (cf. Hamo's) into the creek. The reaction of the two brothers to Belarius's fear of retaliation fills him with pride. Their pleasure turns to grief when Fidele-Imogen is discovered, apparently dead, and they perform graceful obsequies and depart. Imogen awakes, and, seeing the headless body of Cloten in her husband's garments, thinks him Posthumus, killed by Cloten and Pisanio. In true romance-style Lucius and his officers chance by and find the youth aswoon. Lucius befriends him and they bury Cloten's body ere they go.

Her son's absence has put the Queen into a fevered madness (IV. 3). Cymbeline cares more for this and Imogen's absence than for imminent war. Pisanio too is worried at not having heard from Posthumus or Imogen. 'Fortune brings in some boats that are not steer'd,' he says, aptly of this whole story. Meanwhile in Wales Guiderius and Arviragus insist on going to war, despite Belarius's fear that all their identities may be discovered.

Shakespeare has now made the necessary preparations for all his characters to come together. Posthumus, as Pisanio reminded us, has been offstage since II. 5, but in V. 1 he reappears, cherishing the bloody handkerchief sent him by Pisanio, whose ready obedience he regrets since he now wishes that he had overlooked her 'wrying but a little' (4). He has joined the 'Italian gentry', but rather than fight against Imogen's people he will disguise himself as a British peasant and fight for the honour of his house. This he does, for in the confused battle-scene V. 2, he has disarmed Iachimo and he helps Belarius and his sons turn the tide of battle and rescue Cymbeline. In a long speech (V. 3. 1–58) which is an outstanding example of Shakespearian epic narrative made from Holinshed's prose (*infra*, p. 48) he tells us what happened. Deep in gloom because he is still alive, Posthumus will fight no more but await death from either side. Challenged by British soldiers he declares himself a Roman and is haled before Cymbeline and so to prison.

There we find him in V. 4, welcoming bondage as a way to death. In sleep he has a vision in which his dead family (in dreary rhymed 'fourteeners') pray Jupiter to 'take off his miseries', which Jupiter (in slightly superior rhymed decasyllabics) promises to do: 'He shall be lord of Lady Imogen,/And happier much by his affliction made.'

When Posthumus wakes he finds on his breast a tablet inscribed with an oracle promising a happy end under riddling conditions. He resolves to live, and greets his gaolers merrily when they come to hang him, and is unfettered and taken before the King. This leads into the great Recognition-scene (V. 5) which has been so diversely criticized: by Steevens as

'a catastrophe which is intricate without confusion', by
Thorndike as 'so ingeniously intricate that it is ineffective on
the stage', and by Bernard Shaw as 'a tedious string of unsurprising dénouements sugared with insincere sentimentality
after a ludicrous stage-battle'. For a detailed account of the
scene which puts its vigour and effectiveness on the stage
beyond question I refer the reader to Granville Barker's
exposition. Here, as often elsewhere, Shakespeare makes use
of dramatic irony and expectation in the audience, who know
most of the facts to be revealed, and who enjoy the successive
pleasant surprises of the stage-personages as their ignorance is
illumined.

The scene is in six sections which flow effortlessly into one
another, not however without some minor surprises even to
ourselves, and delicious irony, as when our knowledge that
Posthumus is the 'poor soldier' sought by Cymbeline at V. 5. 3
is not made general till later. First comes the revelation to
Cymbeline of his Queen's wickedness (25–68); then the 'discovery' of Imogen, preceded by the King's half-recognition of
'Fidele' and Lucius's fear that his page is abandoning him.
When she takes Cymbeline aside it is to ask him (as in the
sources) to let her question Iachimo, and the Italian elaborates
his tale of treachery (130–210), ignorant that Posthumus is
listening. The latter's frenzied self-accusation culminates in
his striking the 'scornful page' to the ground (much as Pericles
rebuffed his unknown daughter when she tried to console him
—*Per* V. 1. 83–4, 101), which brings forward Pisanio to assert
her identity, only to be accused by Imogen of poisoning her.
Such unexpected turns prevent tediousness. The recognition of
Imogen by her husband and her father is followed at once by
the story of Cloten's death, which puts the two boys and
Belarius in grave danger for slaying a prince, even if 'a most
uncivil one' (292–3). Our expectation that Belarius must now
reveal himself and his kidnapping of the two children is fulfilled, and, this being romance, he is commended by Cymbeline
('thou art my brother'). Shaw mocked at Guiderius's mole
(364–9), but there is playful symmetry here, for a mole identified Imogen earlier, with very different results.

The next revelation is that Posthumus was the 'forlorn
soldier' who helped in the battle, and this is vouched for by

Iachimo, who is spared to better his way of life. This ushers in the general benevolence: 'Pardon's the word to all.'

But all's not over yet. The miraculous tablet with its riddle is produced to prove by means of an excruciating pun (*'mulier'*, *'mollis aer'*, 'tender air') that the gods foretold 'peace and plenty'. And Cymbeline, having beaten off those world-conquering Romans and proved British prowess, agrees 'to pay our wonted tribute', blaming the wicked Queen for his national-istic error. So, as the Roman soothsayer says, politicly re-interpreting his vision of IV. 2. 346–52, 'The imperial Caesar, should again unite/His favour with the radiant Cymbeline,/ Which shines here in the west' (474–6) as 'A Roman and a British ensign wave/Friendly together.' Political romance adds a touch of pageantry to the private romance of love and friend-ship.

On the whole, the smooth blending of the several ingredients of *Cymbeline* is a triumph of ingenuity and transition-work. In bringing together material so diverse Shakespeare was always alive to its ethical implications and often went further than his sources in emphasizing moral values. His choice in this play of semi-fictitious British history as a setting for an Italianate tale of deception, cruelty, and feminine fidelity may have been originally prompted simply by his company's need of a 'history' play with romantic main-plot; but in working it out he added to the Posthumus–Imogen story an adventitious element of national importance. A Jacobean audience would certainly not regard the Romano-British conflict as a warning against refus-ing tribute to a foreign power, but it might deprecate Cymbe-line's breach of a solemn treaty while admiring the patriotism behind his defiance:

> the Pannonians and Dalmatians for
> Their liberties are now in arms; a precedent
> Which not to read would show the Britons cold. (III. 1. 74–6)

That this situation was regarded by the dramatist as secondary was shown by his delay in introducing it; and its main force, apart from the opportunity it gives to reveal the manhood of the two boys and the hitherto weak Posthumus, comes at the end of Act V when Cymbeline gracefully agrees to pay tribute so that the two nations may go forward together in friendship.

This would appeal to King James I who longed to be the peace-
maker of Europe, dreaming even of reconciliation with the
Pope—between Britain and Rome, indeed.

In dramatizing Boccaccio and *Frederyke* Shakespeare wished
to avoid the Oriental adventures of the heroine which would
largely increase the cast and make the play almost as dis-
cursive as Heywood's *Four Prentices*. The dénouement must be
in Britain, so the heroine must stay there and wander into some
wild part of the country. Memories of mountain-pastoral and
of *1 Henry IV*, suggested the Welsh hills as a suitable region, with
Milford Haven (used by Richmond) as the point of invasion
and of meeting. This would provide a different kind of pastoral
from that in *As You Like It*, and together with details from *The
Rare Triumphes* and maybe *Mucedorus* combined to produce the
cave of Belarius and the charming interlude with the two boys.
Shakespeare used such romantic commonplaces, moreover, to
present a new variation on the popular theme of country life as
opposed to court life. Sidney had praised the joys of 'solitariness' and Dekker had described the happy simplicities of rural
life. Shakespeare himself, while giving Rosalind and Orlando
a joyous wooing in the greenwood, had pointed out the dangers
of starvation and wild beasts, and the matter-of-fact dirt and
drudgery of the shepherd's occupation while mocking at the
literary pastoral of Phoebe and Silvius. He makes Imogen wish
that she were 'a neat-herd's daughter' (I. 1. 149), and soon she
has to disguise herself as a boy and steal food from cave-dwellers.
Her adventure leads to some interesting discussions about the
advantages and disadvantages of life in the mountains.
Shakespeare, unlike most pastoralists, gives both sides. When
Belarius (III. 3) joys in its freedom and open-air activities,
the absence of the 'checks' and bribery of the court, the two
princes long for the experience out of which he draws his
wisdom, and decry the unsophisticated skills they have attained:
'We have seen nothing;/We are beastly, subtle as the fox for
prey' (39–40). The audience is meant to sympathize with both
sides, and especially to appreciate with Belarius the proofs that
princely blood will out (82–98).

The contrast between their natural nobility and the ignoble
coarseness of Cloten is well made—he is not of the blood royal—
and the result of his clash with Guiderius is inevitable. As

Belarius says, Cloten was so immature as not to know the meaning—and value—of fear. Belarius himself counsels retirement to the hills, neutrality in the war, but the boys would be ashamed to miss the chance of riding to battle like true knights. It is the desire for experience, which makes a full man, rather than patriotism that urges them to fight, and with them Belarius regains his warrior status though 'the King/Hath not deserv'd my service nor your loves' (IV. 4).

The notion of honour found in them, of proving worthy of one's blood and ancestry, also motivates the grief-struck Posthumus when, wishing to die for Imogen, he will do so as a Briton—'Gods! put the strength o' the Leonati in me'— and like the boys he will show in his peasant disguise, 'less without and more within' (V. 1. 22–33). Fittingly therefore, with the 'rustic mountaineers' he shames the fleeing British into victory, and as his brother in the Vision declares, he has done for Cymbeline what his relatives had previously done for Tenantius. In this way Posthumus, who has behaved like a petty Othello without the Moor's resolution to achieve his own revenge, redeems himself. But his personality is no larger than needful for the part he has to play.

Imogen on the other hand deserves the praise lavished on her by Hazlitt ('Of all Shakespeare's women . . . perhaps the most tender and the most artless')[1] and Wilson Knight ('weak yet courageous . . . fragile yet indestructible', a 'slip of tender royalty' etc.).[2] She is anything but 'a various and erratic tissue of inconsistencies' (Nosworthy). Rather she rises to every occasion, showing a different facet of an opalescent personality which transcends without distracting from the plot to which she contributes so much.

The tendency to dismiss the plot of *Cymbeline* as ridiculous because of its heterogeneous material is often accompanied by dislike of its treatment of Imogen and its insistence on suffering. Granville Barker called it 'a vicious art that can so make sport of its creatures'. But not only tragi-comedy but also hagiology and romance played on the long-suffering and endurance of innocent men and women, the reward of whose virtue made all they had gone through worth while. The dramatization of

[1] *Characters of Shakespeare's Plays*, 'Cymbeline'.
[2] *The Crown of Life*, 1947, pp. 152–7, a fine analysis.

such stories is always in danger of making us realize their improbability, but *Cymbeline*, like *Pericles* and *The Winter's Tale*, was composed (and should be produced) with an idealized formality which should keep us from becoming as involved in any of the characters as we must be in the great tragedies or the 'dark' comedies. Imogen's sufferings are less emphasized than those of Isabella or Helena.

On the other hand *Cymbeline* and the other late plays have been interpreted in recent years as written in a consciously religious mood. Much has been made of the fact, known to Holinshed and Shakespeare, that Jesus Christ was born during the reigns of Cymbeline and Augustus. Robin Moffet finds it the 'central fact . . . reflected in the form and details of the play'.[1] Certainly there is a 'redemptive' quality in the story of Posthumus (as of Leontes) absent in Boccaccio's Bernabò; and the peace and harmony ushered in at the close may possibly have been affected by the knowledge that 'the Saviour of the World . . . [was] borne . . . under a King of peace, as was Augustus, and in a time of peace'.[2] But the Christian relationship should not be exaggerated. Shakespeare is at pains to introduce a pagan vision and to mingle his Christian imagery with references to the Roman gods: for he is working in the romantic tradition which delighted in oracles and visions.

Holinshed no doubt contributed too, for Harrison's *Description of England* and the chronicle itself observed distinctions between pre- and post-Christian Britain and their religious customs. In the account of Brut's vision [Text IA] rites connected with the Oracle of Diana are described and both prayer and answer are given in Latin and English verses. Shakespeare may have modelled Posthumus's vision on this, and aimed at a similar archaic formality in the verses spoken by Posthumus's relatives. But dialogues between gods and between gods and men were common in Renaissance drama on the Continent. An example has been given (*supra* V, pp. 174–7) from Orlando Pescetti's *Il Cesare*, in which Venus and Mars complain to Jupiter about the imminent death of Julius

[1] R. Moffet, 'Cymbeline and the Nativity', ShQ, xiii, 1962, 207–18.
[2] King James I, *A Collection of his Majesties Workes* (1616). Cited by B. Harris, 'What's past is prologue: Cymbeline and Henry VIII' in *Stratford-upon-Avon Studies*, 8; *Later Shakespeare*, 1966, pp. 203–33.

Caesar, and Venus 'rates and revenges' his adulteries as Juno is said to do in *Cymbeline* V. 4. 33–4. Jupiter's reply,

> When men I castigate 'tis as a father
> His son chastises but to make him good

foreshadows 'Whom best I love I cross' (V. 4. 101).

Such divine dialogues usually occur at the beginning of plays to supply providential overtones and excuse a surprising dénouement. In *The Rare Triumphes* the entire first Act is given over to the gods, who comment on the human proceedings at the end of Acts II, III, and IV, and at the beginning of Act V agree to bring about a happy conclusion. Venus and Fortune appear to Phyzantius to achieve this. In *Cymbeline* Posthumus's vision is not prepared for and does not affect the outcome of the plot. Yet the oracular tablet left with Posthumus contributes to the conclusion of the play, since its interpretation leads the happy Cymbeline to make peace and submit to Rome.[1] It must be admitted, however, that the supernatural intervention in *Cymbeline* loses efficacy by coming so late in the play. It looks like an afterthought, perhaps to emulate the vision in *Pericles*, most probably to cater for the current love of the Masque.

I question whether Shakespeare meant the reconciliation in *Cymbeline* to be considered in relation to the Christmas story. He could easily have given a firm hint of it had he wished, but though (being a Christian) he introduces Christian imagery when writing of forgiveness and redemption, he is careful to preserve a pre-Christian tone at the end, with a summons to a Roman service of thanksgiving:

> Laud we the gods,
> And let our crooked smokes climb to their nostrils
> From our bless'd altars . . .
> And in the temple of great Jupiter
> Our peace we'll ratify . . .

The last lines of the play place us firmly in the world of pagan Rome and ancient Britain.

[1] B. Harris, *op. cit.*, pp. 211–13, 223, aptly refers to the oracle in Guarini's *Pastor Fido*: 'Your woe shall end when two of Race divine/Love shall combine: and for a faithless Nymphs apostate state/A faithful Shepherd supererogate' (R. Fanshawe's translation). This oracle is given in Act I. 2, and therefore has more dramatic function than Shakespeare's.

I. Source

From
THE FIRST VOLUME OF CHRONICLES
by R. Holinshed (1587 edn)

A. THE SECOND BOOKE OF THE HISTORIE OF ENGLAND

The first Chapter

[7/1/34] This Brute . . . was the sonne of Silvius, the sonne of Ascanius, the sonne of Aeneas the Trojan, begotten of his wife Creusa, and borne in Troie before the citie was destroied. But as others take it . . . Posthumus the sonne of Aeneas (begotten of his wife Lavinia, and borne after his fathers deceasse in Italie) was called Ascanius, who had issue a sonne named Julius, who . . . was the father of Brute, that noble chieftaine and adventurous leader of the people, which being descended . . . from those Trojans that escaped with life, when that royall citie was destroied by the Greekes, got possession of this worthie and most famous Ile.

[Holinshed tells how Brute, 'hunting in a forest slue his father unwares, and thereupon for feare of his grandfather Silvius Posthumus he fled the countrie'.][1]

[8/2/42] Al things being thus brought to passe according to Brutes desire, wind also and wether serving the purpose, he with his wife Innogen and his people imbarked, and hoising up sailes departed from the coasts of Grecia. Now after two daies and a nights sailing, they arrived at Leogitia . . . an Iland, where they consulted with an oracle. Brute himselfe kneeling before the idoll, and holding in his right hand a boll prepared for sacrifice full of wine, and the blood of a white hinde, spake in this manner as here followeth:

---

[1] The name Posthumus probably suggested that of Shakespeare's hero. On the same page: 'Pyrrhus the sonne of Achilles, having no issue by his wife Hermione, maried Andromache, late wife unto Hector.' On f. 8 occurs the name Antigonus, a Greek captured by Brute.

[The prayer is given in Latin.]

These verses (as Ponticus Virumnius and others also doe gesse) were written by Gildas Cambrius in his booke intituled *Cambreidos*, and may thus be Englished:

> Thou goddesse that doost rule
>   the woods and forrests greene,
> And chafest foaming boares
>   that flee thine awfull sight,
> Thou that maist passe aloft
>   in airie skies so sheene,
> And walke eke under earth
>   in places void of light,
> Discover earthlie states,
>   direct our course aright,
> And shew where we shall dwell,
>   according to thy will,
> In seates of sure abode,
>   where temples we may dight
> For virgins that shall sound
>   thy laud with voices shrill.

After this praier and ceremonie done, according to the pagane rite and custome, Brute abiding his answer, fell asleep: in which sleepe appeared unto him the said goddesse uttering this answer in the verses following expressed:

[They are given in Latin and English.]

> Brute, farre by-west beyond the
>   Gallike land is found,
> An Ile which with the ocean seas
>   inclosed is about,
> Where giants dwelt sometime,
>   but now is desart ground,
> Most meet where thou maist plant
>   thy selfe with all thy rout:
> Make thitherwards with speed
>   for there thou shalt find out
> An everduring seat,
>   and Troie shall rise anew,
> Unto thy race, of whom
>   shall kings be borne no dout,
> That with their mightie power
>   the world shall whole subdew.

After he awaked out of sleepe, and had called his dreame to remembrance, he first doubted whether it were a verie dreame, or a true vision, the goddess having spoken to him with livelie voice.[1] Whereupon calling such of his companie unto him as he thought requisite in such a case, he declared unto them the whole matter with the circumstances, whereat they, greatlie rejoicing, caused mightie bonfires to be made, in the which they cast wine, milke, and other liquors, with divers gums and spices of most sweet smell and savour, as in the pagan religion was accustomed. Which observances and ceremonies performed and brought to an end, they returned streightwaies to their ships, and as soone as the wind served, passed forward on their journie with great joy and gladnesse, as men put in comfort to find out the wished seats for their firme and sure habitations.

B. MULMUTIUS DUNWALLOW[2]

The Third Booke: The First Chapter

[15/1/34] Mulmucius Dunwallow . . . the sonne of Cloton[3] . . . got the upper hand of the other dukes or rulers: and after his fathers deceasse began his reigne over the whole monarchie of Britaine, in the yeere of the world 3529 . . . This Mulmucius Dunwallow . . . prooved a right worthie prince. He builded within the citie of London, then called Troinovant, a temple, and named it the Temple of Peace . . . He also made manie good lawes, which were long after used, called Mulmucius lawes, turned out of the British speech into the Latine by Gildas Priscus, and long time after translated out of Latine into English by Alfred king of England, and mingled in his statutes. He moreover gave privileges to temples, to plowes, to cities, and to high waies leading to the same, so that whosoever fled to them, should be in safegard from bodilie harme, and from thence he might depart into what countrie he would, with indemnitie of his person. Some authors write, that he began to make the foure great high waies of Britaine . . .

After he had established his land, and set his Britains in good and convenient order, he ordeined him by the advise of his lords a crowne of gold,[4] and caused himselfe with great solemnitie to be crowned, according to the custome of the pagan lawes then in use: and because

---

[1] Posthumus thinks it only a dream: V. 4. 123–46.
[2] Referred to in *Cym* II. 1. 54–62 as the king's ancestor.
[3] King of Cornwall, 'rightfull heire' of Ferrex and Porrex.
[4] *In margin:* 'The first king that was crowned with a golden crowne'.

he was the first that bare a crowne heere in Britaine . . . he is named the first king of Britaine.[1]

C. JULIUS CAESAR IN DIFFICULTIES

[In Bk III, Ch. 10–16 Holinshed gives various accounts of Caesar's invasions of Britain. Caesar himself told of his initial difficulty in getting troops ashore and how when he had done so the Britons called for peace and gave hostages.]

[25/2/60] Peace being thus established after the fourth day of the Romans arrivall in Britaine, the 18 ships which . . . were appointed to convey the horssemen over, loosed from the further haven with a soft wind. Which when they approched so neere the shore of Britaine, that the Romans which were in Cesars campe might see them, suddenlie there arose so great a tempest, that none of them was able to keepe his course, so that they were not onelie driven in sunder . . . but also the other ships that lay at anchor, and had brought over the armie, were so pitifullie beaten, tossed and shaken, that a great number of them did not onelie lose their tackle, but also were carried by force of wind into the high sea; the rest being likewise so filled with water, that they were in danger by sinking to perish and to be quite lost . . . There was no way for the Romans to helpe the matter: wherefore a great number of those ships were so bruised, rent and weather-beaten, that without new reparation they would serve to no use of sailing [Ch. 12].

[27/1/7] [Caesar fought on and enforced a truce.] After that these things were thus ordered, Cesar, because the moneth of September

[1] Geoffrey of Monmouth told a story about Mulmutius which anticipated that of Posthumus's disguise in *Cym* Act V. [Kings from other parts of Britain invaded his territory.] Dunwallo marched to meet them with thirty thousand men and gave battle, but after a great part of the day had been spent in fighting and neither party could claim the victory, he called apart six hundred of his bravest youths and bade them all take and don the arms of the enemies they had slain. He himself also flung aside the arms he was wearing and did the like. He then led them into the press of the enemy's ranks, going in among them as though he were of their own party, and when he had reached the place where Rudauc and Stater were leading on their men, gave the word unto his comrades to charge down upon them. They accordingly dashed forward, and the two Kings were slain in the onset and a number of others along with them. But Dunwallo Mulmutius, fearing lest he should be himself slain of his own men, turned back with his comrades and disarmed him. Then, donning again the arms that he had flung aside, he cheereth on his comrades to another charge which he himself led foremost. Scarce a moment later the day was won and the enemy put to flight and scattered.

was well-neare halfe spent and that winter hasted on . . . determined
not to staie anie longer, but having wind and weather for his purpose,
got himselfe aboord with his people, and returned into Gallia.

Thus writeth Cesar touching his first journie made into Britaine.
But the British historie (which *Polydor*[1] calleth the new historie)
declareth that Cesar in a pitched field was vanquished at the first
encounter, and so withdrew backe into France. Beda also writeth,
that Cesar . . . [in] Gallia . . . got togither 80 saile of great ships
and row gallies, wherewith he passed over into Britaine, and there at
the first being wearied with sharpe and sore fight, and after taken
with a grievous tempest, he lost the greater part of his navie, with no
small number of his souldiers, and almost all his horssemen: and
therwith returned into Gallia, placed his souldiors in steeds[2] to
sojourne there for the winter season. Thus saith Bede. The British
historie moreover maketh mention of three under-kings that aided
Cassibellane in this first battell fought with Cesar . . . The same
historie also maketh mention of one Belinus that was generall of
Cassibellanes armie, and likewise of Nenius brother to Cassibellane,
who in fight happened to get Cesars swoord fastened to his shield by
a blow which Cesar stroke at him.[3] Androgeus and Tenancius were
at the battell in aid of Cassibellane. But Nenius died within 15 daies
after the battell of hurt received at Cesars hand [Ch. 13].

[Caesar's next landing was almost unimpeded, but again he
was hindered by storm.]

[28/2/2] The next day, as he had sent foorth such as should have
pursued the Britains, word came to him from Quintus Atrius, that
his navie by rigour of a sore and hideous tempest was greevouslie
molested, and thrown upon the shore, so that the cabels and tackle
being broken and destroied with force of the unmercifull rage of
wind, the maisters and mariners were not able to helpe the
matter. [He defeated the Britons however.] Cassibellane in the end
was forced to fall to a composition, in covenanting to paie a yearelie
tribute of three thousand pounds[4] . . .

[31/1/5] The reverend father Bede writing of this matter, saith
thus: After that Cesar [had] returned into Gallia . . . he caused
ships to be made readie, to the number of 600, with the which

[1] Hence Guiderius's alias? III. 6. 28 etc.
[2] steeds, military stations.
[3] The Queen attributes this to Cassibellane, III. 1. 29-31.
[4] Cf. III. 1. 5-9.

repassing into Britaine, whilest he marched foorth with a mightie armie against the enimies, his ships that lay at anchor being taken with a sore tempest, were either beaten one against another, or else cast upon the flats and sands,[1] and so broken; so that fortie of them were utterlie perished, and the residue with great difficultie were repaired. The horssemen of the Romans at the first encounter were put to the worsse, and Labienus the tribune slaine. In the second conflict he vanquished the Britains, not without great danger of his people[2] . . . the strong citie of Troinovant with hir duke Androgeus delivering fortie hostages, yeelded unto Caesar . . . Thus much touching the war which Julius Cesar made against the Britains, in bringing them under tribute to the Romans. But this tributarie subjection was hardlie mainteined for a season [Ch. 16].

D. CYMBELINE AND GUIDERIUS [Ch. 18]

After the death of Cassibellane, Theomantius or Tenantius the yoongest son of Lud was made king of Britaine in the yeere of the world 3921, after the building of Rome 706, and before the comming of Christ 45 . . . Theomantius ruled the land in good quiet, and paid the tribute to the Romans which Cassibellane had granted, and finallie departed this life after he had reigned 22 yeares, and was buried at London.

Kymbeline or Cimbeline the sonne of Theomantius was of the Britains made king after the deceasse of his father . . . This man (as some write) was brought up at Rome, and there made knight[3] by Augustus Cesar, under whome he served in the warres, and was in such favour with him, that he was at libertie to pay his tribute or not. Little other mention is made of his dooings, except that during his reigne, the Saviour of the world our Lord Jesus Christ the onelie sonne of God was borne of a virgine, about the 23 yeare of the reigne of this Kymbeline . . . some writers doo varie, but the best approoved affirme, that he reigned 35 years and then died, and was buried at London, leaving behind him two sonnes, Guiderius and Arviragus.

But here is to be noted, that although our histories doo affirme, that as well this Kymbeline, as also his father Theomantius, lived in quiet with the Romans, and continuallie to them paied the tributes which the Britains had covenanted with Julius Cesar to pay, yet we

---

[1] III. 1. 21.

[2] III. 1. 22. Holinshed also cites the British chronicles as 'affirming that Cesar comming the second time was by the Britains with martiall prowesse, beaten and repelled, as he was at the first' [30/2/12]. Cf. III. 1. 26, 'twice beaten'.

[3] III. 1. 70–3.

find in the Romane writers, that after Julius Cesars death, when Augustus had taken upon him the rule of the empire, the Britains refused to paie that tribute: whereat as Cornelius Tacitus reporteth, Augustus (being otherwise occupied) was contented to winke; howbeit, through earnest calling upon to recover his right by such as were desirous to see the uttermost of the British kingdome; at length, to wit, in the tenth yeare after the death of Julius Cesar, which was about the thirteenth yeare of the said Theomantius, Augustus made provision to passe with an armie over into Britaine, and was come forward upon his journie into Gallia Celtica: or as we maie saie, into these hither parts of France.

But here receiving advertisements that the Pannonians, which inhabited the countrie now called Hungarie, and the Dalmatians whome now we call Slavons had rebelled, he thought it best first to subdue those rebells neere home, rather than to seeke new countries, and leave such in hazard whereof he had present possession, and so turning his power against the Pannonians and Dalmatians, he left off for a time the warres of Britaine.[1] [Twice more Augustus was prevented thus from crossing to Britain] . . . But whether this controversie which appeareth to fall forth betwixt the Britains and Augustus, was occasioned by Kymbeline, or some other prince of the Britains, I have not to avouch:[2] for that by our writers it is reported that Kymbeline, being brought up in Rome, and knighted in the court of Augustus, ever shewed himselfe a friend to the Romans, and chieflie was loth to breake with them, because the youth of the Britaine nation should not be deprived of the benefit to be trained and brought up among the Romans, whereby they might learne both to behave themselves like civill men, and to atteine to the knowledge of feates of warre.[3]

[33/1/63] Guiderius the first sonne of Kymbeline . . . began his reigne in the seventeenth yeere after th'incarnation of Christ. This Guiderius being a man of stout courage, gave occasion of breach of peace betwixt the Britains and Romans, denieing to paie them tribute, and procuring the people to new insurrections, which by one meane or other made open rebellion, as Gyldas saith. Whereupon the emperour Caligula (as some thinke) tooke occasion to leavie a

---

[1] III. 1. 73-5.

[2] Shakespeare's *Cymbeline* refuses tribute.

[3] The two youths in the play prove that a stay in Rome was not necessary for 'civility' or military prowess. Cf. Posthumus, II. 4. 20-6. Holinshed writes (vol. ii, 'The first inhabitation of Ireland') that in Caesar's time 'the British nation was then unskilful, and not trained to feats of war [and] through lacke of skill easilie gave place to the Romans force'.

power, and . . . he ment not onlie to reduce the Iland unto the former subjection, but also to search out the uttermost bounds thereof, to the behoofe of himselfe, and of the Romane monarchie [Ch. 19]. [All he did however was to gather cockle shells ('the spoile of the Ocean') from the seashore.]

[35/1/58] There be that write, how Claudius subdued and added to the Romane empire, the Iles of Orknie situate in the north Ocean beyond Britaine: which might well be accomplished either by Plautius, or some other his lieutenant. [Gyldas wrote of the Britons at this time as spiritless cowards] so a common proverbe followeth thereof, to wit, That the Britains were neither valiant in warre, nor faithfull in peace . . .

In the British historie we find other report as thus, that Claudius at his comming aland at Porchester, besieged that towne, to the rescue whereof came Guiderius, and giving battell to the Romans, put them to the woorse, till at length one Hamo, being on the Romans side, changed his shield and armour, apparelling himselfe like a Britaine, and so entring into the thickest prease of the British host, came at length where the king was, and there slue him.[1] But Arviragus perceiving this mischiefe, to the end the Britains should not be discouraged therewith, caused himselfe to be adorned with the kings cote-armour and other abiliments, and so as king continued the fight with such manhood, that the Romans were put to flight. Claudius retired back to his ships, and Hamo to the next woods, whom Arviragus pursued, and at length drove him unto the sea side, and there slue him yer he could take the haven[2] which was there at hand; so that the same tooke name of him and was called a long time after, Hamons haven [i.e. Southampton] . . . Thus have you heard how Guiderius or Guinderius . . . came to his end, which chanced (as some write) in the 28 yeere of his reigne [Bk IV. Ch. 2].

[In Ch. 3 Holinshed tells how Arviragus succeeded his brother and 'bare himselfe right manfullie against Claudius and his Romans'.]

[36/1/12] Whereupon Claudius doubting the sequele of the thing, sent messengers unto Arviragus to treat of concord, and so by composition the matter was taken up, with condition that Claudius should give his daughter Genissa in marriage unto Arviragus, and Arviragus should acknowledge to hold his kingdome of the Romans . . . [But apparently Claudius had no daughter named Genissa.]

---

[1] Cf. Posthumus's disguise, V. I. 21–30.
[2] So Cloten is slain near Milford Haven.

And heere to speake my fansie also what I thinke of this Arviragus, and the other kings . . . I will not denie but such persons there were, and the same happilie bearing verie great rule in the land . . . [But he is doubtful about when and where.] For my part therefore, sith this order of the British kinglie succession in this place is more easie to be flatly denied and utterlie reprooved, than either wiselie defended or trulie amended, I will referre the reforming therof unto those that have perhaps seene more than I have, or more deepelie considered the thing, to trie out an undoubted truth.

[In Ch. 4 Holinshed gives (with some scepticism) the British account telling how Arviragus later refused tribute and fought an indecisive battle against Vespasian.]

On the morrow after queene Genissa made them friends, and so the warres ceassed for that time, by hir good mediation.

II. Source

From
THE DESCRIPTION AND HISTORIE OF SCOTLAND
by R. Holinshed (1587 edn)[1]

[154/2/59] From thence the armie of the Danes passed through Angus unto the river of Taie,[2] all the people of the countries by which they marched fleeing afore them. King Kenneth at the same time laie at Sterling, where hearing of these greevous newes, he determined foorthwith to raise his people, & to go against his enimies. The assemblie of the Scottish armie was appointed to be at the place where the river of Erne falleth into the river of Taie. Here when they were come togither in great numbers at the day appointed, the day next following word was brought to the king, that the Danes having passed over Taie, were come before the towne of Bertha,[3] and had laid siege to the same. Then without further delaie, he raised with the whole armie, and marched streight towards his enimies, comming that night unto Loncart a village not far distant from the river of

---

[1] In *The First and Second Volumes of Chronicles, Part III. The Description and Historie of Scotland.*
[2] *In margin:* 'The Danes come to the river of Taie. King Kenneth gathered a great armie.'
[3] *In margin:* 'They laie siege before Bertha.' Bertha was Perth.

Taie, famous ever after, by reason of the battell fought then neere unto the same. The Danes hearing that the Scots were come, detracted no time, but foorthwith prepared to give battell.

[155/1/6] Kenneth as soone as the sunne was up, beholding the Danes at hand, quickelie brought his armie into order.[1] Then requiring them earnestlie to shew their manhood, he promiseth to release them of all tributs and paiments due to the kings cofers for the space of five yeares next insuing: and besides that he offered the summe of ten pounds, or else lands so much woorth in value to everie one of his armie, that should bring him the head of a Dane. He willed them therefore to fight manfullie,[2] and to remember there was no place to atteine mercie; for either must they trie it out by dint of swoord, or else if they fled, in the end to looke for present death at the enimies hands, who would not ceasse till time they had found them foorth, into what place so euer they resorted for refuge, if they chanced to be vanquished. The Scots being not a little incouraged by the kings words, kept their order of battell according as they were appointed, still looking when the onset should be given. Malcolme Duffe prince of Cumberland led the right wing of the Scots; and Duncane lieutenant of Atholl the left: King Kenneth himselfe governed the battell. The enimies on the other part had taken their ground at the foot of a little mounteine right afore against the Scotish campe.[3] Thus both the armies stood readie ranged in the field, beholding either other a good space, till at length the Scots desirous of battell, and doubting least the Danes would not come foorth to anie even ground, advanced forward with somewhat more hast than the case required, beginning the battell with shot, and throwing of darts right freshlie.[4]

[155/1/38] The Danes being backed with the mounteine, were constreined to leave the same, and with all speed to come forward upon their enimies, that by joining they might avoid the danger of the Scotishmens arrowes and darts: by this meanes therefore they came to hand-strokes, in maner before the signe was given on either part to the battell. The fight was cruell on both sides: and nothing hindered the Scots so much, as going about to cut off the heads of the Danes, ever as they might overcome them. Which manner being noted of the Danes, and perceiving that here was no hope of life but

---

[1] *In margin:* 'King Kenneth set his men in aray.'
[2] *In margin:* 'The king exhorted the Scots unto valiantnesse.'
[3] *In margin:* 'The order of the Scotish battell aray. The Danes had the advantage of a little mounteine.'
[4] *In margin:* 'The Scots begin the battell.'

in victorie, they rushed foorth with such violence upon their adversaries, that first the right, and then after the left wing of the Scots,
was constreined to retire and flee backe,[1] the middle-ward stoutly
yet keeping their ground: but the same stood in such danger, being
now left naked on the sides, that the victorie must needes have remained with the Danes, had not a renewer of the battell come
in time, by the appointment (as is to be thought) of almightie
God.

For as it chanced, there was in the next field at the same time an
husbandman, with two of his sons busie about his worke, named
Haie, a man strong and stiffe in making and shape of bodie, but
indued with a valiant courage.[2] This Haie beholding the king with
the most part of the nobles, fighting with great valiancie in the
middle ward, now destitute of the wings, and in great danger to be
oppressed by the great violence of his enimies, caught a plow-beame
in his hand, and with the same exhorting his sonnes to doo the like,
hasted towards the battell, there to die rather amongst other in
defense of his countrie, than to remaine alive after the discomfiture
in miserable thraldome and bondage of the cruell and most unmercifull enimies. There was neere to the place of the battell, a long
lane fensed on the sides with ditches and walles made of turfe,
through the which the Scots which fled were beaten downe by the
enimies on heapes.

Here Haie with his sonnes, supposing they might best staie the
flight, placed themselves overthwart the lane, beat them back
whome they met fleeing, and spared neither friend nor fo:[3] but
downe they went all such as came within their reach, wherewith
diverse hardie personages cried unto their fellowes to returne backe
unto the battell, for there was a new power of Scotishmen come to
their succours, by whose aid the victorie might be easilie obteined of
their most cruell adversaries the Danes: therefore might they choose
whether they would be slaine of their owne fellowes comming to
their aid, or to returne againe to fight with the enimies.[4] The Danes
being here staied in the lane by the great valiancie of the father and
the sonnes, thought verely there had beene some great succors of
Scots come to the aid of their king, and thereupon ceassing from
further pursute, fled backe in great disorder unto the other of their
fellowes fighting with the middle ward of the Scots.[5]

The Scots also that before was chased, being incouraged herewith,

---

[1] *In margin:* 'The two wings of the Scots fled.'
[2] *In margin:* 'Haie with his two sonnes.'
[3] *In margin:* 'Haie staied the Scots from running away.'
[4] *In margin:* 'The Scots were driven to their battell againe.'
[5] *In margin:* 'The Danes fled towards their fellowes in great disorder.'

pursued the Danes unto the place of the battell right fiercelie. Whereupon Kenneth perceiving his people to be thus recomforted, and his enimies partlie abashed, called upon his men to remember their duties,[1] and now sith their adversaries hearts began (as they might perceive) to faint, he willed them to follow upon them manfully, which if they did, he assured them that the victorie undoubtedlie should be theirs. The Scots incouraged with the kings words, laid about them so earnestlie, that in the end the Danes were constreined to forsake the field,[2] and the Scots eagerlie pursuing in the chase, made great slaughter of them as they fled. This victorie turned highlie to the praise of the Scotish nobilitie, the which fighting in the middle ward, bare still the brunt of the battell, continuing manfullie therein even to the end. But Haie, who in such wise (as is before mentioned) staied them that fled, causing them to returne againe to the field, deserved immortall fame and commendation: for by this meanes chieflie was the victorie atchived. And therefore on the morrow after, when the spoile of the field and of the enimies campe (which they had left void) shuld be divided, the chiefest part was bestowed on him and his two sonnes, by consent of all the multitude;[3] the residue being divided amongst the souldiers and men of warre, accerding to the ancient custome used amongst this nation.

The king having thus vanquished his enimies, as he should enter into Bertha, caused costlie robes to be offered unto Haie and his sonnes, that, being richlie clad, they might be the more honoured of the people: but Haie refusing to change his apparell,[4] was contented to go with the king in his old garments whither it pleased him to appoint. So entring with the king into Bertha,[5] he was received with little lesse honor than the king himselfe, all the people running foorth to behold him, whome they heard to have so valiantlie restored the battell, when the field was in maner lost without hope of all recoverie. At his entring into the towne he bare on his shoulder the plow-beame, more honourable to him than anie sword or battell axe might have been to anie the most valiant warrior. Thus Haie being honored of all estates, within certaine daies after, at a councell holden at Scone, it was ordeined, that both he and his posteritie should be accepted amongst the number of the chiefest nobles and peeres of the realme,[6] being rewarded (besides monie

---

[1] *In margin:* 'K. Kenneth called upon his men to remember their duties.'
[2] *In margin:* 'The Danes forsake the field.'
[3] *In margin:* 'The spoile is divided.'
[4] *In margin:* 'Haie refused costlie garments.'
[5] *In margin:* 'The king came to Bertha.'
[6] *In margin:* 'Haie is made one of the nobilitie.'

and other great gifts) with lands and revenues,[1] such as he should
choose sufficient for the maintenance of their estates.[2]

III. Source

From
THE DECAMERON
by Giovanni Boccaccio,
anonymously translated (1620)

The Second Day: The ninth Novell.

*Bernardo, a Merchant of Geneway, being deceived by another
Merchant, named Ambrogiuolo,[3] lost a great part of his goods.
And commanding his innocent Wife to be murthered, she
escaped, and (in the habite of a man) became servant to the
Soldane. The deceiver being found at last, shee compassed such
meanes, that her husband Bernardo came into Alexandria, and,
there, after due punishment inflicted on the false deceiver, she
resumed the garments againe of a woman, and returned home
with her Husband to Geneway.*

Madam Eliza having ended her compassionate discourse, which
indeede had moved all the rest to sighing; the Queene, who was
faire, comely of stature, and carrying a very majesticall countenance,
smiling more familiarly then the other, spake to them thus: . . .
Many times among vulgar people, it hath passed as a common
Proverbe: That the deceiver is often trampled on, by such as he
hath deceived. And this cannot shew it selfe (by any reason) to be
true, except such accidents as awaite on treachery, doe really make

---

[1] *In margin:* 'He had revenues assigned to him.'

[2] Cf. Sir Robert Douglas, *The Peerage of Scotland*, ed. J. P. Wood, Edinburgh, 1813,
1, p. 544: 'The King, as a reward of that signal service, gave him as much land in
the Carse of Gowrie, as a falcon should fly over before she settled, and a falcon
being accordingly let off, flew over an extent of ground six miles in length, afterwards called Errol, and lighted on a stone, still called the Falcon-stone. The king
also assigned three shields or escutcheons for the arms of the family, to intimate
that the father and the two sons had been the three fortunate shields of Scotland;
and the Earl of Errol bears for crest a falcon, and his supporters are two men in
country habits, holding the yokes of a plough over their shoulders, with this
motto, *Serva jugum*, in allusion to their origin.'

[3] Ambroginolo *1620 throughout. Boccaccio* has Ambrogiuolo.

a just discovery thereof. And therefore according to the course of this day observed, I am the woman that must make good what I have saide for the approbation of that Proverbe: no way (I hope) distastfull to you in the hearing, but advantageable to preserve you from any such beguiling.

There was a faire and goodly Inne in Paris, much frequented by many great Italian Merchants, according to such variety of occasions and businesse, as urged their often resorting thither. One night among many other, having had a merry Supper together, they began to discourse on divers matters, and falling from one relation to another; they communed in very friendly manner, concerning their wives, lefte at home in their houses. Quoth the first, I cannot well imagine what my wife is now doing, but I am able to say for my selfe, that if a pretty female should fall into my company: I could easily forget my love to my wife, and make use of such an advantage offered.

A second replyed; And trust me, I should do no lesse, because I am perswaded, that if my wife be willing to wander, the law is in her owne hand, and I am farre enough from home: dumbe walles blab no tales, and offences unknowne are sildome or never called in question. A third man unapt in censure, with his former fellowes of the Jury; and it plainely appeared, that all the rest were of the same opinion, condemning their wives over-rashly, and alledging, that when husbands strayed so far from home, their wives had wit enought to make use of their time.

Onely one man among them all, named Bernardo Lomellino, and dwelling in Geneway, maintained the contrary; boldly avouching, that by the especiall favour of Fortune,[1] he had a wife so perfectly compleate in all graces and vertues, as any Lady in the world possibly could be, and that Italy scarsely contained her equall. But, she was goodly of person, and yet very young, quicke, quaint, milde, and courteous, and not any thing appertaining to the office of a wife, either for domesticke affayres, or any other imployment whatsoever, but in woman-hoode shee went beyond all other. No Lord, Knight, Esquire, or Gentleman, could be better served at his Table, then himselfe dayly was, with more wisedome, modesty and discretion. After all this, hee praised her for riding, hawking, hunting, fishing, fowling, reading, writing, enditing, and most absolute keeping his Bookes of accounts, that neither himselfe, or any other Merchant could therein excell her. After infinite other commendations, he came to the former point of their argument, concerning the easie falling of women into wantonnesse, maintaining (with a solemne oath) that no woman possibly could be more chaste and honest than

[1] *Bocc.* 'di spezial gracia di Dio'. Cf. I. 4. 90–2.

she: in which respect, he was verily perswaded, that if he stayed
from her ten years space (yes all his life time) out of his house; yet
never would shee falsifie her faith to him, or be lewdly allured by
any other man.

Amongst these Merchants thus communing together, there was a
young proper man, named Ambrogiuolo of Placentia, who began to
laugh at the last prayses which Bernardo had used of his Wife, and
seeming to make a mockerie thereof, demaunded, if the Emperour
had given him this priviledge, above all other married men? Bernardo being somewhat offended, answered: No Emperour hath done
it, but the especiall blessing of heaven, exceeding all the Emperours
on the earth in grace, and thereby have I received this favour;
whereto Ambrogiuolo presently thus replyed. Bernardo, without all
question to the contrary, I beleeve that what thou hast said, is true;
but (for ought I can perceive) thou hast slender judgement in the
Nature of things: because, if thou diddst observe them well, thou
couldst not be of so grosse understanding. For, by comprehending
matters in their true kinde and nature, thou wouldst speake of them
more correctly then thou doest. And to the end, thou mayest not
imagine, that we who have spoken of our Wives, doe thinke any
otherwise of them, then as well and honestly as thou canst of thine,
nor that any thing else did urge these speeches of them, or falling
into this kinde of discourse, but onely by a naturall instinct and
admonition, I will proceede familiarly, a little further with thee,
uppon the matter alreadie propounded.

I have evermore understoode, that man was the most noble
creature, formed by God to live in this World, and woman in the
next degree to him: but man, as generally is beleeved, and as is dis-
cerned by apparent effects is the most perfect of both. Having then
the most perfection in him, without all doubt, he must be so much
the more firme and constant. So in like manner, it hath beene, and is
universally graunted, that Woman is more various and mutable,
and the reason thereof may be approved by many naturall circumstances, which were needless now to make any mention of. If a man
then be possessed of the greater stability, and yet cannot containe
himselfe from condiscending, I say not to one that entreates him, but
to desire any other that may please him; and beside, to covet the
enjoying of his owne pleasing contentment (a thing not chancing to
him once in a moneth, but infinite times in a dayes space). What can
you then conceive of a fraile Woman, subject (by nature) to en-
treaties, flatteries, giftes, perswasions, and a thousand other inticing
meanes, which a man (that is affected to her) can use? Doest thou
thinke then that she hath any power to containe? Assuredly, though
thou shouldest rest so resolved, yet cannot I be of the same opinion.

For I am sure thou beleevest, and must needes confesse it, that thy wife is a Woman, made of flesh and blood, as other women are: if it be so, she cannot bee without the same desires, and the weaknesse or strength as other women have, to resist naturall appetites as her owne are.[1] In regard whereof, it is meerely impossible (although she be most honest) but she must needs doe that which other Women doe: for there is nothing else possible, either to be denied or affirmed to the contrary, as thou most unadvisedly hast done.

Bernardo answered in this manner. I am a Merchant, and no Philospher, and like a Merchant I meane to answer thee. I am not to learne, that these accidents by thee related, may happen to fooles, who are voide of understanding or shame: but such as are wise, and endued with vertue, have alwayes such a precious esteeme of their honour, that they wil containe those principles of constancie, which men are meerely carelesse of, and I justifie my wife to be one of them. Beleeve me Bernardo, replyed Ambrigiuolo, if so often as thy wives minde is addicted to wanton folly, a badge of scorne should arise on thy forehead, to render testimony of hir female frailty, I beleeve the number of them would be more, then willingly you would wish them to be. And among all married men in every degree, the notes are so secret of their wives imperfections, that the sharpest sight is not able to discerne them: and the wiser sort of men are willing not to know them; because shame and losse of honour is never imposed, but in cases evident and apparant.

Perswade thy selfe then Bernardo, that what women may accomplish in secret, they will rarely faile to doe: or if they abstaine, it is through feare and folly. Wherefore, hold it for a certaine rule, that that woman is onely chaste, that never was solicited personally, or if she endured any such suite, either shee answered yea, or no. And albeit I know this to be true, by many infallible and naturall reasons, yet could I not speak so exactly as I doe, if I had not tried experimentally, the humours and affections of divers Women. Yea, and let me tell thee more Bernardo, were I in private company with thy wife, howsoever thou presumest to thinke her to bee, I should account it a matter of no impossibility, to finde in her the selfesame frailty.

Bernardoes blood now began to boyle, and patience being a little put downe by choller, thus he replyed. A combat of words requires over-long continuance; for I maintaine the matter which thou deniest, and all this sorts to nothing in the end. But seeing thou presumest, that all women are so apt and tractable, and thy selfe so confident of thine owne power: I willingly yeeld (for the better assurance of my wifes constant loyalty) to have my head smitten off,

[1] Posthumus develops these ideas in his fury in II. 5.

if thou canst winne her to any such dishonest act, by any meanes whatsoever thou canst use unto her; which if thou canst not doe, thou shalt onely loose a thousand duckets of Gold.[1] Now began Ambrogiuolo to be heated with these words, answering thus. Bernardo, if I had won the wager, I know not what I should doe with thy head; but if thou be willing to stand upon the proofe, pawne downe five thousand Duckets of gold, (a matter of much lesse value then thy head) against a thousand Duckets of mine, granting me a lawfull limited time, which I require to be no more then the space of three moneths, after the day of my departing hence. I will stand bound to goe for Geneway, and there winne such kinde consent of thy Wife, as shall be to mine owne content. In witnesse whereof, I will bring backe with me such private and especiall tokens, as thou thy selfe shalt confesse that I have not failed. Provided, that thou doe first promise upon thy faith, to absent thy selfe thence during my limitted time, and be no hinderance to me by thy Letters, concerning the attempt by me undertaken.

Bernardo saide, Be it a bargaine, I am the man that will make good my five thousands Duckets; and albeit the other Merchants then present, earnestly laboured to breake the wager, knowing great harme must needs ensue thereon: yet both the parties were so hot and fiery, as all the other men spake to no effect, but writings was made, sealed, and delivered under either of their hands, Bernardo remaining at Paris, and Ambrogiuolo departing for Geneway. There he remained some few dayes, to learne the streetes name where Bernardo dwelt, as also the conditions and qualities of his Wife, which scarcely pleased him when he heard them; because they were farre beyond her Husbands relation, and shee reputed to be the onely wonder of women; whereby he plainely perceived, that he had undertaken a very idle enterprise, yet would he not give it over so, but proceeded therein a little further.

He wrought such meanes, that he came acquainted with a poore woman, who often frequented Bernardoes house, and was greatly in favour with his wife; upon whose poverty he so prevailed, by earnest perswasions, but much more by large gifts of money, that he won her to further him in this manner following. A faire and artificiall Chest he caused to be purposely made[2] wherein himselfe might be aptly contained, and so conveyed into the House of Bernardoes Wife, under colour of a formall excuse; that the poore woman should be absent from the City two or three dayes, and shee must keepe it safe till she returne. The Gentlewoman suspecting no guile, but that the

[1] In B. they are 'golden florins' ('fiorin d'oro'); in le Macon 'ducatz d'or'.
[2] Iachimo's trunk is already prepared at I. 6. 196. He plausibly asks Imogen to keep it in her house for one night only, thus avoiding the go-between.

Chest was the receptacle of all the womans wealth; would trust it in no other roome, then her owne Bed-chamber, which was the place where Ambrogiuolo most desired to bee.

Being thus conveyed into the Chamber, the night going on apace, and the Gentlewoman fast asleepe in her bed, a lighted Taper[1] stood burning on the Table by her, as in her Husbands absence shee ever used to have: Ambrogiuolo softly opened the Chest, according as cunningly hee had contrived it, and stepping forth in his sockes made of cloath, observed the scituation[2] of the Chamber, the paintings, pictures, and beautifull hangings,[3] with all things else that were remarkable,[4] which perfectly he committed to his memory.[5] Going neere to the bed, he saw her lie there sweetly sleeping, and her young Daughter in like manner by her,[6] she seeming then as compleate and pleasing a creature, as when shee was attired in her best bravery. No especiall note or marke could hee descrie, whereof he might make credible report, but onely a small wart upon her left pappe, with some few haires growing thereon, appearing to be as yellow as gold.[7]

Sufficient had he seene, and durst presume no further; but taking one of her Rings, which lay upon the Table, a purse of hers, hanging by on the wall, a light wearing Robe of silke, and her girdle, all which he put into the Chest; and being in himselfe, closed it fast as it was before, so continuing there in the Chamber two severall nights, the Gentlewoman neither mistrusting or missing any thing. The third day being come, the poore woman, according as formerly was concluded, came to have home her Chest againe, and brought it safely into her owne house; where Ambrogiuolo comming forth of it, satisfied the poore woman to her owne liking, returning (with all the forenamed things) so fast as conveniently he could to Paris.

Being arrived there long before his limmitted time, he called the Merchants together, who were present at the passed words and wager; avouching before Bernardo, that he had won his five thousand Duckets, and performed the taske he undertooke. To make good his protestation, first he described the forme of the Chamber, the curious pictures hanging about it, in what manner the bed stood, and every circumstance else beside. Next he shewed the severall things, which he brought away thence with him, affirming that he had received them of her selfe. Bernardo confessed, that his descrip-

---

[1] II. 2. 19.
[2] II. 2. 25, 'there the window'.
[3] II. 2. 25–6.
[4] II. 2. 27.
[5] Iachimo makes notes at once: II. 2. 24; 43.
[6] No child mentioned in *Cym*; in B. and M. 'a little girl who was with her'.
[7] *Bocc.* has, 'under her left breast there was a mole, round which were a few downy hairs, yellow as gold'.

tion of the Chamber was true, and acknowledged moreover, that these other things did belong to his Wife: But (quoth he) this may be gotten, by corrupting some servant of mine, both for intelligence of the Chamber, as also of the Ring, Purse, and what else is beside; all which suffice not to win the wager, without some other more apparent and pregnant token. In troth, answered Ambrogiuolo, me thinkes these should serve for sufficient proofes; but seeing thou art so desirous to know more: I plainely tell thee, that faire Genevra thy Wife, hath a small round wart upon her left pappe, and some few little golden haires growing thereon.

When Bernardo heard these words, they were as so many stabs to his heart, yea, beyond all compasse of patient sufferance, and by the changing of his colour, it was noted manifestly, (being unable to utter one word) that Ambrogiuolo had spoken nothing but the truth. Within a while after, he saide; Gentlemen, that which Ambrogiuolo hath saide, is very true, wherefore let him come when he will, and he shall be paide; which accordingly he performed on the very next day, even to the utmost penny, departing then from Paris towards Geneway, with a most malicious intention to his Wife. Being come neere to the City, he would not enter it, but rode to a Country house of his, standing about tenne miles distant thence. Being there arrived, he called a servant, in whom hee reposed especial trust, sending him to Geneway with two Horses, writing to his Wife, that he was returned, and shee should come thither to see him.[1] But secretly he charged his servant, that so soone as he had brought her to a convenient place, he should there kill her, without any pitty or compassion, and then returne to him againe.

When the servant was come to Geneway, and had delivered his Letter and message, Genevra gave him most joyfull welcome, and on the morrow morning mounting on Horse-backe with the servant, rode merrily towards the Country house; divers things shee discoursed on by the way, till they descended into a deepe solitary valey, very thickly beset with high and huge spreading Trees, which the servant supposed to be a meete place, for the execution of his Masters command. Suddenly drawing forth his Sword, and holding Genevra fast by the arme, he saide; Mistresse, quickly commend your soule to God, for you must die, before you passe any further.[2] Genevra seeing the naked Sword, and hearing the words so peremptorily delivered, fearefully answered; Alas deare friend, mercy for God's sake; and before thou kill me, tell me wherein I have offended thee, and why thou must kill me? Alas good Mistresse, replied the servant, you have not any way offended me, but in what occasion you have displeased

[1] III. 2. 40–7.
[2] Contrast Pisanio's behaviour in III. 4.

your Husband, it is utterly unknowne to me: for he hath strictly commanded me, without respect of pitty or compassion, to kill you by the way as I bring you, and if I doe it not, he hath sworne to hang me by the necke. You know good Mistresse, how much I stand obliged to him, and how impossible it is for me, to contradict any thing that he commandeth. God is my witnesse, that I am truly compassionate of you, and yet (by no meanes) may I let you live.

Genevra kneeling before him weeping, wringing her hands, thus replyed. Wilt thou turne Monster, and be a murtherer of her that never wronged thee, to please another man, and on a bare command? God, who truly knoweth all things, is my faithfull witnesse, that I never committed any offence, whereby to deserve the dislike of my Husband, much lesse so harsh a recompense as this is. But flying from mine owne justification, and appealing to thy manly mercy, thou mayest (wert thou but so well pleased) in a moment satisfie both thy Master and me, in such manner as I will make plaine and apparent to thee.[1] Take thou my garments, spare me onely thy doublet, and such a Bonnet as is fitting for a man, so returne with my habite to thy Master, assuring him, that the deede is done.[2] And here I sweare to thee, by that life which I enjoy but by thy mercy, I will so strangely disguise my selfe, and wander so far off from these Countries, as neither he or thou, nor any person belonging to these parts, shall ever heare any tydings of me.

The servant, who had no great good will to kill her, very easily grew pittifull, tooke off her upper garments, and gave her a poore ragged doublet, a sillie Chapperone,[3] and such small store of money as he had, desiring her to forsake that Country, and so left her to walke on foote out of the valley. When he came to his Maister, and had delivered him her garments, he assured him, that he had not onely accomplished his command, but also was most secure from any discovery: because he had no sooner done the deed, but foure or five very ravenous Woolves, came presently running to the dead bodie, and gave it buriall in their bellyes. Bernardo soone after returning to Geneway, was much blamed for such unkinde cruelty to his wife; but his constant avouching of her treason to him (according then to the Countries custome) did cleare him from all pursuite of Law.[4]

Poor Genevra was left thus alone and disconsolate, and night stealing fast upon her, shee went to a silly village neere adjoyning,

[1] Imogen wishes to die; Pisanio suggests a way out.
[2] Pisanio has 'doublet, hat, hose', etc. in his cloak-bag (III. 4. 168–71).
[3] A simple hood or cap.
[4] *Bocc.* 'the fact being known, he was much blamed.'

where (by the meanes of a good olde woman) she got such provision
as the place afforded, making the doblet fit to her body, and convert-
ing her petticoate to a paire of breeches, according to the Mariners
fashion: then cutting her haire, and quaintly disguised like unto a
Saylor, she went to the Sea coast. By good fortune, she met there
with a Gentleman of Cathalogna, whose name was Signior Enchararcho, who came on land from his Ship, which lay hulling there
about Albagia, to refresh himselfe at a pleasant Spring. Enchararcho
taking her to be a man, as shee appeared no otherwise by her habite;
upon some conference passing betweene them, shee was entertayned
into his service, and being brought aboord the Ship, she went under
the name of Sicurano da Finale. There shee had better apparrell
bestowne on her by the Gentleman, and her service proved so pleasing and acceptable to him, that hee liked her care and diligence
beyond all comparison.[1]

It came to passe within a short while after, that this Gentleman of
Cathalogna sayled (with some charge of his) into Alexandria, carrying thither certaine Faulcons, which he presented to the Soldan, who
oftentimes welcommed this Gentleman to his table, where he observed the behaviour of Sicurano, attending on his Maisters Tren-
cher, and therewith was so highly pleased; that hee requested to have
him from the Gentleman, who (for his more advancement) willingly
parted with his so lately entertained servant. Sicurano was so ready
and discreet in his daily services, that he grew in as great grace with
the Soldan, as before hee had done with Enchararcho.

At a certaine season in the yeare, as customary order (there observed) had formerly beene, in the City of Acres which was under
the Soldanes subjection, there yeerely met a great assembly of
Merchants, as Christians, Moores, Jewes, Sarazens, and many other
Nations besides, as at a common Mart or Fayre. And to the end, that
the Merchants (for the better sale of their goods) might be there in
the safer assurance, the Soldane used to send thither some of his
ordinarie Officers, and a strong guard of Souldiers beside, to defend
them from all injuries and molestation, because he reaped thereby no
meane benefit. And who should be now sent about this businesse, but
his new elected favourite Sicurano, because she was skilfull and perfect in the Languages.

Sicurano being come to Acres, as Lord and Captaine of the Guard
for the Merchants, and for the safety of their Merchandizes, she discharged her office most commendably, walking with her traine
thorough every part of the Fayre, where she observed a worthy company of Merchants, Sicilians, Pisans, Genewayes, Venetians, and
other Italians, whom the more willingly she noted, in remembrance

---

[1] In *Cym* Lucius takes the place of the Catalan gentleman.

of her native Country. At one especiall time among other, chancing
into a Shop or Booth belonging to the Venetians, she espied (hanging
up with other costly wares) a Purse and a Girdle, which sodainly she
remembered to be sometime her owne; whereat she was not a little
abashed in her minde. But without making any such outward shew,
courteously she requested to know whose they were, and whether
they should be sold, or no.

Ambrogiuolo of Placentia, was likewise come thither, and great
store of Merchandizes hee had brought with him, in a Carracke
appertaining to the Venetians, and hee hearing the Captaine of the
Guard demaund whose they were, stepped foorth before him, and
smiling, answered: That they were his, but not to be solde; yet if hee
liked them, gladly he would bestow them on him. Sicurano seeing
him smile, suspected least himselfe had (by some unfitting behaviour) beene the occasion thereof: and therefore, with a more
setled coutenance, hee said; Perhaps thou smilest, because I that am
a man, professing Armes, should question after such womanish toyes.
Ambrogiuolo replyed, My Lord, pardon mee, I smile not at you, or
at your demaund, but at the manner how I came by these things.

Sicurano, upon this answere, was ten times more desirous then
before, and saide: If Fortune favoured thee in friendly manner, by the
obtaining of these things: if it may be spoken, tell mee how thou
hadst them. My Lord (answered Ambrogiuolo) these things (with
many more besides) were given me by a Gentlewoman of Geneway,
named Madam Genevra, the wife to one Bernardo Lomellino, in
recompence of one nights lodging with her, and she desired me to
keepe them for her sake. Now, the maine reason of my smiling, was
the remembrance of her husbands folly, in waging five thousand
Duckets of Gold, against one thousand of mine, that I should not
obtaine my will of his Wife; which I did, and thereby won the wager.
But hee, who better deserved to be punished for his folly, then shee,
who was but sicke of all womens disease; returning from Paris to
Geneway, caused her to be slaine, as afterward it was reported by
himselfe.

When Sicurano heard this horrible lye, immediately she conceived, that this was the occasion of her husbands hatred to her, and
all the hard haps which she had since suffered: whereupon, shee
reputed it for more than a mortall sinne, if such a villaine should
passe without due punishment. Sicurano seemed to like well this
report, and grew into such familiarity with Ambrogiuolo, that (by
her perswasions) when the Fayre was ended, she tooke him higher
with her into Alexandria, and all his Wares along with him, furnish-
ing him with a fit and convenient shop, where he made great benefite
of his Merchandizes, trusting all his monies in the Captaines

*

custody, because it was the safest course for him, and so hee continued there with no meane contentment.

Much did shee pitty her Husbands perplexity, devising by what good and warrantable meanes she might make knowne her innocency to him; wherein her place and authority did greatly sted her, and she wrought with divers gallant Merchants of Geneway that then remained in Alexandria, and by vertue of the Soldans friendly letters beside, to bring him thither upon an especial occasion. Come he did, albeit in poore and meane order, which soone was better altered by her appointment, and he verie honourably (though in private) entertained by divers of her woorthie friends, till time did favour what she further intended.

In the expectation of Bernardoes arrivall, she had so prevayled with Ambrogiuolo, that the same tale which he formerly told to her, he delivered againe in presence of the Soldan, who seemed to be wel pleased with it. But after shee had once seene her Husband, shee thought upon her more serious businesse; providing her selfe of an apt opportunity, when shee entreated such favour of the Soldan, that both the men might bee brought before him; where if Ambrogiuolo would not confesse (without constraint) that which he had made his vaunt of concerning Bernardoes wife, he might be compelled thereto perforce.

Sicuranoes word was a Law with the Soldane, so that Ambrogiuolo and Bernardo being brought face to face, the Soldane with a sterne and angry countenance, in the presence of a most Princely Assembly, commanded Ambrogiuolo to declare the truth, upon perill of his life, by what meanes he won the Wager for the five thousand Golden Duckets he received of Bernardo. Ambrogiuolo seeing Sicurano there present, upon whose favour he wholly relyed, yet perceiving her lookes likewise to be as dreadful as the Soldans, and hearing her threaten him with most greevous torments except he revealed the truth indeed; you may easily guesse in what condition he stood at that instant.

Frownes and fury he beheld on either side, and Bernardo standing before him, with a world of famous witnesses, to heare his lye confounded by his owne confession, and his tongue to denie what it had before so constantly avouched. Yet dreaming on no other pain or penalty, but restoring backe the five thousand Duckets of gold, and the other things by him purloyned, truly he revealed the whole forme of his falshood. Then Sicurano according as the Soldane had formerly commanded him, turning to Bernardo, saide. And thou, upon the suggestion of this foule lye, what didst thou to thy Wife? Being (quoth Bernardo) overcome with rage, for the losse of my money, and the dishonour I supposed to receive by my Wife; I caused a servant of mine to kill her, and as hee credibly avouched, her body was devoured by ravenous Wolves in a moment after.

These things being thus spoken and heard, in the presence of the Soldan, and no reason (as yet) made knowne, why the case was so seriously urged, and to what end it would succeede: Sicurano spake in this manner to the Soldane. My gracious Lord, you may plainly perceive, in what degree that poor Gentlewoman might make her vaunt, beeing so well provided, both of a loving friend, and a husband. Such was the friends love, that in an instant, and by a wicked lye, hee robbed her both of her renowne and honour, and bereft her also of her husband. And her husband, rather crediting anothers falsehoode, then the invincible trueth, whereof he had faithfull knowledge, by long and very honorable experience; caused her to be slaine, and made foode for devouring Wolves. Beside all this, such was the good will and affection borne to that Woman both by friend and husband, that the longest continuer of them in her company, makes them alike in knowledge of her. But because your great wisedom knoweth perfectly what each of them have worthily deserved: if you please (in your ever-knowne gracious benignity) to permit the punishment of the deceiver, and pardon the partie so deceyved; I will procure such meanes, that she shall appeare here in your presence, and theirs.

The Soldane, being desirous to give Sicurano all manner of satisfaction, having followed the course so industriously, bad him to produce the Woman, and hee was well contented. Whereat Bernardo stoode much amazed, because he verily beleeved that she was dead. And Ambrogiuolo foreseeing already a preparation for punishment, feared, that the repayment of the money would not now serve his turne: not knowing also, what he should further hope or suspect, if the woman her selfe did personally appeare, which hee imagined would be a miracle. Sicurano having thus obtained the Soldanes permission, in teares, humbling her selfe at his feete, in a moment she lost her manly voyce and demeanour, as knowing that she was now no longer to use them, but must truly witnesse what she was indeed, and therefore thus spake.

Great Soldane, I am the miserable and unfortunate Genevra, that for the space of sixe whole yeeres, have wandered through the world, in the habite of a man, falsely and most maliciously slaundered, by this villainous traytor Ambrogiuolo, and by this unkinde cruell husband, betraied to his servant to be slaine, and left to be devoured by savage beasts. Afterward, desiring such garments as better fitted for her, and shewing her breasts, she made it apparant before the Soldane and his assistants, that shee was the very same woman indeede. Then turning her selfe to Ambrogiuolo, with more then manly courage, she demanded of him, when, and where it was, that he lay with her, as (villainously) he was not ashamed to make his vaunt? But hee, having alreadie acknowledged the contrarie, being stricken dumbe with shamefull disgrace, was not able to utter one word.

The Soldane, who had alwayes reputed Sicurano to be a man, having heard and seene so admirable an accident; was so amazed in his minde, that many times he was very doubtfull, whether this was a dreame, or an absolute relation of trueth. But, after hee had more seriously considered thereon, and found it to be reall and infallible: with extraordinary gracious praises, he commended the life, constancy, condition and vertues of Genevra, whom (til that time) he had alwayes called Sicurano. So committing her to the company of honourable Ladies, to be changed from her manly habite; he pardoned Bernardo her husband (according to her request formerly made) although hee had more justly deserved death: which likewise himselfe confessed, and falling at the feet of Genevra, desired her (in teares) to forgive his rash transgression, which most lovingly she did, kissing and embracing him a thousand times.

Then the Soldane strictly commaunded, that on some high and eminent place of the Citie, Ambrogiuolo should be bound and impaled on a stake, having his naked body nointed all over with hony, and never to bee taken off, untill (of it selfe) it fell in peeces, which, according to the sentence, was presently performed. Next, he gave expresse charge, that all his mony and goods should be given to Genevra, which valued above ten thousands double Duckets. Forthwith a solemne Feast was prepared, wherein much honor was done to Bernardo, being the husband of Genevra: and to her, as to a most worthy woman, and matchlesse wife, he gave in costly Jewels, as also vessels of gold and silver plate, so much as did amount to above ten thousand double Duckets more.

When the feasting was finished, he caused a Ship to be furnished for them, graunting them license to depart from Geneway when they pleased; whither they returned most richly and joyfully, being welcomed home with great honour, especially Madam Genevra, whom every one supposed to be dead; and alwayes after, so long as she lived, shee was most famous for her manifold vertues. But as for Ambrogiuolo, the verie same day that hee was impaled on the stake, annointed with honey, and fixed in the place appointed, to his no meane torment: he not onely died, but likewise was devoured to the bare bones, by Flies, Waspes, and Hornets, whereof the Countrey notoriously aboundeth. And his bones, in full forme and fashion, remained strangely blacke for a long time after, knit together by the sinewes; as a witnesse to many thousands of people, which afterward beheld the Carkasse of his wickednesse against so good and vertuous a Woman, that had not so much as a thought of any evill towards him.[1] And thus was the Proverbe truly verified, that shame succeedeth after ugly sinne, and the deceiver is trampled and trod, by such as himselfe hath deceived.

IV. Source

FREDERYKE OF JENNEN
Anon. (1560 edn)

HERE BEGYNNETH A PROPRE TREATYSE OF A MARCHAUNTES WYFE, THAT AFTERWARDE WENTE LYKE A MAN AND BECAME A GRETE LORDE, AND WAS CALLED FREDERYKE OF JENNEN

The prologue

Our lord god sayeth in the gospel, 'What measure ye mete withal, ther with shall ye be mete agayn.' And do your besynes ryghtfully and justly ye shal have a blessyd and a good ende to your rewarde; and occupye your besynes unryghtfully, and ye shall have an yl rewarde therfore, as this story maketh mencion. But now a dayes every man gyve hym selfe to occupye deceytes and unrightfulness, but neverthelesse at the laste commeth ryghtfulness; and he that hath occupied that, he shal have for his rewarde everlastynge blisse, as this lytell story sheweth of a fals marchaunte that deceyved another marchaunte with grete falsenesse and deceyte, but at the last for his falsenesse he was hanged. And that was his rewarde for that false dede, as here after foloweth more playnely.

How foure marchauntes met al together in one waye, whiche were of foure divers londes; and howe they woulde all to Paris.

In the yere of our Lorde God M.CCCC.xxiiii it happened, that foure ryche marchauntes departed out of divers countreis for to do their marchaundise; and as they were goyng their journeys by fortune they mette all together and fel in company together, for thei were al foure goyng towarde Paris in Fraunce; and for company sake they rode al iiii into one ynne, and it was about shraf-tyd in the mooste joyfull tyme of al the yere. And their names were called as here foloweth: the first was called Courant of Spayne, the second was called Borcharde of Fraunce, the thirde was called John of

---

[1] Iachimo is pardoned; but cf. Posthumus's outburst, 'Thou king, send out/For tortures ingenious'—for himself (V. 5. 215–16).

Florence, and the iiii was called Ambrose of Jennen.[1] Then by the consent of the other marchauntes Borcharde of Fraunce went unto the hoste[2] and sayd, 'Hoste! Nowe is the meriest tyme of the yere and we be foure marchauntes of foure divers countreis, and by fortune we met altogether in one place, and oure journey is to Paris. And therefore whyle we be so met let us make good chere together, and ordeine the best meet that ye can get for money against tomorowe, and byd also some of your best frendes that you love moste, that we maye make good chere together or that we departe fro hence; and we shall contente you all your money agayne.' And than the hoste sayd that he woulde do it with a good wil and than went he and bad many of his good frendes and neighbours to diner. And he bought of the best meet that he coulde get for money, and brought it home. And on the morowe he dressed it and made it redy againste dyner after the best maner that he could. And whan that it was diner tyme than came in the gestes to dyner, and the marchauntes came to them and bad them welcome. Than bad the marchauntes the hoste that he should bryng in the meete and lay the table that they myght go to dyner. And than the hoste sayde, 'With a good wyll!' Than went the hoste and layd the table and fetched the meate and set it theron and prayed the marchauntes to take the gestes to them and syt downe together. And sot hey did and made good chere all the daye long with good honeste tyll that it was very late with daunsyng and lepyng. And whan they had doone, the gestes toke their leve of the marchauntes and thanked them for their good chere. And than every man departed home to his house. And than came the marchauntes to the hoste and prayed hym hertely for to come in and thanked hym, that he had ordered and doone all thynges so well and mannerly.

Howe two of the marchauntes, as Johan of Florence and Ambrosius of Jennen, hylde[3] one another v thousande golde gyldens.

Whan all the marchauntes and the gestes had made mery together al the day long, at nyght the gestes toke their leve of the marchauntes and thenked them for theyr good chere that they had made them, and so departed every one to their lodgyng. And as they were departed every man to their house, then wexed it late. And than came the hoste of the house to the marchauntes and asked them if that they would go slepe, and they aunswered unto their hoste, 'Yes'. And than toke he a candell and brought the marchauntes in to a fayre

[1] In Boccaccio they are all Italians. Cf. I. 4. s.d.
[2] Philario is not an innkeeper but an old friend of Posthumus's father (I. 1. 97-9).
[3] held, wagered.

chambre where was iiii beddes rychely hanged with costly curtaynes, that every marchaunt might lye by them selfe. And whan
that they were so altogether in the chambre, than began they to
speke of many thinges, some good, some bad, as it laye in their
myndes. Than sayd Courant of Spayn, 'Sirs, we have be all this day
mery and made good chere, and every one of us hath a fayre wyfe at
home. How fare they nowe at home, we can not tell.' Than said
Bourchard of Fraunce to the other marchauntes, 'What aske you
how they doe? They syt by the fyre and make good chere, and eate
and drynke of the beste and labour not at all; and so get they unto
them hote bloud and than they may take another lystye yong man
and doe their pleasure with him that we knowe not of, for we be
often tymes long from them, and for the cause may they leen[1] a lofe
for a nede secretly to another.' Than sayd Johan of Florence, 'We
may all well be called fooles and ydeotes, that trust our wives in this
maner as we do, for a womans hert is not made of so harde a stone,
but that it wyll melte; for a womans nature is to be unstedfast and
tourneth as the wynde dooeth and careth not for us tyll the time that
we come agayn. And we labour dayly both in wynde and in raine
and put often out lives in jeopardy and in aventure on the sea for to
fynde them withall, and our wyves syt at home and make good chere
with other good felowes, and geve them parte of the money that we
get. And therfore and ye wyll do after my counseyll, let every one of
us take a faire wenche to pas the time withall as well as our wives do,
and they shall knowe no more of that than we knowe of them.'[2] Than
said Ambrosius of Jennen to them, 'By goddes grace that shall I
never dooe whyle that I lyve. For I have at home a good and a
vertuous woman and a womanly. And I know wel that she is not of
that disposition, but that she will eschewe her of all syche yll
abusions till the tyme that I come home agayne, for I knowe wel that
she will have none other man but me alone. And if that I should
breake my wedlocke than were I but litle worthe.' Than sayde John
of Florence, 'Felowe, ye set muche price by your wife at home and
trust her with all that ye have. I wil laye with you a wager of fyve
thousande gyldens,[3] if that ye will abyde me here I shall departe and
ryde to Jennen and dooe with your wyfe my wyll.' Than sayd
Ambrosius to John of Florence, 'I have delyvered to myne hoste five
thousand gyldens to kepe;[4] put ye downe as muche againste it and
I shall tary here tyll the tyme that ye retourne agayne from Jennen,

[1] Lend.
[2] Iachimo attributes these ideas to Posthumus (I. 6. 64–73).
[3] Cf. I. 4. 132–3, 'ten thousand ducats to your ring'.
[4] Posthumus insists on 'covenants', formal 'articles'. Philario reluctantly holds the
stakes.

and if that you by any maner of menes can get your pleasure of my wyfe ye shall have all this money.' Than sayde Johan of Florence, 'I am contente.' And than putte he in his hostes hande other fyve thousande gyldens agaynste Ambrosius money, and than tooke he his leve and departed towarde Jennen. And as he rode thider warde he thought in his mynde by what maner of wyse that he myght come best to speke with Ambroses wyfe, that he myghte have his pleasure of her, and wynne the money that he had layde with Ambrose to a wager, whether it were by ryght or by wrong. And at the laste he had roden so long that he came to Jennen where that Ambroses wyfe dwelte.

How that Johan of Florence was come to Jennen for to speke to Ambroses wyfe, and whan that he came in her presence for to speke to her, he durste not bicause that he founde her so womanly in her behavoure.

And whan that Johan of Florence was come to Jennen, he wente walkyng al aboute to se yf that he coulde spy Ambrosius wyfe.[1] And as he was walkynge, came Ambrosius wyfe to chyrche, so that Johan behelde her, and spake to her and bad her good morow. And she thanked hym and gave unto him agayne swete wordes and womanly behavoure, so that he was a shamed and sayd to hym selfe: 'Alas, poore wretche that I am, what have I done? The money is lost, I se it wel. For she semeth a worshypfull woman and I dare not speke to her of that vylany, whereof I am sory.'[2] And as he walked thus, he thought in hys mynde that yf that he shold wynne the money he must nedes come in to her chambre. And than made he a chest that he wolde have conveyed in to the womans chambre, and he wyst not how. Than remembred he him and sayd, 'I have herde saye that the dyvell can not do that an olde woman can do.' And he thought to prove it. And than went he to the olde clothe market,[3] where he founde an olde woman that solde olde clothes, which he thought best for him. But he sayd, 'How shal I speke beste to here to shewe my mynde?'

How Johan of Florence gave unto the woman a cote of sylke for to sell.

Than broughte Johan of Florence with him a cote of sylke and came to the olde woman and sayd, 'Yf that ye coude sel this cote, I shold gyve you a good drinkynge penny, for it is al to hevy for me.' The woman sayde to hym, 'How! Wyll you sel your sylken cote?' Than

[1] Posthumus has given Iachimo a letter of introduction. I. 6. 22–5.
[2] Iachimo has no such sensitivity. I. 6. 118–68.
[3] Shakespeare omits the old woman and gives Iachimo a plausible excuse to get his trunk into the house. I. 6. 180–99.

answered he, 'Yf that ye may sel it for ii ducates, let it goo.' But the cote was well worth seven ducates. Than was the olde woman glad in her mynde and bad that he shold come agayne the morowe after and he sholde have his monye; and she sayd to her selfe, 'This is my marchaunt!' And than departed he home. And on the nexte daye in the mornynge came Johan of Florence to the olde woman againe. And she gave unto him the ii ducates and she tolde him that she could have no more; but she kepte the cote to her selfe. And than Johan of Florence receyved the two ducates of the olde woman and thanked her. And than he cast downe one of the ducates to her and said unto her, 'Take that and fetche the best meet and drynke that ye can get. For we two must make good chere or that we departe.' And that dyd he for to make the woman dronken, that he myghte have some good counseile of her for to come into Ambroses hous. And at dyner tyme came Johan of Florence to dyne with the olde woman, and there he made good chere and gave unto the olde woman soo moche wyne that she began to wexe mery. And that seynge, Johan of Florence sayd to the olde wyfe that was worser than the devyl, 'Knowe ye not a marchaunt that is called Ambrose?' And the olde woman answered, 'Yes, I know hym wel. He is not at home; but he hath here a fayre woman to his wyfe dwellynge, that is bothe yonge and worshypfull of behavoure, curteyse in answere, gentyl, not proude, good for to speke withall.' Than sayd Johan of Florence, 'Know ye not the way that ye myght convay a chest in to her hous, and I my selfe wil shyt me therin? And whan that the chest hath stande in her hous by the space of iii daies, than come and fetche the chest home againe; and yf that ye can do it, I shal gyve unto you CC ducates for your laboure with a better drinkyng peny.' Than was the olde woman glad with that profer and sayde unto him, 'O my frende, sorowe not for that thynge! Brynge the chest in to my hous and shyt you fast therin and I shall fynde suche wayes that the cheste shall be conveyed in to her house.' Than was Johan of Florence glad and did as the olde women bad him, and fetched the cheste and brought it in to her house and put him selfe therein.

How that the olde woman desyred Ambroses wyfe to kepe a cheste in her house till the tyme that she come from Saynt James.

After that John of Florence had promysed to the olde woman the CC ducates, he woulde see fyrste that she shold erne them before that she shold have them. And the olde woman sought and ymagined many falsenes to have the money. Than went she to Ambroses wyfe with a false herte and greted her, and[1] lovyngly thanked her and bad

[1] 'Ambrose's wife' (omitted).

her welcome to her. For she semed to her for to bee a good honest woman, but she was but a dissimeler of cloked falshede; for it is a commyn saiyng of people that an olde woman can do that the devell hym selfe can not do, as we have in examples more playnely thereof in many diverse bokes, and as this litle boke maketh mencion. Than whan the olde woman had talked a good while with Ambroses wife of many divers matters, than sayde she to her, 'Maistres, my comyng to you at this tyme is for this cause: I did vowe a pilgrimage a longe tyme to the holy apostle Saint James, and nowe take I jorney; and if it please you to sende any offring thither, I shal bere it with a good wil.' And than thanked Ambroses wyfe her and gave unto her a ducate, and said that she should offre that ducate to Saynt James to save her husbande from the perill of the sea and sodayne death. Than toke the olde woman the ducate and sayd, 'Worshypful maistres, I desire you of one thing. I have a cheste here that all my Jewels ben in and all my chefe plates, and I would desyre you to kepe it in youre hous, tyll the tyme that I come home to you agayn. For ye be the woman that I truste and beleve above all other women now beyng alyve.' Than said Ambroses wife, 'That wyll I do with a good will, and I shall set it sure inough, for I will set it in my chamber that it may be the surer kept.'[1] Than was the olde woman glad in her mynde, and thanked her and departed homewarde for the cheste.

Howe John of Florence was in the cheste and howe he was brought into Ambroses house.

And whan this false olde woman hadde ordeyned all thynges after her minde and knewe that Ambroses wife wolde take the cheste into her house, than wente she and put John of Florence in the cheste secretly, that no body wyste thereof, and gave hym in the cheste meate and drinke for three or four daies, soo that he needed nothynge And the cheste was made with a spryng locke, so that John of Florence myght open and shitte in what that he would at his pleasure.[2] And than did the olde woman laye the chest upon a whele-barowe and gate twoo stronge men to cary it to Ambroses house. And whan they were come there with the chest, the olde woman came to Ambroses wyfe and tolde her that she had the chest at the dore. And than Ambroses wyfe bad her brynge the cheste in, and set it in her owne chambre thynking of no deceyte nor falshede. Than went the olde woman to the dore and bade the two men bryng in the cheste and bere it up in to the chambre, and so they dyd. And than whan it was in the chambre, than she payed the men and they

[1] Cf. I. 6. 191–210.
[2] II. 2. 47.

departed from thence. And then tooke the olde woman leve of Ambroses wyfe, and so departed homewarde very glad and mery.

How John of Florence opened the chest in the nyght and came out into Ambroses chambre and stale iii Juwels.

Whan nyght came that everye body was a slepe in their first slepe and at reste, than did John open the chest and went out in to the chamber. And by misfortune Ambroses wife had left her cofer open wherein the Jewels were, and had forgot to shytte it. And that spied wel the false John of Florence, and theyr he stale three costly Jewelles.[1] The one was a purse wrought al with perles and costly stones, beyng worth lxxxiiii ducates. And the other was a gyrdle of fyne golde set with costly perles and stoones, that was worth CCCC ducates. And the thyrde was a rynge with a point of diamond, that was worth L ducates. And the moone shone so clere that he myght see in every corner of the chamber, and there he behelde Ambroses wife that was soundely aslepe. And than it fortuned that her lefte arme lay on the bed, and on that arme she had a blacke warte[2] that the false traitoure John of Florence sawe well, wherwith he rejoysed and sayd, ' O good lorde, what great fortune have I! For now have I sene a pryvy token, whereby he shall byleve me that I have had my pleasure of his wyfe, and so shall I have the money of hym.'[3] Than wente the fals thefe with the Jewelles agayne in to the chest and shyt hym self fast therin. And on the thyrde day after came the olde woman to Ambroses wyfe and gave to her agayne the ducate that she sholde have borne to Saynt James, and sayde, 'Worshypfull maystrys, I have gote a grete sekenes, that I wene wyl tary longe by me. And therfore I wel not take this Jornaye on me this yere. And therfore I praye you that I myghte have my chest agayne, and I thanke you hertely of youre good wyll.' Than delyvered Ambroses wyfe the cheste to the olde woman, mystrustynge nothynge, and knewe not that therof sholde come ony hevynes. And than departed the olde woman home with the chest agayne.[4] And whan it was in the olde womans hous, than opened Johan of Florence the chest and came out; and than he gave to the olde woman CC ducates for her laboure and toke his leve of her and rode to Parys, where that Ambrose taryed hym.

And whan that he was come to Parys than rode he in to the ynne

---

[1] Iachimo takes only the bracelet, II. 2. 33–5.
[2] Cf. II. 2. 37–42.
[3] Iachimo's chief aim is 'the madding of her lord', II. 2. 35–7.
[4] Shakespeare omits minor details such as the conveyance of the chest. But Imogen misses the bracelet, II. 3. 142–50.

where that Ambrose was. And than set he up his horse and came to
Ambrose and called hym a syde and sayde, 'Bycause that ye be a
good frende of myne, and we have kepte company togyder, and that
ye sholde not be a shamed, I call you asyde[1] for to shewe unto you
that I have wonne the money. See, here I have evydente tokens for
to shewe that I have wonne it.' And than toke Johan of Florence
outte the purse, the gyrdell, and the rynge, and shewed those thre
Jeweles unto Ambrose.

Than sayd Ambrose: 'I knowe well that those thre Jewels be my
wyves, but yet I wyll not byleve that ye have hadde your wyl on her;
but ye must tel me some better and pryvyer token than these be.'[2]
And than sayd Johan, 'Ye wyll byleve me and I tel unto you a more
previer token than these be.' Than he tolde unto Ambrose that his
wyfe had upon her lefte arme a blacke wart. And whan that Ambrose
herde that than fel he in a sownde, for he knewe not the falsenes of
Johan.[3] Than Johan toke Ambrose up, and bad hym take a mans
herte unto hym and let it passe, for he coude not therwith amende it.
And whan that Ambrose was up agayne, than he sayde, 'Alas, what
is my fortune! I had went[4] that my wyfe wolde never have deceyved
me as she hath done. For she was bothe worshypfull and vertuous and
beloved bothe of yonge and olde.' And than bad Ambrosius Johan
of Florence that he sholde tel it no ferther to ony bodye, and badde
him goo to the hoste and fetche the money, and so he dyde. And
there was no man but he and Ambrose that knewe who had wonne
the money.

How Ambrose rode home agayne towarde the towne of Jennen.

Than forthwith departed Ambrose from Parys and toke his Journey
towarde Jennen with a soroweful herte. And whan he cam to Jennen,
he wente in to a certayne place of his that he had gyven to kepe
to a certayne man of his that he knewe sure and trusty.[5] And than
came Ambrose in and called the man to him. And than he came;
and whan that he was come he sayd to him, 'My servaunt, I knowe
well that you be trusty and trewe, and you muste do one thyng for
me that I shal commaunde you, and swere on a boke that ye wyl
do it.' And so the servaunte dyde swere that he wolde. Than sayd he
to hym that he sholde byd his maystris come to hym there, and whan

---

[1] Philario is present at II. 4. 27ff. In *Boccaccio* all the merchants are called together.
[2] Cf. Posthumus, prompted by Philario, II. 4. 113–20.
[3] Contrast II. 4. 122ff. and II. 5.
[4] weened, expected.
[5] Posthumus travels to Britain and writes to Pisanio (and his wife) from Milford
Haven, III. 2.

that she was come that he shold slee her and burye her in the sonde. Than sayde the servaunt to his mayster, 'That were grete pyty.' Than sayd Ambrose, 'Yf ye do it not, I shall slee you.' Than sayde the servaunte, 'I wyll.' For he thoughte it was better to slee his maystrys than his selfe to be slayne. And than departed he towarde his maystrys with a sorrowfull herte.

How the man wente to the towne.

And as the man was come to the towne, he came to his maystrys and tolde her that her husbande was come and taryed her at his house without the towne. Than was Ambroses wyfe glad, and wente with the man, and caryed with her a lytell lambe that she was wonte to play withall. And whan they came without the towne in the wod, than saide the servaunt to his maistres, 'O good maistres, my maister hath charged me upon payne of death that I should slee you here and bryng to hym for a token your tongue and a locke of youre heere.'[1] And what she herde that she fell downe on her knees and sayde, 'I have never offended him for to dye; and therfore, good Lady, delyver me from this daunger, as I am gyltlesse.' And as soone as she had done her prayer she sayde to the man, 'My true servaunt, I shall geve you good counseyle. I have a lambe here; we shall kyll it and take his tongue,[2] and I wyll cut a locke of my here and with the bloud anoynt my clothes; and bere these tokens to your maister.' And than sayde the servant to his maistres, 'That shall I doo with a good wil. But ye must departe from hence, that my maister se you not. For if he doo, than shall we bothe lese our lyves.' And than departed she, and than kylde he the lambe and did as she bad him and bare the tokens to his maister. And whan Ambrose sawe theim, than was he more sorier than he was before, because that he spake not with her before that he caused her to be put to death, to examyne her wherfore John of Florence had the Jewels.[3] And the man seing howe his maister that he founde no faulte with the tokens, he thanked God and Our Lady of the good counsayle of the woman.

Howe Ambroses wyfe came in mans clothyng in to Secant.

Than clothed Ambroses wyfe her selfe in mans clothynge and came to Secant to an haven, where she found a shyppe redy to goe. Than

---

[1] She is to be slain near Milford Haven, III. 4. 1–31. Posthumus demands no specific tokens, but 'make me certain it is done'.
[2] This probably suggested the 'lamb' image, III. 4. 97. Pisanio sends a bloodstained handkerchief (V. 1. 1–2).
[3] Contrast V. 1. 2–12.

desired she that she might go with it. And than asked the shypman, 'What is your name?' And she aunswered hym, 'Frederike is my name, and I have had a greate losse both of my frendes and my goodes, so that I am undone.' Than sayde the shypman, 'Ye be a propre man; wil ye serve me? For I have here hawkes that I must bryng to the kynge of Alkare,[1] that shall ye kepe, and I wil geve unto you good wages.' Than sayd Frederyke, 'With a good wyll!' And than toke they their passage and came over and presented the kyng the hawkes, and he rewarded theim well. And as soone as Frederyke was departed, than began the hawkes to drope. Than was the kynge angry, and sente for the Shypman and asked him what haukes he had broughte. 'We bad you bryng of the beste, and see what haukes ye have brought!' Than sayde the Shypman, 'Whan that I hadde theim in the shyppe they were fayre and good, as anye man myght see. And I hyred a propre man that came to me by fortune, that kepte theim diligentely; and for that cause they morne.' Than sayd the kynge, 'Bryng to me the man and let me se hym.' Than sayde the shypman, 'My lege, I will fetche him. But if it please your grace, I am lothe to departe[2] with hym; For he is bothe wyse and subtyll in many causes. And if youre grace have hym, ye muste kepe hym that no persone do to hym wrong.' Than sayde the kyng, 'Gooe fetche hym hether, and we promyse you that no man soo hardy of his head shall dooe hym wronge.' And than toke the shypman leve of the kynge and so departed.

Howe Frederyke was the kynges of Alkares faukenar

Than was the kyng very sory for his haukes, for he went that they would have dyed. And when Frederike was come before the king and sawe hym, than had he a great favoure unto him and brought him to his haukes, and as sone as the haukes sawe him they rejoysed and flapped with their wynges and were hole, wherof the kyng was glad and mervayled gretly therat. And than gave he Frederyke charge of his haukes, and he kept them well, so that the king loved him wel and promoted him and made him a gret officer in his court and after that a knight, and than he made him a lorde. Than in the meane tyme befel in the towne a great death, so that the king wold departe from thense. Than as he departed he called to him lorde Frederyke and made hym lorde defender of all his londe, tyll the tyme that he retourned agayne whan that dethe were paste. And than dyd the kynge and all his lordes take theyr leve of lorde Frederyke, and departed fro thense.

[1] Cairo.
[2] part.

Howe Frederyke overcame the kynges ennemyes that brenned and destroyed many townes after the departyng of the kynge.

Than as the kynge and his lordes were departed, than had his enemyes knowlege that he was departed, and came with a grete hoste and brente, and slewe, and toke many prysoners. And at the last this tydynges came to Frederyke that was lord and defender of the kynges realme. Than assembled he a grete hoost and cam agaynst his enemyes, and slewe them downe afore him lyke a lyon and dyde many mervaylous faytes of armes that daye. For he broke theyr ordynaunce[1] and made theim for to scatter a brode as it had ben loste shep. And so that daye had lord Frederyke grete vyctory, and folowed his enemyes and toke many prysoners of the captaynes and grct lordes, of whom he had grete raunsome. And whan that the warre was done and that lord Frederyke had sette the londe in peace through the grete boldenes and hardynes of hym, than tydynges was brought to the kynge, wherof the kynge was glad of the greate fayte that his newe captayne had done. Than retourned the kynge to his towne agayne where that lorde Frederyke was. And when that lorde Frederyke hade knowlege of his commynge, than receyved he the kynge with great honoure in to the towne. And whan that the kynge was within, he sayde to Frederyke, 'I thanke you, my trewe and faythfull servaunt, of the great dedes of armes that ye have done for me, puttynge your body and lyfe in joperdye. And for that cause I make you lorde protectoure and defender of all my londe. For I am an aged man, and you be yong and lusty and a valyaunt man.' And than thanked Frederyke the kynge and toke the charge on hym, and governed the realme worshipfuly so that al the lordes and knightes loved him wel and al the comens. And he regned xii yere with greate honoure and dayly gettynge more therto.

How Johan of Florence came to Alkaren with marchaundyse.

Upon a tyme wente Johan of Florence to the see wyth his marchaundyse, that was but lyght passage, toward the towne of Alkare. For he coude speke many dyverse languages. And whan he was come to Alkare he wente to the kynges palayce and shewed his marchaundyse. Thanne on a daye as lorde Frederyke and his lordes walked aboute, lorde Frederyke sawe the marchaunte standynge with his marchaundyse. Than wente he wyth his lordes to Johan of Florence. And whan he was come he loked asyde and sawe the gyrdle, the purse, and the ryng, whiche he knewe well inough, and sayd, 'Marchaunt, let me se those three costely Jewels that ye have there,

---

[1] battle-array.

and shewe me I pray you in what londe ye bought them.'[1] Than
sayd Johan of Florence: 'I bought theym not; but yf ye wyste how
daungerously I came by them, ye wolde love me the better ever
after.' Than sayd lorde Frederyke, 'That grete daunger muste ye
tell me.' Than tolde Johan of Florence to lorde Frederyke howe that
he came by them and howe that he layd v thousande geldens with
Ambrose, that he sholde have goten his pleasure of his wyfe, and how
that he gate the Jewels unknowen to his wyfe; 'and than retourned
I to her husbande and tolde hym that I had wonne the money; and
then retourned he home and caused his man for to slee her' (as is
before shewed more playnly). Than sayd lorde Frederyke, 'The
sleynge of hys wyfe was yll done, but the money was goten with a
wonder grete practyse and well.' But for all that lorde Frederyke
spake so, yet he thought not soo. Than said he to the marchaunte,
'Wyll ye tary with us here, and we shall gyve unto you mete and
drynke out of my court. And kepe those Jewelles that ye have here
for me, for they please me wonderly well, and nowe have I no
leasure to gyve to you the money at this time. For they be so costly
that the money wyl be longe a tellynge, and they shal serve for my
paramoure.' Than thanked Johan of Florence lorde Frederyke that
he was so curteyse to him, and sayd, 'These thre Jeweles be so costely
and of to hyghe a price to gyve to his paramoure, without that he
loved her very well.' And than departed lorde Frederyke from the
marchaunt and charged his offycers that they sholde gyve unto the
marchaunte his lyvery for two or thre men every daye. And they
sayde they wolde with a good wyll. So on the morowe came Johan
of Florence for his lyverey; and they gave it unto hym, so that he
neded not for too spende but yf he wolde. Than pryvely called lorde
Frederyke a poste and asked of hym yf that he knewe wel where that
the towne of Jennen was. And he answered, 'Yes lorde, I knowe it
well.' Than sayd lorde Frederyke, 'Thyder must ye as faste as ye may
go, and there is money ynoughe. And whan ye bee there, then aske
for one Ambrose, a wedower, and whan that ye speke with hym
delyver unto hym this letter, and brynge hym with you.' And this
letter was wryten as though the kynge hym selfe had sende it.

How the poste or messenger delyvered the letter to Ambrose.

Through the commaundement of lorde Frederyke departed the
messengere towarde Jennen, and passed over the see and at the laste
came to Jennen. And whan that he was there, he asked where that
Ambrose dwelte, and he asked so longe that at the last he came to
him and presented the letter to hym with the kynges brode seale;

---

[1] V. 5. 136–41; 205.

and he receyved it humbly and opened it. And this was the tenoure as here foloweth, 'We, kynge of Alkaren, desyre of oure frende Ambrose for a nedeful cause that we have to doo, which shall be a grete profyt unto you, wherwith ye shal be made ryche, so that ye wolde spede you and come with this messenger to us, and ye shal have no maner of harme done to you, for we send to you oure brode seale and saufcondute bothe to goo and to come free.' And as Ambrose reed this letter he wondered gretly of the hasty desyre of the kynge. Neverthelesse he dressed his gere and set one in his hous to kepe it tyll the tyme that he retourned agayne; and than departed he with the messenger. And they passed over the see and came to lorde Frederyke, that bad him welcome and made him good chere. And on the morowe came lorde Frederyke to Ambrose and made hym come to dyner with hym. And he his owne persone toke and set hym at the kynges owne table and set hym selfe downe therby, and oftentymes in the dyner he bad that Ambrose sholde be mery. And whan dyner was done than sayd lorde Frederyke to the king, 'My lege, here is come to this towne a marchaunte that hath broughte thre costely Jewelles whiche that I wolde that ye had sene, and therfor wyll I sende for hym and byd hym brynge his thre Jewelles with hym.' And than wente a messenger and bad Johan of Florence that he sholde made hym redy and come before the kynge with his thre Jewels. Than was Johan of Florence glad and thought that he sholde have receyved moche money, and went with the messenger to the kynge in to the halle. And whan he was come, lorde Frederyke sayde unto hym, 'Syr, shewe your marchaundyse and shewe howe that ye came by them to the kyng.' Than sheweth he the three Jewels. And than Ambrose seyng the Jewels woundered, and wente than that the kynge had sent for hym to put him to death, and than fel he for sorowe almoste to the grounde.[1] This markyng lorde Frederyke came and comforted hym and clapped him on the sholder, and sayde he shoulde have no harme, but joye. Than tolde the marchaunt to the king altogether howe that he had gotten the Jewels. Than went the lorde Frederyke with the kyng asyde and asked the kyng what that marchaunt had deserved that hadde dishonoured suche a worshipfull woman and had begyled her in that maner of her Jewels, and after that loste her lyfe therfore. Than saide the kyng to the lorde Frederyke, 'He hath bothe deserved the whele and the galowes, for he caused both murder to be done, and also he stoole the jewels.' Than sayd lorde Frederyke, 'So thynketh me also that he hath deserved it well for to be his rewarde. But if that it please your grace and the lordes to returne againe into the hall, ye shall see and knowe many other marveylous thinges that that false

[1] Posthumus asks for death, V. 5. 211–19.

marchaunt hath done to that worshipfull woman.' Than sayde the kyng, 'With a good wyll that shall we do.' Than retourned the kynge and all his lordes with lorde Frederyke into the hall agayne, for to here more of the marchaunte.

Howe lorde Frederyke came naked before the kyng and his lordes.

With those wordes tourned the king into the hall, where he and his lordes spake of manye dyverse straunge matters. And in the meane whyle went the lorde Frederyke secretly away and came into the chamber, where she did unclothe her al naked saving a clothe before her membres, and than came into the hall before the kyng and al his lordes, and before all the other persones there beynge present, all naked, save that she had a kercher of sylke before her membres. And whan she was come in she wente to the kyng and dyd him reverence. And whan the kyng and his lordes sawe her, they mervayled greatly, wherefore that that fayre woman came in naked before them. Than saide the kynge to his lordes. 'That persone have I sene before often-tymes in other arayment than she is now, and if I should tell trewe, me thynketh it is our protectour and defender lorde Frederyke.' And therfore sayd the kynge to her, 'Shew to us what ye be and wherfore that ye come in here before us al naked in this maner.' Than answered the woman to the kyng and saide, 'I am the same persone —lorde Frederike—that you spake on, your poore subjecte. And I am here come before your great majeste to complaine on this false marchaunt that standeth here with the thre Jewels that be myne, as the purse, the gyrdle, and the rynge, that he had gotten by thefte, whiche is openly knowen before your grace by what maner of craft he came by them. And this other marchaunt that here standeth before you is my husbande, and I my selfe is the same woman that should have be put to death in the wood at the same time, but I escaped by the helpe of God and Oure Ladye from that great perill of death; and from that day to this day I never had conversacion with any man, but have lived chaste, and no man nor woman knewe never none other but that I was a man. And therfore if that it please your grace to do so much for me, that this false marchaunt and traitour may suffre death, as ye knowe well that he hath deserved and none other wise.' Than said the kyng to her, 'That must I nedes do, for right and reason wil desire none other. And therefore, for that yll dede that he hathe done, we will that he be headed, and than after that his body to be layde upon the whele, over him a paire of galowes, because that he hath stolen and also caused murder to be done, and therfore take him by and by.' Than was John of Florence taken and broughte to pryson and all his goodes given to

Ambrose and his wyfe. Then sayde Ambrose to John of Florence, 'O poor wretche and katyf, what helpeth you now al your craft and falshed and al that yll gotten good that ye have gotten by falshed and theft? For now at the last is your traytershype and false dede openly knowen. And nowe therfore must ye suffre a shamefull death, and that shall be your rewarde. Better ye had bene to have done right, and than ye had not come to that ye be at.' Than aunswered John of Florence, 'That is truth. I have well deserved my death.'[1] Than toke the officers John of Florence and brought hym besyde of the galowes where the Justice should be done. And whan that he had made his prayers and all doone, than made the hangman him knele downe, and smote Johans of Florence head of, and after that laied his body upon a whele, and the head he stycked on a stake and set it by, over the head a galowes, all after the maner as the kyng had judged him, and than retourned home again. And in this maner was John of Florence served for his great falshed and thefte that he hadde done to that trewe wyfe and mayde. For it is never seene yet that murdre and thefte was never so long kept, but at laste it is knowen. And they that dooe it at the laste be hanged, or elles they suffre some other shamefull death.

Howe Ambroses wyfe toke leve of the kyng and departed towarde home with her husbande.

And whan that Ambrose had sene that lorde Frederyke was his wyfe, he mervayled gretly therat and wened that she hadde ben deed longe agone. Neverthelesse he was ryght hevy for the grete wronge that he had caused to be done to her in tyme past, and than went he to her and toke her in his armes and kyssed her, and whan he had done he fell before her on his knees and asked her forgyvenes for that grete wronge that he had doone to her so hastely, not spekynge to her before. Than dydde she take hym up and sayd to hym, 'Be contente, my good love! I forgyve you frely as thoughe you had never done it.' And than he rose and thanked her and thought in his mynde not for to tary longer there. Neverthelesse the kynge made them bothe good chere, and gave unto theym many grete gyftes bothe to Ambrose and his wyfe also, for he loved her for the grete trueth and valyaunce that she had done for hym in his abscence, puttynge her lyfe in jeopardy for hym agaynst his ennemyes. And whan she had ben a whyle with the kynge and made good chere, than came she to the kynge and prayed hym of lycence, that she myght departe homeward with her husbande. And whan the kynge herde that she wolde departe fro thense he was sory and was lothe for to let her departe frome thense.

[1] So Iachimo, V. 5. 415–16, but he is spared.

But she desyred so moche that at the laste he gave too her lycence and saufcoundute, that they myght passe throughe all his londe without ony maner of harme or agayne sayenge. Than was Ambrose and his wyfe glad and toke theyr leve of the kynge and wente theyr way and came to the see and toke a shyp and passed over the see to Jennen and hadde good passage; and whan they were come they were receyved and met of the people. Whan they sawe that Ambroses wyfe was come agayne, that was sayde longe before to be dede, they mervayled gretly therof. And after that lyved they longe in vertue and goodnes and loved ever after togyder and thanked God of that grete fortune that they had, and served God devoutely. And after that had Ambrose by hys wyfe foure chyldren, that is to understande iii sonnes and a doughter. And the eldest sone was named Frederyke after the name of his moder. And whan that he began to wexe grete and myghty, than was he sente to Alkaren to the yong kynges court, the sone of the olde kynge that his mother had dwelte withal before, and he was made moch of for that his moder had done before to the old kynge, and gate worshyp dayly more and more for his mothers sake, and became a gret lord and was well beloved of the kyng and all his lordes. And all the kynrede of them ever after came to great worshyp and honour. And than whan that Ambrose and his wyfe sawe that their sonne was so muche made of, than toke they their lefe of the kynge of Alkare, and than departed towarde the towne of Jennen and came therin in the viii. day of January, whiche was upon a Sonday, in the yere of our Lorde God M.CCCC and xxxvii. And thus in this maner hathe this good marchaunt Ambrose and his wyfe lyved together, and these fortunes they have suffered. And than was Ambroses wife seke and died, and commended her soule into the handes of almyghty God, and went to the blisse everlastyng, to the whiche blisse God bryng you and me. Amen.

And thus endeth this lytell story of lorde Frederyke.

V. Analogue

From
EUFEMIA: A COMEDY
by Lope de Rueda,[1]
translated by the editor

[The first four Scenes tell how Leonardo leaves his sister Eufemia for Valencia, where he takes service with Valiano. Valiano is so impressed by the young man's praise of his sister's beauty and virtues that he sends Paulo to bring her so that he may marry her.]

Scene V

[In Calabria Eufemia is lamenting the lack of news from Leonardo when a Gipsy woman comes, who tells Eufemia something about her future. Cristina, Eufemia's maid, is also present.]

GIPSY.   There is a person far from here who loves you greatly, and although he is now greatly favoured by his master, in a short time he will be in danger of his life through a piece of knavery which has been plotted against him. But hush! although it will all be on your account, God who is a true Judge and does not allow any falsehood to be hidden for long, will reveal the truth of it.

EUF.   Ill-omened woman! You say that this person will be put in danger because of me? Who can that be, wretch, but my dear brother?

GIPSY.   Lady, I know no more; but seeing that I did not lie in what I said about your maid, I shall go now. Wait a while and if anything else comes up I shall come and tell you; wait with God's grace.

CRIST.   And you have nothing to tell me; whether I shall be married or a spinster?

GIPSY.   You will be wife to nine husbands, and all alive. What more do you want to know? God console you, lady.

---

[1] *Las Primeras dos elegantes y graciosas Comedias del excellente Poeta y representante Lope de Rueda: sacadas a luz por Juan Timoneda*, Valencia, 1567. Modern edn in *Obras de Lope de Rueda*, Edición de la Real Academia Española, ed. Emilio Cotarelo, 2 vols, Madrid, 1908.

EUF. You can tell me no more about my affairs, and so you'll leave me with my well-being in doubt.

GIPSY. I know no more than to tell you that your trouble will not be so lasting but that in the time of greatest danger prudence and good fortune will change it, and all will become happy and contented, as Divine mercy knows to make it. *[Exit.*

CRIST. A sad look-out for me, my lady! Don't you see what she told me—that I shall be the wife of nine husbands and they all alive? Unlucky me! And how can that be?

EUF. Quiet, I beg! All that these people say can pass for obvious nonsense, yet I am more troubled by what she has told me than ever in my darkest hour before. Let us go. *[Exeunt.*

[The action switches to Valencia where Valiano is receiving his old servant Paulo, just returned from Calabria.]

VALIANO. Tell me Paulo; is it possible that you have been in the house of this Eufemia, sister of that wicked and perfidious Leonardo, of whom I have thought so highly?

PAULO. I tell you yes, Sir.

VAL. And you have really slept with her in her bed?

PAULO. Yes, I have slept with her in her bed. What more do you wish?

VAL. Indeed, my faithful Paulo, tell me, however did you manage it?

PAULO. Sir, it happened to me with her as it does with the rest of them. I had no need to make many turns before she saw me pass in the street, and looked out of a window and sent me a little maid-servant who (and this is another proof) is called Cristina.

VAL. And the maid, what did she say to you?

PAULO. That I was wanted in that house. And since I already knew, as I have told your honour, that there was no need of much matchmaking, I went in, especially since the lady knew me from my previous approaches and had accepted my money. I stayed there that night as a guest, and three more besides, and clearly saw the marks on her body and I promise you, Sir, I have come to tell you what happened.

VAL. Be brief.

PAULO. To be brief, what she gave me so that I could put it in my hat or cap was a piece of hair that grows from a large mole on her left shoulder, and because it was a token that her brother Leonardo, your favourite, could not deny, I resolved to bring it. You see it here. So now I have fulfilled my duty as your vassal. Do you, my lord make sure that no traitor can laugh at you, much less let one of your

EUF. Say what you wish. Don't doubt to be pardoned if you can throw any light on what I learn from this agonized letter.

CRIST. Know then, my lady, that although I have to confess a mistake, I am not so blameworthy for sinning through ignorance as if I had done so through malice.

EUF. Get to the point. This is no time to be wasting words. Don't keep me in suspense waiting for what you have to say, for I am dying to hear it.

CRIST. You must understand then, that some days ago a foreign-looking man asked for you, inquiring if it would be possible to see or speak to you. Knowing you to be in retirement, I told him that I thought it impossible. He was very insistent that I tell him the marks on your person, and not content with that, he worked on me to get from you a piece of the hair that you have in the mole on your right[1] shoulder. Not thinking that it might do offence to your honour nor to anything else, and seeing him so troubled, I thought good to steal it from you while you were asleep, and gave it to him.

EUF. Tell me no more; some great evil must have followed on it. Let us leave at once, for I am determined to go to him whom I have cherished all my life, and get there as secretly as possible within these twenty days. Let us see if we can somehow save the life of my dear brother, who writes so outrageously and woundingly to me through not knowing the truth.

CRIST. If you do this, and make haste on the way, I am sure everything will be put right, with God's help.

MELCH. Must I go there too?

CRIST. Yes brother, for who else have we to serve us on the road?

MELCH. On my honour, although a man might be learning how to make maps of navigation, he would not follow this way more than once! But I'll go.   [*Exeunt.*

[Paulo now enters and boasts of his success in getting rid of Leonardo.]

PAULO. Oh, how well my affairs are going and how well I've managed to make myself valued! How clever I've been to get rid of that foreigner Leonardo! How happily I have made my fortune, and what great credit I have regained with Valiano! . . . But perhaps I have an unreliable witness in Vallejo the lackey? Well, in return for the two doubloons I promised him when he accompanied me on the road, he says that he will murder anyone who contradicts what I've

[1] Paulo mistakenly said 'left shoulder'.

said. But someone I don't know is coming. I don't want to be over-heard by anyone, since my luck's in.

Scene VIII

CRIST. Madam, here we are; in this place you can wait until Valiano comes out and you can tell him whatever you wish to say.

EUF. May the Almighty Lord who knows and understands all things expose and bring to light that great treachery, in such a way that the truth will be made manifest and my dear brother be set free, since both he and I are guiltless of this false accusation.

CRIST. Be strong, my lady. The time has come when the truth will be revealed . . .

EUF. Listen, footsteps. People are coming, and the one on the right must, by his manner, be Valiano, the lord of all these lands.

CRIST. And the man with him is the foreigner to whom, because of his importunity, I gave the tokens from your body.

EUF. Hush! They are talking as they come.

VAL. Tell me, Paulo, is everything properly arranged?

PAULO. Yes Sir, I have taken proper care so that the traitor will pay for it and you may rest without any anxiety.

VAL. You have done well. But who are these people?

PAULO. I do not know, Sir; they look like foreigners.

VAL. I swear that the one in front looks like a lass of parts. Fetch her here so that we may get to know each other.

EUF. Noble Sir, I am a stranger here in your country. I ask you for justice.

VAL. I rejoice infinitely if it is in my power to do you any favour; for although you may be a foreigner, your manner and your neatness will prompt anybody to do you service; so ask what you will, and where justice is concerned nothing will be denied you.

EUF. Justice, my lord, for I am grievously injured.

VAL. For you to be injured in my territory is a thing not to be endured.

VALLEJO. Up, my lord. Let us arm the household and, if you give me a free hand, you shall see how quickly I turn out the corners of this city, and do it without any complaints.

VAL. Peace, Vallejo. Tell me, madam, who has been guilty of offending you?

EUF. Sir, that traitor who stands beside you.

PAULO. You are jesting with me, lady, or you wish to entertain people.

EUF. I am not jesting, traitor; for after sleeping many times with me in my bed, on the last occasion you stole a very rich jewel from beneath my bedhead.

PAULO.   What are you saying? Perhaps you have mistaken me for someone else! I neither know you nor who you are. How could I have stolen anything, when I have never in my life thought of doing so?

EUF.   Ah, you traitor! Was it not enough to profit by my person as you did, without also robbing me of my belongings?

VAL.   Paulo, reply; is what this lady says true?

PAULO.   I tell you, Sir, it is the greatest shock in the world. I neither know her nor saw her in all my life.

EUF.   Ah, my lord, the traitor denies it so as not to give me back my jewel.

PAULO.   Don't you call anybody a traitor, for if there is any treachery you do it, since you insult in this way a man who never saw you before.

EUF.   So, traitor, you have not slept with me?

PAULO.   I tell you, I neither know you nor know who you are.

EUF.   Sir, make him swear on oath that he will tell the truth.

VAL.   Place your hand on your sword, Paulo.

PAULO.   I swear, Sir, by everything that one can swear by, that I have not slept with her, nor been near her house; nor do I know her, or what she is talking about.

EUF.   Then, you scoundrel, let your ears listen to what your devil's mouth has said, since with your own words you have condemned yourself.

PAULO.   In what way? What are you saying? What do I owe you?

EUF.   Say, wretch, if you don't know me, how you have uttered such monstrous lying and false witness against me?

PAULO.   I? False witness? The woman is mad.

EUF.   I'm mad, am I? Have you not said that you have slept with me?

PAULO.   I have said that? Sir, if I have, may I be condemned and suffer an evil death at the hands of the hangman, in your presence!

EUF.   Then if you have not slept with me, why is there such a scandal in this country because of the testimony you have given without even knowing me?

PAULO.   Away with your testimony and your fooleries!

EUF.   Tell us, you lawless wretch, have you not said that you slept with Leonardo's sister?

PAULO.   Yes, I have said so, and also brought back proofs from her person.

EUF.   And those proofs, how did you get them? If you see me,

Leonardo's sister, standing before you, how is it that you do not recognize me, since you have so often said that you have slept with me?

VAL.   Here is some great treachery, from what I hear.

CRIST.   Scoundrel, so you never asked me to give you tokens of my lady, though now, because I have come in disguise you do not recognize me? I, seeing you apparently so urgent and distressed, cut off a piece of hair from the mole on her right shoulder, and gave it to you without thinking that it could harm anyone.

VAL.   Foul traitor, you cannot now deny me the truth, since you yourself have confessed with your own mouth.

VALLEJO.   You'll buzz no more, you insect! Also he tried to get me to help him catch the gentleman in his snare.

VAL.   How was that?

VALLEJO.   When we were together on the way, he asked me to testify that he has slept with Leonardo's sister, and for that he promised me some hose, but it would have gone hard with me if instead of hose he had got me a hundred lashes.

VAL.   Take the villain away and let him pay *lex talionis* with the punishment I had intended for my faithful Leonardo. Release Leonardo from prison; let him be at once restored in all honour; and cut off this traitor's head immediately in the place already prepared for Leonardo.

VALLEJO.   Your orders shall be carried out at once, Sir.

[*Exeunt.*

VAL.   As for this noble lady, since she has so nobly undertaken to save the life of her brother, may she remain in our territories and be their mistress and mine. Nevertheless I cannot hope in this way fully to compensate for the grief that her brother, in prison, and she in saving him, have had to endure.

VALLEJO.   (re-entering) My lord, he is in gaol; the giver of false witness, the wretch Paulo, is already in the hands of the magistrate, with all those attentions that your lordship has commanded.

VAL.   Good. Have new liveries made for all the servants of my house; and you, my lady, give me your hand and let us go in together; for I want you and your brother to dine with me with abundant rejoicing, and then to do what I must so as to obtain what Leonardo promised me.

EUF.   Whatever you command, my lord, will make me happy.

[*Exeunt.*

VALLEJO.   My master goes in embracing the girl. But I gain most by this business, since I have escaped having a hundred lashes for false testimony. I must go, or there will be something wrong in the house.—Listeners, do not go away without eating and then taking a turn in the square, if you would like to see them behead a traitor and set free a loyal man, and reward one who has been assiduous and prudent in undoing such a plot. And so, good-bye!

End of the Comedy of Eufemia

VI. Analogue

From
CERTAINE TRAGICALL DISCOURSES
OF BANDELLO
translated into English by Geoffrey Fenton (1567)

Discourse XIII

[Don Diego, grieved at the cruelty of Genivera, becomes a hermit in the Pyrenees.]

His complaints coulde not so staye the swifte course of tyme, but, or he was ware, the heighte of the sun showed the declyning of the daye; whiche moved hym to increase his pase, leaving the common wayes to folowe the pathes leaste acquainted with traveile . . . wandringe in that sorte by the space of three or foure dayes and nightes; th'ende whereof broughte theim at laste to the foote of a large mountaine, inhabited onely with savage beastes and creatures unreasonable, discoveringe rounde about a platt or soile of pleasante prospecte and moste proper to shroode the solitarie life of the wandrynge knyghte: for if he delited in the shade, he hadd there the benefytt of a number of pleasante trees whiche nature seamed to lende hym as a speciall solace in that wyldernes; when his sorowe desyered the use of a more open prospecte, the plaine forrestes and chases, wyth theyr wholle heardes of deare of all sortes, offred to give hym skoape to recorde his greeffe; and, for chaunge of recreation, he mighte viewe there the hideus and highe rockes, whose steepnes and craggie scituation albeit moved a terrour to the beholders, yet were they not without cause of greate delite, by reason of the pleasant grene, garnished with the tappisery of diverse flowers, spreadyng theim selves all alonge the heighte of the sayde mountes. But that whiche moved moste his affection to that place was a merveilous faire and rowmey cave, environed on all sides with beeche, cypres, pyneaple, and ceder trees, wyth other braunches yeldynge frutes of diverse kyndes; righte afore the mouth or openyng of the which, tendying to the valley, appered a nomber of pleasante graftes, whose rootes, receiving moisture by a cleare streame passing wyth softe noyse all alonge the dore of the cave, gave suche bountifull norriture to the twigges and tender braunches, that th'only topps bowed downe and dipped theim selves as uppon dutie in a fountaine of wonderfull clearenes, fedyng continuallye the saide streame: all whiche seamed to offer suche solace to the solytarye intente of Diego, that, without further advise, he determined to performe there the penance he wente to doo, and to converte that house builded by nature to the monasterye of his profession; wherein he mente to ende the voyage of his devocions, commandyng his man to alight, who, unsadlinge their horses, gave theim the keye of the wilde forestes, whereof hetherto they harde no newes.

Touchinge their saddells, with the harnesse and other furniture of their horsses, they bestowed within a litle cell or corner in their cave, where, also, leaving their ordinarye apparell, they putt on their habittes of pilgrim. There his man made provision accordynge to the condicion of their state and necessitye of the place, dyggynge, for his first indevor certeine soddes and lomppes of claye, wherwith he entrenched and rampierd their felden shopp,[1] to defende theym againste the furye of wilde beastes, who other wayes myghte oppresse theym in the nighte. He made, also, twoo beddes, or lytle couches, of softe mosse, wyth a testure[2] and sides of wodde, which he hewde in no lesse fyne proporcion then yf the skill of the carpenter had assisted the worke. They hadd no other releeffe or foode, for longe tyme, then of the frute whiche the wilde trees did yelde theym; onelesse sometime, for a chaunge of dyot, they were gladde to feede of rawe rootes, whiche they digged out of th'intrailles of the earth, untill extreme hunger preferred a meane to supplie their thinne fare—which was that his man made a crosbowe, with the whiche they killed often times the hare and conie fedynge at releeff.[3] Some time they beguiled the wilde goate in the mountaines, and were often the bane of a greater beaste in the foreste, whose blood they pressed betwene twoo peces of woode, made for the nonst, devidynge theim into morsells, whiche they rosted with the heatte of the sun, and so furnished in sober manner their leane table, disgestynge theyr rude and unholsome dyott wyth a cuppe of colde water, whereof they had no lesse plentye, with no more charges, then when they commaunded over whole cellars of delicate wyne in the pallayes of Dom Diego; who increased the dweile[4] of his presente miserye wyth teares of continuall

---

[1] rural abode.
[2] head-board.
[3] at ease.
[4] deuil, sorrow.

complainte, inveighinge againste the malice of his fortune. Wherein he used as a common exercise to walke all alone in the moste daungerous places of the desertes, enterteynynge his solytarye thoughtes, or rather of intente to offer hym selfe a praye to the jawes of some lyon, or tygre, or merciles beare discendynge from the mountaines.

[Don Roderico goes in search of Don Diego.]

Dom Roderico, wandring thus in the wildernes of the mountes, dispercing his traine to discover some places of habitacion, was advertised by one of his people, being within twelvescore yardes of the hermits cave, of a tracke and steppes of men, not without some merveile notwithstandyng, for that th'infertillety of the place showed no aboad nor repaire for civil people. Whereupon, as they debated, and were in devise to appoint one of the companie to follow the trace somwhat further, they sawe one enter the mouth of the cave, which was Dom Diego, who came from the top of the hill affore mencioned, wher he had newly performed his morninge complaint, with his face directly toward the coste where he judged was th'oracle of the saint to whom he dressed his devocions. The knight sente one of his valletts to approche the cave and know what they were that lived so solitarily, and withall to demaunde the highe waye to Barcelonia. But he, discoveringe afar the scituation of the hoale, so wel fortefied and rampierd with stones and blockes cowched in the forme of a trenche, fearing the same to be the receptacle, or forte, of some that kept house by the highe waye side, living of large revenue, durst neither come nere it nor aske the waye as he was commanded by his maister: to whom as he retorned with more fear of his shadow then true reporte of that he had in charge, so the valiant knight, of more corage then his cowardly servant, put spurres to his horsse, gallopyng to the veraye dore of the cave, where he ceassed not to call and knocke, till he sawe comme owte a man so disfigured with leannes of his face, and other exterior deformotie of his bodye, that his veray regard moved compassion to Roderico; who, asking what he was, demaunded also the common waye to Barcelonia. This was the servant of Diego; who aunswered that he could yelde him no reason of the waye to Barcelonya, and lesse instructe him touchinge the costes of the countrey: 'for that' (saith he) (not without some sighes and other doleful regardes) 'we are two pore brethern, whom the adventure of fortune hath brought hether to do pennance, and mortifie our present age for the synnes and offences of our youth passed.' Which wordes of two pore bretherne, broughte thether as strangers by the guide of Fortune, with the presente remembrance of Diego and his servante, argued such suspicion to Roderico that he alighted; not for that he thoughte to encounter him whom he was most desiered to embrase, but to see only the singularities of the rocke and the mistery of the closse castel, builded in the bellye of the earth. Where, finding him whom he serched (without knowing, notwithstandynge, what he was) entered into conference together of the difference between the felicitie of the solitary lif and miseries which they fynde that participate with the wretched follies of this worlde: 'for' (sayeth he) 'the mynde withdrawen from the viewe of worldly vanities takes his only pleasure in the contemplacion of heavenly thinges, being alwaies more apte to observe the commandementes of God, with a sincere reverence to their maker, then those whiche haunte the common conversation of men. Wherein, truely (when all is said) continuall frequentacion one with an other, delites, ambicions, covetousness, and superfluities of all vices whiche we finde in this confused amasse and corrupte worlde, do cause us to mistake our selves, forget our dutie towardes our Creator, fall into a perillous disdaine of pitie and charitie, and some time to diverte the sinceritie of the true religion, and abuse th'integritie and undoubted interpretation of the gospell: which I leave to be debated at large by the theologians, to whom such charge doth cheifly apperteine.'

VII. Probable Source

From
THE RARE TRIUMPHES OF LOVE AND FORTUNE
Anon. (1589)[1]

The first Acte

Enter Mercury, then riseth a Furie: then enter the assembly of the Gods, Jupiter with Juno, Apollo with Minerva, Mars and Saturne, after Vulcan with Venus. The Fury sets debate amongst them, and after Jupiter speakes as followeth.

JUP.   Ye Gods and Goddesses, whence springes this strife of late?
Who are the authors of this mutenye?
Or whence hath sprung this civill discorde here,
Which on the sodaine strook us in this feare?

---

[1] Title page: *The Rare Triumphes of Love and Fortune. Plaide before the Queenes most excellent Maiestie: wherein are manye fine Conceites with great delight.* Printed by E. A. for Edward White ... 1589. Text from *MalSoc* edn (1930).

If Gods that raigne in Skyes doo fall at warre,
No mervaile then though mortall men doo jarre.

[Tysiphone enters and explains that Pluto is offended because his daughter Fortune is insulted by Venus.]

. . . Thy daughter Venus, thy proud daughter Venus heere,
Blabs it abroad and beareth all the world in hand,   40
She must be thought the only Goddesse of the world:
Exalting and suppressing whom she likes best,
Defacing altogeather Lady Fortunes grace,
Breaking her anckers[1] downe, dishonouring her name,
Whose governement thy selfe, thy selfe doost knowe.
How saist thou, doost thou not?

[Venus proclaims her superiority.]

. . . I neede not stand to make rehearsall here of all,   119
For Gods and ghosts, yea, men and beasts unto my power are thrall.
. . . I make the noble love the bastarde in degree:
I tame and temper all the tunges, that raile and scoffe at me.
What bird, what beast, what worme, but feeleth my delight?
What lives or draweth breth, but I can pleasure or despight?
Yet divers thinges there be that Fortune cannot tame,
As are the riches of the minde, or else an honest name,
Or a contented hart, still free from Fortunes power;
But such as clime before they crale, must drink the sweet with
    sower.
Thy self O Jupiter didst graunt sometimes to me,
Of all things heer beneath the Moone, I should the ruler be . . .
Is this my soveraignitie, is this so glorious: 137
Is this becomming thy renown, to quit thy daughter thus?

[Fortune is more modest.]

FORT.   I cannot but confesse dread Gods I am not she,   151
That seekes with Venus to compare in her supremecie.
I am not of that power, yet am I of some might,
Which she usurping chalengeth to keep me from my right . . .
Loe, such am I that overthrowes the hiest reared tower: 169
That changeth and supporteth Realmes in twinkling of an hower.
And send them hasty smart whom I devise to spoyle:
Not threatning or forewarning them but at a sodain smile.

[1] buildings, 'altars'?
*

Where joy doth most abound there I doo sorrow place,
And them I cheefely persecute that pleasure did embrace.

. . . .

    JUP.   I will not in till thinges be well discernde,
Affection shall not marre a lawfull cause: 200
By examples this may best be learnde,
In elder ages led within your lawes.
Therfore a while heerof I meane to pause.
And bring in, Mercury, in open view,
The Ghosts of them that Love and Fortune slew.[1]

    [Mercury introduces five shows: Troilus and Cressida who
'Cryes out on Love that framed their decay'; Alexander who
'Curseth fell Fortune that did him delude'; Queen Dido, who
'Stabb'd her selfe and yeelded unto love'; Pompey and Caesar,
'By froward Fortune spoyled in their prime'; and Leander and
Hero, 'that felte the force of Love and Fortune both'.]

    JUP.   Content ye both; I'le heare no more of this,   252
And Mercury surcease, call out no more:
I have bethought me how to woorke their wishe,
And you have often proov'd it heertofore.
Heere in this land within that Princely bower,
There is a Prince beloved of his love,
On whom I meane your soverainties to prove.
Venus, for that they love thy sweet delight,
Thou shalt endeavour[2] to encrease their joy:
And Fortune thou to manifest thy might,
Their pleasures and their pastimes thou shalt destroye,
Overthwarting them with newes of fresh anoye.
And she that most can please them or dispight,
I will confirme to be of greatest might . . .

The second Acte

Enter Hermione and Fidelia.

    HERM.   Why then my deere, what is the greatest price in love?
    FID.   Absence of others greefs, the gretest that loving harts can
        prove.
    HERM.   But absence cannot minishe love or make it lesse in
        ought:

---

[1] In Posthumus's vision the minor spirits speak mainly in rhymed fourteeners,
Jupiter in five-foot lines. Cf. Nosworthy, *New Arden*, pp. xxxv–vii.
[2] endure *1589*.

FID. Yet neverthlesse it leaves a doubt within the others thought.

HERM. And what is that?

FID. Least change of ayre should change the absent minde.[1]

HERM. That fault is proper but to them whom jelousy make blinde.

FID. O pardon it for that the cause from whence it springs is such,—

HERM. From whence is that?

FID. My author[2] sayes, from loving overmuch.   294

HERM. Your author I will not admit, that restes as it to prove.

FID. Yet sure is it that jelousie, proceedes of fervent love.

HERM. Can that be fervent love wherin suspition leads the minde?

FID. Most fervent love wher so much love doth make the fancy blind.

HERM. But faithfull love can never be wherin suspect doth dwell.

FID. The faithfull lovers doo suspect because they love so well.

HERM. My deere Fidelia, as I thinke thy love is such to me,
So fervent, faithfull and unstain'd, as purer none can be:
Admit occasions fall out then, that I must parte from thee,
Tell me wilt thou meane space suspect inconstancie in me?

FID. If so I doo impute it to the force of lovers lawes,
That oftentimes are toucht with feare, wheras there is no cause.

Armenio listening.

ARM. What have I heard? what doo mine eyes beholde?
Dishonour to the house from whence I came!   310
Unshamefast girle, forgetfull, all to bolde,
And thou false traitour, author of the same,
Sufferest not for guerdon of thy due
The King my Fathers gratious countenance;
But must thou clime ungratefull and untrue
These steps, at firste thine honour to advance?
Hath Fortune promiste so much hope at firste,
To make thy conquest of a Princes childe?
And should I stand to question how thou durst
To leave to thinke she might be so beguilde?   320
But woords may not suffice to wreak this wrong,
Hid under cloake of over handy love:
Thou upstart fondling and forborne too long,[3]
To give such cause thy Princess ire to move!

---

[1] Cf. I. 3. 28-9.
[2] mother *1589*. No mother in the play. Probably Fidelia is carrying a book.
[3] Cloten somewhat resembles Armenio. Posthumus, an orphan, has been brought up by the king.

FID.   Nay nay, good brother, take it not so hot.
The fault is mine, and I will beare the blame:
And to returne you an answer: well I wot
How to defend the honour of my name.
But for my love I am resolved in this,
How ever you account of his defaultes,   330
With vowed affection wholy to be his,
As one in whome I spye more speciall partes
Then fall in fondlings of the baser kindes:
To have a woord[1] not squaring with the place.
But measure men by their unstained mindes.
Let fortune be to vertue no disgrace,
For fortune when it likes her majestie,
With cloudes can cover birth and highest degree . . .

HERM.   Earst had I thought my Lord a man so wise as you,   345
Sonne to a Prince, Scholer to him that deepth of learning knewe,
Among many lessons, none this rule could wisely finde,
To have the governement of wrath and rancor of your minde . . .
My Lord, that thus you should mislike the cause is very small.
The unremoved love I beare my Lady heere,
Whose countenance my comfort is, that holds my love as deare,
Commaunds me to disgest such hard and bitter woords,
As not with credit of your state, your honour heer affords.
Else, Prince, perswade thy selfe: my minde were not so base,
To pocket but for such respectes so hard and foule disgrace.
And Lady, this[2] Hermione for ought that men doo know,
By birth may be as nobly borne, as Prince Armenio.

ARM.   Traitour thou shalt not joy that proud comparison.
FID.   My good Hermione, come hence, let him alone.   363
ARM.   Nay Dame, it likes me not that you should goe.
HERM.   Whether thou wilt Armenio she shall, though thou say no.
ARM.   What, shall she, villaine?[3]
FID.   Helpe, helpe, alas!

Enter Phizantius, a Lord, and Penulo.

PHIZ.   What sturre is heere? what meanes this broile begun?
Give me to know the occasion of this strife,   370
How falles it out? Armenio my sonne
Hath wound receiv'd by stroke of naked knife?
Say to me straight: what one hath doone this deed?
His blowes are big that makes a Prince to bleed.

[1] mind?
[2] this Lady *1589*.
[3] In *Cym* Cloten draws on Posthumus. I. i. 160–4.

FID.   My soveraigne father, pardon his offence,
Whose greefe of minde is greater then his wound.
My rightfull quarrell yeeldes me safe defence,
And heere they stand that giltie must be found.
      ARM.   Traytor (O King) unto your Majesty,
Whose proud attempt dooth touch your grace so neere:
As what may be the greatest villanye   381
Upon recitall shall be opened heere.
My sister and your farre unwoorthy childe,
Forgetting love and feare of Gods and thee,
And honor of her name, is thus beguilde
To love this Gentleman whom heere you see,
Hermione, whom for a Jewell of some price,
Olde Hermet gave[1] your Highnesse long agoe:
And for I gave rebuke to your devise,
In gallant thought he would not take it so.   390
But as it seemes to doo my body good,
I thanke him, dainde him selfe to let me blood.
      PHIZ.   Hermione? and hast thou doone this deed?
And couldst thou shrine such treason in thy thought?
Armenio, jest not: with thy hurt take heed.
And thou, fond girle whose stained blood hath wrought,
How hath mine age and honor been abused,
My princely care Hermione of thee!
The fault so great it cannot be excusde,
And you inforst the shame therof to see.   400
But farre we feare some farther ill may fall
Through love and hate of one and of the other:
Her foolishe love I meane, and therwithall
The hot disdaine and stomacke of her brother.
Hermione, way[2] what our pleasure is.
Whilome thou knowest we entertainde thee willingly:
Now seeing thou hast doon so farre amisse,
To reach above thy reach unorderly,
In milder wordes because we love thee well,
Loe, we discharge thee of our princely Court: 410
Thou maist no longer with Fidelia dwell,
Forbidden to her presence to resorte.
Holde my rewarde, that am no bitter Judge,
And wend thy way where ere thou likest to goe.[3]
This only way I take to ende the grudge,
And stop the love that eache to other owe . . .

---

[1] give *1589*.   [2] weigh.
[3] So Posthumus is banished, but he has married Imogen.

[Hermione grieves at leaving the Court and Fidelia, who is told by her father to choose a husband 'among the jolly brave resorte /Of sundry knightes of noble personage'. Armenio and Hermione are left alone on the stage.]

ARM. Sir, now you are packing let me know your walke: 479
For I have that may not be past without some talke.
Nor stands it with mine honour to let thee beare it cleere:
But I will make thee know Armenios blood is deare.
HERM. My Lord, I make no chalenge with offence,
But first I will prepare for my defence.
ARM. So sir, you are aforehand, keepe you so:
And reckon of Armenio for thy vowed foe.
Goe, wend thy wayes, obscurer then the night,
And Fortune for revenge plague thee with spite.   [*Exit*.

[The parasite Penulo offers help and Hermione asks him to bring Fidelia 'to the cave /Where whilome lovers we were wont to meete /In secret sorte eche other for to greete'. Penulo however intends to tell Armenio of it.]

Strike up Fortunes triumphes with Drummes and Trumpets.

[Fortune boasts of her power as shown in this Act, but Venus warns her: 'You have begun but I must make an end.']

The thirde Acte

Enter Bomelio solus like an Hermite.

[He bemoans his unhappy lot and 'fickly Fortunes froward checke and her continuall spite'.]

. . . Beholde me wretched man that serv'd his Prince with paine,   590
That in the honor of his praise esteemde my greatest gaine.
Beholde me wretched man that for his publicke weale,
Refused not with thousand foes, in bloody warres to deale.
Beholde me wretched man, whose travell, paine and toyle
Was ever prest to save my frends from force of forrain spoile.
And see my just rewarde, looke on my recompence:
Beholde by this for labours past, what guerdon commeth thence.
Not by my fearcest foes in doubtfull fight with us,
But by my fawning freendes I was confounded thus.

One woord of his dispite in question calde my name, 600
Two woordes of his untrusty tung brought me to open shame.
Then was I banished the Citie, Court and towne:
Then every hand that held me up, began to pull me downe . . .
Heer have I liv'd almost five yeeres disguisde in secret wise.[1]
And now somewhat it is, but what I cannot tell,
Provokes me forward more than wont to leave my darksome cell,
And in my crooked age insteed of mirth and joy, 610
With broken sighes in dolefull tunes to sing of mine annoy.

[He sings a melancholy song, then sends his servant Lentulo to the town to buy food. On his way Lentulo meets Penulo, whom he fools and beats. Penulo offers to prefer him to a place at Court and Lentulo goes with him. Armenio enters, seeking Hermione, followed by Fidelia, who is hoping to see her lover. Instead she encounters Bomelio.]

BOM. . . . What doo I see? thou Nymphe or Lady faire, 813
Or else thou goddess of the grove, what makes thee to repaire
To this unhaunted place thy presence heere unfit?
FID. Ancient father, let it not offend thee any whit,
To finde me heere alone. I am no Goddesse I,
But a mortall maide subject to miserie.
And better that I might lament my heavy mone,
I secret came abroad to recreate my selfe a while alone.
BOM. Take comfort daughter mine, for thou hast found him than,
That is of others all that live, the most accursedst man.
O, I have heard it saide, our sorrowes are the lesse,
If in our anguishe we may finde a partner in distresse.
FID. O father, but my greefe releeved cannot be, 825
My hope is fled, my helpe in vaine, my hurt my death must be:
Yet not the common death of life that heere is led;
But such a death as ever killes, and yet is never dead.

[She refuses to stay with Bomelio. Armenio enters and bids her come home with him.]

FID. O brother! 843
ARM.   Brother, peace!
FID.   Good father help me now.

---

[1] Cf. Belarius, III. 3. 55–73.

BOM.   Have I no weapons, wretch that I am? Well, youth, Ile
    meet with you.
ARM.   Must you be gone? Is this your meeting place?
Come, get you home, and pack you, sir, apace.
Wear't not for reverence of thine age, I sweare
Thou shouldst accursse the time I met you heere.
But, i'faith sister, my Father shall welcome you.[1]
BOM.   Go tell thine arrand if thou canst.
FID.   Hermione adewe!
Ten times adewe, farwell for ever now.
ARM.   I thanke thee Fortune that thou didst this deed allowe.
                                                  [*Exit.*

[Bomelio, left alone, calls on the gods of Hell and strikes
Armenio dumb. Hermione enters and is told that Fidelia has
been forced to return home. He blames Fortune for his woes.]

BOM.   Accuse not Fortune, sonne, but blame thy love ther-
    fore,   936
For I perceive thou art in love, and then thy trouble is more.
HERM.   Father, if this be love, to lead a life in thrall,
To think the rankest poyson sweet, to feed on hunny gall,
To be at warre and peace, to be in joy and greefe,
Then farthest from the hope of helpe where neerest is releefe,
To live and dye, to freese and sweat, to melt and not to move,
If it be this to live in love, father, I am in love.
BOM.   Why did you not possesse your Lady then at home?
HERM.   At home, where is it, sir? Alas, for I have none.
Brought up I know not how, and borne I know not where,
When I was in my childehood given unto my Prince then heere
Of whom I can not tell, wherfore I little know,
But now cast out to seeke my fate unhappy where I goe.
There dare I not be seene, heere must I not abide.   950
Did ever more calameties unto a man betide?
BOM.   My hart will burst if I forbeare amidst this misery.
Beholde, thy father thou hast found, my sonne Hermione.
Thy father thou hast found, thy father I am he.
HERM.   But is it possible my father you should be?
BOM.   Even from my first exile heere have I liv'd forlorne,
And once I gave thee to my prince, for thou was noble borne.
And now he gives me thee, and welcome home againe.
HERM.   This is my recompence for all my former paine.

[1] Cf. Cloten, III. 5. 143–5.

Deere father glad I am to finde you heere alive,   960
By your example I may learne with froward chance to strive.

BOM.   Come sonne, content thee now, within a cave to dwell,
I will provide for thy redresse, and all thinges shal be well.
A darksome den must be thy lofty lodging now.   964

FID.   Father I am well content to take such parte as you.
Here is a breathing pit after hard mischance.
O gratious Venus once vouchsafe thy servants to advance.

Strike up a noise of Viols, Venus triumphe.

[Venus assures the audience that she will support the lovers
against Fortune. Fortune declares, 'My sport is not begun.']

[In Act IV Bomelio, disguised as an Italian doctor, tells the
King that Armenio's dumbness can be cured only by washing
his tongue with blood 'from the tenderest part' of his greatest
enemy, i.e. from the breast of Fidelia. When Fidelia refuses,
'Because unto my deerest freend so spitefull he hath been',
Bomelio offers to persuade her, or to drug her so that he may
take the blood. Left alone with Fidelia he tells her who he is
and takes her to meet Hermione at his cell. Meanwhile Hermione has found his father's magic books and burnt them all.]

HERM.   O Gods, that deepest greefes are felt in closest smart,   1331
That in the smiling countenance may lurk the wounded hart!
I see the noble minde can counterfaite a blisse,
When overwhelmed with a care his soule perplexed is . . .
Not in that wanton youth, not in that plesant mate
Could Fortune with her ficklenesse his wonted minde abate.
He rather challengeth to doo her very woorst,   1350
And makes a semblance of delight, although indeede accurst.
My father therupon devised how he might
Revenge and wreak him self on her, that wrought him such dispite.
And therfore I perceive he strangely useth it,
Inchaunting and transfourming that his fancy did not fit,[1]
As I may see by these his vile blasphemous Bookes.
My soule abhorres as often as mine eye upon them lookes.
What gaine can countervaile the danger that they bring?
For man to sell his soule to sinne, ist not a greevous thing,
To captivate his minde and all the giftes therin,
To that which is of others all the most ungratious sinne,

[1] Like Prospero in *Tem*, but note the difference in attitude towards magic.

Which so intangleth them that therunto apply,
As at the last forsaketh them in their extremety?
Such is this art, such is the studie of this skill,
This supernaturall devise, this Magicke such it will.
In ransacking his Cave, these Bookes I lighted on:
And with his leave Ile be so bolde whilste he abroad is gon,
To burne them all: for best that serveth for this stuffe.
I doubt not but at his returne to please him well enough.
And Gentlemen I pray, and so desire I shall,   1370
You would abhor this study, for it will confound you all.

*Enter Lentulo with a Ring in his mouth, a Marigolde in his hand, and a faire
shute of apparell on his backe: after he hath a while made some dum shew,
Penulo commeth running in with two or three other.*

[Lentulo has stolen the finery and wears it at his disguised
master's command in hope of winning Fidelia thereby. He is
arrested. Bomelio brings Fidelia to his cave.]

    BOM.   Hermione, Hermione, my Sonne I say,   1452
Come foorth and see thy freendes that for thee stay.

Enter Hermione.

    HERM.   Welcome my Father, but ten times welcome thou,
The constant Lady mine that liveth now.
    FID.   And lives Hermione, lives my Hermione!
What can be added more to my felicitie?
    HERM.   Thy life my life, such comfort doost thou give,
    FID.   Happy my life, because I see thee live.   1460
    BOM.   Whilste recorde the sweetnesse of their blisse,
I will apply to further as they wish
Their sweet delight by magickes cunning so,
That happy they shall live in spite of foe.

[He leaves them rejoicing in their reunion, but soon returns.]

Enter Bomelio.

    BOM.   Gogs blood, villins, the devil is in the bed straw. Wounds,
I have been robd, robd, robd, where be the theeves? My books,
bookes, did I not leave thee with my bookes? where are my bookes,
where be my bookes, villin, arrant villin?
    HERM.   O father my deere father, harke.   1498

BOM. Father, my deere father! Soule, give me my Bookes, lets have no more tarrying, the day begins to be dark, it raines, it begins with tempestes, thunder and lightning, fire and brimstone, and all my bookes are gone, and I cannot helpe my selfe, nor my freendes. What a pestilence, who came there?

HERM. Ile tell you father if you please to heare.

BOM. What canst thou tel me? tel me of a turd. What and a come! I conjure thee foule spirit down to hell, ho ho ho the devil, the devil, a coms, a coms, a coms upon me and I lack my books. Help, help, help, lend me a Swoord, a swoord, oh I am gone.

FID. Alas, how fell he to this madding mood? 1510

HERM. The heavens and earth deny to doo us good.

FID. O father, my good father, look on me.

BOM. What ment I, not to shut up the doore, and take the keies with me, and put the bookes under the bed straw? Out you hore, a hore, a hore, gogs blood, Ile dresse you for a hore. I have a cause to curse hores as long as I live. Come away, come away, give me my bookes, my bookes give me, give me, give.

FID. Help, help me good Hermione. [*Exit.*

HERM. I come of worldes of miserie, 1520
Confounded in the top of my delight.
The Fates and Fortune thus against me fight. [*Exit.*

Fortunes Triumph, sound Trumpets, Drummes, Cornets and Gunnes.

[Fortune gloats over her rival, but Venus declares, 'They shall be once againe releev'd by me.']

Musicke, Musick.

The fifth Acte

[Mercury tells Venus and Fortune that Jupiter has decided to end their conflict.][1]

MERC. Then thus our Father Jupiter concludes, 1564
To stay the stroake of your unceasing strife:
As heretofore betwixt these lovers twaine
Ye have exprest your powers upon their life,
So now he willes you to withholde your handes:
Enough suffiseth to confirme your might:
And to conjoyne ye both in freendly handes,

[1] Cf. the Vision of Posthumus and Jupiter's promise of a happy end, V. 4.

Of faithfull love wherin the Gods delight.
His pleasure is, that Lady Venus you
Shall be content never to hinder them
To whome Dame Fortune shall for freendship showe,
Of wretched to procure them happy men.
Ne shall you Fortune once presume to take
The credit of the honor in your hand:
If Lady Venus doo them quite forsake,
You shall not seeme in their defence to stand.
But whome soever one of you preferre,   1580
The other shall be subject unto her.
For thus hath Jupiter determined now.
    VEN.   I must and will subscribe my will to you.
    FORT.   And I most gladly therof doo allow . . .

[Bomelio is put to sleep by Mercury and Hermione is told to
take some of Fidelia's blood and besprinkle all his face to restore his sanity. They are interrupted by Phizantius, Armenio,
etc., led to the cave by Bomelio's absconding servant Lentulo.
Phizantius banishes Hermione again and orders Fidelia to be
taken away. Venus and Fortune show themselves and Venus
reveals Hermione's parentage. Fortune tells how Armenio's
dumbness may be cured. Fidelia allows her blood to be taken,
Bomelio is restored to his former place at Court, and Lentulo
asks his forgiveness for running away.]

    VENUS.   Thus every thing united is by love.   1833
Now Gods and men are reconciled againe:
On whome because I did my pleasure prove,
I will reward you for your former paine.
Receive the favours of our deitie,
And sing the praise of Venus soveraintie.
    FORT.   And for I plaid my parte with Lady Love,
While eche did strive for cheefe authoritie: 1840
Your good deserts Dame Fortune so dooth move,
To give these signes of liberalitie.
Thus for amendes of this your late unrest,[1]
By Love and Fortune ye shall all be blest.
And thus heerof this inward care I have,
That wisdome ruleth Love and Fortune both:
Though riches faile and beauty seeme to save,[2]

[1] Cf. Jupiter, V. 4. 101–2.
[2] Possibly means 'dry up', or an error for 'fade'.

Yet wisdome forward still unconquered goeth . . .
And sith by Love and Fortune our troubles all doo cease   1850
God save her Majestie that keepes us all in peace.

VIII. Analogue

From
JERUSALEM DELIVERED
by Torquato Tasso,
translated by Edward Fairfax (1600)

Godfrey of Bulloigne or The Recoverie of Jerusalem.
Done into English Heroicall verse, by Edward Fairefax
Gent . . . 1600. [Orthography modernized in these ex-
cerpts.]

A. Book VII. [Erminia, seeking the wounded Tancred, is
forced to flee from two Italian Crusaders. She sleeps by the
River Jordan.]

5

The birds awak'd her with their morning song,
    Their warbling music pierc'd her tender ear;
The murmuring brooks and whistling winds among
    The rattling boughs and leaves their parts did bear;
Her eyes unclos'd beheld the groves along
    Of swains and shepherd grooms that dwellings were;
And that sweet noise, birds, winds, and waters sent,
Provok'd again the virgin to lament.

6

Her plaints were interrupted with a sound
    That seem'd from thickest bushes to proceed;
Some jolly shepherd sung a lusty round,
    And to his voice had tun'd his oaten reed;
Thither she went; an old man there she found,
    At whose right hand his little flock did feed,
Sat making baskets, his three sons among,
That learn'd their father's art, and learn'd his song.[1]

---

[1] Cf. the more vigorous life of Belarius and the two young men in III. 3. 6.

7

Beholding one in shining arms appear,
    The seely man and his were sore dismay'd;
But sweet Erminia comforted their fear,
    Her ventail up, her visage open laid.—
You happy folk, of heav'n beloved dear,
    Work on, quoth she, upon your harmless trade;
These dreadful arms I bear no warfare bring
To your sweet toil, nor those sweet tunes you sing:

8

But, father, since this land, these towns and towers,
    Destroyed are with sword, with fire, and spoil,
How may it be, unhurt that you and yours
    In safety thus apply your harmless toil?—
My son, quoth he, this poor estate of ours
    Is ever safe from storm of warlike broil;
This wilderness doth us in safety keep,
No thund'ring drum, no trumpet breaks our sleep:

9

Haply just heav'ns, defence and shield of right,
    Doth love the innocence of simple swains;
The thunderbolts on highest mountains light,
    And seld or never strike the lower plains;
So kings have cause to fear Bellona's might,
    Not they whose sweat and toil their dinner gains,
Nor ever greedy soldier was enticed
By poverty, neglected and despised:

10

O poverty! chief of the heav'nly brood,
    Dearer to me than wealth or kingly crown,
No wish for honour, thirst of other's good,
    Can move thy heart, contented with mine own:
We quench our thirst with water of this flood,
    Nor fear we poison should therein be thrown;
These little flocks of sheep and tender goats
Give milk for food, and wool to make us coats:

11

We little wish, we need but little wealth,
  From cold and hunger us to clothe and feed;
These are my sons, their care preserves from stealth
  Their father's flocks, nor servants more I need:
Amid these groves I walk oft for my health,
  And to the fishes, birds, and beasts give heed,
How they are fed in forest, spring, and lake,
And their contentment for ensample take:[1]

12

Time was (for each one hath his doting time,
  These silver locks were golden tresses then)
That country life I hated as a crime,
  And from the forest's sweet contentment ran;
To Memphis' stately palace would I climb,
  And there became the mighty caliph's man,
And though I but a simple gardener were,[2]
Yet could I mark abuses, see and hear:

13

Enticed on with hope of future gain,
  I suffer'd long what did my soul displease;
But when my youth was spent, my hope was vain;
  I felt my native strength at last decrease;
I 'gan my loss of lusty years complain,
  And wish'd I had enjoy'd the country's peace;
I bade the court farewell, and with content
My later age here have I quiet spent.—

14

While thus he spake, Erminia, hush'd and still,
  His wise discourses heard with great attention;
His speeches grave those idle fancies kill,
  Which in her troubled soul bred such dissension.
After much thought reformed was her will;
  Within those woods to dwell was her intention,
Till fortune should occasion new afford,
To turn her home to her desired lord.

---

[1] Shakespeare is less conventional and Belarius's two companions are not contented with their lot (III. 3. 27–44).
[2] Belarius was a celebrated soldier until he was falsely accused of treachery (III. 3. 44–73); but he has been happy enough in the Welsh mountains.

15

She said therefore—O shepherd fortunate!
 That troubles some didst whilom feel and prove,
Yet livest now in this contented state,
 Let my mishap thy thoughts to pity move,
To entertain me as a willing mate
 In shepherd's life, which I admire and love;
Within these pleasant groves perchance my heart
Of her discomforts may unload some part:

16

If gold or wealth, of most esteemed dear,
 If jewels rich thou diddest hold in prize,
Such store thereof, such plenty have I here,
 As to a greedy mind might well suffice.—
With that down trickled many a silver tear,
 Two crystal streams fell from her watery eyes;
Part of her sad misfortunes then she told,
And wept, and with her wept that shepherd old.

17

With speeches kind he 'gan the virgin dear
 Towards his cottage gently home to guide;
His aged wife there made her homely cheer,
 Yet welcom'd her, and plac'd her by her side.
The princess don'd a poor pastora's gear,
 A 'kerchief coarse upon her head she tied;
But yet her gestures and her looks, I guess,
Were such as ill beseem'd a shepherdess:[1]

18

Not those rude garments could obscure and hide
 The heav'nly beauty of her angel's face,
Nor was her princely offspring damnified
 Or ought disparag'd by those labours base:
Her little flocks to pasture would she guide,
 And milk her goats, and in their folds them place;
Both cheese and butter could she make, and frame
Herself to please the shepherd and his dame.[2]

---

[1] Imogen is disguised as a man; the two boys love her as a brother.
[2] Cf. Belarius, 'you must be our housewife' (IV. 2. 45; 49–51).

19

But oft, when underneath the green-wood shade
  Her flocks lay hid from Phœbus' scorching rays,
Unto her knight she songs and sonnets made,
  And them engrav'd in bark of beech and bays;
She told how Cupid did her first invade,
  How conquer'd her, and ends with Tancred's praise:
And when her passion's writ she over read,
Again she mourn'd, again salt tears she shed.—

B. Book VIII. [The captain Aliprando tells Godfrey how he
found Rinaldo's armour on a body near Gaza.]

52

Thither, to seek some flocks or herds we went,
  Perchance close hid under the greenwood shaw,
And found the springing grass with blood besprent,
  A warrior tumbled in his blood we saw;
His arms, though dusty, bloody, hack'd and rent,
  Yet well we knew when near the corse we draw,
To which (to view his face) in vain I started,
For from his body his fair head was parted;[1]

53

His right hand wanted eke, with many a wound
  The trunk through pierced was from back to breast;
A little by his empty helm we found
  The silver eagle shining on his crest;
To spy at whom to ask we gazed round,
  A churle towards us his steps addrest,
But when us armed by the corse he spied,
He ran away his fearful face to hide:

54

But we pursu'd him, took him, spake him fair,
  Till comforted at last he answer made,
How that the day before he saw repair
  A band of soldiers from that forest's shade,
Of whom one carried by the golden hair
  A head but late cut off with murd'ring blade;

[1] Cf. the killing and finding of Cloten (IV. 2. 96–123; 295–332).

The face was fair and young, and on the chin
No sign of beard to bud did yet begin,

55

And how in sendal wrapt away he bore
  That head with him hung at his saddle-bow;
And how the murd'rers, by the arms they wore,
  For soldiers of our camp he well did know.
The carcass I disarm'd, and weeping sore,
  Because I guess'd who should that harness owe,
Away I brought it, but first order gave
That noble body should be laid in grave.

C. Book XIX. [Erminia tells the spy Vafrino of Ormondo's plot to kill Godfrey.]

86

And now in deserts waste and wild arrived,
  Far from the camp, far from resort and sight,
Vafrine began—'Gainst Godfrey's life contrived,
  The false compacts and trains unfold aright.—[1]
Then she, those treasons, from their spring derived,
  Repeats, and brings their hid deceits to light:—
Eight knights (she says), all courtiers brave, there are,
But Ormond strong the rest surpasseth far;

87

These, whether hate or hope of gain them move,
  Conspired have and fram'd their treason so,
That day when Emiren by fight shall prove
  To win lost Asia from his Christian foe;
These, with the cross scor'd on their arms above,
  And arm'd like Frenchmen, will disguised go
Like Godfrey's guard that gold and white do wear,
Such shall their habit be, and such their gear;

88

Yet each will bear a token in his crest,
  That so their friends for Pagans may them know;

[1] Cf. Posthumus's disguise—for a different purpose (V. 1).

But in close fight when all the soldiers best
  Shall mingled be, to give the fatal blow
They will creep near, and pierce Godfredo's breast,
  While of his faithful guard they bear false show,
And all their swords are dipt in poison strong,
Because each wound shall bring sad death ere long.

D. Book XIX. [Vafrino and Erminia find Tancred, apparently
dead.]

102

Through the highways Vafrino would not pass,
  A path more secret, safe, and short he knew;
And now close by the city's wall he was
  When sun was set, night in the east up-flew;
With drops of blood besmear'd he found the grass,
  And saw where lay a warrior murder'd new,
That all be-bled the ground; his face to skies
He turns, and seems to threat though dead he lies:

103

His harness and his habit both bewray'd
  He was a Pagan. Forward went the squire,
And saw whereas another champion laid
  Dead on the land, all soil'd with blood and mire:
This was some Christian knight, Vafrino said;
  And, marking well his arms and rich attire,
He loos'd his helm and saw his visage plain,
  And cry'd—Alas! here lies Tancredie slain!—

104

The woeful virgin tarried and gave heed
  To the fierce looks of that proud Saracine,
Till that high cry, full of sad fear and dread,
  Pierc'd through her heart with sorrow, grief and pine;
At Tancred's name thither she ran with speed,
  Like one half mad or drunk with too much wine;
And when she saw his face, pale, bloodless, dead,
She lighted, nay, she tumbled from her steed:

105

Her springs of tears she looseth forth, and cries—
    Hither why bring'st thou me, ah fortune blind!
Where dead, for whom I liv'd, my comfort lies,
    Where war for peace, travail for rest I find:
Tancred, I have thee, see thee, yet thine eyes
    Look not upon thy love and handmaid kind;
Undo their doors, their lids fast closed sever;
Alas! I find thee for to lose thee ever.[1]

106

I never thought that to mine eyes (my dear)
    Thou couldst have grievous or unpleasant been,
But now would blind or rather dead I were,
    That thy sad plight might be unknown, unseen:
Alas! where is thy mirth and smiling cheer?
    Where are thine eyes' clear beams and sparkles sheen?
Of thy fair cheek where is the purple red,
And forehead's whiteness? are all gone, all dead?

107

Tho' gone, tho' dead, I love thee still; behold
    Death wounds but kills not love; yet if thou live,
Sweet soul, still in his breast, my follies bold
    Ah pardon, love's desires and stealth forgive;
Grant me from his pale mouth some kisses cold,
    Since death doth love of just reward deprive;
And of thy spoils, sad death, afford me this,
Let me his mouth, pale, cold, and bloodless, kiss:

108

O gentle mouth! with speeches kind and sweet
    Thou didst relieve my grief, my woe, and pain;
Ere my weak soul from this frail body fleet,
    Ah comfort me with one dear kiss or twain;
Perchance, if we alive had hap'd to meet,
    They had been giv'n which now are stol'n: O vain,
O feeble life, betwixt his lips out fly!
O let me kiss thee first, then let me die!

[1] Contrast the fierce anger of Imogen at IV. 2. 306–32.

109

Receive my yielded spirit, and with thine
  Guide it to heav'n, where all true love hath place.—
This said, she sigh'd and tore her tresses fine,
  And from her eyes two streams pour'd on his face.
The man, revived with those show'rs divine,
  Awak'd, and opened his lips a space;
His lips were open, but fast shut his eyes,
And with her sighs one sigh from him up-flies.

THE WINTER'S TALE

INTRODUCTION

NO early Quarto of this play is known. Registered in the Stationers' Register on 8 November 1623 along with fifteen other plays 'as are not formerly entered to other men', it was printed in F1 at the end of the Comedies. It had been set up from a transcript by Ralph Crane made either from a playhouse text, players' parts, or Shakespeare's foul papers. The result was a good text, with Act and Scene divisions marked, and with most of the characters in a scene listed at the beginning.[1]

The Winter's Tale was seen by Simon Forman on Wednesday, 15 May 1611 at the Globe Theatre, and he wrote a long digest of its plot.[2] An entry in the Revels Account Book (now thought genuine) records a performance on 5 November 1611 at Court. In the Induction to *Bartholomew Fair* (1612–14) Ben Jonson boasted, 'He is loth to make nature afraid in his Plays, like those that beget Tales, Tempests, and such like Drolleries.' But the influence of Jonson's *Masque of Oberon*, performed at Whitehall on 1 January 1611 with Prince Henry as Oberon, has been seen in the dance of 'twelve Rustics habited like Satyrs' (IV. 3. 345–9): 'One three of them by their own report, sir, hath danced before the king.' Jonson had twelve Satyrs who praised the Prince, then sang a song to the Moon, and 'the Song ended, they fell suddenly into an antick dance, full of gesture, and swift motion, and continued it, till the crowing of the cock . . .' Perhaps some of Jonson's dancers were King's Men, and repeated their antics in Shakespeare's play. There is no proof that Robert Johnson's music for *Oberon* was used again in *The Winter's Tale*.[3]

Recently Professor G. Wickham has claimed that the piece

---

[1] Cf. J. H. P. Pafford, *New Arden WT*, 1963, pp. xvi–xix.
[2] *WSh*, ii, pp. 337–41.
[3] Cf. J. P. Cutts in *Les Fêtes de la Renaissance*, ed. J. Jacquot, Paris, 1956, pp. 298–300.

was written 'for performance in the autumn of 1610 before the King and the Heir Apparent, then aged 16' during the festivities after the investiture of Prince Henry as Prince of Wales, which took place in June. The argument[1] runs that a reconciliation between two hostile countries (Sicily and Bohemia) would be topical, since James regarded the union of England and Scotland as one of his special missions; also that the statue of Hermione was a reflection of the King's decision to celebrate the memory of his mother (executed in 1586) by having a statue of her placed in Westminster Abbey as well as one of Queen Elizabeth. I find more substance in the second than in the first of these suggestions. Elizabeth's image was carved by Cornelius Cure, the royal master-mason, before his death in 1607. His son William did the excellent statue of Mary, Queen of Scots,[2] which may have been completed before September 1609, when Sir Julius Caesar entered in a list of 'Debtes owing by his Matie' an item 'For fynishing a Tombe for the Queenes Matie mother to the king, 146£',[3] but this may refer to the tomb itself and not the statue on it. It seems certain that Cure had finished Queen Mary's effigy by 1611 when he 'made the monument of Sir Roger Ashton at Cranford, Middlesex, with seven figures kneeling, for £180'.[4] The Queen's body was brought from Peterborough on 11 October 1612 and re-interred in the Abbey. On 11 August 1613, William Cure received the sum of £85. 10. 0 'in full payment of £825. 10. 0 for making the tomb of His Majesty's dearest Mother'. 'On May 24 1616, one James Mauncey, painter, was paid the sum of £265 for painting and gilding this monument.'[5]

The making of the two statues would be known to Shakespeare and it is quite possible that, when he invented Hermione's 'statue' he had Queen Mary's in mind and meant it, as Professor Wickham suggests, as an 'emblem' for his audience of the King's piety towards his mother. Any closer identification of Hermione with the murdered Queen, or of the King with the

---

[1] *TLS*, 18 Dec. 1969, 1456; *Elizabethan Theatre III*, ed. D. Galloway, Toronto, 1973, pp. 82–99.
[2] Praised by M. Whinney, *Sculpture in England, 1530–1830*, 1964, pp. 16–17.
[3] B. M. MS. Lansdowne 164, f. 493.
[4] H. Walpole, *Anecdotes of Painting*, 1888, i, p. 185n.
[5] *Notes on the Authentic Portraits of Mary, Queen of Scots (by) Sir G. Scharf*, ed. Lionel Cust, 1903.

remorseful Leontes, would have been most unwise. James had
not done much to help his mother when she was in captivity
and condemned to death.

It is going too far to suggest that the play 'figures the mystical
marriage of Prince Henry (Florizel) to the three kingdoms
whose original unity was lost but has been found (Perdita)
thanks to Time and King James's own "piaculous action" '.[1]
If there was such an allegorical intention why did not Shakespeare make Florizel (like Greene's Dorastus) rule over two
kingdoms at the end of the play?

The play would certainly have some topicality with respect
to the question of Prince Henry's marriage. As early as 1601
proposals were made for a match with a daughter of the
Duke of Florence.[2] In 1603 the Spaniards suggested a daughter
of the Duke of Savoy,[3] and the French king proposed a double
match between Henry and Princess Elizabeth and two of his
children. When Sir Charles Cornwallis was Ambassador in
Spain (1605–9) a Spanish marriage was mooted and the French
put up a rival proposition.[4] After the installation in June 1610
negotiations became firmer, with Savoy and France as chief
contenders, and in April 1611 Savoy suggested a double match.
As a friend of the Prince, Sir Walter Raleigh wrote from the
Tower against the idea. The Prince himself would not oppose
his father's wishes, and in one of his last letters he wrote duti-
fully to the King, but added, 'your Majesty may think my
part to play, which is to be in love with any of them, is not
yet at hand'.[5] Obviously he did not altogether relish the prospect of a purely political marriage. Maybe one reason why
Shakespeare did not use the incident in *Pandosto* where Prince
Dorastus refused to marry a Danish princess at his father's
bidding was to avoid any close application to Prince Henry's
situation in a play which pleaded for romantic love against
royal expediency.

I incline to place the period of composition between June
1610 and May 1611, later rather than earlier. The play was

---

[1] G. Wickham, 'Shakespeare's Investiture Play', *TLS*, 18 Dec. 1969, 1456.
[2] *State Papers relating to Scotland*, II. 804.
[3] *State Papers, Venetian*, x. 55.
[4] Sir C. Cornwallis, *Discourse of the most Illustrious Henry, late Prince of Wales* (1641).
[5] *Somers Tracts*, 210. Cf. E. C. Wilson, *Prince Henry and English Literature*, Cornell
University Press, Ithaca, 1946, pp. 55–6, 96–100.

performed at Court during the celebrations of the Princess Elizabeth's marriage to the Elector Palatine in February 1613.

There is no evidence (other than what some critics regard as flaws) that there was an earlier version of *The Winter's Tale* which Shakespeare revised (clumsily, it would appear), or that he had a collaborator. Forman's summary of what he saw at the Globe omits the statue, but since his account of *Cymbeline* omits the dénouement no argument can be drawn that on 15 May 1611 the play lacked the climactic scene. The 'resurrection' of Hermione is prepared for by previous hints, and the rapid dismissal of the Perdita-recognition scene need not be attributed to a change of mind by the dramatist. Of this more later.

Shakespeare's main source was Robert Greene's romance *Pandosto, The Triumph of Time* (1588), which had as running title, 'The History of Dorastus and Fawnia'. Editions of this popular work appeared in 1592, 1595, 1607, and often later. Shakespeare used one of the first three editions, for the 1607 and later editions made the Oracle say, 'The King shall die without an heir', not 'live' as in the play and the earlier editions. Text I below is from the B.M. copy of 1588, supplemented by pages from the 1592 copy in the Folger Shakespeare Library, since the B.M. copy lacks signature B.

Shakespeare, who had introduced wronged wives into *All's Well* and *Cymbeline*, must have known many variations on the 'patient Griselda' theme. Greene probably drew on *The Adventures of the Lady Egeria* (?1580) in which the Duke Lampanus,

> attached with such hot broyles of *Egerias* love, could not stay his sliding steps in one sacred contentment, fearing lest others should love that which himselfe liked, or that Egeria favoured that, which hee falsly suspected . . . but cheefly incensed, thorow faithles falsehood of one *Andronius*,

became madly jealous of his wife, whom he accused of adultery with Lord Travenna. They were both cast into prison, where Travenna was murdered. Egeria wrote verses to her husband with the blood of her marriage finger. At her trial she kissed the miniature of her husband which she wore round her throat, and made a noble speech which convinced her judges, but not her husband, and she suffered much before they were reconciled. There is no reason to suppose that Shakespeare used this tale, which is inferior to *Pandosto*.

For the pastoral wooing of Dorastus and Fawnia Greene had a vast literature at his disposal. He probably knew the *Idylls* of Theocritus and the *Daphnis and Chloe* of Longus; but he owed more to modern romances such as the Spanish *Mirrour of Knighthood* by Diego Ortuñez de Calahorra and others, and the *Amadis de Gaule*. The name of the young prince Garinter comes from the Ninth Book of the latter.

Pandosto is one of Greene's best long stories. Whereas in *Gwydonius or The Card of Fancy* (1584) he concentrated on rhetoric and emotional display, in *Pandosto* he gave more attention to the story, which moves swiftly and with varied incident, though Greene still occasionally gives free rein to his antithetical, figurative style. The characters are distinct, if not deeply explored, and he pays some attention to probability, e.g. in making Pandosto's jealousy rise gradually, and in sketching the growth of the child Fawnia through sixteen years.

Pandosto falls naturally into five phases. The first is a study of needless jealousy, as Pandosto, King of Bohemia, becomes jealous of his old friend King Egistus of Sicily, who is visiting him, and resolves to have him poisoned. Fortunately his cup-bearer Franion, ordered to do the deed, warns Egistus and helps him to escape. The innocent Queen, Bellaria, who is expecting a baby, is imprisoned and her husband issues a proclamation that she and Egistus have committed adultery and conspired his death. The Gaoler, hoping to stir Pandosto's sympathy, tells him that Bellaria is in labour, but this infuriates the King, who relents only so far as to let his newborn daughter be placed in a boat and cast adrift on the sea. At each stage of the tale the emotions of the chief characters are expressed in rhetorical soliloquies. Bellaria, brought to trial, is condemned by her husband, but he is persuaded by his nobles to consult the Oracle of Apollo at Delphos (Delos). Six emissaries are sent; the Oracle finds Bellaria chaste, Egistus blameless and Pandosto treacherous. On their return Pandosto, sure that the Oracle will support him, summons his wife for judgment. Bellaria protests her innocence, and the Oracle's message

confirms it. Pandosto is struck with remorse, but too late. He
is informed that his only son, Garinter, has died, and Bellaria
herself collapses and dies. Pandosto erects a tomb with an
appropriate epitaph, and we leave him to his 'dolorous passions'.

The short second phase concerns the exposed infant, who is
picked up on the coast of Sicily by a poor shepherd (Porrus),
whose shrewish wife is persuaded by the rich mantle and the
gold that accompany it, to keep and rear the child as their
own. The girl, Fawnia, grows up, lovely and modest, till she
is sixteen. Greene's style in this section is less ornate and stylized
than before, and there are touches of humour, e.g. in the wife's
reception of her husband with his find.

The third phase describes the wooing of Fawnia by Egistus's
son Dorastus and the trouble this causes. Dorastus offends his
father by refusing to marry a princess of Denmark, then, seeing
Fawnia acting as mistress of a rustic feast, he falls in love with
her and she with him. In long soliloquies they express their
feelings about each other and the difference in their social
positions. At their second meeting she praises the simple
country life. He hints that as a prince he might command her
obedience in love. Fawnia admits that she might love him
'when Dorastus becomes a shepherd', but she knows that she
loves him already. After a conflict between his love and his
sense of rank, Dorastus dresses in shepherd's rags and soon overcomes Fawnia's class-conscious scruples by asking her to be his
wife. They decide to flee to Italy, but their frequent meetings
disturb Porrus, who persuades his wife that they ought to
inform the King how Fawnia was found. Meanwhile Dorastus's
old servant Capnio has found him a ship, which they board.
Porrus, on his way to tell the King, meets Capnio, who lures
him to the ship, and he is carried away from Sicily along with
his daughter and her lover.

The fourth phase begins when Egistus, finding his son fled
with his mistress and her 'father', falls ill with grief. The lovers
are driven by a great storm to the 'coast of Bohemia'. Remembering the old quarrel between his father and Pandosto,
Dorastus calls himself a 'gentleman of Trapalonia' and his
betrothed an Italian from Padua. Hearing of her beauty Pandosto (still a widower) has them arrested and brought before

him. Desiring her, he casts Dorastus into prison and woos her with 'unlawful lust', which she rejects. This gives Greene a chance for some fine rhetoric of temptation and resistance; it provides a striking situation with a trace of the incest-motive; it also blackens Pandosto's character anew.

The fifth phase unties the knots. Egistus, hearing that his son has been imprisoned, sends ambassadors asking that the young man be freed and that Fawnia and her father be executed. Pandosto, infuriated by Fawnia's resistance, agrees, but Porrus tells how he found her, and displays the tokens by which Pandosto realizes that she is his daughter. Her marriage to Dorastus, sealing the reconciliation between the two kingdoms, is celebrated in Sicily. Pandosto, remorseful again and no doubt feeling the inconveniences of the situation, commits suicide. They take his body back to Bohemia, where Dorastus assumes the Crown.

Both in Greene and in Shakespeare the pastoral material is basically orthodox. The child saved from death by exposure and brought up by a herdsman appears in classical drama and story. Herodotus related that Cyrus the Persian was sent off by his grandfather Astyages, but a cowherd and his wife substituted the royal child for their own still-born infant and reared Cyrus for ten years before the secret was discovered (Clio. I. §107–14). Shakespeare probably knew Angell Day's translation of *Daphnis and Chloe* (1587) in which the shepherd Lamon finds the infant girl being suckled by one of his she-goats among the ivy and grasses of a thicket. Later Daphnis's goats are scared by the hounds of young men out hunting (cf. III. 3. 58–74).[1]

Both the lost princess reared by shepherds and the amorous prince disguising himself as a shepherd appear in *The Second Part of the Mirrour of Knighthood* (1583). In Chapter XVI two newly born children are stolen by the Giant Galtenor from the chamber of the Empress Claridiana (f. 87^r), and suckled very healthily by a lady and a lioness. The boy is called Claridiano, the girl Rosalvira. At the age of six they are taken by the Giant on his travels in a chariot drawn by griffins. Rosalvira wanders off one day and is found by a shepherd, who (like

[1] Cf. S. L. Wolff, *The Greek Romances in Elizabethan Prose Fiction*, Columbia University Press, New York, 1912, pp. 451–5.

Greene's Porrus) consults his wife. Not discovering any relatives, they bring up the child as a shepherdess. In Chapter XX Prince Claridiano, enamoured of an unknown Pastora (shepherdess), is provided with shepherd's clothing by the Princess of Jerosolima, who loves him vainly, and he goes among the King's shepherds, 'in his hand a shepheards crooke. Also he carried with him a little lute, which he used at times for to recreate himselfe.' He plays as sweetly as Orpheus 'when with his lute he made the infernall furyes to sleepe. Claridiano with his lute did not onely bring the furies, but also the Queene Proserpina, and the auncient Pluto, he brought into a great perplexitie' (f. 282ᵛ). Rivalling the other amorous shepherds in 'sorrowful and grievous song', he attracts the fair Pastora by his music.

After Greene another anticipation of Shakespeare's pastoral occurs in *The Faerie Queene* (VI. Cantos x–xii) where Calidore comes upon the fair damsel Pastorella sitting enthroned as queen of the feast:

> Upon a little hillock she was placed,
> Higher then all the rest, and round about
> Environ'd with a girland, goodly graced,
> Of lovely lasses, and themm all without
> The lustie shepheard swaynes sate in a rout,
> The which did pype and sing her prayses dew . . . (St. 8)

Melibœe was her supposed father,

> Yet was not so, but as old stories tell,
> Found her by fortune, which to him befell,
> In th' open fields an Infant left alone . . . (St. 14)

Falling in love with her, Calidore lodges with them and listens to Melibœe's dispraise of royal courts in favour of country simplicities. But he cannot move Pastorella's heart until he dresses as a shepherd and helps her with tasks about the farm. Her suitor Coridon is jealous but Calidore treats him with courtesy, even after he proves a coward when Pastorella is in danger from a lion. Calidore also saves her from brigands who have carried them off. She turns out to be the daughter of the Princess Claribell and she is reunited to her parents after many years' absence.

Shakespeare seems to have been attracted to *Pandosto* by its potentialities for romantic tragi-comedy of the kind which he had already written in *Pericles* and *Cymbeline*.[1] Indeed it contained many of the same ingredients: the separation of a child from its parents, variety of setting, including movement from one country to another, false accusations in marriage (*Cym*), a wife lost and found, dissension between parent and child about marriage (*Cym*), the supernatural in oracle or vision, quasi-tragic complications with a happy outcome, variety of social setting. Moreover Greene's novel suggested similar themes affecting characterization or incidental discussion: contrast between youth and age, court and country, true and false nobility, questions of birth and breeding.

Greene's narrative involved a shift of attention, after the death of the Queen and the exposure of her infant-daughter, to the life-story of the latter and her wooing after many years which links her with a major character in the first part of the tale (Egistus). Then the two threads are brought firmly together for the discovery of the daughter's identity and her reunion with her father. In making a play out of this bifocal narrative Shakespeare increases the gap between the first and second halves by leaping over the sixteen years between the discovery of Perdita and her wooing. In some respects this brings *The Winter's Tale* close to *Pericles* in structure, for in both the father is separated from his wife and daughter for many years, and he is the centre of attention in the first three Acts, the daughter is the centre in Act IV, and they come together in Act V. Moreover in both plays the reunion of father and daughter is followed by the reunion of father and mother, and whereas 'the union of father and daughter is the result of mere chance, that of husband and wife is the result of direction'.[2]

Shakespeare's main departures from Greene are as follows: names and settings are changed; the king's jealousy is speeded up, with consequent loss of probability; Leontes himself sends to consult the Oracle before his wife's trial, and does not, like Pandosto, do so only when his wife demands it; unlike Pandosto Leontes rejects the Oracle's verdict, and his im-

[1] See the excellent discussion by Pafford in *New Arden*, pp. xliv–l.
[2] E. Schanzer, 'The Structural Pattern of *WT*', *Review of English Literature*, April 1964.

mediate bereavements are seen as punishments for blasphemy. Paulina is a new character and her continuing part is original; the child is not cast adrift in a boat but taken to Bohemia by Antigonus, another new character. Shakespeare introduces a bear to kill him, and a storm to sink the ship. Polixenes is present at the shearing-feast, which, with the entertainment offered there, is also new; likewise Autolycus and his tricks. *Pandosto* lacks the broad humour of *The Winter's Tale*, and also the discussion of ethical topics. The emotional intensity and poetic feeling of the piece are of course Shakespeare's own. His handling of these and other features will be made clear by a survey of the action, but separate consideration must be given to some aspects which may involve other sources.

Thus, most of the characters' names come from North's Plutarch, especially from the Lives of Camillus, Agis and Cleomenes[1]—e.g. Camillus, Antigones, Cleomenes and Dion, Archidamus, Aemylia and maybe Paulina (Paulinus). Polixenus, a general of the tyrant Dionysius of Sicily, 'became his enemy and fled in alarm out of Sicily'. Leontes is not in Plutarch, but Leontium is, the city of the Leontini. Hermione in Plutarch is a male name, as in Homer. Shakespeare may have thought of the loving wife of Cadmus, founder of Thebes, but more probably he recalled Hermione the daughter of Helen and Menelaus who was promised as wife to Orestes and then married to Pyrrhus.[2] In Ovid's *Heroides*, *Ep.* 8, she writes bitterly about her separation from Orestes and tells him how she grew up without a mother's care after Helen eloped with Paris. The double pathos of wife without husband and daughter without mother may have appealed to Shakespeare, but his Hermione, unlike Ovid's, does not seek relief in copious tears. An Autolycus is mentioned in Plutarch's *Life of Lucullus*, but our rogue undoubtedly came from Ovid's *Metamorphoses*, Bk XI (Golding, 359–63).

Mamillius may come from Greene's romance *Mamillia* (1583). Mopsa, the old Shepherd's wife in *Pandosto*, gives her name to one of Perdita's shepherdess friends. Perdita herself has an invented name (like Marina and Miranda), based on

[1] Cf. Pafford, *New Arden*, App. 1, pp. 163–5.
[2] E. E. Duncan-Jones, 'Hermione in Ovid and Shakespeare', *N&Q*, n.s. 13, 1966, 138–9. Cf. Holinshed, *supra*, p. 38n. for Hermione and Antigonus.

the Oracle's words, 'if that which is lost be not found'. Dorcas, another shepherdess, is named after the woman 'full of good works and almsdeeds', a great needlewoman, in *Acts* ix, 36–9. Shakespeare must have realized Greene's debt to the *Amadis de Grecia*, and he probably turned up that popular romance and took from it his young hero's name, Florizel, and maybe other hints too.

Why did Shakespeare change round the settings of Greene's story, placing Leontes in Sicily and Polixenes in Bohemia? The most probable explanation is that Sicily was well known for crimes of jealousy and revenge, while Bohemia with its fabled sea-coast was currently a frequent centre for romantic adventure.[1] It has been suggested that Shakespeare chose Sicily as Perdita's birthplace in order to identify her with Proserpina, but there is little to support this mythological interpretation except Perdita's allusion at IV. 3. 116–18.[2]

Adventures with wild animals occurred in many medieval romances and their Renaissance imitators.[3] Among the latter is Lodge's *Rosalynde* (1590), where Rosader saves his erring brother Saladyne from a lion (as does Orlando in *As You Like It*) (*supra*, II, pp. 215–17). In Sidney's *Arcadia* (1590 version, from which Shakespeare took the Edmund–Gloster story in *Lear*) there are several resemblances to details in *The Winter's Tale*. Pyrocles, disguised as the Amazon Zelmane, finds his friend Musidorus disguised as a shepherd ('and his rayments, though they were meane, yet received they hansomnes by the grace of the wearer') (Lib. 1. Ch. 18). Zelmane is invited by King Basilius to watch some Pastorals enacted in a natural theatre (Ch. 19). Musidorus gets admission too, calling himself Dorus. Zelmane is just speaking to his beloved Philoclea, 'when sodainely there came out of a wood a monstrous Lion, with a she-Beare not far from him, of litle lesse fiercenes'. Zelmane cuts off the lion's head and presents it to Philoclea. Musidorus slays

---

[1] 'A modern parallel to the sea-coast of Bohemia would be the Swiss Navy or Wigan Pier.' (S. L. Bethell, *The Winter's Tale: A Study* (1947), pp. 32–5.)

[2] *Infra*, p. 135. Cf. F. D. Hoeniger, in his perceptive essay 'The Meaning of *WT*', Toronto U.Q. xx, Oct. 1950, 21–6.

[3] There is a bear in F. de Silva's *Lisuarte de Grecia* (1542). The Prologue to the *Heptameron* of Marguerite Q. of Navarre (1558) tells how two ladies were pursued by a bear in the Pyrenees. It killed all their servants and they fled at such a rate that at the gate of the Abbey their horses dropped dead under them.

the bear and presents one of its paws to his love, Pamela, who tells how he killed the beast and how the foolish Dametas played the coward most comically. After this they have Pastorals in the evening by torchlight, and Dametas acts as director. Analogous to *The Winter's Tale* are the mingling of a disguised prince with shepherds, the sudden appearance of a bear, arousing terror and laughter in quick succession, the Pastoral festivity with dancing and singing, its first sports including a leaping dance of shepherds in honour of Pan and his Satyrs [Text II].

In Spenser's *The Faerie Queene* (VI. Canto iv) Calepine is out walking in the woodland 'To take the ayre, and heare the thrushes song' when he sees 'A cruell Beare, the which an infant bore/ Betwixt his bloudie jawes, besprinckled all with gore' (17). Chasing the beast Calepine forces it to lay down its spoil,

> Wherewith the beast, enrag'd to loose his pray,
> Upon him turned, and with greedie force
> And furie, to bee crossed in his way,
> Gaping full wyde, did thinke without remorse,
> To be aveng'd on him, and to devoure his corse. (20)

Calepine kills the bear by thrusting a stone down its throat and fighting it on the ground.

> Then tooke he up betwixt his armes twaine
> The litle babe, sweet relicke of his pray;
> Whom pitying to heare so sore complaine,
> From his soft eyes the teares he wypt away,
> And from his face the filth that did it ray.

He finds the child to be unharmed, and leaves him with the childless Matilda, wife of Sir Bruin, and the adopted boy becomes a famous knight.

This passage, combining the discovery and cherishing of a baby with danger from a bear may have passed through Shakespeare's mind when planning the exposure of Perdita.

Bohemia and a bear came together in Emmanuel Forde's romance *Parismenos, the Second Part of* . . . *Parismus* (1599, 1609, 1615) in which the newly married Pollipus and Violetta are separated in a wood while he is pursuing a bear which has put Violetta in peril [Text III].

In the theatre a bear appeared in *Mucedorus*, a highly popular romantic play (1598, 1606, 1610).

In the 1598 version the play begins with Segasto (Amadine's suitor) running away and Amadine running after him, both pursued by a bear. Mucedorus kills the bear 'off' and appears with its head in his hand. He offers the head to Amadine, and thus begins their love-story, the main theme of the comedy. In the edition of 1610 two scenes were inserted before the original Act I. Sc. 1. In the first, Mucedorus proclaims his intention to go, dressed as a shepherd, and seek the beauteous Amadine Princess of Arragon. In the second the clown Mouse is seen running away from the bear and showing terror. In order to keep his eye on the bear he runs backwards but the bear comes in behind him and he falls over it before making his escape. The scene with Segasto and Amadine follows [Text IV].

There has been much discussion about the use of live bears (no doubt from the bearpit) on the Jacobean stage. In Jonson's Masque, *Oberon the Fairy Prince*, performed before the royal family on 1 January 1611 at Whitehall, in which Prince Henry was Oberon, there were numerous Satyrs and Sylvans ('armed with their clubs and dressed in leaves'), and Oberon enters 'in a chariot, which to a loud triumphant music began to move forward, drawn by two white bears and on either side guarded by three Sylvans, with one going in front'.

It is just possible that these were two real white bears, for they were guarded by six keepers and could be well harnessed. But white (polar) bears are hard to tame and more unreliable than brown (Indian) bears. I agree with those inquirers who hold that most stage bears were men disguised.[1] The masque audience was used to seeing men in animals' heads and skins. The (white) bear in *Mucedorus* was almost certainly not a real bear, as Mouse hints before it enters: 'A Beare? nay, sure it cannot be a Beare, but some Divill in a Beares Doublet.' It would be a brave Mouse indeed who would undertake daily to walk backwards on to a real bear and fall over it. Proponents

---

[1] See D. Biggins, 'Exit Pursued by a Beare', *ShQ*, xiii, 1962, 3–14; R. Hosley, Introduction to *Oberon*, in *A Book of Masques*, Cambridge University Press, 1967, pp. 49–50.

of the 'live bear theory' could speedily end the controversy by trying the feat once or twice. It is very unlikely that the bear in *The Winter's Tale* was a real one, and Quiller-Couch's idea that Shakespeare introduced the animal because there was a tame bear on hire at the bearpit ignores the prevalence of bears in romances. Nor is it needful to ascribe Antigonus's bear to Jonson's Masque, where the bears serve as emblems of a northern Prince able to tame the wildest of creatures. Shakespeare's bear is more like those of Sidney, Forde, and *Mucedorus*, and its appearance may help to date the play as written after the revival on the public stage of *Mucedorus* (played before the King by the King's Men on Shrove Sunday, 3 February 1611).

The link between the Satyrs in *Oberon* and those in *The Winter's Tale* has already been mentioned. It suggests that Shakespeare's play came second.

A parallel use of imagery has been noted between *Mucedorus* I. 1. 47, 'My minde is grafted on a humbler stocke', and *WT* IV. 3. 92–3, 'You see, sweet maid, we marry/A gentler scion to the wildest stock.' Shakespeare may have remembered the grafting-image and the ambiguous phrase in *Mucedorus* when working on the art–nature theme in relation to the Prince's love for the shepherdess Perdita. Also bearing on our play is the close proximity of violence, terror and broad comedy shown in Mouse's soliloquy in I. 2 (1610 version) and in I. 4, where the cowardly Segasto pretends to Mouse that nothing untoward has occurred. Mouse indeed has much in common with the Clown in *The Winter's Tale*. Maybe the same actor played both parts.

It seems probable that Shakespeare knew two blank-verse narrative poems by Francis Sabie, a Lichfield schoolmaster, who in 1595 published *The Fisherman's Tale* and its sequel, *Flora's Fortune*. These have been dismissed as mere paraphrases of *Pandosto*. Certainly they follow Greene very closely in most of the main incidents, and often verbally, but there are new turns in the narrative and other distinctive qualities, as the excerpts below will show [Text V]. In *The Fisherman's Tale* Cassander tells how he fell in love with a shepherdess, Flora, and after becoming a shepherd, won her, and eloped with her by ship, carrying her indignant foster-father Thirsis with them; and how the ship was wrecked in a tempest and he became a hermit on the rocks. There is much plagiarism of the middle part of *Pandosto*, but Sabie's description of the shepherd's life is more naturalistic than Greene's. He has little mechanical euphuism but some Marlowesque lyricism of the 'Come live with me' kind. There is no sheep-shearing feast, and the wooing is concentrated into one long conversation during which Flora generalizes about natural differences in rank and Cassander declares that in love all men are made equal.

In the Preface to the sequel Sabie asserts that he wrote its predecessor 'To expell ... the accustomed tediousness of colde Winters nightes'. So it was a winter's tale, and this may conceivably have suggested Shakespeare's title, and hence the seasonal contrasts so important in the play.

Flora's Fortune takes Flora and Thirsis to Greece where she refuses to marry, but mourns her lost lover. The poet now goes back to the beginning of Greene's romance, and varies it somewhat. There is no Egistus, but an old counsellor of King Palemon (Eristo) who in her husband's absence tries to seduce Queen Julina, and, failing, accuses her of adultery.[1] She is cast into prison and tried. Two emissaries are sent to consult the Oracle of Apollo. Her baby is born and set adrift before the Oracle declares her chaste. Palemon is remorseful but the Queen dies. Sabie now follows Greene's account in telling of Flora's discovery and bringing-up by Thirsis and Mopsa. After the shipwreck she is wooed by Eristo's son, who, being refused, accuses her and Thirsis of treason. They are about to be burned at the stake when Thirsis tells how he found the girl. Palemon realizes that she is his daughter. She is married to Cassander.

In a valuable essay Mr E. A. J. Honigmann[2] has made a moderate claim for Sabie's influence on *The Winter's Tale*. The most impressive parallels are included in my excerpts. Verbal likenesses appear in Sabie's initial storm and that in III. 3, but 'some of the correspondences are of course typical of this kind' (Honigmann). When the hero is debating the

---

[1] Cinthio's tragi-comedy *Selene* (1583) has similarities. The ambitious secretary Gripo accuses Queen Selene of adultery. There is an attempt to assassinate the King, who escapes and lives abroad for many years, believing his wife unfaithful. Selene rules alone, longing to prove her innocence, and finally is reunited to her husband. Sabie probably took the false accusation from *Lady Egeria*.

[2] 'Secondary Sources of *The Winter's Tale*', *PhilQ*, xxxiv, 1955, 27–38.

pros and cons of loving a shepherdess, Sabie takes over Greene's allusion to gods who demeaned themselves when in love. Shakespeare's IV. 3. 25–30 is nearer to Sabie in calling Apollo a 'swain', not a 'shepherd'; and 'take a Wesils shape' may have suggested 'taken/The shapes of beasts upon them'. Leontes, like Sabie's Palemon, sends two messengers to Apollo's temple (*WT*, II. 1. 179–88), whereas Pandosto sends six; and like Palemon Leontes 'sends to Apollo before Perdita is born', whereas 'in Greene the idea of sending to Apollo is raised only after Fawnia has been exposed to the elements' (Honigmann). The shepherd's reproof to Perdita for not busying herself as hostess (IV. 3. 55–64) may be a reminiscence of Flora's foster-mother's reproof and complaint about her own hard life (*infra*, p. 209).

Some of the verbal resemblances are slight; but there is enough evidence to suggest that Shakespeare may have known Sabie's poems. If so he may have been encouraged by *The Fisherman's Tale* to develop its vignettes of rustic life, for Cassander disguises himself as a real English shepherd, buys 'sheepe and cotes', and sets up as a newcomer to the district before wooing the maiden. Later he disguises himself as a crippled beggar to visit Flora's house, and receives alms.

> Then praying for my maister and my Dame,
> I went away still leaning on my crutch,
> But when I came int' fields out of their sights,
> My crutch, my weeds, and scrip I threw away.
> Then who had seene me would not have supposde,
> I had bene hee which halted so ere while.

Obviously Cassander enjoys his deceit. Is this the germ of Autolycus? But Shakespeare was quite as capable as Greene or Sabie of seeing the dramatic value of different aspects of country life. He had already used them in *As You Like It*, suiting his style to the courtly and rustic personages. In *The Winter's Tale* he achieved a delightful whimsicality by combining material from *Pandosto* and from Greene's Conny-catching pamphlets [Text VI].

Lyly had introduced rascals into his comedies of myth and legend. Thus in *Gallathea* (1584) three young men decide, 'We must live by cosenage; we have neither lands nor wit, nor masters, nor honesty' (I. 4). They encounter older rogues, an Alchemist, an Astronomer, and a Fortune-teller, and by the end are glad to find a master. The satire on seducers, quacks and lawyers in Daniel's pastoral tragi-comedy *The Queen's Arcadia* (1605) was more serious and laboured.

In his gusto, impertinence, and frank self-interest, Autolycus recalls picaresque heroes like Lazarillo de Tormes and Nashe's Jack Wilton.[1] His name and general nature were, however, suggested by Ovid's *Metamorphoses*, Bk XI where Chione bore to Mercury 'A sonne hyght Autolycus, who provde a wyly pye,/ And such a fellow as in theft and filching had no peere'.

In Homer, Autolycus 'outdid all men in theft and skill in swearing'; and he had a worthy grandson in Odysseus, who was certainly a 'wyly pye'. Shakespeare's rogue is brought in mainly for delight in his tricks and to broaden the picture of country life, for he is a rural version of Greene's cockney sharpers. He does the lovers some good, if not altogether voluntarily, and, as we shall see in more detail, he ensures that the Shepherd will be present in Sicilia to make possible the recognition of Perdita. As a 'gentleman', dressed in borrowed garments, he does not convince the Shepherd (IV. 3. 758–9), and in the end he is not preferred, for (like Falstaff) he is a rogue in his grasping irresponsibility, and must kowtow to the rustics whom he has previously despised and cheated.

It is possible that Shakespeare took a hint for the presence of Polixenes at the feast (IV. 3) and his behaviour, at first kindly and then forbidding, from John Day's comedy *Humour out of Breath* played by the Children of the King's Revels in 1607 or 1608, and published in 1608. In this play Octavio Duke of Venice advises his sons Francisco and Hippolito to turn from war to love (I. 1). Accordingly they dress as shepherds: 'We take example from immortal *Jove*,/Who, like a shepheard, would repair to love' (I. 3). Their father accompanies them in disguise, telling the audience, 'Impute it not to any ruffian veine,/But to a fathers wakefull providence' (II. 1). He wants them to have experience but not to make bad matches. However, they woo the daughters of Octavio's enemy the exiled Anthonio Duke of Mantua, Hermia and Lucida,

---

[1] *The Pleasaunt Historie of Lazarillo de Tormes*, trans. David Rouland of Anglesey, 1586. *The Unfortunate Traveller*, 1594.

who are poorly dressed and fishing with rod and line. Both fathers are against their children marrying beneath them, but when Anthonio knows who the young men are he agrees. In IV. 1 Octavio throws off his disguise and forbids the marriages, rather like Polixenes [Text VII].

Shakespeare's most important deviation from Greene is his new ending, with the statue scene (V. 3) and Leontes's recognition of Hermione. The repentance of Pandosto is noted by Greene but not emphasized, and nothing is made of it when he meets his unknown daughter after sixteen years. Instead, he keeps her lover in prison, and tries to seduce her, then, being refused, is willing to have her killed to please Egistus. Leontes, however, aided by that embodied conscience Paulina (a character created for the purpose), is made to suffer the torments of remorse until the last moments of the play, and, looking back over the dialogue, it is obvious that from the moment when Paulina brought news of Hermione's supposed death (III. 3. 170ff.) the intention was to bring her back.

Shakespeare's reasons for this drastic departure from his source were complex. He had already written in *Pericles* a romantic tragi-comedy with two recognition scenes (for daughter and mother), and *Cymbeline* worked out a reconciliation between enemies (Britain and Rome), between parent and child (Cymbeline and Imogen), and husband and wife (Posthumus and Imogen). If the new play was to have such an ending it would be impossible to take over Greene's backsliding Pandosto, whose lust is more despicable than his former jealousy, and to have him mar his daughter's marriage either by living on or committing suicide. On the other hand, to leave Leontes in penitential misery without any recompense would be both harsh and undramatic. A miracle was needed to make reconciliation and pardon possible. Above all, Shakespeare seems to have wished to make his tragi-comedy not simply like 'an old tale', mere entertainment for a winter's evening, but a thought-provoking piece with strong ethical and religious overtones.

Years before, in *Much Ado*, he had restored Hero to the repentant Claudio by introducing him to a 'cousin' ('Almost the copy of my child that's dead' (V. 1. 4)), who is in fact Hero herself, kept hidden till required. He now invents a variant on this, the 'living statue' of the desired woman.

Several parallels to the image-story have been found in Spanish and French romances of the sixteenth century. The ninth book of the *Amadis de Gaule*, by Feliciano de Silva (1542) is especially interesting, having more than one episode with statues. In one a princely pair are turned to marble by enchantment, then restored partly to life, but without power to talk or eat.[1] Closer to Shakespeare is the adventure cited below [Text VIII] where two statues are substituted for living persons who think each other dead until the deception is exposed and they are reunited. No English translation is known before 1693, but the hero's name is Florisel; he becomes a shepherd to woo his mistress; there is a good deal of pastoral talk and atmosphere; and she accompanies him on his travels. The combination of Florisel, the princely shepherd, and an image-trick makes it seem likely that Shakespeare knew the *Amadis de Gaule*, perhaps in the French translation.[2]

To substitute a living person for a statue (though surely not beyond Shakespeare's powers of invention) may have been suggested also by the anonymous play *The Tryall of Chevalry* (1605, probably played 1599–1601), where, however, the sex of the 'statue' is different. Set in medieval France the piece mingles pseudo-history with romantic love story.

Prince Ferdinand, son of the King of Navarre, loves Princess Katharine, daughter of the King of France.[3] She, however, is in love with his friend Pembroke, and when Ferdinand gets his friend to intercede for him she lets Ferdinand know her secret. Believing his friend to be false, Ferdinand challenges him and in the duel both are wounded. Pembroke is tended by a forester, Ferdinand by a fisherman; each recovers, unknown to the other. Meanwhile Katharine has run away from court, and a villain has told her father that Ferdinand has ravished her; whereupon war breaks out between Navarre and France.

---

[1] Sir H. Thomas, *Shakespeare and Spain*, 1922, p. 23. Cf. J. de Perott, 'Die Hirtendichtung des Feliciano de Silva und Shakespeares Wintermärchen', *Archiv*, 30, 1913, 53–6. Thomas rejects de Perott's claim that Shakespeare knew this episode.
[2] *Le neufiesme livre d'Amadis de Gaule, auquel sont contenuz les gestes de Dom Florisel de Niquée, surnommé le Chevalier de la Bergère . . .* trans. G. B. de Buillon, Paris, 1551. I have used the 1577 Lyon edition.
[3] *The History of the Tryall of Chevalry* (1605), ed. A. H. Bullen. *Old English Plays*, iii, 1884, ed. J. S. Farmer, *TFT*, 1912. Cf. E. Koeppel, 'Ein Vorbild für Shakespeares Statue der Hermione', *Archiv*, 97, 1896, 329–32.

Pembroke, in disguise, thinking that he has killed his friend, resolves to spend his life guarding the place where he believes his friend is buried. When Katharine comes to the spot he uses a portrait of his (dying) friend to turn her love from himself to Ferdinand, and promises to erect a statue of the latter there. When Ferdinand returns they are quickly reconciled and Ferdinand is persuaded to act as his own statue when Katharine comes to lay flowers at the tomb. In her grief she is about to kill herself but Ferdinand reveals himself. Together they heal the breach between their parents. The passages about the image are given below [Text IX].

There are slight parallels to *The Winter's Tale*: princely lovers; a quarrel between old friends because one believes that the other has betrayed him; the substitution of a living person for a statue and the consequent reunion of parted lovers. (Note also that Ferdinand appears as the young hero of *The Tempest*.) Whatever Shakespeare took, however, he transformed.

Inevitably the bringing of a statue to life would recall the story of Pygmalion and Galatea, which Shakespeare knew in Ovid's *Metamorphoses*, Bk X. Relevant parts of this are given below in Golding's version [Text X]. Ovid's appreciation of the statue's lifelike ambiguity, and the physical nature of Pygmalion's love, must have influenced *The Winter's Tale*, where Perdita wishes to kiss the image's hand (V. 3. 46) and Leontes gradually realizes that it is alive and breathing and longs to kiss it (V. 3. 64–80).

The dramatist would also find in Pettie's *Petite Pallace of Pettie his Pleasures* (1576, reprinted 1608)[1] a Pygmalion story, modernized and set in Piedmont. A nobleman who has long worshipped platonically a married woman finds her sensually in love with another man, and is so incensed that he blasphemes against love and women. He makes an image on which to bestow his affection. Venus brings it to life after he has 'repented of his former rebellion against the majesty of the goddess'. Pettie spends little time on the statue's beauty or the miraculous transformation, but there is a parallel to Leontes's blasphemy against Apollo. His book also contains the tale of Admetus and Alcestis in which Admetus will be granted by

---

[1] Pettie, G., *A Petite Pallace of Pettie his Pleasures*, 1576, 1578?, 1580?, 1608, 1613, modern edn by I. Gollancz, 1908, 2 vols.

destiny 'a double life if he can find one to die for him, which Alcestis herself performeth'.

And Proserpina, the goddess of hell, especially pitying the parting of this loving couple, for that she herself knew the pain of parting from friends, being by Dis stolen from her mother Ceres, put life into his wife again, and with speed sent her unto him.[1]

Alcestis may have provided one set of associations for the complex surrounding Hermione in V. 3. Perdita is associated with Proserpina when she exclaims: 'O Proserpina!/For the flowers now that frighted thou let'st fall/From Dis's waggon' (IV. 3. 116–18). The idea comes from Ovid's *Metamorphoses*, Bk V (Golding, 487–502) where the kidnapping takes place in a Sicilian paradise:

While in this garden *Proserpine* was taking hir pastime,
In gathering eyther Violets blew, or Lillies white as Lime,
And while of Maidenly desire she fillde her Maund[2] and Lap,
Endevoring to outgather hir companions there, by hap
Dis spide hir: lovde hir: caught hir up: and all at once well neere:
So hastie, hote, and swift a thing is Love, as may appeare.
The Ladie with a wailing voyce afright did often call
Hir Mother and hir waiting Maides, but Mother most of all,
And as she from the upper part hir garment would have rent,
By chaunce she let her lap slip downe, and out the flowres went.
And such a sillie simplenesse hir childish age yet beares,
That even the verie losse of them did move hir more to teares.

Proserpina's mother, the goddess Ceres, searches the world for her until the river Arethusa tells her that Dis has taken her daughter to the underworld, where she is now Queen. (In other versions Ceres herself visits Hades.) Ultimately Jove intervenes and Proserpina is to 'remaine/One halfe yeare with hir mother and the resdue with her Feere' (husband). The restoration of Perdita to her mother after long absence during which Hermione has been 'dead' may well have reminded Shakespeare of Proserpina and Ceres.

I do not, however, regard the play as a fertility myth. The

---

[1] Gollancz, *op. cit.*, I, p. 195.
[2] wicker basket.

seasons of the year and of man's life are introduced poetically but not allegorically, and Perdita is not *identified* with Proserpina.[1] It remains to show how Shakespeare interwove the strands of his various material in the tapestry of his play.[2]

The first Scene, between the Bohemian lord Archidamus and the Sicilian Camillo, sets an initial tone of friendship and hospitality and lets us know that Polixenes and Leontes have been cementing their boyhood friendship by the former's visit to Sicily. The high promise of Leontes's young heir Mamillius is mentioned, and the importance of an heir to the land. There are plenty of ironies here for coming scenes to make plain. I. 2 carries on this note of gracious amity for a hundred or so lines, as Polixenes insists that after nine months' stay he must leave tomorrow, and that he must refuse Leontes's request for another week, or half-week:

> There is no tongue that moves, none, none i' the world,
> So soon as yours could win me. (I. 2. 19–20)

Hermione does not speak until pressed to do so by her husband. Then she gibes gently at Polixenes's stubbornness and declares that he must stay, 'My prisoner or my guest'. Soon he submits, and she holds him apart, hearing about his boyish friendship with Leontes: 'We knew not/The doctrine of ill-doing, no, nor dream'd/That any did.' There is irony here too, but the only change for the worse that he will admit is that both have been 'tempted' into love for their wives. Past innocence will soon be contrasted with bitter experience, for, though they do not know it, Leontes's mind is already tainted with infidelity to both friendship and love. The innocence of this conversation, and Hermione's attitude, make it clear that she loves her husband; but he has not heard what they are saying, and now breaks in. When he hears that Polixenes will stay he comments wryly, 'At my request he would not', but expresses pleasure. In jesting

---

[1] If Shakespeare read N. Comes, *Mythologiae* (1588), IV. 16, 'De Proserpina', he would find reference to Cicero's elaborate description of Sicily's fertility 'whereby flowers bloom there almost all months of the year' (*Verrem*, V). This would make the choice of Bohemia as setting for Perdita's shearing-feast and flower-poetry extraordinary if there were an allegorical intention.

[2] For a detailed examination see Fitzroy Pyle, *The Winter's Tale: A Commentary on the Structure*, 1969.

about her 'last good deed' he reminds her that she was three months before she would accept him as her husband, promise 'I am yours for ever' (105), and give him her hand.

So far the text makes no certain sign of jealousy in Leontes, and although his first speeches are somewhat laconic, it is hard to prove that he is already jealous when the play begins.[1] But a jealous man might take some of Hermione's speeches ambiguously, e.g. 28–9; 39–42. Now, however, his sexual animosity leaps out full-fledged when Hermione gives Polixenes her hand and moves away talking to him with every sign of affection. Whereas in *Pandosto* the King's jealousy grew gradually and affected his daily demeanour, here there is a sudden conviction that Hermione's friendship goes too far; 'To mingle friendship far is mingling bloods' (110), and her innocent freedoms fill his mind with imaginings as foul as those of Othello after he has been primed by Iago. Shakespeare is now interested, not in the origins of jealousy and its mental development, but in its effects. Leontes's jealousy, like Lear's division of his kingdom and his love-test, is a postulate which we must accept. Yet Shakespeare, unlike Greene, gives us several facets of jealous psychology at work, in Leontes's worried affection for Mamillius, playing with whom serves to let him soliloquize freely as his conviction of his wife's infidelity grows (129–47; 186–208). Like Othello he admits that his wife's freedom *might* be virtuous—but dismisses the notion; and when he invokes 'Affection' (139–43) he admits the truth about his own state—that Passion can make the impossible seem truth, making substance out of nothing, but then he twists it against Hermione and Polixenes in the surge of his obsession.

In hiding his confusion Leontes makes the first mention of Polixenes's son Florizel, who is to be the hero later; and the real affection of the two fathers for their boys contrasts with the suspicion with which Leontes sends Hermione and Polixenes into the garden. (Their often walking in the garden while Pandosto was occupied in state business first sowed resentment in *his* mind.) Here it is a test, to watch them as they go, so as to whip himself into a frenzy before action.

Camillo his faithful servant (not, like Greene's Franion,

[1] Shakespeare leaves it open for the actor to suggest the 'melancholy passion' which Greene mentioned.

his cupbearer, but a court official acting as cupbearer to Polixenes) tries to dissuade him from his delusion, but Leontes's fury grows with opposition, and Camillo has to promise to poison Polixenes on condition that Hermione will be forgiven. Unlike Franion, Camillo is a privileged counsellor and the interview shows a wisdom in him which is to be displayed often in later scenes, while Leontes's madness deepens as he invents evidence to support 'this diseas'd opinion'. When Polixenes, suspecting from Leontes's changed behaviour (shown in *Pandosto* only to Bellaria) that something is wrong, asks what it is, Camillo urges him to escape, and he will assist and accompany him. Greene lets Egistus delay for six days before taking ship: Polixenes gets away at once. The speed and urgency of the first three Acts keep the tension high.

The beginning of II. 1, suggested by Bellaria's 'playing with her young son Garinter', gives a few moments of peaceful home-life, letting us know for the first time that Hermione is far advanced in pregnancy, before Leontes bursts in and turns his rage against the departed Polixenes into a flat accusation of his wife (' 'tis Polixenes/Has made thee swell thus' (60–1)). Hermione meets the inexplicable charge with courage, and goes to prison obediently, with gentle reproach but no tears ('I am not prone to weeping' (107)). Contrast *Pandosto*, where there is no confrontation between Bellaria and her husband, who sends a guard to arrest her, and, though she goes 'most willingly', she spends her time 'with sighs and tears'. Leontes's lords, led by old Antigonus, beseech the King to call her back, but Leontes takes on himself all responsibility for what is to happen, discarding their good counsel (167–9). He admits that his accusation was based on 'Camillo's flight/Added to their familiarity' and his own conjectures; yet he is convinced, and his sending to the Oracle is merely to obtain certain confirmation and to prove his reasonableness (173–86).

Shakespeare omits the long lament by Bellaria before her child is born and the visit to Pandosto by the kind-hearted jailer.

Instead he introduces a new character, Antigonus's wife Paulina, who tries in vain to see her mistress, but is present just after the birth of Perdita. This strong-minded, impatient, outspoken but generous court-lady persuades the Queen and the jailer to let her take the baby to Leontes in the hope of softening his hard heart.

Since Polixenes has eluded him, Leontes is bent on avenging himself on his wife (II. 3), and we learn that the boy Mamillius is ill before Paulina (much to her husband's embarrassment) forces her way into the King's presence. There is a good deal of humour in the altercation between the enraged monarch, who calls his child a bastard and orders her out, and his wife's indignant defender, who calls him mad, a traitor to himself, and all but a tyrant (66–129), while Antigonus the ineffectual husband stands by helpless.

After Paulina has gone, Leontes (like Pandosto) is prevented from having the child burnt by the protests of his nobles; but whereas Pandosto has her cast adrift in 'a little cock-boat', Leontes makes Antigonus promise to abandon the baby in 'some remote and desert place quite out/Of our dominions' (175–6). The obedient Antigonus takes the child away, and immediately news comes that the messengers have returned from Delphos after twenty-three days' absence. Leontes at once orders a 'just and open trial' of Hermione to be held. Greene described Bellaria's grief at parting with her new-born infant. Shakespeare leaves that to our imagination.

Act III begins by suggesting the sacred atmosphere of Delphos and the Oracle, whose verdict the messengers do not know, since (as in *Pandosto*) it was sealed up by the priest. However, we approach the trial scene (III. 2) with some anticipation of good news and a happy outcome. In *Pandosto* Bellaria made two appearances in court, one after her baby had been taken from her, during which she begged for the Oracle to be consulted, the other to hear Apollo's judgment. Shakespeare moves at once to the second occasion, when the indictment is read, Bellaria makes her defence, and the Oracle's scroll is opened. Shakespeare expands the scene and Hermione's part in it. As before, Leontes makes a great show of justice while being himself accuser, prosecutor and judge in his own case.

In meeting the indictment Hermione uses material from Bellaria's 'cheerful answer', notably in the assurance that 'powers divine/Behold our human actions' (27–8). But Bellaria's clipped antitheses are expanded into a well-poised oration, interrupted by Leontes, but making a reasoned and total rejection of his absurd accusations. This is no shrinking Desdemona but a mature matron with an intelligence sharper than her husband's as she concludes:

> if I shall be condemn'd
> Upon surmises, all proofs sleeping else
> But what your jealousies awake, I tell you
> 'Tis rigour and not law. Your honours all,
> I do refer me to the oracle:
> Apollo be my judge! (110–15)

In Greene the reader knows the Oracle's verdict before the second trial scene. In Shakespeare the ritual of presenting the scroll must precede our certain knowledge; but the oracle is in almost the same words. Its effect, however, is different. Pandosto at once repents, for his 'conscience was a witness against him of his witless fury and false suspected jealousy'; Leontes, on the other hand, is harder to cure of his passion. He rejects the Oracle and is demanding that the trial go on, when word is brought that the boy Mamillius is dead. At this his resistance collapses; he regards his loss as a punishment for his injustice, but when Hermione swoons he at first makes light of it ('she will recover:/I have too much believ'd mine own suspicion'). After the Queen has been carried out, however, he realizes the enormity of his crimes, which he confesses to the god. Paulina, not knowing how he has changed, comes back to attack him with stinging words, to announce the death of Hermione (173–200), and to offer Leontes nothing but repentance and despair without forgiveness.

When she sees that he is truly remorseful she calms down, and asks pardon for her violent words: but in promising not to mention his victims again she is careful to make sure that he will not forget them (216–30), thus initiating her pattern of behaviour over the next sixteen years. In referring to the burial of his wife and son in a chapel, he is recalling the 'rich and famous sepulchre' in Greene, on which, as Leontes promises, 'The causes of their death appear, unto/Our shame perpetual' (*infra*, p. 172).

So ends the little tragedy of Leontes and Hermione. Shakespeare, like Greene, now traces the adventures of the rejected baby, which in *Pandosto* is driven in its boat to the shore of

Egistus's land (Sicily). Leontes's daughter is deliberately brought by Antigonus to the coast of Bohemia, Polixenes's land, because, having had a terrifying dream in which a lamenting Hermione bade him call the babe 'Perdita' and leave it in Bohemia, he believes that the vision came from Apollo, that Hermione is dead, and that the child is Polixenes's daughter. Moreover the dream-Hermione has told him that because of his part in 'this ungentle business' he will never return home.

It is no doubt natural for Antigonus to conclude that Hermione 'has suffer'd death', i.e. been executed, but his conclusion that she was guilty since she wanted the baby left in Bohemia shows that he is tainted in mind though amiable and pitiful. The tempest was probably suggested by the storm which drove Fawnia's 'cock-boat' to land. It makes the scene more exciting and the child's situation more perilous, and it serves, by sinking the ship after Antigonus's death, to remove all possibility of Leontes being informed of his daughter's whereabouts. The noises of the storm and of the hunt combine to make *'Exit, pursued by a Bear'* not laughable but a sharp and frightening climax to a scene of pity and foreboding. The punishment of Antigonus has been as speedy as that of the children who insulted Elisha: 'And there came forth two she-bears out of the wood, and tare forty and two children of them' (2 *Kings* ii, 23-4). The death of Antigonus also marks the dismissal of the tragic spirit from the play, which at once turns towards rustic comedy and romance.

Greene's romance changed its style somewhat when the 'poore mercenary shepheard . . . wandered downe toward the sea cliffe to see if perchaunce the sheepe was browsing on the sea Ivy', found the baby, took it home, and was ill received by his wife who

> beganne to crowe against her goodman, and taking up a cudgel (for the most maister went breechles) sware solemnly that shee would make clubs trumps, if hee brought any bastard brat within her dores.

Here we are not far from the style of the Conny-catching pamphlets which Greene defended because 'a sertaine decorum is to be kept in everie thing, and not to applie a high stile in a base subject'.[1] In *Pandosto* he did not have to 'write basely of such base wretches who live onely to live dishonestly'; but he suited his style to the different setting of his story. The Shepherd in III. 3 is not so pathetically poor as Greene's, and his character is developed with a real sense of country types, showing an observant, somewhat sardonic humour, whereas his son the Clown is a simpleton, kindly but bewildered. The antithetical balance of Greene's romance style affects them both, though they speak a dialect, as Greene's Porrus and Mopsa do not.

The Shepherd's first remarks look forward, though he does not know it, to the trouble he will have later from youngsters connected with this day's work. His son's account of what he had seen joins sea and land, storm and the bear in a horror which becomes grotesquely comic as he speaks of the drowning sailors and the bear dining 'on the gentleman'.

And the father provides rich material for modern symbolists when he turns our attention away from 'such heavy matters' with 'Now bless thyself! thou mettest with things dying, I with things new born' (110). Pity mixed with natural cupidity marks the ignorant pair, who will bury the dead and do good deeds on this lucky day. So the bear is not merely a burlesque figure;[2] it is both terrifying and funny, and with this scene 'throws a bridge across the two halves of the play'.[3]

The introduction of Time as Chorus at the opening of Act IV[4] may have been suggested by his appearance with the Chorus of *The Thracian Wonder*, a play probably written shortly before *The Winter's Tale*,[5] and based on Greene's romance *Menaphon*. In it Time enters during the Chorus between the first and second Acts 'with an hourglass, sets it down, and exit'. Shakespeare's Time is the popular emblematic figure with scythe and hour-glass often described as Father of Truth. He speaks in heroic couplets, and, like Gower in *Pericles* and the Chorus in *Henry V*, he stands outside the action, interpreting it to the audience. At one moment he seems to be the author when he

---

[1] *The Second Part of Conny-catching*, 1592, Dedication.
[2] S. L. Bethell's view in *The Winter's Tale: A Study*, 1947, pp. 50–62.
[3] E. M. W. Tillyard, *Shakespeare's Last Plays*, 1938; N. Coghill, 'Six Points of Stagecraft in *WT*', *Sh Survey* 2, 1958, 31–41.
[4] I follow Craig's scene-divisions in the three-volume Oxford edn. In many edns the Chorus is IV. 1.
[5] Cf. O. L. Hatcher, 'Sources and Authorship of *TW*', *MLN*, xxiii, 1908, 16ff.

says, 'I mention'd a son of the king's', referring back to I. 2. 34; 164–71. He links past, present and future, telling us of Leontes's lasting grief, Florizel's name, and that Perdita has grown up 'a shepherd's daughter'. He talks of his power as planter and destroyer of law and custom, but Shakespeare, unlike Greene, manipulates events more through character than through Time. 'We are to think of Time as a story-teller' and the play as a tale put on the stage, and although Time apologizes wittily to lovers of the Unities, in fact 'he *emphasizes* the temporal gap', for this 'is not, like *Pericles*, a chronicle play'.[1] What matters is not how Perdita and Florizel grew up or how Hermione spent her years in hiding, but what is to happen now on the stage.

The dependence on character is instanced in IV. 1 when Camillo, Polixenes's trusted counsellor, shows his yearning for a sight of his own land, Sicily. He is too indispensable to be allowed to go, and Polixenes seems to doubt the penitence of Leontes (23–4). Like Henry IV he is disturbed by his son's behaviour, but Florizel's absence from the court is due to his frequenting 'the house of a most homely shepherd', who has a daughter 'of most rare note'. We gather from this that Shakespeare has omitted not only to describe Perdita's growing up but also her first meeting with the Prince. He has also ignored the King's attempt to have his son marry a Danish princess. Polixenes has 'not this cause to be offended with his son, but, unlike Egistus, he resolves to go in disguise and interview the old shepherd. By bringing the King into contact with the young people at the shearing-feast, Shakespeare adds greatly to the dramatic tension of that scene.

Moving back to the country, we are introduced in IV. 2 to Autolycus singing his song of the seasons and thievery and announcing his prigging philosophy like any old Vice, before putting it into practice against Perdita's foster-brother the Clown. As a stealer of sheets from drying-grounds he is the rural equivalent of the Curber, who, Greene tells us in his Conny-catching pamphlets,[2] with the help of his Warp (assistant) steals household stuffs by means of his hooked staff [Text

---

[1] F. Pyle, *The Winter's Tale: A Commentary on the Structure*, 1969, pp. 71–3.
[2] *The Second and last part of Conny-catching* . . . R. G. (1592). Gipsies have often been accused of stealing linen, and in African towns today the 'Curber' still walks at night with his hooked stick.

VI AII]. The thieves' slang for such booty was 'snappings';
hence Autolycus is a 'snapper-up of unconsidered trifles'
(IV. 2. 26).

The Clown on his way to buy things for the sheep-shearing
feast helps to make a pleasant picture of country life and pastimes, with his reference to the prowess of the shearers in male
three-part songs, and the puritan among them who is not
averse to singing psalms to hornpipes.[1]

The trick played on the Clown comes straight from Greene's
'kinde conceit of a Foist performed in Paules' [Text VI AI].
In this robbing of a good Samaritan Autolycus shows himself
off as a 'Foist' or pickpocket. His versatility knows no bounds,
and there is every reason for believing that the account he
gives of himself as an ex-servant of the Prince 'whipped out of
the court' and of his later professions, is substantially true.

The long and delightful shearing-feast (IV. 3) was not in
Greene, but Dorastus first saw Fawnia dressed as 'mistress of
the feast' after 'a meeting of all the farmer's daughters in
Sicilia', and this gave Shakespeare the idea of bringing out the
differences between court and country, and showing the charm
of unsophisticated pleasures, while presenting Florizel and
Perdita as pastoral lovers and bringing father and son together
at the climax. Other ideas emerged too, as we shall see later.

Only now do we meet the two young people, who are already
sworn lovers, greatly occupied, however, with Perdita's scruples
about the inequality of their ranks and births. For Florizel the
shearing-feast (soon after midsummer, as commonly in England) is 'a meeting of the petty gods/And you the queen on't'
(IV. 3. 4–5). She is like Greene's Flora, fresh as at the end of
spring, but she dislikes to see the Prince wearing a shepherd's
humble garb. They met by chance, and she fears that his father
might also chance that way, showing not only dramatic irony
but also a feminine realism which Florizel will not acknowledge.
Like Greene's Dorastus, he likens his disguise to the amorous
transformations of the gods (25–33), though his intentions are
strictly honourable. Perdita's fears are hard to banish, and she
has to be called to a sense of her duties as hostess by her foster-

[1] Cf. *Gude and Godly Ballatis* (1567), a Scottish collection which has a section, 'The
Psalmes of David, with other new Pleasand Ballatis'. This included religious
adaptations of such songs as 'Johne, cum kiss me now', and 'The hunt is up'.

father, who contrasts her behaviour with that of his wife Mopsa, now dead (55–68).

The disguised Polixenes and Camillo enter with the guests and are taken for farmers (69–77). In a charming ritual of welcome Perdita offers them suitable flowers: to Polixenes and Camillo at first 'rosemary and rue', herbs which (signifying remembrance and grace respectively, but rue also means repentance and pity) Polixenes notes are suitable for old age and winter-keeping. Her apology, saying that she will not grow the autumn flowers most suited to their age because they are 'nature's bastards', initiates a discussion about Art and Nature to which I shall return later. Enough for the moment to suggest that her conversation with Polixenes proves to the visitors not only her sexual modesty but also her intelligence and strength of mind. She is not to be moved by the best metaphysical arguments. A bastard is still a bastard, however excused, and she'll have none of them. Delightful irony here, since she has herself been thrown out as a bastard; irony, too, in Polixenes's defence of mingling high and low stocks when he is there to prevent that happening (83–103). She flatters the visitors by giving them midsummer flowers, pretending that they are 'men of middle age'.

Camillo is captivated, but she turns aside his compliment and passes among the guests, distributing her flowers to the young ones and wishing that she had all the blossoms of Spring to offer to them, especially to Florizel. Into their few lines of love-speech Shakespeare puts more feeling and proof of deep affection than Greene managed in several conventional scenes. Even Polixenes is impressed by her natural grace, and begins to talk to the Shepherd, who praises her, and drops a hint not lost on the audience (165–80), and shows that he does not know who Florizel may be.

The climax of the scene is cunningly delayed by the arrival of Autolycus, this time as an itinerant ballad-monger and pedlar of fancy stuffs. This causes a tiff between the Clown and his Mopsa (contrasting with the nobler love of Florizel and Perdita), introduces some comical satire on popular street-ballads and their credulous purchasers, and prepares for another *coup* by the engaging scalliwag Autolycus. Moreover, the songs now sung are like part of the entertainment at the feast, which continues with the dance of twelve farm-people dressed as Satyrs. This indicates a general debt to the Masques, if not specifically to Jonson's *Oberon*, and still more to the pastoral romance, whether Spenserian or Arcadian.

Meanwhile Polixenes has been talking to the Shepherd, and what he has heard convinces him that he must act now to separate the two lovers. Accordingly he leads them on, encouraging them to swear their love, and letting the Shepherd start making an oral contract of marriage, before asking whether Florizel's father should not be consulted. When Florizel persistently refuses to tell his father, Polixenes in a rage reveals himself and forbids the marriage.

The reactions of the victims of his wrath are characteristic. The old Shepherd is crushed and fearful. Perdita is shaken but more indignant than afraid for herself; she fears for her lover and is willing to give him up: 'I'll queen it no inch further,/ But milk my ewes, and weep' (456–7). Florizel is all the more determined to marry his mistress; if he break his faith, 'Let nature crush the sides o' the earth together,/And mar the seeds within' (485–6).

So far the scene has drawn almost nothing from Greene; now it returns near to his romance, where Dorastus tells 'an old servant, Capnio' of his need to flee, and the latter gets a ship and helps them to escape as Franion helped Egistus many years before. Shakespeare divides Capnio's functions between Camillo and Autolycus. The former, when he perceives the Prince resolved on flight overseas, sees a way of himself getting to Sicily while aiding the young lovers to be married under Leontes's protection.

His hope of reconciling Polixenes to the runaway match, Florizel realizes, will be 'almost a miracle' (541), but he agrees to go to Sicily. While Camillo and Florizel are discussing money problems Autolycus enters and tells the audience how he sold all his ballads and trinkets to the rustics, and, having taken good note of the fullest purses, was able to do some profitable pocket-picking as well. He has in fact performed the trick of Greene's ballad-monger in *The Art of Conny-catching*, whose music and quickfire salesmanship are an aid to his partner the cutpurse. Autolycus works alone, but with equal success [Text VI B].

He is now brought into the plot, for his clothes will provide a disguise by which Florizel can reach the harbour. So Autolycus is forced to change his shabby garments for the Prince's festive dress, Perdita is given her lover's hat and they steal away. Camillo lets us know that he intends to tell the King where they have gone, so that Polixenes may pursue them, and he will accompany him to his native land. Autolycus is left behind to congratulate himself on his luck and on his skill at his craft. He is ready for more knavery when the Clown enters, urging his father to tell the King the truth about Perdita. They are seeking the royal palace, but Autolycus stops them, and, pretending to be a courtier in his fine clothes, terrifies them into giving him money and, telling them that the King has 'gone aboard a new ship to purge melancholy', takes them to the Prince's ship to prevent their making any trouble. He likes to exaggerate his own rascality, but he obviously sympathizes with the lovers, and if he can both 'do the prince my master good' and get gold and maybe 'advancement' by it, he will help them.

Greene's lovers are brought to Pandosto's country by Fortune and a storm which drives them to 'the coast of Bohemia'. There is no need for a storm in *The Winter's Tale*, although a hint of one remains (V. 1. 152–4). In V. 1 the atmosphere in Sicilia is prepared when Leontes, still mourning after sixteen years, is asked by his Lords to marry again so as to get an heir. Paulina objects to this, reminding them of the Oracle, which she claims implicitly forbade re-marriage (35–49). Leontes, who does not want another wife, swears never to marry without Paulina's leave (a device taken from *Much Ado* (V. 1. 269–93)), and 'Unless another/As like Hermione as is her picture' should be found. There are other ambiguous touches shadowing forth some startling dénouement.

The arrival of Florizel and Perdita brings such praise of the latter's beauty that Paulina becomes jealous for her lost mistress's memory (93–111). Unlike Dorastus, who hides his birth and nationality, fearing Pandosto's old enmity to his father, Florizel, following Camillo's advice, declares that he has been sent by Polixenes and that Perdita 'came from Libya'. Leontes greets them most hospitably, eager for reconciliation, but while he is praising the young couple before him, one of his Lords enters with a request from Polixenes (who has landed in

Sicily), that Florizel be arrested. Florizel has to admit his deception and that he and Perdita are not married. He begs Leontes to intercede for them. Leontes, rebuking him gently for disobedience and a choice of bride 'not so rich in worth as beauty', says that if Polixenes were to grant him some precious things he would beg for Perdita. At this Paulina is indignant ('Your eye hath too much youth in't') and she reminds him of his dead Queen's beauty. 'I thought of her,/Even in these looks I made,' he answers. Obviously Leontes has been struck by a striking resemblance between Perdita and Hermione.

There is no lust here,[1] no rivalry with Florizel for his 'precious mistress', but a tribute to her worth and a hint of recognition. Compare the melodramatic episode in *Pandosto* where the King suddenly conceives a passion for his unknown daughter thinking her the mistress of the poor knight Meleagrus (Dorastus) (*infra*, p. 193). Instead of imprisoning Florizel, Leontes takes him to meet his father, prepared to be his advocate if he has not behaved badly. His gentleness here is the first proof that he is a new man. When Paulina reminds him of Mamillius in this scene he says that her continual reproofs 'Will bring me to consider that which may/Unfurnish me of reason' (123).[2] But his interview with Florizel and Perdita has in a sense brought him back to life by making him think of other problems than his own. This is 'Shakespeare's transmutation of Greene's incest-theme. . . . Time past is bridged; a youthful Hermione is ever-present to Leontes' mind.'[3] By his delight in Perdita and his helpful attitude he has proved himself worthy of the revelations to come.

After this it is certainly surprising that the 'recognition' of Perdita (the climax of Greene's romance), and all that has happened to the girl since III. 3 are disclosed in narrative as three court Gentlemen tell Autolycus and each other how the old Shepherd produced his tokens; the mantle and jewels were recognized; Perdita's resemblance to her mother was per-

---

[1] Pafford (*New Arden*, p. lxxiii) sees Leontes as not fully penitent; and 'Worst of all is his desire for Perdita.' Contrast Pyle, *op. cit.*, p. 108.

[2] As Pyle points out (*op. cit.*, p. 105n.), 'This delicate touch . . .[may] derive from the clumsy conclusion of *Pandosto*' where Pandosto, remembering his sins, kills himself.

[3] J. L. Lawlor, '*Pandosto* and the Nature of Dramatic Romance', *PhilQ*, xli, 1962, 96–113.

ceived, so that there was mingled joy and grief in Leontes's cry, 'O thy mother, thy mother!' (1–55); and so on through the whole sequence of revelations until they all went off to see Paulina's statue of Hermione. Shakespeare's reasons for treating matters in this way have often been discussed. Surely not because of their improbability. In *Cymbeline* he had made a masterly long scene out of events almost as improbable. Maybe just because he had recently done this he did not want to do it again. But I suspect that there was another more important dramatic reason. Although the Florizel–Perdita story has been presented with great tenderness and insight into character and situation, it is not so profound or poignant as its parent-story about Leontes and Hermione. By resolving to bring Hermione back to the world the dramatist involved himself in a double dénouement, such as he had handled effectively in *Pericles*, where the 'discovery' of Marina on board Pericles's ship is soon followed by his reunion with Thaisa in the Temple of Diana at Ephesus. This second recognition in *Pericles* occupies only fifty or so lines of V. 3, and the suspense and intensity of the first (V. 1) are so much greater that the Temple scene, despite the divine intervention that brings it about, seems somewhat hastily contrived. Obviously Shakespeare wished in his new play to make the meeting of Leontes and Hermione both ethically and dramatically the climax. So he not only lengthened that incident so as to allow free play to the emotions involved, but also 'played down' the conventional long-lost-child scene in order to make more of the lost wife's 'resurrection'.

Accordingly he has it told by sophisticated courtiers who emphasize that it is suited to ballad-makers, and 'so like an old tale, that the verity of it is in strong suspicion', though it actually happened. They tell it excitedly, fussily, taking a humorous pleasure in the succession of surprising events, which are narrated in a courtly, somewhat precious manner, substituting a Jacobean, more subtle form of euphuism for the obvious antitheses of Greene, yet still with some of his balanced rhetoric, e.g.

But O! the noble combat that 'twixt joy and sorrow was fought in Paulina. She had one eye declined for the loss of her husband, another elevated that the oracle was fulfilled. (V. 2. 75–8)

Even Antigonus is not forgotten in this tying up of loose ends: the Clown has produced 'a handkerchief and rings of his that Paulina knows'.

Only Autolycus has been left out of the general joy, for although he guessed something of the old Shepherd's secret he was not able to inform Florizel on the ship (nor apparently did the old man, but we do not wonder at that in the theatre). So the pleasant rogue is chagrined by the sight of the Clown and his father in their fine clothes, for they are now 'gentlemen born'; and whereas before he terrified them, now they patronize him, but 'gently' as befits their new dignity, and he is glad to ask pardon and become their follower.[1]

Paulina, who seems to be a collector of works of art (V. 3. 9–12), has a statue of Hermione carved by the Italian artist Julio Romano.[2] Like the monuments in Greene, it is in a chapel at her house, 'lonely, apart'. When she takes Perdita and Leontes to see it and to dine with her, there is much talk about the contrast between cold stone and warm life, especially as the onlookers become more and more aware how lifelike the image is, standing in 'her natural posture'. When Leontes notices that Hermione seems older than she was when she died, Paulina attributes this to the sculptor's art. Perdita is with difficulty stopped from kissing the statue's hand, and Leontes and Polixenes are both fascinated by the movement seeming to affect its veins, eyes and breathing, 'as we are mock'd with art' (68). The dramatist uses Paulina's predicament most cunningly to get more suspense—she must not risk a premature disclosure by some movement, or by letting the statue be

---

[1] For C. L. Barber this reflects the social mobility apparent in Jacobean England. He also notes the 'elegant, contrived style' of the courtiers and the 'humanity and naturalness' of the cottagers' 'manners'. '*The Winter's Tale* and Jacobean Society', in *Shakespeare in a Changing World*, ed. A. Kettle, 1964.

[2] No satisfactory reason for Shakespeare's choice of Julio Romano (d. 1546) as the sculptor has been found, for he was essentially a painter, though he sometimes made gesso reliefs. Hermione's statue is in stone, 'a piece many years in doing'. Vasari, *Lives of the Painters*, 1550, gave two epitaphs on Romano's tomb at Mantua, one of which said that Jupiter envied Julio when he 'saw sculptured and painted statues breathe' (*spirare*). Cf. K. Elze, *Essays on Shakespeare*, 1874, pp. 284–9; Martin Pares in *Listener*, 22 Dec. 1966. 'Breathing' is of course important in V. 3. 63–5; 79. Vasari was not translated into English before 1850, but Shakespeare may have found Romano in a book of eulogies. The insistence on the freshness of statue and painting may be a reference to Cure's and Mauncey's recent effigy of the King's mother.

touched. When they will not let her draw the curtain she knows that she must soon come to a climax, and makes use of 'white magic' and music to work the miracle which will wake the stone, like Pygmalion's image: ' 'Tis time; descend; be stone no more; approach' (99); and there is a hint of Alcestis in 'Bequeath to death your numbness, for from him/Dear life redeems you.'

Once the awed Leontes dares to touch his wife there is no need of words from them for a while. But the others are somewhat afraid of witchcraft. 'If she pertain to life let her speak too,' says Camillo, and when her long-lost daughter kneels before her, Hermione at last speaks, requiring explanations which Paulina puts off. She has likened it all to 'an old tale', credible only because it is seen to happen. Now to round off the story, she is given a new husband, Camillo, and Leontes ends the play with happy words, once more asking pardon for his past misdeeds.

Looking back over these details we see at once that *The Winter's Tale* has structurally something in common with those early comedies, *The Comedy of Errors*, *The Taming of the Shrew*, and *A Midsummer Night's Dream*, in which there are two actions, one set within the other as in a frame. In the early comedies the frame-action was minor in extent if not in importance, but it contrasted in tone with the inset-action. Here there is deliberate contrast between the story of Leontes and that of his daughter, but the former is at least as important as the latter. By insisting first on Leontes's sins and then on his repentance, Shakespeare conceals the broken-backed nature of the original tale, and while presenting two different foci of interest brings them together in Act V and merges them in a unity absent from *Pandosto*.

As Professor E. Schanzer has pointed out,[1] *The Winter's Tale*, like *Pericles*, depends greatly on contrasts and parallels between the two major themes of the play. Thus the wintry desolation of Leontes in his rage and despair is contrasted with the imagery of flowery seasons and natural fertility in Act IV. The storm which ends III. 3 is soon followed by the gaiety of shearing-time (IV. 2-3). Polixenes in the latter half of the piece displays a tyranny almost as threatening as Leontes's

---

[1] E. Schanzer, 'The Structural Pattern of The Winter's Tale', *Review of English Literature*, April 1964; and *WT Casebook*, ed. K. Muir, 1968, pp. 87-97.

in the first half. Camillo links both parts together as good counsellor both to Leontes and Polixenes, and to Polixenes and Florizel: and there is irony in that, having saved Polixenes from his friend's fury, he later saves Florizel from Polixenes's anger. His functions towards them are parallel to Paulina's towards Leontes. He sends Florizel and Perdita to Sicily and guides Polixenes there too; she controls the life of Leontes and brings him to her chapel where she effects the miracle of reunion. The 'death' of Hermione in III. 2 is contrasted with her re-creation in V. 3. The real supernatural of Apollo's Oracle and the awesome account of the temple (III. 1. 2ff.) are paralleled by the religious atmosphere of Paulina's chapel and the pretended miracle which has all the effect of a real one.

There are other parallels: in the short prose scenes at the beginning of each half of the play (I. 1; IV. 2), when the conversation turns 'upon a happy and harmonious relationship, which is soon to be violently disrupted' (Schanzer); in the two climaxes—the trial scene and the statue scene, with Hermione at the centre of each. These are not just for mechanical symmetry. They help to give the action an aesthetic neatness and circularity which avoid the straggling effect of Greene's romance and make *The Winter's Tale*, despite the lapse of years, a more closely knit piece than *Cymbeline*. Moreover, Schanzer writes, 'the principal effect of the pattern of repetition . . . is to increase our sense of the fragility, the precariousness, of human happiness'. But the total effect is not of a circle but of a spiral, since the statue scene leaves us in a very different mood from the trial scene. Thanks to Paulina, Leontes's repentance, and the natural goodness of the young people, we have broken out of the dismal round which seemed about to be repeated.

Some recent critics have abstracted specific ethical or religious themes from the story and asserted that Shakespeare's purpose was mainly to embody or discuss them. I see the ethical discussion rather as a product of the story, emerging from time to time in the act of composition, and making part of a totality in which story and character, the poetic ideas and feelings evoked by these, produce ethical considerations which are no more important to the dramatist than the rest.[1]

[1] Cf. N. Frye, 'The Argument of Comedy', *Eng. Inst. Essays, 1948*, New York, 1949.

So the contrast between Leontes's suspicion and jealousy and Hermione's love and fidelity helps to make credible the plot and also to bridge the gap of years, since, unlike Pandosto, Leontes learns through penitence and the perpetual reminders of Paulina, how to endure suffering, how to be patient. *Pericles* was bound together mainly by the anguish of Pericles himself, but he sank into *accidie* until saved by his daughter. Here Leontes's penitence has not ruined him as a King (V. 1), and the patience he has learned makes the long-delayed dénouement credible, as in 'an old tale' at least.

The repentance does not make the play into an allegory, however; its spiritual implications help to bolster the story by giving the mind something more to feed on than a tissue of romantic improbabilities. Similarly the reappearance of Hermione disguised as a statue, with all its associations of Pygmalion's image and Alcestis's return from the dead, does not turn the play into an allegory of resurrection. But it is an illustration of the power of love and patience, and, though Hermione is at the centre, the ethical emphasis is on Leontes, not on her, for we are fortunately not called on to explore her experiences during sixteen years' seclusion. She exists now chiefly as a reward for Leontes's repentance and Perdita's goodness. So she says nothing when 'awakened' except to forestall their questions by asking her own, and the play ends quickly in the first joyous flush of reunion.

Similarly, in organizing his plot and characters Shakespeare developed contrasts which he found in Greene about the differences between court and country, birth and breeding, youth and age, nature and art. These themes entered into his dialogue, and undoubtedly affected his portrayal of characters, but without turning the latter into personifications of abstract qualities or making their symbolic value more important than their human fullness. The question of true nobility which had appeared in *Cymbeline* comes up once more. In the first three acts we see royalty behaving in despicable fashion (Leontes) and with proper dignity (Hermione, Polixenes). In Act IV differences in rank and birth trouble Perdita, but not Florizel, who (like the King in *All's Well*) knows what true nobility is and sees it in the queenly qualities of his mistress, who after their marriage will indeed be 'the daughter of a king' (V. 1.

207–9). And there are several references to her behaviour as being at odds with her apparent station in society. Shakespeare in fact has it both ways. True worth is independent of rank; yet there is a homely virtue (shown by the Shepherd in III. 3) and a courtly virtue. High birth and upbringing are good things, and when Polixenes says:

> Nothing she does or seems
> But smacks of something greater than her self:
> Too noble for this place . . . (IV. 3. 157–9)

he is pointing to real differences in manners which few before our present century would have scorned. Perdita, however, is already 'the daughter of a king' and her behaviour is a triumph of nature over nurture.

Out of this concern with effects of birth sprang the charming discussion about flowers which contains a piquant irony, in that the 'bastard' shepherdess is against all 'bastard' mixtures, even in horticulture, while the King who favours making 'Conceive a bark of baser kind/By bud of nobler race' will oppose his son's marriage to her.

Other aspects of art and nature, arising from Shakespeare's decision to have the statue scene, are mentioned in the play. Art in general, any human skill applied to constructive ends, is justified by Polixenes's assertion that 'over that art/Which you say adds to nature, is an art/That nature makes.' 'The art itself is nature', since 'great creating nature' works through our human powers as well as through subhuman forces (IV. 3. 86–97).

The alleged statue of Hermione by Julio Romano is an instance of human skill seeking to copy nature, not to 'mend it'. The artist is nature's ape, praised (like Apelles in Lyly's *Campaspe*) for his verisimilitude. Here Shakespeare's idea of art is not so lofty as that of Sidney, who, if he called it a 'second nature', stressed its idealizing power as superior to nature, since 'her world is brasen; the Poets only deliver a golden' (*Apology for Poetry*). But only verisimilitude is in question here since the statue turns out to be its own 'living image'.

Still other facets of art are alluded to in the conduct of Autolycus—who may indeed have been invented with this in mind—for he lives by art misdirected—the gentle art of Conny-catching, which he demonstrates in divers skilful ways; and not .the least of his professional skills is his art of singing attractive songs and ballads, 'pitiful and true'. 'Why should I carry lies abroad?' he asks, yet he does so. This is a homely art compared with Romano's, but pleasant enough.

And there is the art by which Paulina has preserved Hermione over the years, and at last, with pretence of magic art and 'lawful spell', brings the image to breathe and live, so that Leontes cries out:

> O! she's warm.
> If this be magic, let it be an art
> Lawful as eating. (V. 3. 109–11)

Lastly, above and circumscribing it all is the art of the dramatist, conscious as never before of the improbabilities inherent in his sources and trying to make them plausible by switching our attention to the variety of human nature with its jealousy and vengefulness and remorse, its idyllic love and adventure, its capacity for penitence, forgiveness and gracious healing. Yet in its unlikely twists and turns, its miraculous wish-fulfilment, it remains like 'an old tale'. Hence much of the dramatist's craftsmanship is devoted to invoking the audience's co-operation in 'a willing suspension of disbelief', by means of an apparent artlessness that conceals great art. And the whole world of action is suspended in a benevolent universe in which the gods smile on the good, and the Christian ethic of chastity, fidelity, courage, repentance, and reconciliation suffuses the romance with religious overtones which never become the hard rigidity of allegory; for the people are real persons though moving through a fairy-tale, and the poetry or prose that they speak issues naturally from their personalities in the circumstances in which they are placed.

I. Source

PANDOSTO. THE TRIUMPH OF TIME
by Robert Greene (1588)[1]

Pandosto. The Triumph of Time. Wherein is discovered
by a pleasant Historie, that although by the meanes of
sinister fortune, Truth may be concealed yet by Time in
spight of fortune it is most manifestly revealed. Pleasant
for age to avoyde drowsie thoughtes, profitable for youth
to eschue other wanton pastimes, and bringing to both
a desired content. *Temporis filia veritas.* By Robert Greene,
Maister of Artes in Cambridge. *Omne tulit punctum qui
miscuit utile dulci.* Imprinted at London by Thomas
Orwin for Thomas Cadman, dwelling at the Signe of the
Bible, neere unto the North doore of Paules, 1588.

The Historie of Dorastus and Fawnia.

Among al the passions wherewith humane mindes are perplexed,
there is none that so galleth with restlesse despight, as the infectious
soare of Jealousie: for all other griefes are eyther to bee appeased
with sensible perswasions, to be cured with wholesome counsel, to be
relieved in want, or by tract of time to be worne out, (Jealousie only
excepted) which is so sawsed with suspitious doubtes, and pinching
mistrust, that whoso seekes by friendly counsaile to rase out this
hellish passion, it foorthwith suspecteth that he geveth this advise
to cover his owne guiltinesse. Yea, who so is payned with this restlesse torment doubteth all, dystrusteth him-selfe, is alwayes frosen
with feare, and fired with suspition, having that wherein consisteth
all his joy to be the breeder of his miserie. Yea, it is such a heavy
enemy to that holy estate of matrimony, sowing betweene the married
couples such deadly seeds of secret hatred, as Love being once rased
out by spightful distrust, there oft ensueth bloudy revenge, as this
ensuing Hystorie manifestly prooveth: wherein Pandosto (furiously

[1] Since the unique B. M. copy of this edition lacks Signature B, the text of those
pages is given (160–7) from the copy of the 1592 edition in the Folger Library, by
kind permission.

incensed by causelesse Jealousie) procured the death of his most loving and loyall wife, and his owne endlesse sorrow and misery.

In the Countrey of Bohemia there raygned a King called Pandosto, whose fortunate successe in warres against his foes, and bountifull curtesie towardes his friendes in peace, made him to be greatly feared and loved of all men. This Pandosto had to Wife a Ladie called Bellaria, by birth royall, learned by education, faire by nature, by vertues famous, so that it was hard to judge whether her beautie, fortune, or vertue, wanne the greatest commendations. These two lincked together in perfect love, led their lives with such fortunate content, that their Subjects greatly rejoyced to see their quiet disposition. They had not beene married long, but Fortune (willing to increase their happines) lent them a sonne, so adorned with the gifts of nature, as the perfection of the Childe greatly augmented the love of the parentes, and the joys of their commons;[1] in so much that the Bohemians, to shewe their inward joyes by outwarde actions, made Bone-fires[2] and triumphs throughout all the Kingdome, appointing Justes and Turneyes for the honour of their young Prince: whether resorted not onely his Nobles, but also divers Kings and Princes which were his neighbours, willing to shewe their friendship they ought to Pandosto, and to win fame and glory by their prowesse and valour. Pandosto, whose minde was fraught with princely liberality, entertayned the Kings, Princes, and noble men with such submisse curtesie and magnifical bounty, that they all sawe how willing he was to gratifie their good wils, making a generall feast for his Subjects, which continued by the space of twentie dayes; all which time the Justes and Turneys were kept to the great content both of the Lordes and Ladies there present. This solemne tryumph being once ended, the assembly, taking their leave of Pandosto and Bellaria: the young sonne (who was called Garinter)[3] was nursed up in the house to the great joy and content of the parents.

Fortune envious of such happy successe, willing to shewe some signe of her inconstancie, turned her wheele, and darkned their bright sunne of prosperitie, with the mistie cloudes of mishap and misery. For it so happened that Egistus King of Sycilia, who in his youth had bene brought up with Pandosto,[4] desirous to shewe that neither tracte of time, nor distance of place could diminish their former friendship,[5] provided a navie of ships, and sayled into Bohemia to visite his old friend and companion, who hearing of his arrivall, went himselfe in person, and his wife Bellaria, accompanied

---

[1] I. 1. 34–7.
[2] V. 2. 24.
[3] The name of Florisel's cousin in *Amadis de Grecia.*
[4] I. 1. 21–4.
[5] I. 1. 24–31.

with a great traine of Lords and Ladies, to meet Egistus: and espying him, alighted from his horse, embraced him very lovingly, protesting that nothing in the world could have happened more acceptable to him then his comming, wishing his wife to welcome his olde friend and acquaintance: who (to shewe how she liked him whom her husband loved) intertayned him with such familiar curtesie, as Egistus perceived himselfe to bee verie well welcome.[1] After they had thus saluted and embraced eche other, they mounted againe on horsbacke and rode toward the Citie, devising and recounting, howe being children they had passed their youth in friendely pastimes: where, by the meanes of the Citizens, Egistus was receyved with triumphs and showes in such sort, that he marvelled how on so small a warning they coulde make such preparation.

Passing the streetes thus with such rare sightes, they rode on to the Pallace, where Pandosto entertained Egistus and his Sycilians with such banqueting and sumptuous cheare, so royally, as they all had cause to commend his princely liberality; yea, the verie basest slave that was knowne to come from Sycilia was used with such curtesie, that Egistus might easily perceive how both hee and his were honored for his friendes sake.[2] Bellaria (who in her time was the flower of curtesie), willing to show how unfaynedly shee looved her husband by his friends intertainement, used him likewise so familiarly, that her countenance bewraied how her minde was affected towardes him: oftentimes comming her selfe into his bed chamber, to see that nothing should be amis to mislike him. This honest familiarity increased dayly more and more betwixt them; for Bellaria, noting in Egistus a princely and bountifull minde, adorned with sundrie and excellent qualities, and Egistus, finding in her a vertuous and curteous disposition, there grew such a secret uniting of their affections, that the one could not well be without the company of the other: in so much that when Pandosto was busied with such urgent affaires, that hee could not bee present with his friend Egistus, Bellaria would walke with him into the Garden,[3] where they two in privat and pleasant devises would passe away the time to both their contents. This custome still continuing betwixt them, a certaine melancholy passion entring the minde of Pandosto, drave him into sundry and doubtfull thoughts.[4] First, he called to minde the beauty of his wife Bellaria, the comelines and braverie of his friend Egistus, thinking that Love was above all Lawes, and therefore to be staied with no Law: that it was hard to put fire and flaxe together without

[1] Cf. III. 2. 62–5.
[2] The play begins nine months after this arrival (in Sicily, not Bohemia).
[3] I. 2. 177–8.
[4] Speeded up in I. 2. 109ff.

burning; that their open pleasures might breede his secrete dis-
pleasures. He considered with himselfe that Egistus was a man, and
must needes love: that his wife was a woman, and therefore subject
unto love, and that where fancy forced, friendship was of no force.

These and such like doubtfull thoughtes a long time smoothering
in his stomacke, beganne at last to kindle in his minde a secret mistrust, which increased by suspition, grewe at last to be a flaming
Jealousie, that so tormented him as he could take no rest.[1] He then
began to measure all their actions, and to misconstrue of their too
private familiaritie, judging that it was not for honest affection, but
for disordinate fancy, so that hee began to watch them more narrowely, to see if hee coulde gette any true or certaine proofe to confirme
his doubtfull suspition.[2] While thus he noted their lookes and gestures,
and suspected their thoughtes and meaninges, they two seely soules
who doubted nothing of this his treacherous intent, frequented daily
eache others companie, which drave him into such a franticke passion, that he beganne to beare a secret hate to Egistus, and a lowring
countenance to Bellaria, who marveiling at such unaccustomed
frowns,[3] began to cast beeyond the Moone, and to enter into a
thousand sundrie thoughtes, which way she should offend her husband: but finding in her selfe a cleare conscience, ceassed to muse,
until such time as she might find fit opportunitie to demaund the
cause of his dumps. In the meane time Pandostoes minde was so farre
charged with Jealousy, that he did no longer doubt, but was assured
(as he thought) that his Friend Egistus had entered a wrong pointe
in his tables, and so had played him false play:[4] whereupon desirous
to revenge so great an injury, he thought best to dissemble the grudge
with a faire and friendly countenance:[5] and so under the shape of a
friend, to shew him the tricke of a foe.[6] Devising with himself a long
time how he might best put away Egistus without suspition of
treacherous murder, hee concluded at last to poyson him: which
opinion pleasing his humour, he became resolute in his determination, and the better to bring the matter to passe he called unto him
his cupbearer, with whom in secret he brake the matter: promising
to him for the performance thereof to geve him a thousande crownes
of yearely revenues; his cupbearer,[7] eyther being of a good conscience,
or willing for fashion sake, to deny such a bloudy request, began with
great reasons to perswade Pandosto from his determinate mischief:

[1] II. 3. 1.
[2] In I. 2. Leontes has reached this state.
[3] I. 2. 148–51; 365–76.
[4] The 'play' image is altered in I. 2. 187–9.
[5] I. 2. 172ff.
[6] I. 2. 350.
[7] I. 2. 345.

shewing him what an offence murther was to the gods: how such unnaturall actions did more displease the heavens than men,[1] and that causeles crueltie did seldome or never escape without revenge: he layd before his face, that Egistus was his friend, a king, and one that was come into his kingdome to confirme a league of perpetuall amitie betwixt them, that he had and did shew him a most friendly countenaunce: how Egistus was not onely honoured of his owne people by obedience, but also loved of the Bohemians for his curtesie. And that if he now should, without any just or manifest cause, poyson him, it would not only be a great dishonor to his Majesty, and a meanes to sow perpetuall enmitie betweene the Sycilians and the Bohemians, but also his owne subjectes would repine at such trecherous crueltie. These and such like perswasions of Franion (for so was his cup-bearer called) could no whit prevaile to disswade him from his devilish enterprise:[2] but remaining resolute in his determination, his fury so fiered with rage, as it could not be appeased with reason, he began with bitter taunts to take up his man, and to lay before him two baytes; preferment, and death: saying that if he would poyson Egistus, he should advaunce him to high dignities: if he refused to do it of an obstinate minde, no torture should be too great to requite his disobedience.[3] Franion, seeing that to perswade Pandosto any more, was but to strive against the streame, consented, as soone as oportunity would give him leave, to dispatch Egistus,[4] wherewith Pandosto remained somewhat satisfied, hoping now he should be fully revenged of such mistrusted injuries, intending also assoon as Egistus was dead, to give his wife a sop of the same sawce, and so be rid of those which were the cause of his restles sorrow. While thus he lived in this hope, Franion being secret in his chamber, began to meditate with himselfe in these termes.

Ah Franion, treason is loved of many, but the traitor hated of all: unjust offences may for a time escape without danger, but never without revenge. Thou art servant to a king, and must obey at commaund: yet Franion, against law and conscience, it is not good to resist a tyrant with armes, nor to please an unjust king with obedience. What shalt thou do? Folly refuseth gold, and frensie preferment: wisedome seeketh after dignitie, and counsel looketh for gaine. Egistus is a stranger to thee, and Pandosto thy soveraigne: thou hast little cause to respect the one, and oughtest to have great care to obey the other. Thinke this Franion, that a pound of gold is worth a

---

[1] From here to p. 167 line 16 follows the 1592 edn (Folger Library copy) since *1588* lacks Signature B.
[2] Cf. I. 2. 279–333.
[3] I. 2. 348–9.
    I. 2. 333–49.

tunne of Lead, great gifts are little Gods, and preferment to a meane
man is a whetstone to courage: there is nothing sweeter than promo-
tion, nor lighter than report: care not then though most count thee
a traytor, so all call thee rich. Dignitie (Franion) advaunceth thy
posteritie, and evill report can hurt but thyselfe. Know this, where
Eagles builde, Faulcons may prey: where Lyons haunt, Foxes may
steale. Kings are knowen to commaunde, servaunts are blamelesse
to consent: feare not thou then to lift at Egistus, Pandosto shall beare
the burthen. Yea, but Franion, conscience is a worme that ever
biteth, but never ceaseth: that which is rubbed with the stone
Galactites will never be hot. Flesh dipped in the Sea Ægeum will
never bee sweete: the hearbe Tragion, being once bit with an Aspis,
never groweth, and conscience once stayned with innocent bloud, is
alwayes tyed to a guiltie remorse. Preferre thy content before riches,
and a cleare minde before dignitie; so beeing poore, thou shalt have
rich peace, or else rich, thou shalt enjoy disquiet.

Franion having muttered out these or such like words, seeing
either he must die with a cleare minde, or live with a spotted conscience, he was so combred with divers cogitations that hee could
take no rest:[1] untill at last he determined to breake the matter to
Egistus; but fearing that the king should either suspect or heare of
such matters, he concealed the devise till oportunitie would permit
him to reveale it. Lingring thus in doubtfull feare, in an evening he
went to Egistus lodging, and desirous to breake with him of certaine
affaires that touched the king, after all were commaunded out of the
chamber, Franion made manifest the whole conspiracie which
Pandosto had devised against him, desiring Egistus not to accompt
him a traytor for bewraying his maisters counsell, but to thinke that
he did it for conscience, hoping that although his maister inflamed
with rage, or incensed by some sinister reportes, or slaunderous
speeches, had imagined such causelesse mischief: yet when time
should pacifie his anger, and try those talebearers but flattering
Parasites, then he would count him as a faithfull servaunt, that with
such care had kept his maisters credit. Egistus had not fully heard
Franion tell forth his tale, but a quaking feare possessed all his
limmes,[2] thinking that there was some treason wrought, and that
Franion did but shaddow his craft with these false colours: wherefore
he began to waxe in choller, and sayd that he doubted not Pandosto,
sith he was his friend, and there had never as yet bene any breach of
amitie:[3] he had not sought to invade his lands, to conspire with his
enemies, to disswade his subjectes from their allegiance; but in word

---

[1] Contrast Camillo's dignity and brevity, I. 2. 351–63.
[2] I. 2. 457.
[3] Polixenes is prepared for the disclosure by I. 2. 365–76. Cf. I. 2. 446–7.

and thought he rested his at all times: he knew not therefore any cause that should moove Pandosto to seeke his death, but suspected it to be a compacted knavery of the Bohemians to bring the King and him at oddes.

Franion staying him in the midst of his talke, told him that to dally with Princes was with the swannes to sing agaynst their death, and that if the Bohemians had intended any such secret mischief, it might have bene better brought to passe then by revealing the conspiracie: therefore his Majestie did ill to misconstrue of his good meaning, sith his intent was to hinder treason, not to become a traytor; and to confirme his premises, if it please his Majestie to fly into Sycilia for the safegard of his life, he would goe with him: and if then he found not such a practise to be pretended, let his imagined trecherie be repayed with most monstrous torments.

Egistus hearing the solemne protestation of Franion, began to consider, that in love and kingdomes, neither faith, nor lawe is to bee respected: doubting that Pandosto thought by his death to destroy his men, and with speedy warre to invade Sycilia.[1] These and such doubts throughly weighed, he gave great thankes to Franion, promising if hee might with life returne to Syracusa, that hee would create him a Duke in Sycilia;[2] craving his counsell how he might escape out of the countrey. Franion, who having some small skill in Navigation, was well acquainted with the Ports and Havens, and knew every daunger in the Sea, joyning in counsell with the Maister of Egistus Navie, rigged all their ships,[3] and setting them afloate, let them lye at anker, to be in the more readinesse when time and winde should serve.

Fortune although blind, yet by chaunce favoring this just cause, sent them within six dayes a good gale of wind;[4] which Franion seeing fit for their purpose, to put Pandosto out of suspition, the night before they should sayle, he went to him and promised, that the next day he would put the device in practise, for he had got such a forcible poyson, as the very smell thereof should procure sodaine death. Pandosto was joyfull to heare this good newes, and thought every houre a day till he might be glutted with bloudy revenge, but his suit had but ill successe: for Egistus fearing that delay might breede daunger, and willing that the grasse should not be cut from under his feete, taking bagge and baggage,[5] with the helpe of Franion, conveyed himself and his men out of a posterne gate of the Citie[6] so

---

[1] No political motive appears in *WT*.
[2] Cf. I. 2. 439-41; 461-2.   [3] Cf. I. 2. 449.
[4] No such delay in *WT*.
[5] Camillo has a trunk ready! I. 2. 435-6.
[6] I. 2. 437-9.

secretly and speedely that without any suspition they got to the sea shoare, where, with many a bitter curse taking their leave of Bohemia, they went aboord. Weighing their Ancres and hoysting sayle, they passed as fast as winde and sea would permit towardes Sycilia; Egistus being a joyfull man that he had safely past such trecherous perils.

But as they were quietly floating on the sea, so Pandosto and his Citizens were in an uprore: for seeing that the Sycilians without taking their leave were fled away by night, the Bohemians feared some treason, and the King thought that without question his suspition was true, seeing his Cup-bearer had bewrayed the summe of his secret pretence:[1] whereupon be began to imagine, that Franion and his wife Bellaria had conspired with Egistus, and that the fervent affection she bare him, was the onely meanes of his secret departure,[2] in so much that, incensed with rage, he commaunded that his wife should be carried to straight prison, untill they heard further of his pleasure.[3]

The guarde unwilling to lay their hands on such a vertuous Princesse, and yet fearing the kings furie, went very sorrowfully to fulfill their charge. Comming to the Queenes lodging, they found her playing with her young sonne Garinter,[4] unto whom with teares doing the message, Bellaria astonished at such a hard censure, and finding her cleare conscience a sure advocate to pleade in her case, went to the prison most willingly: where with sighs and teares[5] she past away the time till she might come to her triall.

But Pandosto, whose reason was suppressed with rage, and whose unbridled folly was incensed with furie: seeing Franion had bewrayed his secrets, and that Egistus might wel be rayled on, but not revenged, determined to wreake all his wrath on poore Bellaria.[6] He therefore caused a generall Proclamation to be made through all his Realme, that the Queene and Egistus had by the helpe of Franion, not onely committed most incestuous adulterie, but also had conspired the Kings death: wherupon the traitor Franion was fled away with Egistus, and Bellaria was most justly imprisoned.[7] This proclamation being once blazed through the countrey,[8] although the vertuous disposition of the Queene did halfe discredit the contents, yet the sodaine and speedie passage of Egistus, and the secret depar-

[1] II. 1. 32–6.
[2] II. 1. 45–51.
[3] Contrast Shakespeare's fine scene of confrontation, II. 1. 55–124.
[4] Hence II. 1. 1–31, etc.
[5] Contrast Hermione, II. 1. 107–8.
[6] II. 3. 2–9.
[7] Cf. II. 1. 46 and the indictment, III. 2. 11–20.
[8] III. 1. 15–17; III. 2. 100–1.

16464

The Winter's Tale

ture of Franion, induced them (the circumstances throughly considered) to thinke that both the Proclamation was true, and the King greatly injured: yet they pitied her case,[1] as sorowful that so good a Ladie should be crossed with such adverse Fortune.

But the King, whose restlesse rage would admit no pity, thought that although he might sufficiently requite his wifes falshood with the bitter plague of pinching[2] penurie, yet his minde should never be glutted with revenge, till he might have fit time and oportunitie to repay the treacherie [of][3] Egistus with a fatall injurie. But a curst Cow hath oft times short hornes, and a willing mind but a weake arm: for Pandosto although he felt that revenge was a spurre to warre, and that envie alwayes proffereth steele, yet he saw, that Egistus was not onely of great puissance and prowesse to withstand him, but also had many Kings of his alliance to ayde him, if neede should serve: for he married to the Emperours daughter of Russia.[4] These and the like considerations something daunted Pandosto his courage, so that he was content rather to put up a manifest injurie with peace, than hunt after revenge with dishonor and losse; determining since Egistus had escaped scot-free, that Bellaria should pay for all at an unreasonable price.

Remayning thus resolute in his determination, Bellaria continuing still in prison, and hearing the contents of the Proclamation, knowing that her mind was never touched with such affection, nor that Egistus had ever offered her such discurtesie, would gladly have come to her answer, that both she might have knowne her unjust accusers, and cleared her selfe of that guiltlesse crime.

But Pandosto was so enflamed with rage, and infected with Jealousie, as he would not vouchsafe to heare her nor admit any just excuse;[5] so that she was faine to make a vertue of her neede, and with patience to beare these heavie injuries. As thus she lay crossed with calamities (a great cause to increase her griefe) she found her selfe quicke with childe: which assoone as she felt stir in her bodie, she burst foorth into bitter teares, exclaiming against fortune in these tearmes.

Alas, Bellaria, how infortunate art thou, because fortunat! better hadst thou bene borne a begger than a Prince: so shouldest thou have bridled Fortune with want, where now shee sporteth her selfe with thy plentie. Ah happy life where poore thoughts, and meane desires live in secure content, not fearing Fortune because too low for

[1] II. 1. 64–7; 125–56.
[2] Leontes is 'pinch'd' at II. 1. 50.
[3] Not in *1592*.
[4] Cf. Hermione, 'The Emperor of Russia was my father', III. 2. 118.
[5] Leontes forbids Paulina to go to her, II. 3. 42–6.

Fortune! Thou seest now Bellaria, that care is a companion to honor, not to povertie, that high cædars are frushed[1] with tempests, when low shrubs are not toucht with the wind: pretious Diamonds are cut with the file, when despised peables lie safe in the sand: Delphos is sought to by Princes, not beggers: and Fortunes altars smoke with Kings presents, not with poore mens gifts. Happy are such, Bellaria, that curse Fortune for contempt, not fear, and may wish they were, not sorrow they have bene. Thou art a Princesse, Bellaria, and yet a prisoner, borne to the one by discent, assigned to the other by despite; accused without cause, and therefore oughtest to die without care: for patience is a shield against Fortune, and a guiltlesse minde yeeldeth not to sorow. Ah, but Infamie galleth unto death, and liveth after death: Report is plumed with Times feathers, and Envie oftentimes soundeth Fames trumpet: thy suspected adulterie shall fly in the ayre, and thy knowne vertues shall ly hid in the Earth; one Moale stayneth a whole face, and what is once spotted with Infamy can hardly be worne out with time. Die then Bellaria, Bellaria die! for if the Gods should say thou art guiltlesse, yet envie would heare the Gods, but never beleeve the Gods. Ah haplesse wretch, cease these tearmes: desperat thoughts are fit for them that feare shame, not for such as hope for credite. Pandosto hath darkned thy fame, but shal never discredite thy vertues. Suspition may enter a false action, but proofe shall never put in his plea: care not then for envie, sith report hath a blister on her tongue: and let sorrow baite them which offend, not touch thee that art faultlesse. But alas, poore soule, howe canst thou but sorrow? Thou art with child, and by him that in steed of kind pitie, pincheth thee in cold prison.

And with that, such gasping sighes so stopping her breath, that she could not utter mo words, but wringing her hands, and gushing foorth streames of teares, shee passed away the time with bitter complaints. The Jaylor pitying these her heavie passions, thinking that if the king knew she were with child, he would somwhat appease his furie, and release her from prison,[2] went in all hast, and certified Pandosto what the effect of Bellarias complaint was: who no sooner heard the Jaylour say she was with child, but as one possessed with a phrenzie, he rose up in a rage, swearing that she and the basterd brat she was withall should dye, if the Gods themselves said no; thinking assuredly by computation of time, that Egistus, and not he, was father to the child.

This suspitious thought galled afresh this halfe healed sore, in so much as he could take no rest, until he might mitigate his choler with a just revenge, which happened presently after. For Bellaria was

---

[1] smashed, struck down.

[2] So Paulina, II. 2. 39–42.

brought to bed of a faire and beautifull daughter, which no sooner
Pandosto heard, but he determined that both Bellaria and the yong
infant should be burnt with fire.[1]

His Nobles, hearing of the Kings cruell sentence, sought by perswasions to divert him from this bloody determination:[2] laying before his face the innocencie of the child, and vertuous disposition of
his wife, how she had continually loved and honored him so tenderly,
that without due proof he could not, nor ought not to appeach her
of that crime. And if she had faulted, yet it were more honorable to
pardon with mercy, then to punish with extremity, and more Kingly,
to be commended of pity, than accused of rigor. And as for the child,
if he should punish it for the mothers offence, it were to strive against
nature and justice: and that unnaturall actions do more offend the
Gods then men: how causelesse crueltie, nor innocent bloud never
scapes without revenge.

These and such like reasons could not appease his rage, but he
rested resolute in this, that Bellaria beeing an adulteresse, the child
was a bastard, and he would not suffer that such an infamous brat
should call him father. Yet at last (seeing his noble men were im-
portunate upon him) he was content to spare the childs life, and yet
to put it to a worser death.[3] For he found out this devise, that seeing
(as he thought) it came by Fortune, so he would commit it to the
charge of Fortune, and therefore he caused a little cock-boate to be
provided, wherein he meant to put the babe, and then send it to the
mercie of the seas, and the destinies.

From this his Peeres in no wise could perswade him, but that he
sent presently two of his Gard to fetch the child, who being come to
the prison, and with weeping teares recounting their maisters
message: Bellaria no sooner heard the rigorous resolution of her
mercilesse husband, but she fell downe in a swound, so that all
thought she had bin dead,[4] yet at last being come to her selfe, she
cried and scriched out in this wise.

Alas, sweete infortunate babe, scarse borne before envied by
fortune: would the day of thy birth had bin the tearme of thy life!
then shouldest thou have made an end to care and prevented thy
fathers rigor. Thy faults cannot yet deserve such hatefull revenge,
thy dayes are too short for so sharpe a doome, but thy untimely death
must pay thy mothers debtes, and her guiltlesse crime must be thy
gastly curse. And shalt thou, sweete babe be committed to fortune,
when thou art already spighted by Fortune? Shall the seas be thy

[1] II. 3. 94–5.
[2] II. 3. 146–52.
[3] II. 3. 153–82. The method of exposure is different in *WT*.
[4] Cf. her 'death' in the play, III. 2.

harbour, and the hard boate thy cradle? Shall thy tender Mouth, in steede of sweete kisses, be nipped with bitter stormes? Shalt thou have the whistling windes for thy Lullabie, and the salt sea fome in steede of sweet milke?[1] Alas, what destinies would assigne such hard hap? What father would be so cruell? Or what Gods will not revenge such rigor? Let me kisse thy lips (sweet Infant) and wet thy tender cheekes with my teares, and put this chaine about thy litle necke, that if fortune save thee, it may helpe to succour thee. Thus, since thou must goe to surge in the gastfull seas, with a sorrowfull kisse I bid thee farewell, and I pray the Gods thou mayst fare well.

Such, and so great was her griefe, that her vital spirits being suppressed with sorrow, she fell downe in a traunce, having her sences so sotted with care, that after she was revived, yet shee lost her memorie, and lay for a great time without moving, as one in a traunce. The gard left her in this perplexitie, and carried the child to the King, who quite[2] devoide of pity commanded that without delay it should bee put in the boat, having neither saile nor rudder to guid it, and so to bee carried into the midst of the sea, and there left to the wind and wave as the destinies please to appoint.[3] The very shipmen, seeing the sweete countenance of the yong babe, began to accuse the King of rigor, and to pity the childs hard fortune: but feare constrayned them to that which their nature did abhorre: so that they placed it in one of the ends of the boat, and with a few green bows made a homely cabben to shrowd it as they could from wind and weather: having thus trimmed the boat they tied it to a ship, and so haled it into the mayne Sea, and then cut in sunder the coarde, which they had no sooner done, but there arose a mighty tempest, which tossed the little Boate so vehemently in the waves, that the shipmen thought it coulde not long continue without sincking, yea the storme grewe so great, that with much labour and perill they got to the shoare.

But leaving the Childe to her fortunes. Againe to Pandosto, who not yet glutted with sufficient revenge, devised which way he should best increase his Wives calamitie. But first assembling his Nobles and Counsellors, hee called her for the more reproch into open Court, where it was objected against her, that she had committed adulterie with Egistus, and conspired with Franion to poyson Pandosto her husband, but their pretence being partly spyed, shee counselled them to flie away by night for their better safety. Bellaria, who standing like a prisoner at the Barre, feeling in her selfe a cleare Conscience to withstand her false accusers: seeing that no lesse then

[1] III. 2. 97–100; III. 3. 53–5.
[2] The 1588 text is resumed here.
[3] II. 3. 182, 'Where chance may nurse or end it.'

death could pacifie her husbands wrath, waxed bolde, and desired that she might have Lawe and Justice, for mercy shee neyther craved nor hoped for; and that those perjured wretches, which had falsely accused her to the King, might be brought before her face, to give in evidence.

But Pandosto, whose rage and Jealousie was such, no reason, nor equitie could appease: tolde her, that for her accusers they were of such credite, as their wordes were sufficient witnesse, and that the sodaine and secret flight of Egistus and Franion confirmed that which they had confessed: and as for her, it was her parte to deny such a monstrous crime, and to be impudent in forswearing the fact, since shee had past all shame in committing the fault:[1] but her stale countenance should stand for no coyne, for as the Bastard which she bare was served, so she should with some cruell death be requited. Bellaria no whit dismayed with this rough reply, tolde her Husband Pandosto, that he spake upon choller, and not conscience: for her vertuous life had beene ever such, as no spot of suspition could ever staine.[2] And if she had borne a friendly countenaunce to Egistus, it was in respect he was his friende, and not for any lusting affection: therefore if she were condemned without any further proofe, it was rigour, and not Law.[3]

The noble men which sate in judgment, said that Bellaria spake reason, and intreated the king that the accusers might be openly examined, and sworne, and if then the evidence were such, as the Jury might finde her guilty (for seeing she was a Prince she ought to be tryed by her peeres), then let her have such punishment as the extremitie of the Law will assigne to such malefactors. The king presently made answere, that in this case he might, and would, dispence with the Law, and that the Jury being once panneld, they should take his word for sufficient evidence, otherwise he would make the proudest of them repent it. The noble men seeing the king in choler were all whist, but Bellaria, whose life then hung in the ballaunce, fearing more perpetuall infamie then momentarie death,[4] tolde the king, if his furie might stand for a Law, that it were vaine to have the Jury yeeld their verdit; and therefore she fell downe upon her knees, and desired the king that for the love he bare to his young sonne Garinter, whome she brought into the world, that hee would graunt her a request,[5] which was this, that it would please his majestie to send sixe of his noble men whome he best trusted, to the

[1] III. 2. 53–6.
[2] III. 2. 32–4.
[3] III. 2. 107–13.
[4] III. 2. 108–10.
[5] Leontes's emissaries are already back from Delphi, II. 3. 192–200.

Isle of Delphos, there to enquire of the Oracle of Apollo, whether she had committed adultery with Egistus, or conspired to poyson with Franion: and if the God Apollo, who by his devine essence knew al secrets, gave answere that she was guiltie, she were content to suffer any torment, were it never so terrible. The request was so reasonable,[1] that Pandosto could not for shame deny it, unlesse he would bee counted of all his subjects more wilfull then wise. He therefore agreed, that with as much speede as might be there should be certaine Embassadores dispatched to the Ile of Delphos; and in the meane season he commanded that his wife should be kept in close prison.[2]

Bellaria having obtained this graunt was now more carefull for her little babe that floated on the Seas, then sorrowful for her owne mishap. For of that she doubted: of her selfe shee was assured, knowing if Apollo should give Oracle according to the thoughts of the hart, yet the sentence should goe on her side, such was the clearenes of her minde in this case. But Pandosto (whose suspitious heade still remained in one song) chose out six of his Nobility, whom hee knew were scarse indifferent men in the Queenes behalfe, and providing all things fit for their journey, sent them to Delphos. They willing to fulfill the Kinges commaund, and desirous to see the situation and custome of the Iland, dispatched their affaires with as much speede as might be, and embarked themselves to this voyage, which (the wind and weather serving fit for their purpose) was soone ended. For within three weekes[3] they arrived at Delphos, where they were no sooner set on lande, but with great devotion they went to the Temple of Apollo, and there offring sacrifice to the GOD,[4] and giftes to the Priest, as the custome was, they humbly craved an aunswere of their demaund: they had not long kneeled at the Altar, but Apollo with a loude voice[5] saide: Bohemians, what you finde behinde the Alter take and depart. They forthwith obeying the Oracle founde a scroule of parchment, wherein was written these words in letters of Golde,—

The Oracle.

Suspition is no proofe: Jealousie is an unequall judge: *Bellaria* is chast: *Egistus* blameless: *Franion* a true subject: *Pandosto* treacherous: his babe an innocent, and the King shal live without an heire: if that which is lost be not founde.[6]

---

[1] III. 2. 113–17.
[2] II. 1. 192–5.
[3] Cf. Leontes, II. 3. 197–8.   [4] III. 1. 6–8.
[5] III. 1. 8–11.   [6] III. 2. 131–4.

As soone as they had taken out this scroule, the Priest of the God commaunded them that they should not presume to read it, before they came in the presence of Pandosto: unlesse they would incurre the displeasure of Apollo.[1] The Bohemian Lords carefully obeying his commaund, taking their leave of the Priest, with great reverence departed out of the Temple, and went to their ships, and assoone as winde would permit them, sailed toward Bohemia, whither in short time they safely arrived, and with great tryumph issuing out of their Ships went to the Kinges pallace, whom they found in his chamber accompanied with other Noble men: Pandosto no sooner saw them, but with a merrie countenaunce he welcomed them home, asking what newes: they told his Majestie that they had received an aunswere of the God written in a scroule, but with this charge, that they should not read the contents before they came in the presence of the King, and with that they delivered him the parchment: but his Noble men entreated him that sith therein was contayned either the safetie of his Wives life, and honesty, or her death, and perpetuall infamy, that he would have his Nobles and Commons assembled in the judgement Hall, where the Queene brought in as prysoner should heare the contents: if shee were found guilty by the Oracle of the God, then all should have cause to thinke his rigour proceeded of due desert: if her Grace were found faultlesse, then shee should bee cleared before all, sith she had bene accused openly. This pleased the King so, that he appointed the day, and assembled al his Lords and Commons, and caused the Queene to be brought in before the Judgement seat, commaunding that the inditement shoulde bee read, wherein she was accused of adultery with Egistus, and of conspiracy with Franion:[2] Bellaria hearing the contentes, was no whit astonished, but made this chearefull aunswer:

If the devine powers bee privy to humane actions (as no doubt they are)[3] I hope my patience shall make fortune blushe, and my unspotted life shall staine spightful discredit. For although lying Report hath sought to appeach mine honor, and Suspition hath intended to soyle my credit with infamie: yet where Vertue keepeth the Forte, Report and Suspition may assayle, but never sack: how I have led my life before Egistus comming, I appeale Pandosto to the Gods and to thy conscience.[4] What hath past betwixt him and me, the Gods only know, and I hope will presently reveale: that I loved Egistus I can not denie: that I honored him I shame not to confesse: to the one I was forced by his vertues, to the other for his

[1] III. 1. 18–21; III. 2. 123–9.
[2] III. 2. 11–20.
[3] III. 2. 27–31.
[4] III. 2. 44–7.

dignities.[1] But as touching lascivious lust, I say Egistus is honest, and hope my selfe to be found without spot: for Franion, I can neither accuse him nor excuse him, for I was not privie to his departure,[2] and that this is true which I have heere rehearsed, I referre myself to the devine Oracle.[3]

Bellaria had no sooner sayd, but the King commaunded that one of his Dukes should read the contentes of the scroule: which after the commons had heard, they gave a great showt, rejoysing and clapping their hands that the Queene was cleare of that false accusation: but the king whose conscience was a witnesse against him of his witlesse furie, and false suspected Jealousie, was so ashamed of his rashe folly, that he entreated his nobles to perswade Bellaria to forgive, and forget these injuries:[4] promising not onely to shew himselfe a loyall and loving husband, but also to reconcile himselfe to Egistus, and Franion: revealing then before them all the cause of their secrete flighte, and how treacherously hee thought to have practised his death, if the good minde of his Cupbearer had not prevented his purpose. As thus he was relating the whole matter, there was worde brought him that his young sonne Garinter was sodainly dead,[5] which newes so soone as Bellaria heard, surcharged before with extreame joy, and now suppressed with heavie sorrowe, her vital spirites were so stopped, that she fell downe presently dead, and could never be revived.[6]

This sodaine sight so appalled the Kings Sences, that he sancke from his seat in a swound,[7] so as he was fayne to be carried by his nobles to his Pallace, where hee lay by the space of three dayes without speache: his commons were as men in dispaire, so diversely distressed: there was nothing but mourning and lamentation to be heard throughout al Bohemia: their young Prince dead, their vertuous Queene bereaved of her life, and their King and Soveraigne in great hazard: this tragicall discourse of fortune so daunted them, as they went like shadowes, not men; yet somewhat to comfort their heavie hearts, they heard that Pandosto was come to himselfe, and had recovered his speache, who as in a fury brayed out these bitter speaches:

O miserable Pandosto, what surer witnesse then conscience? what thoughts more sower then suspition? What plague more bad then Jealousie? Unnaturall actions offend the Gods more than men, and causelesse crueltie never scapes without revenge: I have committed

---

[1] III. 2. 60–5.   [2] III. 2. 72–4.   [3] III. 2. 114.
[4] Contrast Leontes at III. 2. 137–8.
[5] III. 2. 142–3.
[6] III. 2. 146–7; 199.
[7] sound *1588*.

such a bloudy fact, as repent I may, but recall I cannot. Ah Jealousie, a hell to the minde, and a horror to the conscience, suppressing reason, and inciting rage: a worse passion then phrenzie, a greater plague than madnesse. Are the Gods just? Then let them revenge such brutishe crueltie: my innocent Babe I have drowned in the Seas; my loving wife I have slaine with slaunderous suspition; my trusty friend I have sought to betray, and yet the Gods are slacke to plague such offences. Ah unjust Apollo, Pandosto is the man that hath committed the faulte: why should Garinter, seely childe, abide the paine?[1] Well, sith the Gods meane to prolong my dayes, to increase my dolour, I will offer my guiltie bloud a sacrifice to those sackles soules, whose lives are lost by my rigorous folly.

And with that he reached at a Rapier, to have murdered himselfe, but his Peeres being present, stayed him from such a bloudy acte:[2] perswading him to think, that the Common-wealth consisted on his safetie, and that those sheepe could not but perish, that wanted a sheepheard; wishing that if hee would not live for himselfe, yet he should have care of his subjects, and to put such fancies out of his minde, sith in sores past help, salves do not heale, but hurt: and in things past cure, care is a corrosive:[3] with these and such like perswasions the Kinge was overcome, and began somewhat to quiet his minde: so that assoone as he could goe abroad, hee caused his wife to be embalmed, and wrapt in lead with her young sonne Garinter:[4] erecting a rich and famous Sepulchre, wherein hee intombed them both, making such solemne obsequies at her funeral, as al Bohemia might perceive he did greatly repent him of his forepassed folly: causing this epitaph to be ingraven on her Tombe in letters of Golde:[5]

THE EPITAPH.

HERE LYES ENTOMBDE BELLARIA FAIRE,
FALSLY ACCUSED TO BE UNCHASTE:
CLEARED BY APOLLOS SACRED DOOME,
YET SLAINE BY JEALOUSIE AT LAST.
WHAT ERE THOU BE THAT PASSEST BY,
CURSSE HIM, THAT CAUSDE THIS QUEENE TO DIE.

This epitaph being ingraven, Pandosto would once a day repaire to the Tombe, and there with watry plaintes bewaile his misfortune; coveting no other companion but sorrowe, nor no other harmonie,

---

[1] Cf. Paulina, III. 2. 177–96.
[2] Cf. III. 2. 205–8.   [3] III. 2. 220–1.
[4] III. 2. 234.   [5] III. 2. 234–6.

but repentance.[1] But leaving him to his dolorous passions, at last let us come to shewe the tragicall discourse of the young infant.[2]

Who being tossed with Winde, and Wave, floated two whole daies without succour, readie at every puffe to bee drowned in the Sea, till at last the Tempest[3] ceassed and the little boate was driven with the tyde into the Coast of Sycilia, where sticking uppon the sandes it rested. Fortune minding to be wanton, willing to shewe that as she hath wrincles on her browes, so shee hath dimples in her cheekes, thought after so many sower lookes, to lend a fayned smile, and after a puffing storme, to bring a pretty calme: shee began thus to dally. It fortuned a poore mercenary Sheepheard, that dwelled in Sycilia, who got his living by other mens flockes, missed one of his sheepe, and thinking it had strayed into the covert,[4] that was hard by, sought very diligently to find that which he could not see, fearing either that the Wolves[5] or Eagles had undone him (for hee was so poore, as a sheepe was halfe his substaunce), wandered downe toward the Sea cliffes, to see if perchaunce the sheepe was browsing on the sea Ivy,[6] whereon they greatly doe feede, but not finding her there, as he was ready to returne to his flocke, hee heard a child crie; but knowing there was no house nere, he thought he had mistaken the sound, and that it was the bleatyng of his Sheepe. Wherefore looking more narrowely, as he cast his eye to the Sea, he spyed a little boate, from whence as he attentively listened, he might heare the cry to come: standing a good while in a maze, at last he went to the shoare, and wading to the boate, as he looked in, he saw the little babe lying al alone, ready to die for hunger and colde, wrapped in a Mantle of Scarlet, richely imbrodered with Golde, and having a chayne about the necke.

The Sheepeheard, who before had never seene so faire a Babe, nor so riche Jewels,[7] thought assuredly, that it was some little God, and began with great devocion to knock on his breast. The Babe, who wrythed with the head, to seeke for the pap, began againe to cry afresh, whereby the poore man knew that it was a Childe, which by some sinister meanes was driven thither by distresse of weather; marvailing how such a seely infant, which by the Mantle, and the Chayne, could not be but borne of Noble Parentage, should be so hardly crossed with deadly mishap. The poore sheepheard perplexed thus with divers thoughts, tooke pitty of the childe, and determined

[1] III. 2. 236–40.
[2] Shakespeare also does this.
[3] Cf. III. 3. 4–6; 48; 81–9.
[4] Cf. III. 3. 62–4; the sheep are scared by the hunt.
[5] Referred to at III. 3. 65.
[6] III. 3. 66.
[7] V. 2. 36.

with himselfe to carry it to the King, that there it might be brought up, according to the worthinesse of birth; for his ability coulde not afforde to foster it, though his good minde was willing to further it.

Taking therefore the Chylde in his armes, as he foulded the mantle together, the better to defend it from colde, there fell downe at his foote a very faire and riche purse, wherein he founde a great summe of golde:[1] which sight so revived the shepheards spirits, as he was greatly ravished with joy, and daunted with feare: Joyfull to see such a summe in his power, and feareful if it should be knowne, that it might breede his further daunger. Necessitie wisht him at the least, to retaine the Golde, though he would not keepe the childe: the simplicity of his conscience scared him from such deceiptfull briberie. Thus was the poore manne perplexed with a doubtfull Dilemma, until at last the covetousnesse of the coyne overcame him: for what will not the greedy desire of Golde cause a man to doe?[2] So that he was resolved in himselfe to foster the child, and with the summe to relieve his want: resting thus resolute in this point he left seeking of his sheepe, and as covertly, and secretly as he coulde, went by a by way to his house, least any of his neighbours should perceave his carriage: as soone as he was got home, entring in at the doore, the childe began to crie, which his wife hearing, and seeing her husband with a yong babe in armes, began to bee somewhat jelousse, yet marveiling that her husband should be so wanton abroad, sith he was so quiet at home: but as women are naturally given to beleeve the worste, so his wife thinking it was some bastard, beganne to crowe against her goodman, and taking up a cudgel (for the most maister went breechles) sware solemnly that shee would make clubs trumps, if hee brought any bastard brat within her dores. The goodman, seeing his wife in her majestie with her mace in her hand, thought it was time to bowe for feare of blowes, and desired her to be quiet, for there was non such matter; but if she could holde her peace, they were made for ever:[3] and with that he told her the whole matter, how he had found the childe in a little boat, without any succour, wrapped in that costly mantle, and having that rich chaine about the neck: but at last when he shewed her the purse full of gold, she began to simper something sweetely, and taking her husband about the neck, kissed him after her homely fashion: saying that she hoped God had seene their want, and now ment to relieeve their poverty, and seeing they could get no children, had sent them this little babe to be their heire. Take heede in any case (quoth the shepherd) that you be secret, and blabbe it not out when you meete with your

[1] III. 3. 112–19.
[2] III. 3. 117–23.
[3] III. 3. 117, 'You're a made old man.'

gossippes, for if you doe, we are like not only to loose the Golde and Jewels, but our other goodes and lives.[1] Tush (quoth his wife), profit is a good hatch before the doore: feare not, I have other things to talke of then of this; but I pray you let us lay up the money surely, and the Jewels, least by any mishap it be spied.

After that they had set all things in order, the shepheard went to his sheepe with a merry note, and the good wife learned to sing lullaby at home with her yong babe, wrapping it in a homely blanket in sted of a rich mantle; nourishing it so clenly and carefully as it began to bee a jolly girle, in so much that they began both of them to be very fond of it, seeing, as it waxed in age, so it increased in beauty. The shepheard every night at his comming home, would sing and daunce it on his knee, and prattle, that in a short time it began to speake, and call him Dad, and her Mam: at last when it grew to ripe yeeres, that it was about seven yeares olde, the shepheard left keeping of other mens sheepe, and with the money he found in the purse, he bought him the lease of a pretty farme, and got a smal flocke of sheepe, which when Fawnia (for so they named the child) came to the age of ten yeres, hee set her to keepe, and shee with such diligence performed her charge as the sheepe prospered marveilously under her hand. Fawnia thought Porrus had been her father, and Mopsa her mother, (for so was the shepheard and his wife called) honoured and obeyed them with such reverence, that all the neighbours praised the duetifull obedience of the child. Porrus grewe in a short time to bee a man of some wealth, and credite;[2] for fortune so favoured him in having no charge but Fawnia, that he began to purchase land, intending after his death to give it to his daughter; so that diverse rich farmers sonnes came as woers to his house: for Fawnia was something clenly attired, beeing of such singular beautie and excellent witte, that whoso sawe her, would have thought shee had bene some heavenly nymph, and not a mortal creature: in so much, that when she came to the age of sixteene yeeres,[3] shee so increased with exquisite perfection both of body and minde, as her natural disposition did bewray that she was borne of some high parentage;[4] but the people thinking she was daughter to the shephard Porrus, rested only amazed at hir beauty and wit; yea she won such favour and commendations in every mans eye, as her beautie was not only praysed in the countrey, but also spoken of in the Court: yet such was her submisse modestie, that although her praise daily increased, her mind was no whit puffed up with pride, but humbled her selfe as became a country mayde and the daughter of a poore

[1] III. 3. 122–4.   [2] IV. 1. 39–41.
[3] IV. Chorus, 'I slide/O'er sixteen years.'
[4] IV. 3. 156–9.

sheepheard. Every day she went forth with her sheepe to the field, keeping them with such care and diligence, as al men thought she was verie painfull, defending her face from the heat of the sunne with no other vale, but with a garland made of bowes and flowers; which attire became her so gallantly, as shee seemed to bee the Goddesse Flora her selfe for beauty.[1]

Fortune, who al this while had shewed a frendly face, began now to turne her back, and to shewe a lowring countenance, intending as she had given Fawnia a slender checke, so she would give her a harder mate: to bring which to passe, she layd her traine on this wise. Egistus had but one only son called Dorastus,[2] about the age of twenty yeeres: a prince so decked and adorned with the gifts of nature: so fraught with beauty and vertuous qualities, as not onely his father joyed to have so good a sonne, and al his commons re-joyced that God had lent them such a noble Prince to succeede in the Kingdom.[3] Egistus placing al his joy in the perfection of his sonne: seeing that he was now mariage-able, sent Embassadors to the king of Denmarke, to intreate a mariage betweene him and his daughter, who willingly consenting, made answer, that the next spring, if it please Egistus with his sonne to come into Denmarke, hee doubted not but they should agree upon reasonable conditions. Egistus rest-ing satisfied with this friendly answer, thought convenient in the meane time to breake with his sonne: finding therefore on a day fit oportunity, he spake to him in these fatherly tearmes:

Dorastus, thy youth warneth me to prevent the worst, and mine age to provide the best. Oportunities neglected, are signes of folly: actions measured by time, are seldome bitten with repentance: thou art young, and I olde: age hath taught me that, which thy youth cannot yet conceive. I therefore will counsell thee as a father, hoping thou wilt obey as a childe. Thou seest my white hayres are blossomes for the grave, and thy freshe colour fruite for time and fortune, so that it behooveth me to thinke how to dye, and for thee to care how to live. My crowne I must leave by death, and thou enjoy my King-dome by succession, wherein I hope thy vertue and prowesse shall bee such, as though my subjectes want my person, yet they shall see in thee my perfection. That nothing either may faile to satisfie thy minde, or increase thy dignities, the onely care I have, is to see thee well marryed before I die, and thou become olde.

Dorastus, who from his infancy, delighted rather to die with Mars in the Fielde then to dally with Venus in the Chamber, fearing to dis-please his father, and yet not willing to be wed, made him this reverent answere.

[1] IV. 3. 1–3.		[2] Florizel. IV. Chorus, 22–3.
[3] IV. 3. 7–8.

Sir, there is no greater bond then duetie, nor no straiter law then nature: disobedience in youth is often galled with despight in age. The commaund of the father ought to be a constraint to the childe: so parentes willes are laws, so they passe not all laws: may it please your Grace therefore to appoint whome I shall love, rather then by deniall I should be appeached of disobedience: I rest content to love, though it bee the only thing I hate.[1]

Egistus hearing his sonne to flie so farre from the marke, began to be somewhat chollericke, and therefore made him his hasty aunswere.

What Dorastus canst thou not love? Commeth this cynicall passion of prone desires, or peevish frowardnesse? What durst thou think thy selfe to[o] good for all, or none good inough for thee? I tell thee, Dorastus, there is nothing sweeter then youth, nor swifter decreasing, while it is increasing. Time past with folly may bee repented, but not recalled. If thou marrie in age, thy wives freshe couloures will breede in thee dead thoughtes and suspition, and thy white hayres her lothesomnesse and sorrowe. For Venus affections are not fed with Kingdomes, or treasures, but with youthfull conceits and sweet amours. Vulcan was allotted to shake the tree, but Mars allowed to reape the fruite. Yeelde Dorastus to thy Fathers perswasions, which may prevent thy perils. I have chosen thee a Wife, faire by nature, royall by birth, by vertues famous, learned by education, and rich by possessions, so that it is hard to judge whether her bounty, or fortune, her beauty, or vertue bee of greater force: I mean, Dorastus, Euphrania, daughter and heire to the King of Denmarke.[2]

Egistus pausing here a while, looking when his son should make him answere, and seeing that he stoode still as one in a trance, he shooke him up thus sharply.

Well Dorastus take heede, the tree Alpya wasteth not with fire, but withereth with the dewe: that which love nourisheth not, perisheth with hate: if thou like Euphrania, thou breedest my content, and in loving her thou shalt have my love, otherwise—and with that hee flung from his sonne in a rage, leaving him a sorrowfull man, in that he had by deniall displeased his Father, and halfe angrie with him selfe that hee could not yeelde to that passion, whereto both reason and his Father perswaded him: but see how fortune is plumed with times feathers, and how shee can minister strange causes to breede straunge effects.

It happened not long after this that there was a meeting of all the Farmers Daughters in Sycilia, whither Fawnia was also bidden as the mistres of the feast,[3] who having attired her selfe in her best garments,[4]

[1] This resembles Prince Henry's attitude to marriage, 1610–12.
[2] No suggestion of this in *WT*.
[3] IV. 2. 38; IV. 3. 3–5; 68.   [4] IV. 3. 1–2.

went among the rest of her companions to the merry meeting: there spending the day in such homely pastimes as shepheards use. As the evening grew on, and their sportes ceased, ech taking their leave at other, Fawnia desiring one of her companions to beare her companie, went home by the flocke, to see if they were well folded, and as they returned, it fortuned that Dorastus (who all that daye had bene hawking,[1] and kilde store of game) incountred by the way these two mayds, and casting his eye sodenly on Fawnia, he was halfe afraid, fearing that with Acteon he had seene Diana; for hee thought such exquisite perfection could not be founde in any mortall creature. As thus he stoode in a maze, one of his Pages told him, that the maide with the garland on her heade was Fawnia, the faire shepheard, whose beauty was so much talked of in the Court. Dorastus desirous to see if nature had adorned her minde with any inward qualities, as she had decked her body with outward shape, began to question with her whose daughter she was, of what age and how she had bin trained up, who answered him with such modest reverence and sharpnesse of witte, that Dorastus thought her outward beautie was but a counterfait to darken her inward qualities, wondring how so courtly behaviour could be found in so simple a cottage[2] and cursing fortune that had shadowed wit and beauty with such hard fortune. As thus he held her a long while with chat, Beauty seeing him at discovert, thought not to lose the vantage, but strooke him so deeply with an invenomed shafte, as he wholy lost his libertie, and became a slave to Love, which before contemned love, glad now to gaze on a poore shepheard, who before refused the offer of a riche Princesse; for the perfection of Fawnia had so fired his fancie as he felt his minde greatly chaunged, and his affections altered, cursing Love that had wrought such a chaunge, and blaming the basenesse of his mind, that would make such a choice: but thinking these were but passionat toies that might be thrust out at pleasure, to avoid the Syren that inchaunted him, he put spurs to his horse, and bad this faire shepheard farewell.

Fawnia (who all this while had marked the princely gesture of Dorastus) seeing his face so wel featured, and each lim so perfectly framed, began greatly to praise his perfection, commending him so long, till she found her selfe faultie, and perceived that if she waded but a little further, she might slippe over her shooes: shee therefore seeking to quench that fire which never was put out, went home, and faining her selfe not well at ease, got her to bed: where casting a thousand thoughts in her head, she could take no rest: for if she waked, she began to call to minde his beautie, and thinking to

[1] IV. 3. 14–16.
[2] IV. 3. 586–90.

beguile such thoughts with sleepe, she then dreamed of his perfection: pestered thus with these unacquainted passions, she passed the
night as she could in short slumbers.

Dorastus (who all this while rode with a flea in his eare) could not
by any meanes forget the sweete favour of Fawnia, but rested so
bewitched with her wit and beauty, as hee could take no rest. He
felt fancy to give the assault, and his wounded mind readie to yeeld
as vanquished: yet he began with divers considerations to suppresse
this frantick affection, calling to minde, that Fawnia was a shepheard,
one not worthy to bee looked at of a Prince, much less to bee loved
of such a potentate, thinking what a discredite it were to himself, and
what a griefe it would be to his father, blaming fortune and accusing
his owne follie, that should bee so fond as but once to cast a glaunce
at such a country slut. As thus he was raging against him selfe, Love
fearing if shee dallied long, to loose her champion, stept more nigh,
and gave him such a fresh wounde as it pearst him at the heart, that
he was faine to yeeld, maugre his face, and to forsake the companie
and gette him to his chamber: where being solemnly set, hee burst
into these passionate tearmes.

Ah, Dorastus, art thou alone? No not alone, while thou art tried
with these unacquainted passions. Yeld to fancy, thou canst not by
thy fathers counsaile, but in a frenzie thou art by just destinies. Thy
father were content, if thou couldest love, and thou therefore discontent, because thou doest love. O devine Love, feared of men
because honoured of the Gods, not to be suppressed by wisdome, because not to be comprehended by reason: without Lawe, and therefore above all Law. How now Dorastus, why doest thou blaze that
with praises, which thou hast cause to blaspheme with curses? Yet
why should they curse Love that are in Love? Blush Dorastus at thy
fortune, thy choice, thy love: thy thoughts cannot be uttered without
shame, nor thy affections without discredit. Ah Fawnia, sweete
Fawnia, thy beautie Fawnia. Shamest not thou Dorastus to name
one unfitte for thy birth, thy dignities, thy Kingdomes? Dye
Dorastus, Dorastus die. Better hadst thou perish with high desires,
then live in base thoughts. Yea but, beautie must be obeyed, because
it is beauty, yet framed of the Gods to feede the eye, not to fetter the
heart. Ah but he that striveth against Love, shooteth with them of
Scyrum against the wind, and with the Cockeatrice pecketh against
the steele. I will therefore obey, because I must obey. Fawnia, yea
Fawnia shall be my fortune, in spight of fortune. The Gods above dis-
dain not to love women beneath. Phoebus liked Sibilla, Jupiter Io,
and why not I then Fawnia? one something inferiour to these in
birth, but farre superiour to them in beautie, borne to be a Shepheard,
but worthy to be a Goddesse. Ah Dorastus, wilt thou so forget thy

selfe as to suffer affection to suppresse wisedome, and Love to violate thine honour? How sower will thy choice be to thy Father, sorrow-full to thy Subjects, to thy friends a griefe, most gladsome to thy foes! Subdue then thy affections, and cease to love her whome thou couldst not love, unlesse blinded with too much love. Tushe I talke to the wind, and in seeking to prevent the causes, I further the effectes. I will yet praise Fawnia; honour, yea and love Fawnia, and at this day followe content, not counsaile. Doo Dorastus, thou canst but repent: and with that his Page came into the chamber, whereupon hee ceased from his complaints, hoping that time would weare out that which fortune had wrought. As thus he was pained, so poore Fawnia was diversly perplexed: for the next morning getting up very earely, she went to her sheepe, thinking with hard labours to passe away her new conceived amours, beginning very busily to drive them to the field, and then to shifte the foldes, at last (wearied with toile) she sate her down, where (poore soule) she was more tryed with fond affections: for love beganne to assault her, in so much that as she sate upon the side of a hill, she began to accuse her owne folly in these tearmes.

Infortunate Fawnia, and therefore infortunate because Fawnia, thy shepherds hooke sheweth thy poore state, thy proud desires an aspiring mind: the one declareth thy want, the other thy pride. No bastard hauke must soare so high as the Hobbie, no Fowle gaze against the Sunne but the Eagle, actions wrought against nature reape despight, and thoughts above Fortune disdaine. Fawnia, thou art a shepheard, daughter to poore Porrus: if thou rest content with this, thou art like to stande, if thou climbe thou art sure to fal. The Herb Anita growing higher then sixe ynches becommeth a weede. Nylus flowing more then twelve cubits procureth a dearth. Daring affections that passe measure, are cut shorte by time or for-tune: suppresse then Fawnia those thoughts which thou mayest shame to expresse. But ah Fawnia, love is a Lord, who will com-maund by power, and constraine by force. Dorastus, ah Dorastus is the man I love, the woorse is thy hap, and the lesse cause hast thou to hope. Will Eagles catch at flyes, will Cedars stoupe to brambles, or mighty Princes looke at such homely trulles? No, no, thinke this, Dorastus disdaine is greater then thy desire, hee is a Prince respect-ing his honour, thou a beggars brat forgetting thy calling. Cease then not onely to say, but to thinke to love Dorastus, and dissemble thy love Fawnia, for better it were to dye with griefe, then to live with shame: yet in despight of love I will sigh, to see if I can sigh out love.

Fawnia somewhat appeasing her griefes with these pithie per-swasions, began after her wonted maner to walke about her sheepe, and to keepe them from straying into the corne, suppressing her affection with the due consideration of her base estate, and with the impossibilities of her love, thinking it were frenzy, not fancy, to covet that which the very destinies did deny her to obteine.

But Dorastus was more impatient in his passions; for love so fiercely assayled him, that neither companie, nor musicke could mittigate his martirdome, but did rather far the more increase his maladie: shame would not let him crave counsaile in this case, nor feare of his Fathers displeasure reveyle it to any secrete friend; but hee was faine to make a Secretarie of himselfe, and to participate his thoughtes with his owne troubled mind. Lingring thus awhile in doubtfull suspence, at last stealing secretely from the court without either men or Page, hee went to see if hee could espie Fawnia walking abroade in the field; but as one having a great deale more skill to retrive the partridge with his spaniels, then to hunt after such a straunge pray, he sought, but was little the better: which crosse lucke drave him into a great choler, that he began to accuse love and fortune. But as he was readie to retire, he sawe Fawnia sitting all alone under the side of a hill, making a garland of such homely flowers as the fields did afoord. This sight so revived his spirites that he drewe nigh, with more judgement to take a view of her singular perfection, which hee found to bee such as in that countrey attyre she stained all the courtlie Dames of Sicilia. While thus he stoode gazing with pearcing lookes on her surpassing beautie, Fawnia cast her eye aside, and spyed Dorastus, which[1] sudden sight made the poore girl to blush, and to die her christal cheeks with a vermilion red; which gave her such a grace, as she seemed farre more beautiful. And with that she rose up, saluting the Prince with such modest curtesies, as he wondred how a country maid could afoord such courtly behaviour. Dorastus, repaying her curtesie with a smiling countenance, began to parlie with her on this manner.

Faire maide (quoth he) either your want is great, or a shepheards life very sweete, that your delight is in such country labors. I can not conceive what pleasure you should take, unless you meane to imitate the nymphes, being yourself so like a Nymph. To put me out of this doubt, shew me what is to be commended in a shepherdes life, and what pleasures you have to countervaile these drudging laboures.

Fawnia with blushing face made him this ready aunswere. Sir, what richer state then content, or what sweeter life then quiet? we shepheards are not borne to honor, nor beholding unto beautie, the less care we have to feare fame or fortune: we count our attire brave inough if warme inough, and our foode dainty, if to suffice nature: our greatest enemie is the wolfe; our onely care in safe keeping our flock: in stead of courtly ditties we spend the daies with cuntry songs:

[1] with *1588*.

our amorous conceites are homely thoughtes; delighting as much to talke of Pan and his cuntrey prankes, as Ladies to tell of Venus and her wanton toyes. Our toyle is in shifting the fouldes, and looking to the Lambes, easie labours: oft singing and telling tales, homely pleasures; our greatest welth not to covet, our honor not to climbe, our quiet not to care. Envie looketh not so lowe as shepheards: Shepheards gaze not so high as ambition: we are rich in that we are poore with content, and proud onely in this, that we have no cause to be proud.

This wittie aunswer of Fawnia so inflamed Dorastus fancy, as he commended him selfe for making so good a choyce, thinking, if her birth were aunswerable to her wit and beauty, that she were a fitte mate for the most famous Prince in the worlde.[1] He therefore beganne to sifte her more narrowely on this manner.

Fawnia, I see thou art content with Country labours, because thou knowest not Courtly pleasures: I commend thy wit, and pitty thy want: but wilt thou leave thy Fathers Cottage and serve a Courtlie Mistresse?

Sir (quoth she) beggars ought not to strive against fortune, nor to gaze after honour, least either their fall be greater, or they become blinde. I am borne to toile for the Court, not in the Court, my nature unfit for their nurture: better live then in meane degree, than in high disdaine.

Well saide, Fawnia (quoth Dorastus) I gesse at thy thoughtes; thou art in love with some Countrey Shephearde.

No sir (quoth she) shepheards cannot love, that are so simple, and maides may not love that are so young.

Nay therefore (quoth Dorastus) maides must love, because they are young, for Cupid is a child, and Venus, though olde, is painted with fresh colours.

I graunt (quoth she) age may be painted with new shadowes, and youth may have imperfect affections; but what arte concealeth in one, ignorance revealeth in the other.

Dorastus seeing Fawnia held him so harde, thought it was vaine so long to beate about the bush: therefore he thought to have given her a fresh charge: but he was so prevented by certaine of his men, who missing their maister, came posting to seeke him; seeing that he was gone foorth all alone, yet before they drewe so nie that they might heare their talke, he used these speeches.

Why Fawnia, perhappes I love thee, and then thou must needes yeelde, for thou knowest I can commaunde and constraine. Trueth sir (quoth she) but not to love; for constrained love is force, not love: and know this sir, mine honesty is such, as I hadde rather dye then

[1] Cf. IV. 4. 585-92.

be a concubine even to a King, and my birth is so base as I am unfitte
to bee a wife to a poore farmer. Why then (quoth he) thou canst not
love Dorastus. Yes saide Fawnia, when Dorastus becomes a shepheard, and with that the presence of his men broke off their parle, so
that he went with them to the palace, and left Fawnia sitting still on
the hill side, who seeing that the night drewe on, shifted her fouldes,
and busied her selfe about other worke to drive away such fond
fancies as began to trouble her braine. But all this could not prevaile,
for the beautie of Dorastus had made such a deepe impression in her
heart, as it could not be worne out without cracking, so that she was
forced to blame her owne folly in this wise.

Ah Fawnia, why doest thou gaze against the Sunne, or catch at the
Winde? starres are to be looked at with the eye, not reacht at with
the hande: thoughts are to be measured by Fortunes, not by desires:
falles come not by sitting low, but by climing too hie: what then shal
al feare to fal, because some happe to fall? No luck commeth by lot,
and fortune windeth those threedes which the destinies spin. Thou
art favored Fawnia of a prince, and yet thou art so fond to reject
desired favours: thou hast deniall at thy tonges end, and desire at thy
hearts bottome; a womans fault, to spurne at that with her foote,
which she greedily catcheth at with her hand. Thou lovest Dorastus,
Fawnia, and yet seemest to lower. Take heede, if hee retire thou wilt
repent: for unles hee love, thou canst but dye. Dye then Fawnia: for
Dorastus doth but jest: the Lyon never prayeth on the mouse, nor
Faulcons stoupe not to dead stales.[1] Sit downe then in sorrow, ceasse
to love, and content thy selfe, that Dorastus will vouchsafe to flatter
Fawnia, though not to fancy Fawnia. Heigh ho! Ah foole, it were
seemelier for thee to whistle as a Shepheard, then to sigh as a lover.
And with that she ceassed from these perplexed passions, folding her
sheepe, and hying home to her poore Cottage.

But such was the incessant sorrow of Dorastus to thinke on the
witte and beautie of Fawnia, and to see how fond hee was being a
Prince: and how froward she was being a beggar, then he began to
loose his wonted appetite, to looke pale and wan; instead of mirth,
to feede on melancholy: for courtly daunces to use cold dumpes: in
so much that not onely his owne men, but his father and all the court
began to marvaile at his sudden change, thinking that some lingring
sickenes had brought him into this state: wherefore he caused Phisitions to come, but Dorastus neither would let them minister, nor so
much as suffer them to see his urine: but remained stil so oppressed
with these passions, as he feared in him selfe a farther inconvenience.
His honor wished him to ceasse from such folly, but Love forced him
to follow fancy: yea and in despight of honour, love wonne the con-

[1] decoy-birds.

quest, so that his hot desires caused him to find new devises, for hee presently made himselfe a shepheards coate, that he might goe unknowne, and with the lesse suspition to prattle with Fawnia, and conveied it secretly into a thick grove hard joyning to the Pallace, whither[1] finding fit time, and opportunity, he went all alone, and putting off his princely apparel got on those shepheards roabes, and taking a great hooke in his hand (which he had also gotten) he went very anciently[2] to find out the mistres of his affection: but as he went by the way, seeing himselfe clad in such unseemely ragges, he began to smile at his owne folly, and to reprove his fondnesse, in these tearmes.

Well said Dorastus, thou keepest a rich decorum, base desires and homely attires: thy thoughtes are fit for none but a shepheard, and thy apparell such as only become a shepheard. A strange change from a Prince to a pesant! What is it? thy wretched fortune or thy wilful folly? Is it thy cursed destinies? Or thy crooked desires, that appointeth thee this penance? Ah Dorastus thou canst but love, and unlesse thou love, thou art like to perish for love. Yet fond foole, choose flowers, not weedes; Diamondes, not peables; Ladies which may honour thee, not shepheards which may disgrace thee. Venus is painted in silkes, not in ragges; and Cupid treadeth on disdaine, when he reacheth at dignitie. And yet Dorastus, shame not at thy shepheards weede: the heavenly Godes have sometime earthly thoughtes: Neptune became a ram, Jupiter a Bul, Apollo a shepheard: they Gods, and yet in love: and thou a man appointed to love.[3]

Devising thus with himselfe, he drew nigh to the place where Fawnia was keeping her shepe, who casting her eye aside, and seeing such a manerly shepheard, perfectly limmed, and comming with so good a pace, she began halfe to forget Dorastus, and to favor this prety shepheard, whom she thought shee might both love and obtaine: but as shee was in these thoughts, she perceived then, that it was the yong prince Dorastus, wherfore she rose up and reverently saluted him. Dorastus taking her by the hand, repaied her curtesie with a sweete kisse, and praying her to sit downe by him, he began thus to lay the batterie.

If thou marvel Fawnia at my strange attyre, thou wouldest more muse at my unaccustomed thoughtes: the one disgraceth but my outward shape, the other disturbeth my inward sences. I love Fawnia, and therefore what love liketh I cannot mislike. Fawnia, thou hast promised to love, and I hope thou wilt performe no lesse: I have ful-

---

[1] whether *1588*.
[2] like an old man; but cf. next page. 'anxiously' perhaps.
[3] IV. 3. 25–31.

filled thy request, and now thou canst but graunt my desire. Thou wert content to love Dorastus when he ceast to be a Prince, and to become a shepheard, and see I have made the change, and therefore not to misse of my choice.

Trueth, quoth Fawnia, but all that weare Cooles[1] are not Monkes: painted Eagles are pictures, not Eagles. Zeusis Grapes were like Grapes, yet shadowes: rich clothing make not princes: nor homely attyre beggers: shepheards are not called shepheardes, because they weare[2] hookes and bagges, but that they are borne poore, and live to keep sheepe: so this attire hath not made Dorastus a shepherd, but to seeme like a shepherd.

Well Fawnia, answered Dorastus, were I a shepherd, I could not but like thee, and being a prince I am forst to love thee. Take heed Fawnia be not proud of beauties painting, for it is a flower that fadeth in the blossome. Those which disdayne in youth are despised in age: Beauties shadowes are trickt up with times colours, which being set to drie in the sunne are stained with the sunne, scarce pleasing the sight ere they beginne not to be worth the sight, not much unlike the herbe Ephemeron, which flourisheth in the morning and is withered before the sunne setting. If my desire were against lawe, thou mightest justly deny me by reason, but I love thee Fawnia, not to misuse thee as a Concubine, but to use thee as my wife: I can promise no more, and meane to performe no lesse.

Fawnia hearing this solemne protestation of Dorastus, could no longer withstand the assault, but yeelded up the forte in these friendly tearmes.

Ah Dorastus, I shame to expresse that thou forcest me with thy sugred speeche to confesse: my base birth causeth the one, and thy high dignities the other. Beggars thoughts ought not to reach so far as Kings, and yet my desires reach as high as Princes. I dare not say, Dorastus, I love thee, because I am a shepherd; but the Gods know I have honored Dorastus (pardon if I say amisse) yea and loved Dorastus with such dutiful affection as Fawnia can performe, or Dorastus desire: I yeeld, not overcome with prayers, but with love, resting Dorastus handmaid ready to obey his wil, if no prejudice at all to his honour, nor to my credit.

Dorastus hearing this freendly conclusion of Fawnia embraced her in his armes, swearing that neither distance, time, nor adverse fortune should diminish his affection: but that in despight of the destinies he would remaine loyall unto death. Having thus plight their troath each to other, seeing they could not have the full fruition of their love in Sycilia, for that Egistus consent woulde never bee

[1] cowls.
[2] were *1588*.

graunted to so meane a match,[1] Dorastus determined, assone as time
and oportunitie would give them leave, to provide a great masse of
money, and many rich and costly jewels, for the easier cariage, and
then to transporte themselves and their treasure into Italy, where
they should leade a contented life, until such time as either he could
be reconciled to his Father, or else by succession come to the Kingdome.[2] This devise was greatly praysed of Fawnia, for she feared if
the King his father should but heare of the contract, that his furie
would be such as no lesse than death would stand for payment: she
therefore tould him, that delay bred daunger: that many mishaps
did fall out betweene the cup and the lip, and that to avoid danger,
it were best with as much speed as might be to pass out of Sycilia,
least fortune might prevent their pretence with some newe despight:
Dorastus, whom love pricked forward with desire, promised to dispatch his affaires with as great hast, as either time or oportunitie
would geve him leave: and so resting upon this point, after many
imbracings and sweete kisses they departed.

Dorastus having taken his leave of his best beloved Fawnia, went
to the Grove where hee had his rich apparel, and there uncasing
himself as secretly as might be, hiding up his shepheards attire, till
occasion should serve againe to use it, he went to the pallace, shewing
by his merrie countenaunce, that either the state of his body was
amended, or the case of his minde greatly redressed: Fawnia poore
soule was no less joyful, that being a shepheard, fortune had
favoured her so, as to reward her with the love of a Prince, hoping in
time to be advaunced from the daughter of a poore farmer to be the
wife of a riche King: so that she thought every houre a yeere, till by
their departure they might prevent danger, not ceasing still to goe
every daye to her sheepe, not so much for the care of her flock, as
for the desire she had to see her love and Lord Dorastus: who oftentimes, when oportunitie would serve, repaired thither to feede his
fancy with the sweet content of Fawnias presence: and although he
never went to visit her, but in his shepheards ragges, yet his ofte
repaire made him not onely suspected, but knowne to divers of their
neighbours: who for the good will they bare to old Porrus, tould him
secretly of the matter, wishing him to keepe his daughter at home,
least she went so ofte to the field that she brought him home a yong
sonne: for they feared that Fawnia being so beautifull, the yong
prince would allure her to folly. Porrus was striken into a dump at
these newes, so that thanking his neighboures for their good will he
hyed him home to his wife,[3] and calling her aside, wringing his

[1] IV. 3. 17–20; 36–46.
[2] Cf. IV. 3. 504ff.
[3] In *WT* she is dead, IV. 3. 55.

handes and shedding foorth teares, he brake the matter to her in these tearmes.

I am afraid wife, that my daughter Fawnia hath made her selfe so fine, that she will buy repentance too deare. I heare newes, which if they be true, some will wish they had not proved true. It is tould me by my neighbours, that Dorastus the Kinges sonne begins to looke at our daughter Fawnia: which if it be so, I will not geve her a halfe-peny for her honestie at the yeeres end. I tell thee wife, nowadaies beauty is a great stale to trap yong men, and faire wordes and sweete promises are two great enemies to a maydens honestie: and thou knowest where poore men intreate, and cannot obtaine, there Princes may commaund, and wil obtaine. Though Kings sonnes daunce in nettes, they may not be seene: but poore mens faultes are spied at a little hole: Well, it is a hard case where Kinges lustes are lawes, and that they should binde poore men to that, which they themselves wilfully breake.[1]

Peace husband (quoth his wife) take heede what you say: speake no more than you should, least you heare what you would not: great streames are to be stopped by sleight, not by force: and princes to be perswaded by submission, not by rigor: doe what you can, but no more than you may, least in saving Fawnias mayden-head, you loose your owne head. Take heede I say, it is ill jesting with edged tooles, and bad sporting with Kinges. The Wolfe had his skinne puld over his eares for but looking into the Lions den. Tush wife (quoth he) thou speakest like a foole. If the King should knowe that Dorastus had begotten our daughter with childe (as I feare it will fall out little better) the Kings furie would be such as no doubt we should both loose our goodes and lives: necessitie therefore hath no lawe, and I will prevent this mischiefe with a newe devise that is come into my head, which shall neither offend the King, nor dis-please Dorastus. I meane to take the chaine and the jewels that I found with Fawnia, and carrie them to the King, letting him then to understand how she is none of my daughter, but that I found her beaten up with the water alone in a little boate wrapped in a rich Mantle, wherein was inclosed this treasure. By this meanes I hope the King will take Fawnia into his service, and we whatsoever chaunceth shal be blamelesse. This device pleased the good wife very well, so that they determined assoone as they might know the King at leisure, to make him privie to this case.

In the meane time Dorastus was not slacke in his affaires, but applyed his matters with such diligence, that he provided all thinges fitte for their journey. Treasure and Jewels he had gotten great store, thincking there was no better friend than money in a strange

[1] Contrast the Shepherd, IV. 3. 458–69.

countrey: rich attire he had provided for Fawnia, and, because he could not bring the matter to passe without the helpe and advice of some one, he made an old servant of his called Capnio,[1] who had served him from his childhood, privie to his affaires: who seeing no perswasions could prevaile to divert him from his setled determination, gave his consent and dealt so secretly in the cause, that within short space hee had gotten a ship ready for their passage: the Mariners seeing a fit gale of winde for their purpose, wished Capnio to make no delayes, least if they pretermitted this good weather, they might stay long ere they had such a fayre winde. Capnio fearing that his negligence should hinder the journey, in the night time conveyed the trunckes full of treasure into the shippe, and by secrete meanes let Fawnia understand, that the next morning they meant to depart: she upon this newes slept verie little that night, but gotte up very early, and wente to her sheepe, looking every minute when she should see Dorastus, who taried not long, for fear delay might breede daunger, but came as fast as he could gallop, and without any great circumstance[2] took Fawnia up behinde him and rode to the haven, where the shippe lay, which was not three quarters of a mile distant from that place. He no sooner came there, but the Marriners were readie with their Cockboate to set them aboard, where being coucht together in a Cabben they past away the time in recounting their old loves, til their man Capnio should come.

Porrus who had heard that this morning the King would go abroad to take the ayre, called in haste to his wife to bring him his holyday hose and his best Jacket, that he might goe like an honest substantiall man to tell his tale. His wife, a good cleanly wenche, brought him all things fitte, and spungd him up very handsomlie, giving him the chaines and Jewels in a little boxe, which Porrus for the more safety put in his bosom. Having thus all his trinkets in a readines, taking his staffe in his hand he bad his wife kisse him for good lucke, and so hee went towards the Pallace.[3] But as he was going, fortune (who meant to shewe him a little false play) prevented his purpose in this wise.

He met by chaunce in his way Capnio,[4] who trudging as fast as he could with a little coffer under his arme to the ship, and spying Porrus whome he knewe to be Fawnias Father, going towardes the Pallace, being a wylie fellow, began to doubt the worst, and therefore crost him the way, and askt him whither he was going so early this morning. Porrus (who knew by his face that he was one of the

---

[1] Camillo in *WT*.
[2] No disguising. Cf. IV. 3. 640–64.
[3] Cf. IV. 3. 694–716.
[4] Autolycus at IV. 3. 720ff.

Court) meaning simply, told him that the Kings son Dorastus dealt hardly with him; for he had but one daughter who was a little beautifull, and that his neighboures told him the young Prince had allured her to folly, he went therefore now to complaine to the King how greatly he was abused.

Capnio (who straight way smelt the whole matter) began to soothe[1] him in his talke, and said, that Dorastus dealt not like a Prince to spoyle any poore manes daughter in that sort: he therefore would doe the best for him he could, because he knew he was an honest man. But (quoth Capnio) you lose your labour in going to the Pallace, for the King meanes this day to take the aire of the Sea, and to goe aboord of a shippe that lies in the haven.[2] I am going before, you see, to provide all things in redinesse, and if you will follow my counsaile, turne back with me to the haven, where I will set you in such a fitte place as you may speake to the King at your pleasure. Porrus giving credit to Capnios smooth tale, gave him a thousand thanks for his frendly advise, and went with him to the haven, making all the way his complaintes of Dorastus, yet concealing secretlie the chaine and the Jewels. Assone as they were come to the Sea side, the marriners seeing Capnio, came a land with their cockboate, who still dissembling the matter, demaunded of Porrus if he would go see the ship? who unwilling and fearing the worst, because he was not well acquainted with Capnio, made his excuse that he could not brooke the Sea, therefore would not trouble him.

Capnio seeing that by faire meanes hee could not get him aboord, commaunded the mariners that by violence they should carrie him into the shippe, who like sturdy knaves hoisted the poore shepheard on their backes, and bearing him to the boate, lanched from the land.

Porrus seeing himselfe so cunningly betraied durst not crie out, for hee sawe it would not prevaile, but began to intreate Capnio and the mariners to be good to him, and to pittie his estate, hee was but a poore man that lived by his labour: they laughing to see the shepheard so afraide, made as much haste as they could, and set him aboorde. Porrus was no sooner in the shippe, but he saw Dorastus walking with Fawnia, yet he scarse knew her: for she had attired her selfe in riche apparell, which so increased her beauty, that shee resembled rather an Angell than a mortall creature.

Dorastus and Fawnia, were halfe astonished to see the olde shepherd, marvailing greatly what wind had brought him thither, til Capnio told them al the whole discourse: how Porrus was going to make his complaint to the King, if by pollicie he had not prevented him, and therefore now sith he was aboord, for the avoiding of further danger it were best to carrie him into Italy.

[1] soth *1588*.   [2] IV. 3. 770–2.

Dorastus praised greatly his mans devise, and allowed of his counsaile; but Fawnia (who stil feared Porrus, as her father) began to blush for shame, that by her meanes he should either incure daunger or displeasure.

The old shephard hearing this hard sentence, that he should on such a sodaine be caried from his Wife, his country, and kinsfolke, into a forraine Lande amongst straungers, began with bitter teares to make his complaint, and on his knees to intreate Dorastus, that pardoning his unadvised folly he would give him leave to goe home: swearing that hee would keepe all thinges as secret as they could wish. But these protestations could not prevaile, although Fawnia intreated Dorastus very earnestly, but the mariners hoisting their maine sailes waied ankers, and hailed into the deepe, where we leave them to the favour of the wind and seas, and returne to Egistus.[1]

Who having appointed this day to hunt in one of his Forrests, called for his sonne Dorastus to go sport himselfe, because hee saw that of late hee began to loure; but his men made answer that hee was gone abroade none knew whither, except he were gone to the grove to walke all alone, as his custome was to doe every day.

The King willing to waken him out of his dumpes, sent one of his men to goe seeke him, but in vaine, for at last he returned, but finde him he could not, so that the King went himselfe to goe see the sport; where passing away the day, returning at night from hunting, hee asked for his sonne, but he could not be heard of, which drave the King into a great choler: whereupon most of his Noblemen and other Courtiers poasted abroad to seek him, but they could not heare of him through all Sicilia, onely they missed Capnio his man, which againe made the King suspect that hee was not gone farre.

Two or three daies being passed, and no newes heard of Dorastus, Egistus began to feare that he was devoured with some wilde beastes,[2] and upon that made out a great troupe of men to go seeke him; who coasted through all the Country, and searched in everie daungerous and secrete place, untill at last they mette with a Fisherman that was sitting in a little covert hard by the sea side mending his nettes, when Dorastus and Fawnia tooke shipping: who being examined if he either knewe or heard where the Kings Sonne was, without any secrecie at all revealed the whole matter, how he was sayled two dayes past, and had in his company his man Capnio, Porrus and his faire Daughter Fawnia. This heavie newes was presently caryed to the King, who halfe dead for sorrow commaunded Porrus wife to be sent for: she being come to the Pallace, after due examination, confessed that her neighbours had oft told

---

[1] Shakespeare does so in V. 1, cutting out what happened on the ship.
[2] Like the bear in III. 3.

her that the Kings Sonne was too familier with Fawnia, her Daughter: whereuppon, her husband fearing the worst, about two dayes past (hearing the King should goe an hunting) rose earely in the morning and went to make his complaint, but since she neither hearde of him, nor saw him.

Egistus perceiving the womans unfeyned simplicity, let her depart without incurring further displeasure, conceiving such secret greefe for his Sonnes recklesse follie, that he had so forgotten his honour and parentage, by so base a choise to dishonor his father, and discredit himselfe, that with very care and thought he fel into a quartan fever, which was so unfit for his aged yeeres and complexion, that he became so weake, as the Phisitions would graunt him no life.

But his sonne Dorastus little regarded either father, countrie, or Kingdome in respect of his Lady Fawnia, for fortune smyling on this young novice, lent him so lucky a gale of winde, for the space of a day and a night, that the maryners lay and slept upon the hatches; but on the next morning about the breake of the day, the aire began to be overcast, the winds to rise, the seas to swel, yea presently there arose such a fearfull tempest, as the ship was in danger to be swallowed up with every sea, the maine mast with the violence of the wind was thrown over boord, the sayles were torne, the tacklings went in sunder, the storme raging still so furiously that poore Fawnia was almost dead for feare, but that she was greatly comforted with the presence of Dorastus. The tempest continued three dayes, al which time the Mariners everie minute looked for death, and the aire was so darkned with cloudes that the Maister could not tell by his compasse in what Coast they were. But upon the fourth day about ten of the clocke, the wind began to cease, the sea to waxe calme, and the sky to be cleare, and the Mariners descryed the coast of Bohemia, shooting of their ordnance for joy that they had escaped such a fearefull tempest.[1]

Dorastus hearing that they were arrived at some harbour, sweetly kissed Fawnia, and bad her be of good cheare: when they tolde him that the port belonged unto the cheife Cittie of Bohemia where Pandosto kept his Court, Dorastus began to be sad, knowing that his Father hated no man so much as Pandosto, and that the King himself had sought secretly to betray Egistus: this considered, he was halfe afraide to goe on land, but that Capnio counselled him to chaunge his name and his countrey, until such time as they could get some other barke to transport them into Italy. Dorastus liking this devise made his case privy to the Marriners, rewarding them bountifully for their paines, and charging them to saye that he was a

[1] Did Shakespeare recall this storm which led to happiness when planning *The Tempest*?

Gentleman of Trapalonia called Meleagrus. The shipmen willing to shew what friendship they could to Dorastus, promised to be as secret as they could, or hee might wish, and uppon this they landed in a little village a mile distant from the Citie, where after they had rested a day, thinking to make provision for their mariage, the fame of Fawnias beauty was spread throughout all the Citie, so that it came to the eares of Pandosto, who then being about the age of fifty, had notwithstanding yong and freshe affections:[1] so that he desired greatly to see Fawnia, and to bring this matter the better to passe, hearing they had but one man, and how they rested at a very homely house, he caused them to be apprehended as spies,[2] and sent a dozen of his garde to take them: who being come to their lodging, tolde them the Kings message. Dorastus no whit dismayed, accompanied with Fawnia and Capnio, went to the court (for they left Porrus to keepe the stuffe) who being admitted to the Kings presence, Dorastus and Fawnia with humble obeysance saluted his majestie.

Pandosto amased at the singular perfection of Fawnia, stood halfe astonished, viewing her beauty, so that he had almost forgot himselfe what hee had to doe: at last with stearne countenance he demaunded their names, and of what countrey they were, and what caused them to land in Bohemia. Sir (quoth Dorastus) know that my name is Meleagrus, a Knight borne and brought up in Trapalonia, and this gentlewoman, whom I meane to take to my wife is an Italian borne in Padua, from whence I have now brought her.[3] The cause I have so small a trayne with me is for that, her friends unwilling to consent, I intended secretly to convey her into Trapalonia; whither as I was sailing, by distresse of weather I was driven into these coasts: thus have you heard my name, my country, and the cause of my voiage. Pandosto starting from his seat as one in choller, made this rough reply.

Meleagrus, I feare this smooth tale hath but small trueth, and that thou coverest a foule skin with faire paintings. No doubt this Ladie by her grace and beauty is of her degree more meete for a mighty Prince, then for a simple knight, and thou like a perjured traitour hath bereft her of her parents, to their present griefe, and her insuing sorrow. Till therefore I heare more of her parentage and of thy calling, I wil stay you both here in Bohemia.

Dorastus, in whome rested nothing but Kingly valor, was not able to suffer the reproches of Pandosto, but that he made him this answer.

---

[1] Contrast Leontes, V. 1. 56–62; 81–4.
[2] Prospero accuses Ferdinand thus, *Tem* I. 2. 451–3.
[3] Florizel proclaims his identity but says that Perdita 'came from Libya', V. 1. 157.

It is not meete for a King, without due proofe to appeach any man of ill behaviour, nor upon suspition to inferre beleefe: straungers ought to bee entertained with courtesie, not to bee intreated with crueltie, least being forced by want to put up injuries, the Gods revenge their cause with rigor.

Pandosto hearing Dorastus utter these wordes, commaunded that he should straight be committed to prison, untill such time as they heard further of his pleasure, but as for Fawnia, he charged that she should be entertained in the Court, with such curtesie as belonged to a straunger and her calling. The rest of the shipmen he put into the Dungeon.

Having thus hardly handled the supposed Trapalonians, Pandosto contrarie to his aged yeares began to be somewhat tickled with the beauty of Fawnia, in so much that hee could take no rest, but cast in his old head a thousand new devises: at last he fell into these thoughtes.

How art thou pestred Pandosto with fresh affections, and unfitte fancies, wishing to possesse with an unwilling mynde, and a hot desire troubled with a could disdaine! Shall thy mynde yeeld in age to that thou hast resisted in youth? Peace Pandosto, blabbe not out that which thou maiest be ashamed to reveale to thy self. Ah, Fawnia is beautifull, and it is not for thine honour (fond foole) to name her that is thy Captive, and an other mans Concubine. Alas, I reach at that with my hand which my hart would faine refuse: playing like the bird Ibys in Egipt, which hateth Serpents, yet feedeth on their egges.

Tush, hot desires turne oftentimes to colde disdaine: Love is brittle, where appetite, not reason, beares the sway. Kinges thoughtes ought not to climbe so high as the heavens, but to looke no lower then honour: better it is to pecke at the starres with the young Eagles, then to prey on dead carkasses with the Vulture: tis more honourable for Pandosto to dye by concealing Love, then to enjoy such unfitte Love. Dooth Pandosto then love? Yea. Whome? A maid unknowne, yea and perhapps, immodest, stragled out of her owne countrie: beautifull, but not therefore chast: comely in bodie, but perhappes crooked in minde. Cease then Pandosto, to looke at Fawnia, much lesse to love her: be not overtaken with a womans beauty, whose eyes are framed by arte to inamour, whose hearte is framed by nature to inchaunt, whose false teares knowe their true times, and whose sweete wordes pearce deeper then sharpe swordes.

Here Pandosto ceased from his talke, but not from his love: for although he sought by reason, and wisedome to suppresse this franticke affection, yet he could take no rest, the beautie of Fawnia had made such a deepe impression in his heart. But on a day, walking abroad into a Parke which was hard adjoyning to his house, he sent by one of his servants for Fawnia, unto whome he uttered these wordes.

Fawnia, I commend thy beauty and wit, and now pittie thy distresse and want: but if you wilt forsake Sir Meleagrus, whose poverty, though a Knight, is not able to maintaine an estate aunswerable to thy beauty, and yeld thy consent to Pandosto, I wil both increase thee with dignities and riches. No sir, answered Fawnia: Meleagrus is a knight that hath wonne me by love, and none but he shal weare me:[1] his sinister mischance shall not diminishe my affection, but rather increase my good will. Thinke not though your Grace hath imprisoned him without cause, that feare shall make mee yeeld my consent: I had rather be Meleagrus wife, and a beggar, then live in plenty, and be Pandostos Concubine.

Pandosto, hearing the assured aunswere of Fawnia, would, notwithstanding, prosecute his suite to the uttermost: seeking with faire words and great promises to scale the fort of her chastitie, swearing that if she would graunt to his desire, Meleagrus should not only be set at libertie, but honored in his courte amongst his Nobles: but these alluring baytes could not intise her minde from the love of her newe betrothed mate Meleagrus: which Pandosto seeing, he left her alone for that time to consider more of the demaund. Fawnia, being alone by her selfe, began to enter into these solitarie meditations.

Ah, infortunate Fawnia, thou seest to desire above fortune is to strive against the Gods and Fortune. Who gazeth at the sunne weakeneth his sight: they which stare at the skie, fall oft into deepe pits: haddest thou rested content to have been a shepheard, thou needest not to have feared mischaunce. Better had it bene for thee, by sitting lowe, to have had quiet, then by climing high to have fallen into miserie. But alas, I feare not mine owne daunger, but Dorastus displeasure. Ah sweete Dorastus, thou art a Prince, but now a prisoner, by too much love procuring thine owne losse. Haddest thou not loved Fawnia thou haddest bene fortunate. Shall I then bee false to him that hath forsaken Kingdomes for my cause? No; would my death might deliver him, so mine honor might be preserved.

With that, fetching a deepe sigh, she ceased from her complaints, and went againe to the Pallace, injoying a libertie without content, and profered pleasure with smal joy. But poore Dorastus lay all this while in close prison, being pinched with a hard restraint, and pained with the burden of colde, and heavie Irons, sorrowing sometimes that his fond affection had procured him this mishappe, that by the disobedience of his parentes, he had wrought his owne

[1] I. 2. 307.

despight: an other while cursing the Gods and fortune, that they should crosse him with such sinister chaunce: uttering at last his passions in these words.

Ah unfortunate wretch, borne to mishappe, now thy folly hath his desert: Art thou not worthie for thy base minde to have bad fortune? could the destinies favour thee, which hast forgot thine honor and dignities? Wil not the Gods plague him with despight that payneth his father with disobedience? Oh Gods, if any favour or justice be left, plague me, but favour poore Fawnia, and shrowd her from the tirannies of wretched Pandosto, but let my death free her from mishap, and then, welcome death! Dorastus payned with these heavie passions, sorrowed and sighed, but in vaine, for which he used the more patience.

But againe to Pandosto, who broyling at the heat of unlawfull lust coulde take no rest but still felte his minde disquieted with his new love, so that his nobles and subjectes marveyled greatly at this sudaine alteration, not being able to conjecture the cause of this his continued care. Pandosto, thinking every hower a yeare til he had talked once againe with Fawnia, sent for her secretly into his chamber, whither though Fawnia unwillingly comming, Pandosto entertained her very courteously, using these familiar speaches, which Fawnia answered as shortly in this wise.

Pandosto

Fawnia, are you become lesse wilfull and more wise, to preferre the love of a King before the liking of a poore Knight? I thinke ere this you thinke it is better to be favoured of a King then of a subject.

Fawnia

Pandosto, the body is subject to victories, but the mind not to be subdued by conquest: honesty is to be preferred before honour, and a dramme of faith weigheth downe a tunne of gold. I have promised Meleagrus to love, and will performe no lesse.

Pandosto

Fawnia, I know thou art not so unwise in thy choice, as to refuse the offer of a King, nor so ingrateful as to dispise a good turne: thou art now in that place where I may commaunde, and yet thou seest I intreate. My power is such as I may compell by force, and yet I sue by prayers: Yeelde Fawnia thy love to him which burneth in thy love. Meleagrus shall be set free, thy countrymen discharged: and thou both loved and honoured.

Fawnia

I see, Pandosto, where lust ruleth it is a miserable thing to be a virgin, but know this, that I will alwaies preferre fame before life, and rather choose death then dishonour.

Pandosto seeing that there was in Fawnia a determinate courage to love Meleagrus, and a resolution without feare to hate him, flong away from her in a rage: swearing if in shorte time she would not be wonne with reason: he would forget all courtesie, and compel her to graunt by rigour: but these threatning wordes no whit dismayed Fawnia;[1] but that she still both dispighted and dispised Pandosto. While thus these two lovers strove, the one to winne love the other to live in hate: Egistus heard certaine newes by Merchauntes of Bohemia, that his sonne Dorastus was imprisoned by Pandosto, which made him feare greatly that his sonne should be but hardly intreated: yet considering that Bellaria and hee was cleared by the Oracle of Apollo from that crime wherewith Pandosto had unjustly charged them, hee thought best to send with all speed to Pandosto, that he should set free his sonne Dorastus, and put to death Fawnia and her father Porrus: finding this by the advise of Counsaile the speediest remedy to release his sonne, he caused presently two of his shippes to be rigged, and thoroughly furnished with provision of men and victuals, and sent divers of his nobles Embassadoures into Bohemia;[2] who willing to obey their King, and relieve[3] their yong Prince: made no delayes, for feare of danger, but with as much speed as might be, sailed towards Bohemia: the winde and seas favored them greatly, which made them hope of some good happe, for within three daies they were landed: which Pandosto no soner heard of their arrivall, but hee in person went to meete them,[4] intreating them with such sumptuous and familiar courtesie, that they might well perceive how sory he was for the former injuries hee had offered to their King, and how willing (if it might be) to make amendes.

As Pandosto made report to them, how one Meleagrus, a Knight of Trapolonia, was lately arived with a Lady called Fawnia in his land, comming very suspitiously, accompanied onely with one servant, and an olde shepheard. The Embassadours perceived by the halfe, what the whole tale ment, and began to conjecture, that it was Dorastus, who for feare to bee knowne, had chaunged his name:

---

[1] Cf. Perdita's courage, IV. 3. 449.
[2] Polixenes goes himself, V. 1. 178–89.
[3] receive *1588.*
[4] V. 1. 229–31.

but dissembling the matter, they shortly arived at the Court, where after they had bin verie solemnly and sumptuously feasted, the noble men of Sicilia being gathered togither, they made reporte of their Embassage: where they certified Pandosto that Meleagrus was sonne and heire to the King Egistus, and that his name was Dorastus: how contrarie to the Kings minde he had privily convaied away that Fawnia, intending to marrie her, being but daughter to that poore shepheard Porrus: whereupon the Kings request was that Capnio, Fawnia, and Porrus, might bee murthered and put to death, and that his sonne Dorastus might be sent home in safetie.[1]

Pandosto having attentively and with great mervaile heard their Embassage, willing to reconcile himselfe to Egistus, and to shew him how greatly he esteemed his favour: although love and fancy forbad him to hurt Fawnia, yet in despight of love hee determined to execute Egistus will without mercy; and therefore he presently sent for Dorastus out of prison, who mervailing at this unlooked for curtesie, found at his coming to the Kings presence, that which he least doubted of, his fathers Embassadours: who no sooner sawe him, but with great reverence they honored him: and Pandosto embracing Dorastus, set him by him very lovingly in a chaire of estate. Dorastus ashamed that his follie was bewraied, sate a long time as one in a muse, til Pandosto told him the summe of his Fathers embassage: which he had no sooner heard, but he was toucht at the quicke, for the cruell sentence that was pronounced against Fawnia: but neither could his sorrow nor perswasions prevaile, for Pandosto commaunded that Fawnia, Porrus, and Capnio, should bee brought to his presence; who were no sooner come, but Pandosto having his former love turned to a disdainfull hate, began to rage against Fawnia in these tearmes.

Thou disdainfull vassal, thou currish kite,[2] assigned by the destinies to base fortune, and yet with an aspiring minde gazing after honour: how durst thou presume, being a beggar, to match with a Prince? By thy alluring lookes to inchant the sonne of a King to leave his owne countrie to fulfill thy disordinate lusts?[3] O despightfull minde, a proud heart in a beggar is not unlike to a great fire in a smal cottage, which warmeth not the house, but burneth it: assure thy selfe that thou shalt die, and thou old doating foole, whose follie hath bene such, as to suffer thy daughter to reach above thy fortune, looke for no other meede, but the like punishment.[4] But Capnio, thou which hast betrayed the King, and has consented to the unlawfull

---

[1] V. 1. 180–5.
[2] Cf. the thievish kite in IV. 2. 23.
[3] Cf. IV. 3. 429–33; 441–8.
[4] IV. 3. 427–9. Leontes is more sympathetic, V. 1. 229–32.

lust of thy Lord and maister, I know not how justly I may plague thee: death is too easie a punishment for thy falsehood, and to live (if not in extreme miserie) were not to shew thee equitie. I therefore award that thou shall have thine eyes put out, and continually while thou diest, grinde in a mil like a brute beast. The feare of death brought a sorrowfull silence upon Fawnia and Capnio, but Porrus seeing no hope of life, burst forth into these speeches.

Pandosto, and ye noble Embassadours of Sicilia, seeing without cause I am condemned to die; I am yet glad I have opportunitie to disburden my conscience before my death: I will tel you as much as I know, and yet no more than is true: whereas I am accused that I have bene a supporter of Fawnias pride, and shee disdained as a vilde begger, so it is that I am neither Father unto her, nor she daughter unto me. For so it happened that I being a poore shepheard in Sicilia, living by keeping other mens flockes: one of my sheepe straying downe to the sea side, as I went to seeke her, I saw a little boat driven upon the shoare, wherein I found a babe of sixe daies olde, wrapped in a mantle of skarlet, having about the necke this chaine: I pittying the child, and desirous of the treasure, carried it home to my wife, who with great care nursed it up, and set it to keepe sheepe. Here is the chaine and the Jewels, and this Fawnia is the childe whome I found in the boate. What shee is, or of what parentage, I knowe not, but this I am assured that she is none of mine.[1]

Pandosto would scarce suffer him to tell out his tale, but that he enquired the time of the yeere, the manner of the boate, and other circumstaunces, which when he found agreeing to his count, he sodainelie leapt from his seate, and kissed Fawnia, wetting her tender cheeks with his teares, and crying, My daughter Fawnia, ah sweete Fawnia, I am thy Father, Fawnia. This sodaine passion of the King drave them all into a maze, especially Fawnia and Dorastus. But when the King had breathed himselfe a while in this newe joy, he rehearsed before the Embassadours the whole matter, how he hadde entreated his wife Bellaria for jealousie, and that this was the childe whome hee sent to floate in the seas.[2]

Fawnia was not more joyfull that she had found such a Father, then Dorastus was glad he should get such a wife. The Embassadors rejoyced that their yong prince had made such a choice, that those Kingdomes which through enmitie had long time bin disseuered, should now through perpetual amitie be united and reconciled. The Citizens and subjects of Bohemia (hearing that the King had found againe his Daughter, which was supposed dead, joyfull that there was an heire apparent to his Kingdome) made Bonfires and showes

---

[1] V. 2. 1–8. The Gentleman certainly makes 'a broken delivery of the business'.
[2] V. 2. 31–42.

throughout the Cittie. The Courtiers and Knights appointed Justs
and Turneis to signifie their willing mindes in gratifying the Kings
hap.

Eighteene daies being past in these princely sports, Pandosto,
willing to recompence old Porrus, of a shepheard made him a
Knight:[1] which done, providing a sufficient Navie to receive him
and his retinue, accompanied with Dorastus, Fawnia, and the Sicilian
Embassadours, he sailed towards Sicilia, where he was most princelie
entertained by Egistus;[2] who hearing this comicall event, rejoyced
greatly at his sonnes good happe, and without delay (to the perpetuall joy of the two yong Lovers) celebrated the marriage: which
was no sooner ended, but Pandosto (calling to mind how first he
betraied his friend Egistus, how his jealousie was the cause of
Bellarias death, that contrarie to the law of nature hee had lusted
after his owne Daughter) moved with these desperate thoughts, he
fell into a melancholie fit, and to close up the Comedie with a
Tragicall stratageme, he slewe himselfe,[3] whose death being many
daies bewailed of Fawnia, Dorastus, and his deere friend Egistus,
Dorastus taking his leave of his father, went with his wife and the
dead corps into Bohemia, where after they were[4] sumptuouslie intoombed, Dorastus ended his daies in contented quiet.

FINIS

II. Analogue

From
THE COUNTESSE OF PEMBROKES ARCADIA
by Sir Philip Sidney (1590)

Lib. I.

[Pamela tells how she was saved from a savage bear, and the
courtiers are entertained by the shepherds.]

Being al now come together, & all desirous to know each others
adventures, *Pamelas* noble hart would needs gratefully make knowne
the valiant mean of her safety: which (directing her speach to her

---

[1] Cf. V. 2. 57–9; 130–49. Shakespeare gets good fun out of it.
[2] Cf. V. 2. 42–55.
[3] Contrast Leontes's happier fate, V. 3. 111ff.
[4] Should be 'Pandosto was'. Doubtless he was 'sumptuouslie intoombed' with his
wife Bellaria.

mother) she did in this manner. As soone (said she) as ye were all run away, and that I hoped to be in safetie, there came out of the same woods a foule horrible Beare, which (fearing belike to deale while the Lion was present, as soone as he was gone) came furiously towards the place where I was, and this young shepheard left alone by me; I truly (not guilty of any wisedome, which since they lay to my charge, because they say, it is the best refuge against that beast, but even pure feare bringing forth that effect of wisedome) fell downe flat of my face, needing not counterfait being dead, for indeed I was litle better.

But this shepheard having no other weapon, but that knife you see, standing before the place where I lay, so behaved him selfe, that the first sight I had (when I thought my selfe nearer *Charons* ferry,) was the shepheard shewing me his bloudy knife in token of victory. I pray you (saide *Zelmane*, speaking to *Dorus*, whose valour she was carefull to have manifested) in what sorte, so ill weaponed, could you atchive this enterprise? Noble Ladie (saide *Dorus*) the manner of these beastes fighting with any man, is to stande up upon their hinder feete: and so this did, & being ready to give me a shrewd imbracement, I thinke, the God *Pan*, (ever carefull of the chiefe blessings of *Arcadia*) guided my hand so just to the hart of the beast, that neither she could once touch me, nor (which is the only matter in this worthy remembrance) breed any danger to the Princesse. For my part, I am rather (with all subjected humblenes) to thanke her excellencies, since the duety thereunto gave me harte to save myselfe, then to receive thankes for a deede, which was her onely inspiring.

And this *Dorus* spake, keeping affection as much as he could, backe from comming into his eyes and gestures. But *Zelmane* (that had the same Character in her heart) could easily discerne it, and therefore to keepe him the longer in speach, desired to understand the conclusion of the matter; and how the honest *Dametas* was escaped.

Nay (said *Pamela*) none shall take that office from my selfe, being so much bound to him as I am, for my education. And with that word (scorne borrowing the countenance of myrth) somewhat she smiled, and thus spake on. When (said she) *Dorus* made me assuredly perceive, that all cause of feare was passed (the truth is) I was ashamed to finde my selfe alone with this shepheard: and therefore looking about me, if I could see any bodie; at length we both perceived the gentle *Dametas*, lying with his breast and head as farre as he could thrust himselfe into a bush: drawing up his legges as close unto him as hee coulde: for, like a man of a very kind nature, soone to take pittie of himselfe, he was full resolved not to see his owne death.[1] And when this shepheard pushed him, bidding him to be of

[1] Note a similar proximity of horror and humour in *WT*, III. 3.

good cheere; it was a good while, ere we could perswade him, that *Dorus* was not the beare: so that he was faine to pull him out by the heeles, & shew him the beast, as deade as he could wish it: which you may beleeve me, was a very joyful sight unto him. But then he forgate al curtesie, for he fel upon the beast, giving it many a manfull wound: swearing by much, it was not wel such beasts shuld be suffered in a common welth. And then my governour, as full of joy, as before of feare, came dauncing and singing before us as even now you saw him. Well wel (said *Basilius*) I have not chosen *Dametas* for his fighting, nor for his discoursing, but for his plainenesse and honestie, and therein I know he will not deceave me.

But then he told *Pamela* (not so much because she should know it, as because he would tell it) the wonderfull act *Zelmane* had perfourmed, which *Gynecia* likewise spake off.

[Zelmane has killed the lion. The shepherd Dorus is taken into Basilius's service and Dametas is told to 'receive him like a sonne into his house'.]

Dametas, no whit out of countenance with all that had bene said (because he had no worse to fal into then his owne) accepted *Dorus*: and with all, telling *Basilius*, that some of the shepheards were come; demaunded in what place he would see their sports: who first curious to know whether it were not more requisite for *Zelmanes* hurt to rest, then sit up at those pastimes; and she (that felt no wound but one) earnestly desiring to have Pastorals, *Basilius* commanded it should be at the gate of the lodge: where the throne of the Prince being (according to the auncient manner) he made *Zelmane* sit betweene him & his wife therin, who thought her selfe betweene drowning and burning: and the two young Ladies of either side the throne, and so prepared their eyes and eares to bee delighted by the shepheards. . .

The first Eclogues

Basilius, because *Zelmane* so would have it, used the artificiall day of torches, to lighten the sports their inventions could minister. And yet because many more shepheards were newly come, then at the first; he did in a gentle manner chastise the cowardise of the fugitive shepheards: with making them (for that night) the Torch-bearers, and the others later come, he willed with all freedome of speech and behaviour, to keepe their accustomed method. Which while they prepared to do, *Dametas*, who much disdained (since his late authority) all his old companions, brought his servant *Dorus* in good acquaintance and allowance of them, & himselfe stood like a directer over them, with nodding, gaping, winking, or stamping shewing how he did like, or mislike those things he did not understand. The first sports the shepheards shewed, were full of such leapes & gambols, as being accorded to the Pipe (which they bare in their mouthes, even as they daunced) made a right picture of their chiefe god *Pan*, and his companions the *Satyres*.[1] Then would they cast away their Pipes; and holding hand in hand, daunce as it were in a braule, by the onely cadence of their voices, which they would use in singing some short coplets, whereto the one halfe beginning, the other halfe should answere . . . Then all joyning their voyces, and dauncing a faster measure, they would conclude with some such words:

> *As without breath, no pipe doth move,*
> *No musike kindly without love.*

Having thus varied both their songs and daunces into divers sorts of inventions; their last sport was one of them to provoke another to a more large expressing of his passions: which *Lalus* (accounted one of the best singers amongst them) having marked in *Dorus* dauncing, no lesse good grace & handsome behaviour, then extreame tokens of a travelled minde;[2] began first with his Pipe, and then with his voice, thus to chalenge *Dorus*, and was by him answered in the underwritten sort . . .

[1] Compare the Satyr dance in *WT*, IV. 3. 329–48.
[2] In IV. 3 Florizel takes part in a shepherds' dance with Perdita and her dancing is praised by Polixenes (176).

III. Analogue

From
PARISMENOS
[by Emmanuel Forde] (1609 edn)

Parismenos. The Second Part of the most famous, delect
able, and pleasant Hystorie of Parismus, the renowmed
Prince of Bohemia.

[After Pollipus and Violetta have been married they leave
Thessaly for Bohemia with Parismus.]

Chap. I

Pollipus and Violetta upon a day walkt foorth for recreation, some
halfe mile from the Court, unto a most pleasant shadie greene wood,
which by meanes of the coolenesse and aboundance of sweete
smelling flowers, wherewith it was adorned, and by naturall sleight
was so pavised, with the assistance of little twigges and sprayes, that
neither the heate of the Sonne, nor vehemence of winde could
molest it, that the place seemed to adde increase to their delight,
where they lovingly sat downe, recreating themselves with great
pleasure, and at last fell both asleepe, in middest of which slumber, a
ravenous wilde Beare that haunted those woods, whom extreame
hunger had forced to wander so neare the Courte, winded them, and
guided by unluckie Fate, came to the place where they laye, ready to
seize upon the tender bodie of kinde *Violetta*, who at the verie instant
(by the Divine Providence) awaked, and espying the uglie Beare,
suddainely shriked. *Pollipus* amazed with her crie, started up and
drewe out his swoord, and rescued her from the beastes violence,
pursuing him with such vigor and dexteritie, that the Beare beeing
grevously wounded, shund his blowes, and made hast to get away
from him, but hee intending to win honour by his conquest, regard-
lessly pursued the Beare, untill he was quite out of Violetta's sight.
Who likewise fearing his harme, and pricked forward with a
tender care of his welfare, followed after him, but not knowing
which way he was gone, tooke a quite contrarie way and with
eager steppes laboured to overtake him. He having with much travel
slaine the Beare, smote off his head, and intending to present that
spoyle to his Love, came back to the place where hee had left her,

and missing her, hee should not well tell what to thinke, being perswaded shee was gone to seeke him, wherewith he was wrapt in to an
extreame perplexitie and doubt . . .

[Pollipus throws down the bear's head and rides into the
forest, followed by Parismus his lord. Meanwhile Violetta
wanders on and is seized by Archas the Cruel, who imprisons
her in his castle and endeavours to overcome her chastity.]

IV. Possible Source

From
MUCEDORUS
Anon. (1610 edn)

A most pleasant Comedie of Mucedorus . . . Amplified
with new additions, as it was acted before the king's
Majestie at White-hall on Shrove-Sunday night. By his
Highnes Servants usually playing at the Globe. Very
delectable, and full of conceited Mirth. For William
Jones. 1610.

[This edition (Q 3) adds several scenes including a Prologue
between Comedy and Envy. In I. 1 Mucedorus tells his friend
Anselmo that he intends to seek out the 'beautious Amadine',
Princess of Aragon, and to go in disguise. Anselmo objects.]

ANS.	That action craves no counsell,
	Since what you rightly are will more commaund
	Then best usurped shape.
MU.	Thou still art opposite in disposition:
	A more obscure servile habillament
	Beseemes this enterprise.
ANS.	Then like a Florentine or Mountebancke?
MU.	'Tis much too tedious; I dislike thy judgement:
	My minde is grafted on an humbler stocke.[1]
ANS.	Within my Closet does there hang a Cassocke,
	Though base the weede is; t'was a Shepheards,
	Which I presented in Lord Julios Maske.

[1] Often paralleled to *WT*, IV. 3. 92–3; see *supra*, p. 128.

MU.   That, my Anselmo, and none else but that,
        Maske Mucedorus from the vulgar view!
        That habite suites my minde: fetch me that weede.

                                        [*Exit Anselmo.*

        Better then Kinges have not disdained that state,
        And much inferiour, to obtaine their mate.[1]

Act I, Scene 2[2]

Enter Mouse with a bottle[3] of Hay.

MOUS.   O horrible, terrible! Was ever poore Gentleman so scard
out of his seaven Senses? A Beare? nay, sure it cannot be a Beare, but
som Divell in a Beares Doublet: for a Beare could never have had
that agilitie to have frighted me. Well, Ile see my Father hang'd,
before Ile serve his Horse any more. Well, Ile carry home my Bottle
of Hay, and for once make my Father's Horse turne Puritane and
observe Fasting dayes, for he gets not a bit. But soft! this was she
followed me, therefore Ile take the other Path; and because Ile be
sure to have an eye on him, I will take handes with some foolish
Creditor, and make every step backward.

*As he goes backwards the Beare comes in, and he tumbles over her, and runnes
away and leaves his bottle of Hay behind him.*

Scene 3

Enter Segasto runing and Amadine after him, being persued with a beare.

SEG.   O fly, Madam, fly or els we are but dead.
AMA.   Help, *Segasto*, help! help! help! swet Segasto, or els I die.
SEG.   Alas, madam, there is no way but flight;
        Then hast and save your selfe.

Segasto runnes away.

AMA.   Why then I die; ah help me in distresse!

*Enter Mucedorus like a sheapheard with a sworde drawne and a beares head
in his hande.*

MU.   Stay, Lady, stay, and be no more dismaide . . .

---

[1] Cf. IV. 3. 25–31, but Shakespeare went to *Pandosto*.
[2] Both I. 1 and I. 2 were added in 1610. I. 3 (here cited from 1598) originally began
the play.
[3] a bundle.

[She accepts the bear's head which he offers her, and tells him how the animal pursued her and Segasto. She will see that the shepherd's courage is rewarded.]

Scene 4

[Segasto regrets his cowardice but does not give up hope of winning Amadine. When Mouse runs in he pretends to know nothing of any bear, but invites Mouse to be his man.]

MOUS.   Clubs, prongs, pitchforks, billes! O helpe! a beare, a beare, a beare!

SEG.   Still beares, and nothing else but beares. Tell me, sirra, wher she is.

CLO.   O sir, she is runne downe the woods: I saw her white head and her white belly.

SEG.   Thou talkest of wonders, to tell me of white bears. But, sirra, didst thou ever see any such?

CLO.   No, faith, I never sawe any such, but I remember my fathers woordes: hee bad mee take heede that I was not caught with a white beare.

SEG.   A lamentable tale, no dout.

[Mouse tells how he saw the bear and ran away. 'I saw nothing but her whit head, and whit belly.' Segasto invites him to be his man and go to the King's court.]

CLO.   King of the land! I never see him.

SEG.   If thou wilt dwel with me, thou shallt see him everie day.

CLO.   Shal I go home againe to be torne in peces with beares? no, not I. I wil go home and put on a cleane shirt, and then goe drowne my selfe.

SEG.   Thou shallt not need; if thou wilt dwell with me, thou shalt want nothing.

CLO.   Shal I not? then heares my hand; ile dwel with you. And harke you, sir, now you have entertained me, I wil tell you what I can doe: I can keepe my tongue from picking and stealing, and my handes from lying and slaundering, I warrant you, as wel as ever you had man in all your life . . .

[Segasto gets Captain Tremelio to attack Mucedorus. When the latter in defending himself kills Tremelio, he is accused of murder, and saved from execution by Amadine, who shows

her father the bear's head and tells how 'he reached after me,/
And hardly did I oft escape his pawes,/Till at the length this
shepheard came,/And brought to me his head.' (II. 4)]

V. Probable Source

From
THE FISHERMAN'S TALE and
FLORA'S FORTUNE
by Francis Sabie (1595)[1]

A. From THE FISHERMAN'S TALE

[An aged fisherman tells his life-story to the poet, who, caught
in a storm at sea, has taken shelter on 'A rocke whereon a
cabbin small was built'. The storm is described in conventional
terms].

> But see what chanc'd, a sudden storme arose,
> Skies looked blacke, clouds overwhelmed the skies . . .
> Seas sweld, ropes crackt, sailes rent, shipmen cride out,
> Ay me, poore wretch, my little fleeting barke
> Leapt like a feather, tost with blastes of wind:
> One while it seemde the loftie skies to touch,
> Straightwaies I thought it went to Plutoes lake . . .[2]

[Thinking that the old man must be a god he begs him to
quell the storm. The old man tells him that he is Cassander, an
Earl who fought in the Holy Land against the Pagans and
after long warfare in many lands came to Arcadia,]

> Where manie troupes of love-bewitched swaines
> Sit under shades, and leave-behanged trees,
> Resounding ditties to their trulles on pipes,
> Or telling ancient histories of love . . .
> I sawe one Lasse farre comelier than the rest,
> A peerlesse peece, an heart-delighting gyrle,
> An heavenly Nymph . . .

[1] *The Fisherman's Tale: Of the famous Actes, Life and love of Cassander, a Grecian
Knight*, by Francis Sabie, 1595. *Flora's Fortune. The Second part and finishing of the
Fisherman's Tale. By F.S.* 1595.
[2] Cf. the storm in *WT* III. 3. 2–6; 53–5; 81–92.

She seeing her so vewed on of me,
Began to change her countenance so sweet,
Even like *Aurora* when her *Phoebus* faire
She welcometh, her colour went and came,
Then who had seene her, would have doubtles said,
A goddesse she, no mortal wight had bene.
In beauty she did *Venus* farre surpasse:
In modesty *Diana* she did staine . . .
Good Lord, how long could I have found in heart,
T'have gazed on her mind-rejoycing shape.
Whole dayes, whole yeares, my life I could have spent
In vewing her.[1] But modesty forbad.
I went from thence, but altogether lame,
And wounded with a fire-burning dart,
My sences sad, heart metamorphosed.

[He asked an old man near by about the shepherdess.]

She is (quoth he) supposde the daughter of
Old *Thirsis*, she her selfe doth know no lesse.
She is not so, I heard him oft times say,
(He is my brother) that he founde her young
Wrapt in a skarlet mantle, rich in price,
As once he passed by the silver streame
Of *Humber*, lying in a wherrie boate.
He brought her up; 'ful many wold her have,
But she rejecteth all, I muse at it.

[The story follows Greene closely, in passionate soliloquies and imagery.]

Love conquers all things; it hath conquered
Apollo once, it made him be a swaine.
Yea, mightie *Mars* in armes invincible,
It forced hath to lay aside his speare.
Love made the sea-god take a Wesils shape,
Yea mightie *Jove*, whose rage makes earth to shake,
Love made to take the snow-white shape of Bull:[2]
And shall not then *Cassander* yeeld to love?

[There is some realism in his account of how he turned shepherd.]

[1] Cf. IV. 3. 109–10.
[2] IV. 3. 25–31.

I cut mine haire; instead of silken robes
I bought a sute of cuntry russet cloth:
A paire of slops I put upon my legs,
A leather scrip I hung about my necke,
And for my palfrey, a cut-taile dog I got.
I bought me sheepe, and cotes; I was content
To be a shepherd to obtaine my love.

[Meanwhile Flora too is distressed:]

I am a base and flock-attending drudge,
And he (quoth she) an high-conceited Knight . . .
Art thou in love, fond foole, whom doest thou love?
A stragling Knight, some faithlesse run-away,
What canst thou tel? perhaps he hath deceiv'd
A number of such wanton gyrles as thou?
Ah but hees faire. What then? Doth not the Moth
Sooner corrupt a fine than naughtie cloth? . . .
O no, it cannot be that he is false.
Oh would I had him, were he ne'er so false . . .

[Cassander now woos her as a shepherd recently arrived in
the district, promising her freedom from hardship and danger.]

So (saith she) shunning vast Charibdis gulfe,
I should int' Silla fal, as bad or worse.
Then children come, then charge of keeping house,
Then mickle woes, but little joyes arise.
My mother oft hath told me in a rage,
That I live like a Lady unto her.
I (saith she) care for all things which be done,
I serve the Swine, I give the Pulhens meat,
I fret, I chide, I never am at rest,
And thou doest nought but walke the pleasant fieldes,[1]
Thy greatest labour is a meere delight.
I but (quoth I) thy mother tels thee so,
When she doth chafe and chide with thee, because
She would have thee be pleasde with thine estate,
But if she might a Queene or Empresse be,
She would not leade a single life againe.
  Some other talk would better please my mind,
I am not yet disposde (saith she) to wed,

---

[1] Possibly the basis of IV. 3. 55–64.

Know that thou art not first I have repeld:
Cease therefore, yet I can, nor will not wed.
　Then I replyde, if thou wilt not me love,
A simple swaine, love me a noble Knight.
That Knight I am whom lately thou espiedst,
Range through the plaines upon a courser brave . . .
Setting apart my fame and dignity,
I am content thou seest to be a Swaine.
O would I might be still a Swaine, so that
I might once get thy chiefe desired love.

[Flora still refuses to surrender.]

　Then cease, sir Knight, leave off your fayned sute,
The law of nature seemes it to resist.
Two things contrarie never can agree;
My birth is meane, yours noble, I am poore,
You rich, alas, what kind of match is this?
　Hereat she staid, and I replyed thus:
No *Flora*, no, tis not your meane estate,
Nor ofspring vile which can detract my love.
Love is a god, regarding no estate:
It striketh where, and when, and whom it list,
It maketh rich and poore have all one mind,
It maketh prince and people all alike.
It maketh swaines and high-conceited Knights
To beare one heart, one mind, and both content.

[At length, convinced of his faithfulness, she accepts him, and they meet often, until Thirsis learns of it and takes her place with the sheep. Cassander then disguises himself as a cripple-beggar.]

I laid aside my countrie Swaines attire,
And baser weeds upon me I did put.
With rags and tags my selfe I did abase,
A filthy cloth about my head I knit,
One leg I bolstred out with dyrtie clothes,
As though it had bene swolne with festred sores,
A crouch in hand and wallet at my backe,
So cripple-like I went to Thirsis doore.
　There first I praid and made mine orison,
As beggars use before they crave their almes:

Then crav'd their good will and benevolence,
In doleful wise and lamentable sort.
My Flora, who was always ready prest
To aide the poore whome Fortune frownde upon,
To th' ambrie ran, and cut a slunch of bread
And cheese, she thought a charitable deed.
Here (saith she) pray that I may have my wish.
Then lookt I up; she foorthwith fetcht a sigh,
And knew I was *Cassander* her true love.
Help, my *Cassander*, help me now, she said,
Or *Coridon* must me enjoy, thy love:
My father said I shall tomorrow wed,
Love or love not, for time will breede content.
Nay, weel prevent him if thou wilt (quoth I)
In carelesse bed when parents lie at night,
Unlocke the doores, and secretly come out.
Ile be preparde, Ile carie thee away,
So weel escape and remedie these evils.
This said, she beckned with her hand, as though
That I had said did please her very well,
Then went from me and ran into the house:
And time it was, her mother came apace.
Then praying for my maister and my Dame,
I went away, still leaning on my crutch,
But when I came int' fields out of their sights,
My crutch, my weeds, and scrip I threw away.
Then who had seene me would not have supposde
I had bene hee which halted so ere while.
Unto the port I went, two ships there found,
All furnished and readie to lanche out.

[He arranges a passage to Greece, and at night Flora creeps from the house to where he waits outside. Cassander's horse neighs and wakes old Thirsis, who runs after them. Afraid that he will rouse the neighbourhood with his cries, Cassander carries him aboard and they sail away. A tempest breaks up the vessel. Cassander is swept away but swims to some rocks, where he becomes a hermit, ever mourning his lost love.]

B. From FLORA'S FORTUNE

In his *Preface* the poet writes: 'To expell (scorn-hating Reader) the accustomed tediousnes of colde Winters nightes, and partlie to beguile slouth-causing sleepe, which other wise would have claimed some interest in an unbusied braine, I tooke pen in hand and . . . wrote the late-published Poem of the Fishermans Tale.'

[Flora and her Sire are wrecked on Delphos Isle and consult the Oracle. They proceed to Greece, where Thirsis, becoming famous as Apollo's prophet, buys flocks and herds which Flora tends, while singing sad echo-songs and sighing for Cassander. She rejects all suitors. The poet now tells of her birth after her mother Queen Julina was wrongfully accused of adultery through the lust and treachery of King Palemon's counsellor Eristo (*supra*, p. 129). Julina (unlike Hermione) declares vengefully that she will haunt her husband if he has her executed. Slightly more like Shakespeare is Palemon's decision at the trial to send to consult the Oracle before the baby is born,[1] on the advice of 'a grave and senile Earle'.]

> Thou hast condemn'd thy royall Queene to die,
> Accused by *Eristoes* sole complaint.
> He doth accuse, and she excuse her selfe,
> He moov'd with rage, and she to save her life.
> Now if thou wilt have her to see her fault,
> And all men know that she doth rightly die,
> Let her againe be sent to prison close,
> And send thou to the crime-disclosing God,
> Or *Themis* wise . . .
> *Apollo* or wise *Themis* will declare,
> Her treacherous deed, so shall she justly die . . .
> *Palemon* might full well have bene condemn'd
> Of rigor, should he have mislik'd of this:
> To prison backe he sent *Julina* chaste,
> *Julina*, who with child was verie big;
> Which when *Palemon* saw, and did behold
> Her womb, which sweld with ofspring therein closde,
> He sware by heaven, and all the Gods therein,
> The bastard brat should smart for Sires offence.
> Two Noble men were speedily sent foorth
> To *Themis* Church, her Oracle to fetch,
> And she again to dreadfull dungeon sent,
> Expecting alwaies when she should bring foorth.
>   Th'expected houre now came, she cride and gron'd,
> Intreating *Juno* for deliverance.

[1] Cf. II. 1. 181–6. In Greene it occurs after the child has been cast adrift.

Juno releasde her, *Juno* heard her sute,
She on the flintes, no midwife helping her,
O dolefull case, a daughter sweet brought foorth.
Soone brought *Pandion* keeper of the Jaile
These tidings to *Palemon* fretting king,
He straightway charg'd him take the bastard brat,
Throw't in a box, and let it flote on seas:
For so (saith he) by some sinister chance,
Or death it shal for Sires offences smart.
He foorthwith came, and told the wretched Queen,
These heavie newes: who can expresse her mone?

[Sabie, however, does his best at some length before the baby
is 'layd in wherry boate' and thrust off. Meanwhile the messengers reached the Temple of Themis and obtained at once
from the goddess a sealed Oracle, which, when opened, changed
Palemon's intention of burning his wife into remorse.]

The Noble men unbinding their good Queene,
Gan comfort her with delectable words,
Affirming that *Palemon* did repent
Him of the rigour he to her had showne;
Which she might see in punishing her foes.
Poore wretch, she cast her eies upon the ground,
Refusing on *Palemon* once to looke,
Increasing rivers with her spring of teares:
Her golden lockes once trimd with pretious gems,
With furious hands now from her head she pluckt . . .
Her snowie cheeks, once intermixt with red,
A yellow hue and ashie visage staind.
Naught on her bodie now but bones were seene,
A grieslie Ghost, and bony shape she seem'd,
And in short time, outworne with fretting griefe,
Death finished her miserable life.

[Her funeral and epitaph are described; then the story turns
to the discovery of the child by the shepherd Thirsis, and her
upbringing until the arrival of Cassander.]

VI. Sources

From
A.   THE SECOND PART OF
CONNY-CATCHING
by R[obert] G[reene] (1592)

I   *A kinde conceit of a Foist performed in Paules.*

While I was writing this discovery of foysting, & was desirous of any
intelligence that might be given mee, a Gentleman, a friend of mine,
reported unto me this pleasant tale of a foist, and as I well remember
it grewe to this effect. There walked in the midle walke a plaine
Country farmer, a man of good wealth, who had a well lined purse,
onely barely thrust up in a round slop, which a crue of foists having
perceived, their hearts were set on fire to have it, & every one had a
fling at him, but all in vaine, for he kept his hand close in his pocket,
and his purse fast in his fist like a subtil churle, that either had been
forwarnd of Pauls, or els had afortime smokt some of that faculty.
Well, howsoever it was impossible to do any good with him, he was
so warie. The foists spying this, strained their wits to the highest string
how to compasse this boung, yet could not al their politike conceits
fetch the farmer over, for iustle him, chat with him, offer to shake
him by the hand, all would not serve to get his hand out of his
pocket. At last one of the crue that for his skill might have bene
Doctorat in his misterie, amongst them all choose out a good foist,
one of a nimble hand and great agility, and said to the rest thus:
Masters it shall not be said such a base pesant shall slip away from
such a crue of Gentlemen foists as wee are, and not have his purse
drawen, and therefore this time Ile play the staull my selfe, and if I
hit him not home, count mee for a bungler for ever, and so left them
and went to the farmer and walkt directly before him and next him
three or foure turnes; at last standing still, he cried, Alas honest man
helpe me, I am not well, & with that sunck downe suddenly in a
sown,[1] the pore Farmer seeing a proper yong Gentleman (as hee
thought) fall dead afore him, stept to him, helde him in his armes,
rubd him & chaft him: at this there gathered a great multitude of
people about him, and the whilest the Foiste drewe the farmers
purse and away: by that the other thought the feat was done, he
began to come something to himselfe againe, and so halfe staggering,
stumbled out of Paules, and went after the crue where they had

Cf. Autolycus and the Clown, IV. 2. 35ff.

appointed to meet, and there boasted of his wit and experience. The farmer little suspecting this villany, thrust his hand into his pocket and mist his purse, searcht for it, but lining and shels & all was gone, which made the Country man in a great maze, that he stood stil in a dumpe so long, that a Gentleman perceiving it asked what he aild: What aile I, sir? quoth he, truly I am thinking how men may long as wel as women. Why doest thou coniecture that, honest man, quoth he? Marry sir, answers the farmer, the gentleman even now that sowned heer, I warrant him breeds his wives childe, for the cause of his sodaine qualme that he fel down dead grew of longing. The gentleman demanded how he knew that. Wel enough, sir, quoth he, and hee hath his longing too, for the poore man longed for my purse, and thanks be to God he hath it with him. At this al the hearers laught, but not so merrily as the foist and his fellows, that then were sharing his money.

II(i) *The discovery of the courbing law.*

The Courber, which the common people call the Hooker, is he that with a Curb (as they tearm it) or hook, doth pul out of a window any loose linnen cloth, apparell, or els any other houshold stuffe whatsoeuer, which stolne parcels, they in their Art cal snappings:[1] to the performance of this law there be required, duly two persons, the Curber and the Warpe: the curber his office is to spye in the day time fit places wher his trade may be practised at night, and comming unto anie window if it be open, then he hath his purpose, if shut, then growing into the nature of the blacke Art, hath his trickers, which are engins of Iron so cunningly wrought, that he wil cut a barre of Iron in two with them so easily, that scarcely shal the standers by heare him: then when hee hath the window open and spies any fat snappinges worth the Curbing, then streight he sets the Warp to watch, who hath a long cloke to couer what soeuer he gets: then doth the other thrust in a long hooke some nine foote in length (which he calleth a curbe) that hath at the end a crooke, with three tynes turned contrary, so that tis unpossible to misse, if there be any snappinges abroad. Nowe this long hooke they call a Curbe, and because you shall not woonder how they carrie it for being spied, know this that it is made with joyntes like an angle rod, and can be conveyed into the forme of a truncheon, and worne in the hand like a walking staffe untill they come to their purpose, and then they let it out at the length, and hook or curb whatsoever is loose and within the reach, and then he conveies it to the Warp, and from thence (as they list) their snappings go to the Broker or to the Bawd, and there

[1] 'a snapper-up of unconsidered trifles', IV. 2. 26.

they have as readie money for it, as merchantes have for their ware in the Exchange: . . . Thus you heare what the Curber doth . . . and what inconvenience growes to many by their base villanies: therefore I wish all menservants and maids, to be carefull for their maisters commodities, & to leave no loose ends abroad, especially in chambers where windows open to the streete, least the Curber take them as snappings, and convey them to the cooseninge broker. Let this suffise, and nowe I will recreate your wits with a merry tale or two.

II(ii) *Of the subtiltie of a Courber in coosoning a Maid.*

A merry jest and as subtile, was reported to me of a cunning Courber, who had apparreld himselfe maruellous brave, like some good wel-favoured yong Gentleman, & instead of a man had his Warp to wait upon him: this smooth faced rogue comes into Moore fields, and caused his man to cary a pottle of Ipocras vnder his cloke, and there had learned out amongst others that was drying of cloaths, of a very wel favoured maid that was there with her Flasket of linnen,[1] what her Maister was, where she dwelt, and what her name: having gotten this intelligence, to this maid he goes, courteously salutes her, and after some pretie chat, tels her how hee saw her sundrie times at her Maisters doore, and was so besotted with her beautie, that he had made inquirie what her qualities were, which by the neighbours he generally heard to bee so vertuous, that his desire was the more inflamed, and thereupon in signe of good wil, and in further acquain-tance, hee had brought her a pottle of Ipocras: the maid seeing him a good proper man, tooke it very kindly, and thankt him, and so they drunke the wine, and after a little lovers prattle, for that time they parted.

The maids hart was set on fire, that a Gentleman was become a suter to her, and she began to thinke better of her selfe then ever she did before, and waxed so proud that her other suters were counted too base for her & there might be none welcome but this newcom gentleman her lover: wel, divers times they appointed meetings, that they grew very familiar, and he oftentimes would come to her Maisters house, when all but she & her fellow maids were in bed, so that he and the Warpe his man did almost knowe every corner of the house: it fortuned that so long he dallied, that at length he meant earnest, but not to marry the maid whatsoever he had done els, and comming into the fieldes to her on a washing day, saw a mighty deale of fine Linnen, worth 20. pound as he conjectured: wherupon he thought this night to set downe his rest, and therefore he was very

[1] In the country Autolycus steals linen from hedges, IV. 2. 5-7; 23.

pleasant with his lover, and told her that that night after her Maister
and mistres were in bed, he would come, & bring a bottle of Sacke
with him and drinke with her: the maid glad at these newes, promised
to sit up for him and so they parted till about ten a clocke at night,
when he came and brought his man with him, and one other
Courber with his tooles, who should stand without the dores: to be
briefe, welcom he came, & so welcome as a man might be to a maid:
hee that had more mind to spy the clothes, then to look on her
favour, at last perceived them in a Parlor that stood to the streetward
and there would the maid have had him sit. No, sweeting, quoth he,
it is too neere the street, we can neither laugh nor be merry, but
everie one that passeth by must hear us: upon that they removed
into another roome and pleasant they were, and tippled the Secke
round, til all was out, and the gentleman swore that he would have
another pottle, and so sent his man, who tolde the other Courber
that stood without, where the window was he should worke at, and
away goes he for more secke and brings it very orderly, & then to
their cups they fall againe, while the courber without had not left
one rag of Linnen behinde. Late it grew, and the morning began to
wax gray, and away goes this curber and his man, leaving the maid
very pleasant with his flattering promises untill such time as poore
soule, she went into the Parlor, and mist all her mistres Linnen, then
what a sorrowful hart she had, I refer to them that have greeved at
the like losse.

VI. Sources

From

B.   THE THIRD PART OF CONNY-
CATCHING
by R[obert] G[reene] (1592)

*An other Tale of a coosening companion, who would needs trie his cunning in
this new invented art, and how by his knavery (at one instant) he beguiled
half a dozen and more.*

Of late time there hath a certaine base kind of trade been used, who
though divers poor men, & doubtles honest apply themselves to,
only to relieve their need: yet are there some notorious varlets do the
same, beeing compacted with such kind of people, as this present
treatise manifesteth to the worlde, and what with outward simplicity
on the one side, and cunning close trechery on the other, divers
honest Cittizens and day-labouring men, that resort to such places

as I am to speake of, onely for recreation as opportunity serveth, have bin of late sundry times deceived of their purses. This trade, or rather unsufferable loytring qualitie, in singing of Ballets, and songs at the doores of such houses where plaies are used, as also in open markets and other places of this Cittie, where is most resort: which is nothing els but a sly fetch to draw many togeather, who listning unto an harmelesse dittie, afterwarde walke home to their houses with heavie hearts:[1] from such as are heereof true witnesses to their cost, do I deliver this example. A subtil fellow, belike imboldned by acquaintance with the former deceit, or els beeing but a beginner to practise the same, calling certaine of his companions together, would try whether he could attaine to be maister of his art or no, by taking a great many of fools with one traine. But let his intent and what els beside, remaine to abide the censure after the mater is heard, & com to Gracious street, wher this villanous pranke was performed. A roging mate, & such another with him, were there got upon a stal singing of balets which belike was som pretty toy, for very many gathered about to heare it, & divers buying, as their affections served, drew to their purses & paid the singers for them. The slye mate and his fellowes, who were dispersed among them that stoode to heare the songes: well noted where everie man that bought, put up his purse againe, and to such as would not buy, counterfeit warning was sundrie times given by the rogue and his associate, to beware of the cut pursse, and looke to their pursses, which made them often feel where their pursses were, either in sleeve, hose, or at girdle, to know whether they were safe or no. Thus the craftie copesmates were acquainted with what they most desired, and as they were scattered, by shouldring, thrusting, feigning to let fall something, and other wilie tricks fit for their purpose: heere one lost his purse, there another had his pocket pickt, and to say all in briefe, at one instant, upon the complaint of one or two that sawe their pursses were gone, eight more in the same companie, found themselves in like predicament. Some angrie, others sorrowfull, and all greatly discontented, looking about them, knewe not who to suspect or challenge, in that the villaines themselves that had thus beguiled them, made shewe that they had sustained like losse. But one angrie fellow, more impacient then al the rest, he falles upon the ballade singer, and beating him with his fists well favouredly sayes, if he had not listened his singing, he had not lost his purse, and therefore woulde not be other wise perswaded, but that they two and the cutpurses were compacted together. The rest that had lost their purses likewise, and saw that so many complaine togither: they jumpe in opinion with the other fellow, & begin to tug & hale the ballad singers, when one after one, the

[1] Cf. Autolycus, IV. 3. 611–21.

false knaves began to shrinke awaie with the pursses. By means of some officer then being there present, the two roges wer had before a Justice, and upon his discreete examination made, it was found, that they and the Cutpurses were compacted together, and that by this unsuspected villanie, they had deceived many. The fine Foole-taker himselfe, with one or two more of that companie, was not long after apprehended: when I doubt not but they had their reward aunswerable to their deserving: for I heare of their journey westward, but not of their returne: let this forewarne those that listen singing in the streets.

VII. Possible Source

From
HUMOUR OUT OF BREATH
by John Day (1608)

Humour out of Breath. A Comedie Divers times latelie acted By the Children Of The Kings Revells. Written by John Day. Printed at London for John Helmes, and are to be sold at his shop in Saint Dunstons Church-yard in Fleetstreet. 1608.

ACTUS QUARTUS

Enter Anthonio, Francisco, Hippolito, Hermia, Lucida, and Octavio disguisd.

ANT.   Sons of Octavio, if your princely thoughts
Can stoope to such meane beauty, from this hand
Receive your wives; but should the duke your father—
    FRAN.   Feare not, old man, he was the meanes that breath'd this spirit unto us.
    HIPP.   Wood us to this course.
But should he prove Apostata, denie
Love which he first enforced us to profes,
So firme are our inseparate affections,
To winne our loves wee'd loose the name of sonnes.
    OCT.   Your father thanks you; but, hot-sprighted youthes,
Take counsell from experience, ere you tie
The gordian knot which none but heaven can loose.
*

Crave his consent:[1] when an imperiall hand
Shakes a weake shed, the building cannot stand.
FRAN.   Not stand? it shall: not Jove himselfe can ruine
The ground-worke of our love.
OCT.   Not Jove!
HIPP.   Not Jove!
Should a speak thunder; then go boldly on,
Our love admits no separation.
OCT.   Then to mine office: in the sighte of heaven
Your love is chast?
FRAN.⎫
HIPP.⎭   As innocence white soule.
OCT.   And yours?
HERM.⎫
LUCID.⎭   And ours.
OCT.   Then lend me all your hands,
Whilst thus a fathers tongue forbids the bands.

                            (*Discovers himselfe.*)

Forgetful boyes! but most audacious traytor,
That durst in thought consent to wrong thy prince,
Out of my sight; no land that calls me lord
Shall beare a waight so hatefull as thy selfe:
Live ever banishd. If (three daies expirde)
Thou or these lustfull strumpets—
HIPP.   Father!
OCT.   Boyes,
If you be mine, show't in obedience:
If (three daies past) you live within my dukedome,
Thee as a slave Ile doome unto the gallies,
And these thy brats as common prostitutes
Shall drie their lustfull veynes in the Burdello.[2]
Come, boyes, to Court; he that first gave you lives,
Will to your births provide you equall wives.
FRAN.   They have our loves.
HIPP.   Our oathes.
FRAN.   Our hearts and hands.
OCT.   Tut, lovers othes, like toyes writ down in sands,
Are soone blowne ore; contracts are common wiles
T'intangle fooles; Jove himselfe sits and smiles
At lovers perjuries. Bawd, strumpets, hence,
My bosom's chargde, give way to violence:
Come, doe not mind them.

                        [*Exeunt Anth. and his daughters.*

[1] Cf. IV. 3. 398–423.   [2] This passage is close to IV. 3. 423–48.

FRAN. How? not minde them, father?
When in your court you courted us to love,
You read another lecture: women then
Were angells.
  OCT.   True, but that was before angells
Had power to make them divells; they were then
Fiends to themselves, and angells unto men.
When upon Po thou find'st a cole-black swan,
Th'ast found a woman constant to a man.
  FRAN. And not afore?
  OCT.   Never afore.
  HIPP.   Your tongue
Unspeaks your former speech.
  OCT.   It doth; new theames
Must have new change of Rhetorique; all streames
Flow not alike one way; when I spake like a lover,
It was to breake you from your soldiers humour;
Having made you lovers, I, like envy, speak
To make you hate love: Art still strives to breake
Bad to make better.
  BROTHERS.   You have your wish.
  OCT.   Then onward to the court,
Make use of love as school-boyes do of sport.   [*Exeunt.*

VIII. Possible Source

From
THE NINTH BOOK OF
AMADIS DE GAULE
by F. de Silva,
translated by the editor from the French version
$(1577)^1$

In Ch. III Florisel, son of Amadis of Greece, meets Silvia.
Realizing that he is a man of worth she gets up and curtsies
'so that it was a marvel to see a rustic maiden showing so
much knowledge of how to behave'.]

'Fair damsel, said Don Florisel, surely the God Jupiter has stayed
round here, since your demeanour proves that the high gods have
not left this place.' 'Good sir, said she, I do not know why you say
that. You can obtain only a poor answer to so lofty a speech from
one who is a servant to such poverty and isolation . . .'

[Florisel's companion, Garinter, jealous of their obvious
attraction for one another, interposes, saying that he saw Silvia
first. He and Florisel quarrel and draw their swords, but Silvia
runs between them. Florisel now disguises himself as a Shepherd
in hope of talking to her more freely. She does not recognize
him but knows that he must be noble. He tells her how love has
changed him from being the greatest prince in the world to the
condition in which she now sees him. She fears his wooing:
'Enough that Fortune has abased me so in social position without your seeking to debase my honesty.' He protests his good
intentions and again cites as proof his willing surrender of
power, riches and luxury to be with her. Since she loves Prince
Anastarax he will go with her in search of him. They have
many adventures involving oracles and magic. In one castle
they find a hall of statues, and on two thrones images of Amadis
de Gaul and Queen Oriana. Florisel kisses their hands and the
image of King Amadis sets a helm on his head (Ch. XII).

¹ *Le neufiesme Livre d'Amadis de Gaule, Auquel sont continuez lez gestes de dom Florisel
de Niquée, surnommé le Chevalier de la Bergère, qui fut fils d'Amadis de Grèce et de la belle
Niquée . . . par C. Colet Champenois.* Lyon, 1577.

In Ch. XVIII they hear the story of Manatiles, King of Epirus.]

'Know now, there is a King in this realm of Epirus named Manatiles, who was married to a good, wise Lady of this land, by whom he had a son, all perfection, named Arpilior, who ought to succeed his father on the throne. Now when this young Prince was about eighteen years old, they brought to his mother the Queen one of her nieces, a Princess of perfect beauty, named Galathea, with whom the Prince fell so deeply in love that he could not for long endure it, but declared it openly: at which the Princess was overjoyed, and they began to love each other so much as their like could scarcely be found, enjoying one another secretly so that nobody perceived it. Until, about a year later the King himself became so amorous of the Princess that he sought her love, and strongly urged her to satisfy his amorous desire. The Princess refused, with modesty and virtuous shame, telling him that she would never give herself to any man except him who should have her in marriage.

Grieved by this reply the King began to look round for any means to draw her to him so that he might enjoy her at his pleasure. Accordingly he resolved to retire to the fountain of Epirus where he had an extremely beautiful royal residence.

[The palace is described in detail, with its castled corners, moat stocked with fish, fine garden, etc.]

In the middle of the garden was a square chamber to which one could go under cover from each of the four castles. Near it is a fountain with a strange and remarkable property; for it lights unlit torches and puts out those which are lit. Here the King one day announced his intention to retire with the Queen, his son, and the Princess only, forbidding all others to enter save those employed in the household. And once they were there, enjoying themselves and making good cheer, and the King always seeking to seduce the Princess, it happened that Love, which is always wont to cast a thousand suspicions and jealousies between lovers, put into the Queen's mind such a fancy about the King that she began to give him sour looks and a worse affection. The King for his part treated her with no fondness, and wished to be rid of her so that he might marry the Princess, on whom all his desire was fixed.

Ignorant of his father's passion, the Prince continued to rejoice in the company of Galathea, until one day when he was walking with her in the garden the King saw the two of them together; at which he was suddenly struck with such jealousy of his son that he decided to kill him, and the Queen too, so that he could freely enjoy Galathea. With this in mind he went to the Queen's chamber, where he found her sitting pensive. Without saying a word he raised the sword which he held ready drawn under his cloak, and cut off her head. Thence he went out with his sword all bloody in his hand, and by ill chance walked into a chamber where the Prince and Galathea had retired to take their pleasure together, as they had done on several previous occasions. And indeed the King surprised them there. In an immense fury he cried, 'Ah, traitor! Is this the respect you show me?' And so saying, he raised his arm to strike; but the Prince, agile and dexterous, threw himself quickly aside from the bed and put hand to sword, with which he parried several blows showered on him by his father, and finally, seeing his arm outstretched to increase his attack, he slipped swiftly underneath the weapon and seized his father round the body, thus preventing him from doing him any harm.

The Princess meanwhile ran for help and got four or five noblemen to come, who removed the Prince from his father's hands, begging the King not to punish his only son, the heir to his Kingdom, with death. On this the King, seeing that he could not then carry out his evil purpose, resolved to defer it to another day, but ordered his son to be imprisoned in one of the castles and the Princess in another, until he should have them executed.

Now he had with him a very learned man, a great Necromancer, who, seeing that his anger and cruel purpose were unabated, determined to use his art in such a way as to save the lives of the two young people—while yet making them endure punishment for their sin—and maybe also to satisfy the King by the punishment which he would give them. Wherefore he ordered an image to be made so like the young Prince that it lacked only speech, and another in the likeness of the Princess; and he made them move about as if they were alive. When they were ready he came to the King and said, 'Sire, I have thought long about the judgment and the punishments deserved by your son and the Princess to give satisfaction for the great crime they have committed. I suggest that, to make them suffer greatly and to give yourself lifelong satisfaction by it, you have them taken to the room where you caught them in the act, and there have them beheaded, one in front of the other, then have the bodies and heads carried into the garden-room, where I shall preserve them from corruption, on the understanding that you will go every day at sunset to see them. In this way you will live happily, seeing them so well punished.'

The King agreed to this, and the wise man, having warned the chief officers of the household of his purpose, and made them take an oath not to reveal it, ordered the two images to be brought into his presence and beheaded, then had them carried with the heads into the chamber in the garden. This pleased the King, who thought himself fittingly revenged.

And for the punishment of the two poor lovers the sage gave orders that the Princess, accompanied only by one lady, should go every morning to gaze on the body and head of the image of her lover, whom she thought to be dead. At mid-day the Prince would do the same as his beloved, unperceived by anyone whatsoever. Thus each one goes every day at the appointed hour; that is, the Princess goes to weep and make her moan in the morning for an hour by the image of her lover, without seeing her own image there, and the Prince goes at mid-day for an hour and laments the death of his beloved. That done, each returns to his prison, where they are fed secretly; and the sage intends that this shall continue while the King lives. He has placed a strong guard and close watch on the paths leading to the room, so that nobody may get in there to undo the enchantment.

[Ch. XIX. Florisel and Silvia, reaching the Castle of Cruelty, are assailed by the twelve Knights who keep the passage.

Florisel defeats them all, and the adventurers enter the palace.]

Then Don Florisel asked Silvia and her company to wait for him until he had done his best to bring them news. The Ladies agreed; then he set out, and walking straight to the gate, which he found open without any guard, he entered a fine courtyard. This had in one of its corners a wide stairway by which he mounted to a hall painted richly with various colours; and from there into a chamber hung with black drapery, and a bed curtained about with black, near which was a young Lady of excellent beauty, clad in mourning, her head leaning on the palm of her hand and weeping so sorely that Florisel was much moved with compassion and tears came into his eyes.

Then the young Lady began to say to herself, 'Alas, Galathea, what offence have you committed against Almighty God that he lets you suffer so strange a punishment? O my true love Arpilior, who endured a cruel death for love of me, where now is your faithful soul? Truly I believe that it is in this room, waiting for mine to bear you company in the happy place destined for it before it was born. Alas, why then am I now alive? . . . O Death, why dost thou linger?' . . .

So saying she let herself fall in a swoon, whereupon Florisel was
approaching to help her when the Maidens set to guard her came in,
and, not seeing Florisel there, they laid her on the bed and by their
ministrations brought her to her senses, after which she began to
make complaint and lament. Seeing this Don Florisel went out and
returned to Silvia and her companions, to tell them what he had
seen, and they all felt great pity. Night meanwhile was coming on,
and since they were resolved to go and see that strange and pitiful
thing, they retreated, in order not to be discovered, into the thickness
of the wood until the full dark of night had come.

[Florisel wishes to leave them there, but Silvia insists on
accompanying him. So at midnight the two of them enter the
garden. There Florisel would like to make love to Silvia, but
she fends him off as usual with rebukes and vague half-promises.]

Thus talking they reached the fountain near the room where the
images of Arpilior and Galathea were lying. As they entered day was
already beginning to break and they contemplated for a long time
the bodies and heads of those images, which looked as fresh as if they
had just been carved.

[Concealing themselves they are able to hear the Princess
bewailing her loved one. They spend the rest of the morning
discussing the ways of love. At mid-day Prince Arpilior comes
and embraces the image of his beloved, kissing the head and
blaming his cruel father. At sunset they wait for the King to
arrive.]

Soon after night closed in he came with six Gentlemen, clad in
kilts of orange-coloured camelot, each carrying before him two
flaming torches; the King coming after, clad in a large cloak of cloth
of gold trailing on the ground, and a crown of gold on his head, his
hair white as fine cotton, and his beard likewise, which hung down
to his waist, as, approaching the images of his son and the Princess,
he spoke thus:
'O Sovereign Lord, where was my mind when I allowed such
cruelty to be executed on my own child and on this young Princess
for so slight an offence, and one which I was myself trying to commit!
Ah love, who art the cause of great sorrow and mischance, was it not
enough that I murdered my wife, who was so modest and chaste,
without also staining my hands with my own blood, depriving myself and this noble realm of the legitimate heir? Alas, could I not

have used some gentler correction? Indeed I might—But what am I saying? I could do no less, seeing the gravity of the case. That noble Roman Cassius did well to punish his son publicly for the least offence; likewise Brutus, Manlius, Torquatus and others. Have I done wrong to punish them like that? No; it will become an honour to me when others understand it properly. So I do not trouble myself about it in any way . . .'

As soon as he had finished speaking a band of minstrels arrived who, placing themselves about the fountain, began to sing melodious songs. These ending, the King and all the others retired to the palace, leaving in the chamber a light as bright as day by reason of the precious stones with which the ceiling was decorated; at which Silvia and Florisel were astonished.

After considering all that he had seen Florisel said, 'Indeed, the force of Love is great, and difficult to resist. We see by this experience how true the proverb is which says that Love does not go along with Reason. Love was the cause why this King has committed such inhumanity. Therefore I think it right for me not to tolerate it, and I do not mean to leave those two passionate creatures in torment. I suggest that tomorrow you tell Galathea the whole secret as soon as she comes, and I shall do the same to Arpilior, so that they may do whatever they think proper . . . '

[Ch. XX.] Don Florisel and Silvia spent the greater part of the night discussing love and its power, as they had done the night before. Now day came, and the hour when the Princess Galathea was wont to be in the garden-room to weep and mourn by the image of her lover Prince Arpilior. Silvia went out from the small room where she had been hidden with Don Florisel, and placed herself beside the fountain, to await her coming, and soon she saw the Princess, in the same dress as before, come in great haste to the room, wringing her hands like a woman in distress. To put an end to her grief Silvia went and stood in front of her and with sweet grace and joyous countenance said to her, 'My Lady, I beg you, before you go further, give me the honour of a brief hearing, and I assure you that what I tell you will comfort you and banish all your sorrow.'

At first the poor Galathea was a little astonished to see so lovely and gracious a Lady in that place. The sweet, amiable words however reassured her, and she replied, weeping, 'Alas, dear Lady, how is it possible for you to tell me anything of comfort, considering the great misfortune fallen on me, which nobody in the world could remedy! . . . 'My Lady,' said Silvia, 'give up this false opinion that you have hitherto held, and be assured that you have been deceived, and your lover too, who thinks the same of your fate as you of his—as you will see for yourself if it please you to wait here until noon, when he will come to weep and lament your death, just as you do his.'

The Princess was so struck with joy at hearing this good news that she fell down at Silvia's feet as if in a swoon, and lay a long time with no more power to move than someone in an ecstasy. Seeing this Silvia presumed to moisten her face with water from the nearby fountain; which brought her back to herself, and seemingly in the same state as before she was enchanted.

[Silvia tells her all that has happened and what the Necromancer has done and they walk about in the garden until nearly noon, when Florisel comes and is introduced to Galathea, who expresses her gratitude.]

While they were thus conversing they saw Prince Arpilior coming, clad in mourning as usual; but as soon as Galathea saw him she had no patience to wait to see his face when he entered the room, as she had intended, but running to him she threw herself on his bosom, and held him embraced for a long time, unable to do anything but weep and sob with the great joy she felt . . . [Then she tells him brokenly what has happened.]

Prince Arpilior thought that she was a phantom and stood transfixed, not knowing what to say or do; at which Galathea felt deeply wounded, thinking that he had lost all power of recognition through his great melancholy. She continued to talk to him:

'My love, you seem to doubt what I tell you. Why do you not answer? Come, come and see the deception played on us to keep us for ever in torment—had it not been for this good Knight and this fair Lady who have come to reveal it.' So saying she took him by the hand and led him into the chamber, where he saw the image of Galathea lying just as he had seen it previously when it made him think it the true Galathea. Now recognizing his faithful lover he embraced her fervently and kissed her several times: then thanked Don Florisel and Silvia warmly for the great benefit they had received through their intervention . . .

[Ch. XXI. They wait for the King's coming. Don Florisel slays him, and with Arpilior's help vanquishes his Knights. Arpilior and Galathea are married and the 'good philosopher' who prevented their execution is given the palace and garden. The images are remade so as to represent Arpilior and Queen Galathea crowned and sitting in state, and these images are used at the Coronation of the two lovers.]

IX. Analogue

From
THE HISTORY OF THE TRYALL
OF CHEVALRY
Anon. (1605)[1]

[Pembroke, wrongly believing that he has slain his friend
Ferdinand, resolves to spend his life by the latter's tomb. His
eulogies persuade the Princess Katharine to transfer her love
from himself to the lost Ferdinand.]

PEM.   This buryed here, is noble Ferdinand,
His fathers comfort, and his Countryes hope . . .
He was the verie pride of fortitude,
The house of vertue, and true frendships mirrour:
Looke on his picture, in the armes of death,
When he was ready to give up the ghost,
I causde it to be drawne: if at that time,
In that extremity of bitter pangs,
He lookt so lovely, had so fresh a colour,
So quick a moving eye, so red a lip,
What was his beauty when he was in health?
See with what courage he indur'd the combat,
Smiling at death for all his tyranny.
Had death bin ought but what he was, sterne death,
He would have bin enamour'd with his looks.
    KATH.   A certayne softe remorce[2]
Creeps to my heart, perswades me he was true,
Loving, and vertuous: but my selfe unkind,
Coyly to scorne the proffer of his mind.
    PEM.   O that in Justice of her former hate,
She now would hopelesse doate on Ferdinand!
Ile do the best I can to bring her on . . .

[He succeeds, and Katharine grieves for Ferdinand.]

---

[1] *The History of the Tryall of Chevalry, With the life and death of Cavaliero Dicke
Bowyer. As it hath bin lately acted by the right Honourable the Earle of Darby his servants.*
1605.
[2] Cf. Leontes's remorse, V. 3. 32–8.

PEM.   Give me the picture, I may hang it up.

KATH.   O take it not away: since I have lost
The substance, suffer me to keepe the shaddow:
Me thinks, so long as this is in my hand,
I claspe my Ferdinand betweene my armes:
So long as I behold this lively forme,
So long am I refreshed by his smiles:
So long, me thinks, I heare him speake to me.
Knew I the Paynter drew this counterfeyt,
I would reward him with a mynt of gold.

PEM.   If such a pleasure you receyve by this,
I tell you, Madam, I shall shortly have
His whole proportion cut in Alablaster,
Armed as he was when he encountred here,
Which, kneeling, shall be set upon his tombe.

KATH.   On that condition I will gather flowers,
And once a day come straw them at his feet:
And once a day pay tribute of choyce thankes
To you the furtherer of my happinesse:
Till then, I place the picture where it was . . .

[Ferdinand is not dead. He and Pembroke meet near the tomb and recognize each other. Pembroke describes Katharine's changed attitude.]

FERD.   Has then my shaddow and supposed death
Brought that to pass my living substance could not?

PEM.   It hath, and never Lady more enamour'd,
Then now is Katharine of her Ferdinand.
I told her, and no more then truth I told,
A cunning Carver had cut out thy shape
And whole proportion in white Alablaster,
Which I intended here should be set up.
She earnestly entreated she might have
A sight of it, and dayly be permitted
To deck thy tombe and statue with sweet flowers.
Shee's but even now departed to that end.
And will (I know) be quickly here agayne.
Now, for assurance I dissemble not,
Instead of thy resemblance cut in stone,
Kneele here thy selfe, and heare her pitious mone.

FERD.   Content, I hold your counsell for the best:
Weele once conclude our sorrowes with a jest.

PEM.   Soft, there's a cushen: nay, you must be bare,
And hold your hands up, as the maner is.
FERD.   What if I held a booke, as if I prayed?
PEM.   'Twere best of all; and now I think upon't,
Here is a booke: so, keepe your countenance,
You must imagine now you are transform'd.
Yonder she comes, in any case stir not.

(*Enter Katharine.*)

KATH.   I feare I have detracted time too long,
In my determinde service to my Love:
But Ile redeeme my fault with double care.
See where his statue is set up: kind Knight,
For ever Katharine will record thy truth.
PEM.   How say you, Madam, is't not very like him?
KATH.   As like as if it were himselfe indeed.
And would to God my prayers might be heard,
That as the Image of Pigmalion once,
Life might descend into this sencelesse stone:
But that was faynd, as my desire is fond.
Relentlesse death withholds my Ferdinand;
And no intreaty may recover him.
In token then I doe repent my scorne,
That I was cruell to so kind a friend.
Thou the presenter of his absent person,
Receive these sweets, thy temples be adorn'd
With this fresh garland; thy white Ivory hand
Boast of this Ring, which if thou wert alive,
Should bind our faythes up in a nuptiall knot:
But for thou canst not be reviv'd agayne,
Ile dwell with thee in death: and as my spirit
Mounts to the happy mansion of thy spirit,
So to accompany thy shaddow here,
Ile turne my body to a shaddow too;
And kneeling thus, confront thy silent lookes
With my sad looks: this is the Instrument.
Now Ferdinand, behold thy Katharine comes,
FERD.   And she is welcome unto Ferdinand.[1]
PEM.   Ile play the clark for both, and say Amen.
Nay, muse not, Madam, tis no sencelesse Image,
But the true essence of your wished Love.
KATH.   I am asham'd to looke him in the face.

---

[1] Cf. this with the subtlety of V. 3. 18–111.

FERD.   Hide not those splendant lights; hereafter be
A constant wife; it shall suffice for me.
    KATH.   Heaven cast her off, if Katharine prove not so!
    PEM.   Of that no more: now let us haste from hence,
To quiet the dissension lately sprung
Betweene your parents . . .

X. Source

From
OVID'S METAMORPHOSES
translated by Arthur Golding (1567)

Book X, 265–324

[Pygmalion's Image]

Now in the whyle of wondrous Art an image he did grave
Of such proportion, shape and grace as nature never gave
Nor can to any woman give. In this his worke he tooke
A certaine love. The looke of it was ryght a Maydens looke,
And such a one as that yee would beleeve had lyfe, and that
Would moved bee, if womanhod and reverence letted not:
So artificiall was the work. He woondreth at his Art,
And of his counterfetted corse conceyveth love in hart.
He often toucht it, feeling if the woork that he had made
Were verie flesh or Ivorye still. Yit could he not perswade
Himself to think it Ivory. For he oftentymes it kist,
And thought it kissed him ageine . . .[1]
                              He layd her in a bed
The which with scarlet dyde in *Tyre* was richly overspred,
And terming her his bedfellow, he couched downe hir head
Uppon a pillow soft, as though shee could have felt the same.

[He prayed Venus to give him a wife like his 'wench of
Ivory'.]

Assoone as he came home, streyght way *Pygmalion* did repayre
Unto the Image of his wench, and leaning on the bed,
Did kisse her. In hir body streyght a warmenesse seemd to spred.
He put his mouthe againe to hers, and on her brest did lay

[1] Cf. V. 3. 44–80, etc.

His hand. The Ivory wexed soft: and putting quyght away
All hardnesse, yeelded underneathe his fingars, as wee see
A peece of wax made soft ageinst the Sunne, or drawen to bee
In divers shapes by chaufing it betweene ones handes, and so
To serve to uses. He amazde stood wavering too and fro
Tweene joy and feare to bee beeguyld; ageine he burnt in love,
Ageine with feeling he began his wisshed hope to prove.
He felt it verrye flesh in deede. By laying on his thumb,
He felt her pulses beating. Then he stood no longer dumb,
But thanked *Venus* with his hart: and at the length he layd
His mouth to hers, who was as then become a perfect mayd.
Shee felt the kisse, and blusht therat: and lifting fearefully
Hir eyelidds up, hir Lover and the light at once did spye.
The mariage that her selfe had made the Goddesse blessed so,
That when the Moone with fulsum lyght nyne tymes her course
    had go,
This Ladye was delivered of a Son that *Paphus* hyght,
Of whom the Iland takes that name . . .

THE TEMPEST

INTRODUCTION

THE TEMPEST was first published in the 1623 Folio, but according to an entry in the Revels Account there was played on 'Hallowmas nyght [1 Nov. 1611] att Whithall before the Kinges Majestie a play called the Tempest . . . By the Kings players'. Early in 1613 it was one of fourteen plays performed before the Princess Elizabeth after her marriage on 14 February to the Elector Palatine. The brevity of the piece, some anomalies, and the frequent use of music and song have elicited the suggestion that it was revised for that occasion, possibly abridged, and in particular that the masque in IV. 1 was inserted then.[1] This is of course possible, but although the masque of Ceres and Juno affects the plot little, it fits admirably into the ethical pattern of the play, shows Prospero in gracious mood, and would please the King and Queen (who loved masques) in 1611 as in 1613. Dover Wilson argued that the long passages of narrative exposition may have replaced scenes in a longer play, 'possibly an earlier play of Shakespeare's own'. This is guesswork. The narrative exposition involved in setting the piece on the last day of the action may rather be the result of a deliberate attempt to keep the unities —as Shakespeare had done in *The Comedy of Errors*. As it stands the play is beautifully organized, and I cannot believe that 'at some stage of its evolution *The Tempest* was in all likelihood a loosely constructed drama like *A Winter's Tale* and *Pericles*'.[2]

The play must have been written mainly in 1611, for it was prompted to some extent by the excitement caused by the disappearance at sea in 1609 of Sir Thomas Gates, his return safely from Virginia in the autumn of 1610, and the subsequent publication of pamphlets describing his shipwreck in

[1] Cf. H. D. Gray, 'Some Indications that *The Tempest* was revised', *SPhil*, xviii, 1921, 129–40.
[2] *Camb*, pp. 79–81.

the Bermudas and the state of the Virginian settlement as he found it on his arrival in James Town.[1]

To stories of this expedition *The Tempest* owed many details of the storm and shipwreck, the nature of the island, and the behaviour of those on it. Three pamphlets of 1610 in particular had a close bearing on the play:

1. *A True and Sincere Declaration of the purpose and ends of the Plantation begun in Virginia* 'set forth by the authority of the Governors and councillors' (*S.R.* 14 Dec. 1609). This official publication was written while the *Sea-Venture* was still missing, with the Governor and 'all the Commissioners and principall persons aboard'. Its purpose was to explain the difficulties experienced in setting up a colony in Virginia as due to 'dissension and ambition' among the leaders and 'the Idlenesse and bestiall slouth of the common sort'; to express confidence in Gates's safety; and to protest against the scandalous reports spread by 'unruly youth' recently returned from America.

2. *A Discovery of the Bermudas, otherwise called the Ile of Divels, by Sir Thomas Gates, Sir George Sommers and Captayne Newport, with divers others.* This was a private account by Silvester Jourdain, a survivor, dated 13 October 1610. It gave a vivid description of the shipwreck, described the Bermudas very favourably, and told briefly how the shipwrecked people escaped to the mainland.

3. *A true Declaration of the estate of the Colony in Virginia, with a confutation of such scandalous reports as have tended to the disgrace of so worthy an enterprise* (*S.R.* 8 Nov. 1610). This, another authorized publication, described the shipwreck and the islands, the escape to Virginia, and the parlous state of the settlement when Gates got there. It included matter from Gates's report to the Virginian Council and from unpublished

---

[1] The idea of settling North America went back at least thirty years. In 1578 Sir Humphrey Gilbert studied the possibility; he died in 1583. Next year his half-brother Raleigh sailed from the W. Indies to Carolina and Virginia, finding the Indians friendly. In 1585, however, Sir Richard Grenville's men, settling Roanoke, fell out with the natives, and in 1586 the colonists were so reduced that they went home with Drake. Later attempts were unsuccessful, until the first Virginia Charter gave official authority for new expeditions in 1606, the year of Christopher Newport's voyage with artisans, labourers and gentlemen who chose a site for James Town but quarrelled among themselves. Newport was Vice-Admiral of the 1609 expedition, with Sir George Somers as Admiral and Sir Thomas Gates as Acting-Governor until Lord de la Warr could take over.

letters from the colony. Its purpose was to allay rumours discrediting the enterprise which were making sponsors hesitate to pay their dues and to support another expedition.

4. To these we must add a fourth work which Shakespeare must have read although it was not printed until 1625, when it appeared in *Purchas his Pilgrimes* with chapter headings by Hakluyt and marginal notes by Samuel Purchas. This was the long letter to an 'excellent Lady' sent from Virginia on 15 July 1610 by William Strachey, secretary to Gates at James Town and to the Council there under Lord de la Warr. Its published title was: *A True Reportory of the Wracke and Redemption of Sir Thomas Gates, Knight; upon, and from the Ilands of the Bermudas: his comming to Virginia, and the estate of that Colonie there, and after, under the government of the Lord La Warre.*

After describing in detail the shipwreck, this letter gave a vivid account of the indiscipline, mutiny, and perils from savage Indians suffered by the colonists from June 1609 to July 1610. Its contents were known to the author of *A true Declaration*, for the letter was apparently shown to members of the Virginia Company after Gates got back to England.

Shakespeare probably read all three published tracts, maybe others too, and incorporated details from them into his comedy; and he certainly drew on Strachey's account. How he knew it has often been discussed.[1] He must have known several members of the Council besides the Earls of Southampton and Pembroke, e.g. Sir Dudley Digges and Christopher Brooke, and perhaps Sir Henry Neville. Moreover he would know prominent investors such as William Leveson, who had been appointed in 1607 to raise money for the Company, and Sir Henry Rainsford of Clifford Chambers, two miles from Stratford, who, with Shakespeare, was mentioned in the will of John Combes in 1613. Any of these may have let him read a copy of Strachey's narrative[2] and he used its phrasing to good effect here and there. I give below considerable extracts from Strachey and the two official pamphlets [Texts I–III]; but have not given Jourdain's account since space is limited and he has little not found in Strachey.

[1] Notably by C. M. Gayley in *Shakespeare and the Founders of Liberty in America*, New York, 1917.
[2] See L. Hotson, *I, William Shakespeare*, 1937.

One must guard against ascribing to literary influences features which Shakespeare could well have got from talking with returned voyagers: the storm, the shipwreck near shore, the Island of Devils which proved to be 'habitable and commodious', the dissensions among the marooned people and those in Virginia. The pamphlets are useful in showing what must have been common talk at the time, and that Shakespeare's play had considerable topicality. They also helped to suggest some of the pervading themes. To Strachey the dramatist owed specific details, e.g. the roaring and darkness (I. 2. 3–7; *infra*, p. 276); the fear, amazement, prayers, and utter weariness of the passengers and crew; their common toil; the St Elmo's fire on mast and rigging (I. 2. 196–206); the safe harbour (I. 2. 226–7); the recurrent storms (II. 2. 18–39); the birds caught on the rocks (II. 2. 171–2); a drink made of berries (I. 2. 333–4); a gentleman carrying wood (III. 1. 2–9); a plot against the governor's life (IV. 1. 139–63).[1]

Shakespeare's interest in the American voyages was by no means confined to the expedition of 1609. He knew Richard Eden's translations from Sebastian Münster's *Cosmographia Universalis* and the first three Decades of Pietro Martire and his abstract of Antonio Pigafetta's account of Magellan's voyage round Cape Horn (this gave him the name 'Setebos').[2] He read Hakluyt's *Voyages* and stories later put into *Purchas his Pilgrimes*. Thus the 'men/Whose heads stood in their breasts' (III. 3. 46–7), already mentioned in *Othello*, may have come from Raleigh's *Discovery of Guiana* (1596) printed in Hakluyt, and Trinculo's description of Caliban (II. 2. 35) as 'Legg'd like a man and his fins like arms' recalls Purchas, ii. 1,556 (*c*. 1597), 'A sea-monster . . . armes like a man without haire and at the elbows great Finnes like a fish'. A similar description had been given in *Troilus and Cressida* of Ajax: 'He's grown a very landfish, languageless, a monster' (III. 3. 264). Obviously Shakespeare's reading of travel-books went back some time.

In Captain John Smith's *A True Relation of such Occurrences . . . as hath passed in Virginia since the first planting of that Colony*

[1] For an exhaustive list of parallels see R. R. Cawley, 'Shakspere's Use of the Voyagers', *PMLA*, xli, 1926, 688–726.
[2] See *The First Three English Books on America*, ed. E. Arber, 1895.

(1608)[1] Shakespeare would find evidence of the greed and folly of settlers who, discovering talc in the bed of a stream, thought it to be gold and wasted their energy and supplies in searching for more. Here is a distant parallel to the 'glistering garments' which distract the servants, though Caliban says, 'Let it alone, thou fool; it is but trash' (IV. 1. 225). In Eden's *A treatyse of the newe India* (from Münster, 1553) he would read how Columbus on his third voyage tried in vain to placate some warlike savages with music; then 'the Spaniards drawing nearer unto them, caste certayn apparell into theyr bote . . . although all were in vayne. For they fled all awaye' (Arber, pp. 35–6). In Smith he would read how the treacherous chief Powhatan sent as emissary his daughter Pocahontas 'a childe of tenne yeares old . . . the only Nonpareil of his Country: this hee sent by his most trustie messenger, called Rawhunt, as much exceeding in deformity of person, but of a subtill wit, and crafty understanding.' The contrast between the innocent daughter of the chief and the deformed servant may have been one impulse towards the creation of Miranda and Caliban.

Morton Luce (*Arden*, 1901) suggested that the relations between Miranda and Ferdinand were affected by the story of how Pocahontas later saved Smith from death when he was Powhatan's prisoner and about to be killed. The girl, 'when no entreatie would prevaile, got his head into her armes, and laid her owne upon his to save him from death. Whereupon the Emperour was content he should live to make him hatchets.' This story was, however, not printed before 1624, in Smith's *Generall History of Virginia, Summer Islands and New England*. If Shakespeare knew it, it must have been by oral transmission. There was no suggestion that Pocahontas and Smith fell in love. She married John Rolfe, a settler, in 1613 and died in England four years later. To identify Miranda with Pocahontas is a tempting fancy which must be sternly repressed.

There can be no doubt that when Shakespeare decided to write another romantic comedy after *The Winter's Tale*, the Bermuda shipwreck and the Virginian colony soon came uppermost in his mind. *The Tempest* is not a play about colonization, but when James I and his courtiers saw it performed at Whitehall while the controversy about the settlement was still hot,

[1] Ed. C. Deane, 1866.

they must have seen—and been intended to see—many subtle allusions to it. Of these more later. It is clear, however, that Shakespeare's imagination was still working on lines laid down in the previous 'romances', *Pericles*, *Cymbeline*, and *The Winter's Tale*. In all three he had concerned himself with the love between parents and children, and with children separated from their parents; all three involved plots against the innocent; exile; wandering; contrast between high-born persons and true or apparent plebeians; a pervasive sense of Providence (or the gods) bringing good out of evil; visions or oracles; music. In *Pericles* there were storms and shipwreck, a father driven from his kingdom and wandering the seas for many years having lost his baby daughter, until united to her and her mother. Both there and in *The Winter's Tale* the structure of the play suffered through the lapse of time. The new play was to present or imply these ingredients, but with a tauter structure.

The playwright in search of a plot found in the Virginian pamphlets promising features, including a tempest; shipwreck; a haunted island of ill repute but beautiful and fertile, though uninhabited and almost inaccessible; a mingling of social classes—nobles, gentlemen, tradesmen, labourers, mariners, natives well- and ill-disposed—dissensions leading to dangerous divisions and conspiracies.

At least as important for Shakespeare were the ethical ideas and lessons embodied in the pamphlets, such as the need (especially in perilous situations) of firm leadership and a strong governor. The evil results of a bad president were illustrated by the ill-treatment of John Smith under Wingwood, and the weakness of other leaders. Gates and Somers proved themselves to be good leaders. The importance of hard work and self-control were also shown, for the Virginian colony was almost destroyed by idleness, ignorance, greed, and lust. It was obvious that a colony depends on the kind of men who go there. Bad men will behave badly when placed in an earthly paradise; they take their ambitions, feuds and treacheries with them. Hence Strachey insisted that a glorious colony could not be built by 'an hundred or two of deboist hands, dropt forth by yeare after yeare, with penury, and leisure, ill provided for before they come, and worse to be governed when they are here . . .' (*infra*, p. 293).

Settlers must be recruited from moderate and well-behaved men of all ranks if a proper order is to be established in the New World. However favourable the land and climate, a good society depends upon the virtues, labour, and obedience to law of its people. Some of those marooned in the Bermudas wished to stay for ever, without toil, in perfect freedom of life and worship (being Puritans), but their passions, their 'sloath, riot and vanity' soon proved their ineptitude.

Another topic suggested by the reports of many travellers concerned the 'natural man'. Were the Indians good or bad before they encountered Europeans? Did they live idyllic lives? Travellers' opinions differed according to the tribes they met. On his first voyage Amerigo Vespucci found wild men who were 'allured with gentlenes':

> They fyght not for the enlargeing of theyr dominion, forasmuch as they have no Magistrates: nor yet for th'increase of riches, . . . but onely to revenge the death of theyr predecessours . . . Thei use no lawful conjunction of mariage, but everyone hath as many women as him listeth, and leaveth them agayn at his pleasure . . . They use no kynd of marchaundise or buying and selling, beyng content onely with that which nature hath lefte them. As for Golde, Pearles,[1] precious stones, jewelles and such other thinges, which we in Europe esteme as pleasures and delicates, they sette nought by. They have no kynde of corne . . . They eate no kynd of fleshe except mans fleshe; for they eate all such as they kyll in theyr warres, or otherwise take by chaunce. (Eden, ed. Arber, p. 37)

Here is the basis of Montaigne's famous essay on 'Cannibals' in which he treats the eating of human flesh as a mere peccadillo of an admirable race.

Columbus contrasted the cannibals in the Caribbean with 'meke and humayne people' in other islands. He admired the natives of Hispaniola who lived simply, without money, etc.

> So that if we shall not be ashamed to confesse the truthe, they seeme to lyve in that goulden worlde of the whiche owlde wryters speake so much; wherein men lyved simplye and innocentlye without inforcement of lawes, without quarrelling Judges and

---

[1] Cf. *Othello* V. 2. 345–7.

libelles, content onely to satisfie nature; without further vexation
for knowlege of thinges to come. Yet these naked people also are
tormented with ambition for the desyre they have to enlarge their
dominions: by reason wherof they kepe warre, and destroy one
an other: from the which plag[u]e I suppose the golden world was
not free. For even then also, *Cede, non cedam*, that is 'gyve place',
and 'I wyll not give place', had entred emonge men. (Arber, p. 71)

Many travellers found that friendly Indians turned hostile
after a time, either through greed or through the mistakes or
crimes of the whites. Some seemed incredibly debased. In
Virginia the story of mutual treachery was often repeated and
the sullen, hostile chief Powhatan was not won over by being
crowned with a copper crown sent especially from England.
But that the Virginians were not primitive savages was made
clear by Thomas Hariot, the mathematician, who spent a
year there in 1586–7 and wrote *A briefe and true report of the new
found land of Virginia*, printed in 1588, in which he gave a
valuable account 'of the nature and maners of the people'. He
found that:

> though they have no such tooles, nor any such crafts, Sciences and
> Artes as we, yet in those thinges they doe, they shew excellencie
> and wit . . . Whereby may bee hoped, if meanes of good govern-
> ment be used, that they may in short time bee brought to civilitie,
> and the imbracing of true Religion.

To justify colonization in the name of religion and civilization was one aim of several works written on behalf of the
adventurers to America.[1] To preach the Gospel to every nation
was incumbent upon good Christians; to educate the educable
was a humane task; to domesticate the wilderness, to win
profit by trade and manufactures, to extend the royal realms
by taking possession of empty or ill-used lands, were all praise-
worthy activities. 'Plantations' (Bacon was to write in an Essay
of 1625) 'are amongst ancient, primitive, and heroical works.'
But 'if you plant where savages are, do not only entertain
them with trifles and gingles; but use them justly and graciously,
with sufficient guard nevertheless'; work so that 'the plantation
may spread into generations, and not ever be pieced from

[1] E.g. *A true Declaration* . . ., 1610; *Virginia's Verger*, 1625.

without'. Recalcitrant or treacherous natives, it was generally agreed, should be ruled firmly, even harshly, for Sir Thomas Gates found 'how little a faire and noble intreatie workes upon a barbarous disposition'.

All these ideas came into Shakespeare's mind and affected the characterization and texture of his play. He was not writing a didactic work; nevertheless approval of the Virginian Company's aims, and recognition of its difficulties seem to be implied in his depiction of Prospero, Caliban, and the intruders into the island. Prospero is the good, authoritarian Governor; more, he is like the Providence which in the Bermudan shipwreck brought the ship near to the shore that its people might escape, and gave them the means to live and to escape from their predicament. Hence was derived the conception of Prospero as an all-wise controller of events, plaguing sinners for their own good, and both testing and advising Ferdinand.

Topical suggestions might come from America, but for Shakespeare romance was mainly of the Mediterranean. Not surprisingly therefore he combined themes implied by the voyagers with similar material in the romance-literature which had influenced his recent comedies. No specific source has been found, so we must content ourselves with analogues to the setting, plot and personages of the play. Perhaps there was no one source, but, as in *A Midsummer Night's Dream*, a number of stories from which he interwove suitable features.

One analogue of considerable interest formed a strand in one of those complicated Spanish prose romances dealing with the adventures of knights errant among giants, enchanters and beautiful damsels. *El Espejo de Principes y Caballeros*, begun by Ortuñez de Calahorra in 1562 and continued by P. La Sierra and M. Martinez was gradually translated into English. Margaret Tyler's version of the First Part, *The Mirrour of Princely Deedes and Knighthood* (1578), contained the story of Prince Palisteo, much addicted to magic, who loses his wife and retires with his baby son and daughter to an island where he builds a magic castle. He rears the daughter in solitude. When she grows up he shows her pictures of many valiant knights, and as soon as she shows a preference for one of them her father uses his magic to bring the stranger (King

Trebacio) to the island, although Trebacio is already married to Briana.

Palisteo does this by having the wife kidnapped and carried off in a chariot to the river, where a ship is waiting. Trebacio follows the chariot to the waterside where, seeing an old man in a little boat, he asks to be taken to the ship. The old man (who is Palisteo) agrees. They follow the ship out to sea and sail after it till the chariot lands on an island. Trebacio's vessel rushes ashore and is wrecked, and he is thrown to safety. On the island he finds a palace, in which dwells the fair princess Lindaraza, whose beauty enchants Trebacio so that he forgets his wife and stays for many years until the young Knight of the Sun arrives, slays the giants who guard the castle, finds the amorous pair, and reminds Trebacio of his wife and royal duties. The two leave the palace, which immediately disappears; Lindaraza dies of grief, and the repentant Trebacio is united to his wife.

The parallels to *The Tempest* are obvious. A magician-prince leaves civilization and dwells in an enchanted island, bringing up his daughter in solitude. A young man is brought by magic across the sea and out of a wrecked boat to be the daughter's lover. Palisteo the magician, being the second son of the King of Phrygia, and 'not being born to the Kingdom', may fitly 'seek his own delight without envy, rather than trouble himself with the care of governing'. Trebacio and the lady Lindaraza are totally unlike Ferdinand and Miranda, and the ensuing adventures have little in common with the play; but this is the sort of material drawn on by the dramatist, and a moral note is struck when the need for Trebacio to repent is stated [Text IV].

Also in *The Mirrour of Princely Deedes* is Devil's Island, so called from the ugly monster who has ravaged it and become its master. This monster (Fauno) is the son of a wicked princess and a monster from the Atlas Mountains, brought to her by the Devil, who deceived her into thinking that the child would be his. This offspring of a witch and a diabolical creature is otherwise unlike Caliban, for he is a giant with a legion of devils within him which issue from his mouth when he is fighting the Knight of the Sun. The latter has encountered a terrible storm at sea. Against the wishes of his friends he lands, to face almost certain death, for he is lovesick and weary of life. He slays the monster and stays alone on the island until his mistress comes there [Text V].

Another parallel is found in the *Noches de Invierno* ('Winter Nights' Tales') of Antonio Eslava (1609), Chapter IV,[1] which tells how a magician King of Bulgaria (Dardano), forced into exile by his enemy King Niciphoro of Greece, takes ship with his only daughter (who is not a baby), then goes down to the bottom of the sea, where he builds a marvellous palace and lives there, spurning mankind, until the daughter (Serafina) becomes lonely and restless. His enemy's elder son (Valentiniano) has been robbed of the succession by his father, who favours the younger son (Juliano). Wishing to seek help from the Emperor in Constantinople, Valentiniano goes down to the shore, where he finds a skiff, with an ancient ferryman (Dardano in disguise) who conveys him across the sea. Arriving over his palace, the magician strikes the water with his wand and takes the prince down to the princess. The two young people fall in love and are married.

Meanwhile Juliano has ascended the thrones of Greece and Bulgaria, and, having married in Rome, is returning with his bride when the magician raises a great storm. The ship is struck by lightning, and Neptune would destroy it, but Dardano will not allow this. Instead he reproaches Juliano with his father's crimes and his own usurpation, and foretells a sad fate for him. Soon afterwards both Juliano and his bride die, and Valentiniano obtains the throne.

Here again there are certain likenesses to *The Tempest*; an exiled ruler who lives with his daughter in a remote place, and who procures a suitable bridegroom for his daughter by magic; the use of a storm to bring his enemies to the magician. In such tales the sheer fantasy of extraordinary and varied adventures is what matters. Shakespeare may have taken hints from several such romances, or from one particular romance; but he handled the material with unusual economy and ballasted it with oblique topical allusions and with ethical ideas scarcely hinted at in the romances. He certainly knew *The Mirrour of Princely Deedes*, which was very popular, and maybe Falstaff's 'Phoebus, he, that wandering knight so fair' in *1 Henry*

[1] Ed. A. Gonzalez Palencia, Madrid, 1942 (Colección Literaria, Saeta, 5).

IV I. 2. was a reference to the Knight of the Sun. It has been pointed out[1] that the name Claribel (Claribelle, Claribela) occurs several times in Part IV, Book 2 of the romance. But it is very unlikely that Shakespeare could have read Eslava's story, first published in 1609, and never put into English.

A dramatic analogue has been found in the German comedy *Die Schöne Sidea* by Jacob Ayrer of Nuremberg who died in 1605 and whose *Opus Theatricum* was published in 1618. It may be an adaptation (like his *Julio and Hippolyta*) from an English play performed by English actors in Germany. Such comedians did in fact play a *Celinde und Sedea* in 1604 and 1613.[2]

The main points of contact between Ayrer and Shakespeare are illustrated in the passages given below [Text VI]. They include a magician-prince driven from his land, a reluctant devil-servant, the enemy's son captured and made to serve by carrying logs, a daughter who falls in love with the young man, their marriage, and a reconciliation between the two fathers. A brief sketch of the plot will, however, show how different *The Tempest* is from Ayrer's crude rustic piece in which the romance of Sidea and Prince Engelbrecht is interspersed with peasant farce (as when the wily miller John Molitor is faced by two angry fathers whose daughters are carrying his babies; he escapes by getting the two men to fight each other). The main plot tells how Prince Ludolff, having unjustly struck the ambassador of Leudegast, Prince of Wiltau (Vilna), is conquered and flees into the forest with his daughter Sidea. There he lurks, seeking vengeance, and conjures up a demon who foretells the future. Ludolff captures his enemy's son Engelbrecht and makes him split logs for Sidea, who at first treats him harshly then falls in love and agrees to run away with him. She must know some magic, for when the demon Runcifal is disobedient she strikes him dumb with her staff.

[1] Cf. discussions of *The Mirrour* by Edmund Dorer in *Magazin für die Literaturen des Inland und Auslandes*, no. 5, 1885, pp. 77ff.; G. Becker, 'Zur Quellenfrage von Sh's *Sturm*', *ShJb*, xliii, 1907, 155–68; Josef de Perott, 'The Probable Source of the Plot of Shakespeare's Tempest', *Clark U. Lib. Pubns*, Worcester, Mass., i, 8, Oct. 1905, and *ShJb*, xlvii, 1911, 128–31; most judiciously by Sir Henry Thomas, *Spanish and Portuguese Romances of Chivalry*, Ch. VII, Cambridge, 1920.
[2] See A. Cohn, *Shakespeare in Germany in the Sixteenth and Seventeenth Centuries*, 1865, who gave the German text and an English translation.

When Sidea grows weary while escaping, Engelbrecht leaves
her up a tree while he goes to find a carriage; but when he
gets home his father produces a bride (Julia) and he forgets
Sidea entirely. The Miller sees her and tells her father, who
seeks her in vain and resolves to approach his enemy and offer
reconciliation if Engelbrecht will marry Sidea. Meanwhile she
has been given shelter by a Shoemaker, and goes to the court
with a potion to restore Engelbrecht's memory. Arriving on the
wedding-day in disguise, she gives him the drink; his memory
and love for her are restored; Julia releases him and he marries
Sidea. Ludolff obtains forgiveness from Leudegast for his arrogance and all ends joyfully.

If there was an English comedy behind this, it must have
been a straggling piece like *Mucedorus*. One is tempted to agree
with Professor Frank Kermode: 'the whole play is so naïf and
buffoonish as to be beyond the possibility of serious consideration as the reflection of an important source.'[1] But remembering
the mess made of other English plays by the German players,
one dares not be so positive. *Die Schöne Sidea* throws little light
on Shakespeare's play, but it supports the conclusion that
behind *The Tempest* there was a large international body of
folk-lore and romantic tradition.

The search for sources of Shakespeare's names has led to
attempts to give a shadowy historical background to *The
Tempest*. In Thomas's *History of Italy* (1549), which he probably knew, Shakespeare would find a confused account of
Prosper Adorno, Duke of Genoa, who was deposed by his
rivals the Fregosi in 1561. Sixteen years later he returned as
deputy for the Duke of Milan. His cruelties alienated the
people of Genoa and to save himself he made friends with
Ferdinando, King of Naples. This alienated the Milanese, who
attacked him but were repulsed, and it was his old enemies the
Fregosi who drove him out after a short, inglorious rule.[2]
Thomas also mentions an Alfonso, King of Naples, married to
the daughter of a Duke of Milan, who in 1495 'renounced his

[1] *New Arden Tempest*, 1954, pp. lxiii–iv.
[2] G. Sarrazin, an indefatigable seeker of historical parallels, in 'Neue italienische
Skizzen zu Shakespeare', *ShJb*, xlii, 1906, 179–86, added more information, e.g.
the deposed Prospero fled to the harbour where he had to jump into the water
fully clothed and swim for it, while his enemies threw stones at him (U. Foliètre,
Hist. Gen., lib. xii, p. 256).

state unto his son Ferdinand ... and sailed into Sicily, where he gave himself to study, solitariness and religion'. Ferdinand was expelled by Charles VIII of France, and retired to Ischia. There was also a Prospero Colonna, who aided Gonsalvo de Cordoba in 1495.

It is, of course, possible that Shakespeare recalled the banished Duke of Genoa and his difficulties, when naming Prospero of Milan; he may have got Ferdinand from Thomas also; but it is not necessary to think so. Prosper and Stephano were characters in Jonson's *Every Man in his Humour* (original version) in which Shakespeare played a part; Eden's translation of P. Martire referred to 'Gonsalus Orviedus'[1] and the wars of King 'Ferdinando' of Spain against the Saracens, and 'the woorthy owlde man yet lyving, Sebastiane Cabote'. These suggestions have little or no bearing on the characters themselves.

Prospero is the last of several Dukes and Princes in Shakespeare who judge men and manipulate events (one recalls the Dukes in *A Comedy of Errors* and *Romeo and Juliet*, Duke Theseus in *A Midsummer Night's Dream*, Don Pedro in *Much Ado* who does Claudio's wooing for him, and the Duke in *Measure for Measure* who works deviously to bring a happy end). Prospero is the wise tyrant of the island, foreseeing and 'preventing' all, and many of the ironies in the play are caused by our knowledge of this. He is greatly helped by his magic.

As a magician he is contrasted with Caliban's mother Sycorax, who is mentioned, not only somewhat to distinguish Caliban from the American and African 'savages' to whom his character owes much, but also to distinguish the white magic of Prospero from the black arts of the 'blue-eyed hag'.

There were already benevolent magicians in Elizabethan drama as well as in romances. If Faustus damned himself by his pact with Mephistophelis, Greene's Friar Bacon was a patriot, studying for seven years to 'gird fair England with a wall of brass', but he endangered his soul by using 'pyromantic spells' and 'necromantic charms,/Conjuring and abjuring devils and fiends'. When his brazen head shattered and his perspective glass caused the deaths of Lambert and Serlsby, he repented and gave up his magic:

[1] Cf. also Strachey (*infra*, p. 281).

Bungay, I'll spend the remnant of my life
In pure devotion: praying to my God
That he would save what Bacon vainly lost. (1864–6)

The amusing conjuring match between Friar Bungay, Vandermast, and Bacon influenced Anthony Munday's *John a Kent and John a Cumber* (1594), where the Welsh magician (Kent) helps the cause of true love against parental harshness and the wiles of the Scottish wizard. There is little like Prospero here, but some anticipation of Ariel, as we shall see.

In *The Rare Triumphes of Love and Fortune* (*c*. 1582, sometimes ascribed to Kyd) a nobleman, Bomelio, exiled from court for many years through the treachery of a friend, has lurked for years in a cave not far from court. There he studies magic books and by a Senecan curse he strikes his enemy Armenio dumb. He knows how to cure the spell, but in the end it is the God Mercury who does so. United to his long-lost son Hermione, Bomelio leaves him in his cave, where the youth finds his magic books in the bed-straw, is profoundly shocked, and takes them away to burn them. When his father discovers his loss he goes mad, for 'all my books are gone, and I cannot help myself, nor my friends' (*supra*, pp. 98–101).

In elevation of mind and subtlety of operation Prospero is far above such wizards. He is a philosophic magician like Cornelius Agrippa, schooled in neo-Platonic theurgy.[1] His dealings are not with devils but with the elemental spirits described by Hermes Trismegistus and Porphyry, and he regards himself as an instrument of Divine Providence, though Shakespeare does not describe the nature of his meditations. He uses ceremonial magic, the wand, the robe, and the books, and the popular belief that a wizard's power lay in these appurtenances appears in Caliban's 'Remember/First to possess his books'; 'Burn but his books' (III. 2. 94–100).

Magical tricks are for Prospero but a means to virtuous ends, and when these are attained he will give up his rituals, not because, like Friar Bacon, he needs to repent, but because he has outgrown the lower supernatural. Hence

[1] Cf. R. H. West, *The Invisible World*, 1939; H. C. Agrippa, *De Occulta Philosophia*, Antwerp, 1531; *New Arden*, pp. xl–li.

> this rough magic . . .
> I here abjure; and . . .
>   I'll break my staff,
> Bury it certain fathoms in the earth,
> And, deeper than did ever plummet sound,
> I'll drown my book. (V. i. 50–7)

This comes at the end of an invocation to the 'weak masters'
(minor spirits) by whom he has done his magic; and the fact
that the invocation is itself a milder version of Medea's call to
the demons when she is seeking to prolong the life of Theseus's
father in Ovid's *Metamorphoses*, Bk VI, indicates that Prospero
(and his creator) recognized the sinister implications of even
the most benevolent use of the lower supernatural, though, as
F. Kermode writes, 'Only those elements which are consistent
with "white magic" are taken over for Prospero, though some
of the remnant is transferred to Sycorax.'[1] Shakespeare seems
to have used both the original Latin and Golding's translation,
so I supply both [Text VII].

Greene's *Friar Bacon and Friar Bungay* throws light on Shakespeare's conception of Ariel and Caliban. There the learned
German magician Vandermast disputes with Friar Bungay
'Whether the spirits of pyromancy or geomancy be most pre-
dominant in magic?' (1123–70). Vandermast praises pyromancy, i.e. divination by fire and use of the spirits that dwell
in the region of fire, the most expansive and lofty of elements in
the Ptolemaic universe:

> If then, as Hermes says, the fire be greatest,
> Purest, and only giveth shape to spirits,
> Then must those daemones that haunt that place
> Be every way superior to the rest.

Bungay is all for the spirits of earth:

> I tell thee, German, magic haunts the ground,
> And those strange necromantic spells
> That work such shows and wondering in the world,
> Are acted by those geomantic spirits
> That Hermes calleth *terrae filii*.

[1] *New Arden*, pp. 147–50.

The fiery spirits are but transparent shades,
That lightly pass as heralds to bear news;
But earthly fiends, closed in the lowest deep,
Dissever mountains, if they be but charg'd,
Being more gross and massy in their power.

Vandermast retorts that

these earthly geomantic spirits
Are dull and like the place where they remain . . .
Therefore such gross and earthly spirits do serve
For jugglers, witches, and vile sorcerers;
Whereas the pyromantic genii
Are mighty, swift, and of far-reaching power.

In practice the German shows himself no more adept than the
Englishman; but the distinction, common in alchemical and
neo-Platonic thought, lies behind the Caliban–Ariel antithesis, though it by no means explains all their characteristics.

Many ingredients went to make up Caliban.[1] He is a
monstrous creature born of a witch's congress with a demon;
he is the 'wild man' of folk-lore; he is a savage, enslaved
Indian; and he is the antithesis of the Utopian 'natural man'
implied in Gonzalo's idyllic fancy (II. 1. 145–69). His mother
Sycorax was a witch born in Argier (Algiers?); this would link
Caliban with the North African monster in *The Mirrour of
Knighthood* [Text V]; but other suggestions about Sycorax have
been made.[2] The preternatural origin fits Caliban's quasi-
symbolical function as the embodiment of sensual grossness
and hostility to truth and goodness; but he has no supernatural powers. He reminds one somewhat of the witch's son
in Spenser's *Faerie Queene*, III. vii, who, when Florimell takes
shelter in his mother's cottage, falls lustfully in love with her
and offers her flowers, birds and squirrels, which she accepts,
but she soon finds occasion to escape into the forest.

Caliban is nearer to the 'wild men' or 'salvage men' who
appear frequently in Spenser's poem. Obviously Spenser (like
Shakespeare) found in folk-tradition and travellers' tales two
opposed views: that they were innocent, unspoiled and happy,

[1] Cf. John E. Hankins, 'Caliban the Bestial Man', *PMLA*, lxii, 1947, 793–801.
[2] Cf. F. Kermode's valuable note in *New Arden*, on I. 2. 258.

and that they were brutal, cannibalistic and lecherous. The latter type appears in Bk IV. vii, where a monster abducts Amoret and keeps her in his cave:

> It was to weet a wilde and salvage man,
> Yet was no man, but onely like in shape,
> And eke in stature higher by a span,
> All overgrowne with haire that could awhape
> An hardy hart, and his wide mouth did gape
> With huge great teeth, like to a tusked bore:
> For he liv'd all on ravin and on rape
> Of men and beasts; and fed on fleshly gore,
> The signe whereof yet stain'd his bloudy lips afore. (St. 5)

Like a 'green man' he had a wreath of ivy about him, and carried a great oaken staff. Amoret escaped, but he pursued and caught her, and was destroyed by the 'gentle Squire' and Amoret's sister Belphoebe.

In contrast is the gentle savage in Bk VI. iv, who, seeing Serena and Sir Calepine being attacked by Sir Turpine, feels an unwonted pity, and being 'invulnerable made by Magicke leare', chases Sir Turpine away and allays Serena's feare of his own roughness:

> But the wilde man, contrarie to her feare,
> Came to her creeping like a fawning hound,
> And by rude tokens made to her appeare
> His deepe compassion of her dolefull stound,
> Kissing his hands, and crouching to the ground;
> For other language had he none, nor speach,
> But a soft murmure, and confused sound,
> Of senselesse words, which nature did him teach,
> T'expresse his passions, which his reason did impeach. (St. 11)

This recalls Caliban's behaviour on first meeting Prospero. Caliban, too, spoke no language until Prospero taught him. But whereas Caliban soon turned against the civilized intruder, Serena's 'salvage man' sheltered her in his lair, and handed her over to Prince Arthur.

Shakespeare would find in Spenser many references to the importance of civilized arts and trades. Even Serena's gentle

savage was a 'bad Stuard' since he 'neither plow'd nor sow'd';
and the cannibals in VI. viii. 35ff. lived by robbery

> ne did give
> Themselves to any trade, as for to drive
> The painefull plough, or cattell for to breed,
> Or by adventrous marchandize to thrive.

They lived by pillage, 'on the labours of poore men to feed'.
Spenser's ideal was not the Utopia of Montaigne's essay on
'Cannibals' which Gonzalo quoted in II. i. 144–69. He held
that the arts of civilization were a higher stage in human life
than even the most innocent life according to nature. Shakespeare agreed with Spenser. Gonzalo's vision of anarchy was a
lovely illusion. The play, like the Virginian pamphlets, stressed
the importance of work. Ferdinand must toil to prove his fitness to marry Miranda. Caliban's loutish idleness, his unwillingness to serve, his schemes of robbery, are typical of his
baseness.

Many of Caliban's characteristics come from travellers'
tales about primitive men, and he is plainly a refutation of
Gonzalo's dream. From Pory's translation of Leo Africanus,
Shakespeare had learned about the savagery of some African
tribes, and he had read other Western voyagers besides those
to Virginia. In the very first English book on America, *Of the
newe landes and of the people founde by the messengers of the kynge of
portyngale named Emanuel*[1] he could read of a people that 'goeth
all naked' except for feather ornaments: 'These folke lyve lyke
beastes without any reasonablenes and the wymmen be also as
comon . . . And they ete also͜one another.' In Richard Eden's
A treatyse of the newe India (1553)[2] Columbus, voyaging 'to the
Canibales' (actually Dominica and other West Indian islands)
found 'certayn young men bound to postes, and kept to be
made fatte' (Arber, p. 30). The Spaniards 'abused the submission and frendshippe of the inhabitants of the Ilandes' (p.
31), whereby the Indians 'became more disobedient and wyld,
degeneratinge from all kind of honestie and faithfulnes'.

---

[1] From the third letter of Amerigo Vespucci. Cf. *The First Three English Books on
America*, ed. E. Arber, 1895, pp. xxv–vii.
[2] A translation of Sebastian Münster's *Cosmographia Universalis*.

Magellan, too, found cannibals, and when sailing down the coast of S. America he saw

> certeyn Indians gatheringe shel fyshes by the sea bankes: beyng men of very high stature, clothed with beastes skinnes. To whom, whereas certayne of the Spaniards went a land, and shewed them belles and paynted papers, they began to daunce and leape about the Spaniardes, with a rude and murmuring songe . . . They interteined their gestes after a barbarous and beastly maner, which nevertheles semed to them princelike. (32–3)

Eden's translation of the first three Decades of Pietro Martire (1555), being published in the reign of Queen Mary, was more favourable to the Spaniards than most, and he thought that the Indians' bondage 'is such, as is much rather to be desired then their former libertie', since the Spaniards 'browghte unto these newe gentyles the victorie of Chrystes death, wherby they beinge subdued with the worldely sworde, are now made free from the bondage of Sathans tyrannie' (p. 50). In Hispaniola the natives were restive under European rule: 'The inhabitants of these Ilandes have byn ever soe used to live at libertie, in playe and pastime, that they can hardely away with the yoke of servitude which they attempt to shake off by all meanes they maye.' They only need Christianity and freedom to make their lives blissful; indeed, the account given of their lives before the Spaniards invaded them suggests that they had need of nothing but to be left alone! Caliban's rebelliousness owes much to such accounts.

The superstitious nature of Caliban and Prospero's use of it may have been suggested by various West Indian beliefs. Thus according to P. Martire, at Guadaloupe, 'they knowe none other god then the Sunne and Moone, although they make certaine Images of gossamine cotton to the similitude of such phantasies as they say appere to them in the nyghte' (*Dec.* 1, Arber, p. 69). Similar 'phantasies and illusions of evyll spirites' were also common in Hispaniola (p. 99). Caliban's mother's god Setebos, however, came from Magellan's voyage,[1] during which he captured two giants in Patagonia by pretending that he would give them some chains if they would shackle them-

'A Briefe Declaration of the Voyage of the Spaniardes round about the World' by Marco Antonio Pigafetta; in R. Eden, *History of the Travayle*, 1577, f. 434.

selves: 'In fine, when they saw how they were deceaved they rored lyke bulles, and cryed uppon thyr greate devyll *Setebos* to helpe them.' At a man's death Setebos 'maketh great mirth and rejoysinge'. One of the giants died of the heat at the Equator; the other lived until famine struck the vessel.

> On a tyme, as one made a crosse before him, and kyssed it, shewynge it unto hym, he suddeynely cryed *Setebos*, and declared by signes that if they made any more crosses, *Setebos* wold enter into his body and make him brust, But when in fine he sawe no hurte coome thereof, he tooke the crosse, and imbrased and kyssed it oftentymes, desyring that he myght bee a Chrystian before his death. He was therfor baptysed and named Paule. (Arber, p. 252)

Caliban is not a Christian, for he is brutish and almost in-educable, and is therefore treated as a slave. This agrees with 'the law, made by *Ferdinando*,[1] onely against *Canibals*; *That all which would not bee Christians, should bee bondslaves*'. Prospero is justified in his attitude to him. Yet the ambiguity of the travel-lers' opinions about the American natives affects Shakespeare's handling of Caliban. He is a base creature, yet, like Shylock, he has a valid point of view and some reason for his grudge against Prospero. Previously he was king of the island; he welcomed the stranger and showed him how to live there; yet he was reduced to servitude and forced to labour. He calls in vain on Setebos, but he is not converted to Christianity, merely to acceptance of his lot.

In this respect Caliban is made a more interesting and complex figure than the Bremio of *Mucedorus* (*c.* 1598), who is a 'wild man' of the most ferocious sort, a bestial cannibal without reason or moral sense, who abducts the heroine Amadine, is somewhat tamed by love for her, and is killed by Mucedorus[2] [Text VIII].

Caliban is not an eater of human flesh, nor were all natives

---

[1] Ferdinand V of Castile (1452–1516). The quotation is from Donne's *Ignatius his Conclave* (1610) in *Poetry and Prose*, ed. J. Hayward, 1932, p. 393.

[2] Doubtless the lost play *Valentine and Orson* (performed at Court, 1600) contained a similar wild man, for in the French romance translated by Henry Watson, EETS, Orig. Ser. 204, 1937, ed. A. Dickson, Orson was a fierce savage tamed by Valentine.

of the Caribbean islands whom the Spaniards called 'Canibales'. Caliban may derive his name from 'cannibal', or from the Romany word 'cauliban' (blackness).[1] In the Names of the Actors he is described as 'A salvage and deformed slave'. Ariel on the other hand is 'an airy spirit'. His origins have been much debated.[2] Ariel is Jerusalem in *Isaiah* xxiv, where the prophet foretells troubles like those brought upon the sinners in *The Tempest*. In *Paradise Lost*, vi, 371 he is a fallen angel defeated by Abdiel, but in Gaelic hymns he was a good angel, with Uriel and Michael.[3] Some writers on angelology made him one of the planetary spirits.[4] Cornelius Agrippa thought him a daemonic guardian of earth. Shakespeare, probably affected by the sound of his name, makes him a spirit of the air who also plays with fire, and Prospero uses him to 'do me business in the veins of th' earth' (I. 2. 255). Like the air-spirits in Burton[5] he can cause tempests, thunder and lightning. W. C. Curry called him 'a rational Platonic daemon'.[6] He is a 'sublunar' spirit who can be controlled by a sage, and even fall under the spell of a powerful witch such as Sycorax. Her treatment of him (I. 2. 269–93) recalls slightly George Gifford's anecdote of a witch who 'confessed that she had a spirite which did abide in a hollow tree, where there was an hole, out of which hee spake unto her'.[7]

It is unnecessary to seek allegorical significance in the elemental antithesis between Caliban (earth and water) and Ariel (air and fire). Since the theory of humours was fundamental to medicine, anthropology, and magical lore, we can accept them as typical of their particular elements without reducing them to metaphysical ideas. They are personages at different levels in the scale of being: Caliban irrational, almost subhuman, Ariel intuitive, superhuman, yet considerably lower than the angels. Basically he is a 'familiar spirit', but of higher type than the ordinary 'familiar' of witchcraft. The latter

[1] *WSh*, i, p. 494.
[2] See Kermode, *New Arden*, App. B.
[3] Cf. A. Carmichael, ed., *Carmina Gadelica*, 1900, I, p. 94, etc. 'Bith Uiril ri m'chasan, /Bith Airil ri m' chul' ('May Uriel be at my feet, Ariel at my back'—to guard me while sleeping).
[4] See Stacy Johnson, 'The Genesis of Ariel', *ShQ*, ii, 1951, 205–10.
[5] *Anatomy of Melancholy*, Pt 1, Sec. 2, Mem. 1, Subsec. 2.
[6] *Shakespeare's Philosophical Patterns*, Baton Rouge, 1937, pp. 186–8.
[7] *A Dialogue concerning Witches and Witchcraftes*, 1593, Signature I[4v].

was exemplified in Anthony Munday's *John a Kent and John a Cumber* (1594). John a Kent, a conjurer working on the side of virtue, has a 'familiar' called Shrimp, and when the two young heroines are being taken under escort to make hateful marriages he sends Shrimp to mislead the party. Making himself invisible, Shrimp surrounds them with sweet music, encourages the two sad maidens by whispering into their ears, and leads them to the tree where both their lovers and their unwanted suitors are waiting. He casts a spell with music upon the latter; they fall asleep; and the lovers are united to the sound of chimes [Text IX].[1]

This episode may have influenced *A Midsummer Night's Dream*, and Shrimp has something in common with Puck. Ariel has more character than either. Like most elementals he is reluctant to serve a human being, and while obeying Prospero until he has repaid him for rescuing him from Sycorax, he often reminds Prospero of his promise to release him, and eagerly seeks his master's approval of his tricks.

It has been pointed out[2] that several comic incidents in the play closely resemble devices common in the Italian *commedia dell' arte*, and the suggestion is made that Shakespeare was influenced by this Italian drama. There can be no doubt that he knew something about it. There had been Italian players in England in the 1570s, and there are numerous allusions to extemporized acting which show that audiences twenty years later knew about their methods.[3] Falstaff in *1H4*, II. 4. 283, asks, 'Shall we have a play extempore?' but this refers to the kind of invention shown when they mimic the King with his son. Polonius's praise of the players, 'For the law of writ and the liberty, these are the only men' (II. 2. 406–7), seems to refer to the distinction made in *'The Case is Altered* (1597) between 'extemporall' and 'premeditated things', where 'extemporall' means *commedia dell' arte*. In fact the Italian comedies of this kind were not purely extempore. Their characters and scenarii were definite and often laid down in

---

[1] T. T. Reed, 'The Probable Origin of Ariel', *ShQ*, xi, 1960, 61–8.
[2] By F. Neri, *Scenari delle Maschere in Arcadia* (1913); K. M. Lea, *Italian Popular Comedy*, 2 vols, 1934; H. D. Gray, 'The Sources of *The Tempest*', *MLN*, 35, 1920, 321–30.
[3] Chambers, *ElSt*, ii, pp. 262–3; i, p. 494. He found traces of an Italian comedian in 1610, but his speciality is uncertain.

writing.[1] Much of the dialogue was extemporized but some was memorized and applicable to several similar situations. The actor showed his skill in manipulating and adapting comic tricks (*lazzi*) and speeches from his considerable repertoire to the needs of the particular plot.

Since there is no proof that Shakespeare ever saw a *commedia dell' arte* acted it cannot be claimed as a specific influence, but, since there are several remarkable resemblances between incidents in *The Tempest* and incidents in scenarii of *commedie dell' arte*, the possibility remains open. In several of these comedies the scene is an island or pastoral country where comic sailors and nobles or shepherds are shipwrecked.[2] A magician casts spells on the intruders into his realm. Miss Lea notes that in *Il Capriccio* 'a banquet rises from the ground and is snatched away as suddenly by spirits' (i, p. 209). In *I Forestieri* the shipwrecked sailors get drunk. In *Pantaloncino* the wizard is praised for assisting the others, then, declaring that he does not wish to exercise his art any more, but to live among other men, he throws away his wand and book. In *Arbore Incantato* the magician Sabino is served, not by the usual Satyrs, but by a wild man. In *Arcadia Incantata* several features of *The Tempest* are anticipated. Thus there is a Magician who controls events to good ends, using spells and spirits to prevent a human sacrifice and carry the victim to safety (Act I). He conjures up a storm, and the scene shows 'a tempestuous sea, with a ship being wrecked'; the mariners are tormented by spirits both when awake and when asleep; much comedy is got from their hunger, and they are tantalized and cheated of food. When they attempt to pick fruit, 'flames appear; they are terrified; the fruit flies through the air; they try to reach it with sticks; a pot of water is broken, and they are frightened' (Act II). In one version they are offered a plate of macaroni, but their hands are tied, and the spirits rob them.[3]

[1] E.g. those discussed by Neri and in Flaminio Scala, *Il Teatro delle Favole rappresentative*, Venetia, 1611 (cf. *supra*, I, pp. 256–60).
[2] In *La Nave* (1554), a regular comedy by P. M. Scandova, the action occurs on board a ship during a tempest and includes a young man searching for the father he has never known, and an old man seeking a son stolen by pirates when a child. Nothing much happens except the obvious 'discovery'. There are also two marine deities; a Siren and a Monster. Cf. G. Crocioni in *La Bibliofilia*, Nov. 1909–Feb. 1910.
[3] Neri, *op. cit.*, pp. 87–93; Lea, *op. cit.*, ii, pp. 670–4.

There are more parallels in *Li Tre Satiri* (*The Three Satyrs*), a translation of which I provide [Text X].[1] A powerful magician has 'spirits in the shape of wild men' to serve him (i.e. the satyrs). A pure girl, Phillis, ignorant of love, is desired by shipwrecked mariners. Two of these steal the magician's book, by means of which they force the satyrs to supply their (foolish) demands. Two are changed into animals when they drink of the magician's magic fountain; another becomes a woman. A conspiracy is made, but the magician draws a magic circle which makes all who enter it dance without stopping, and soon all the intruders are dancing. The magician releases them only when he gets his book back. Then there is a joyful pairing off.

This is crude stuff compared with *The Tempest*, but some of its ingredients come sufficiently close to the Caliban–Stephano–Trinculo sub-plot to make it seem likely that Shakespeare knew some *commedia dell' arte* situations and *lazzi*. H. D. Gray noted in particular the storm and shipwreck; the plot to steal the magician's book (cf. III. 2. 92–9); the native Fausto's desire for Phillis (cf. Caliban's lust, I. 2. 347–8), and his offer to serve the sailors if they will let him have her (cf. II. 2. 123; but Caliban offers her to Stephano, III. 2. 109); the clowns who dress themselves in stolen garments and are mistaken for gods (cf. Stephano and Trinculo and the 'glistering apparel', IV. 1. 222–55); the bringing together of the characters into a magic circle (V. 1. 30–61).

All these, together with parallels to other scenarii, can scarcely be mere coincidences, though some (such as the storm at sea and the stealing of magic books) were commonplaces of romantic story and drama.[2]

Another likely influence on *The Tempest* was the Court masque, which was developed under King James and his extravagant wife to great splendour in settings, costumes, music, and poetic ideas by writers such as Samuel Daniel and Ben Jonson and with the decorative genius of Inigo Jones. Spectacle, song, dance and fine dress were the soul of Masque, but

[1] Miss Lea also translated this scenario, *op. cit.*; Neri, pp. 77–86.
[2] One of the dramatic pieces in the Oxyrhynchus MS. has a storm, also men made drunk on the stage. The magician's book is stolen in *The Rare Triumphes* (*supra*, p. 100).

there was usually a mild ethical or patriotic theme involving opposition between good and evil or other principles, with mythological or allegorical characters presented in an ideal situation which resulted in the 'presentation' of the chief masquers, male and female, and their participation in elaborate dances. Grotesque and comic figures were often introduced for contrast, and Ben Jonson made this 'antimasque' an integral part of the entertainment.

The claim that Shakespeare was influenced by the Jacobean Court masque in this play is based both on the entertainment presented by Prospero to the newly affianced Ferdinand and Miranda in IV. 1, and, more generally, on the entire spirit of the play with its use of music, dance, grotesque antithesis and disguising.

The interrupted show of Iris, Juno, Ceres, Nymphs and Reapers is certainly in the older tradition of Masque before Ben Jonson and Jones elaborated it to the full. 'Ceres and Juno had appeared in *The Vision of the Twelve Goddesses*. Nymphs, called naiads, were footing it in the same author's *Tethys' Festival*, and their companions, the reapers, gave a "country dance" in the anonymous *Four Seasons*.'[1] In Samuel Daniel's *Vision of the Twelve Goddesses* (1604) the Greek deities, each representing a virtue, descended from a mount to music supposed to be played by satyrs. A Sibyl described their special qualities:[2]

> First here imperial Juno in her chair,
> With sceptre of command for kingdoms large
> Descends all clad in colours of the air,
> Crown'd with bright stars, to signify her charge.

Next to the last came Ceres:

> Next plenteous Ceres in her harvest weed,
> Crown'd with th'increase of what she gave to keep
> To gratitude and faith: in whom we read,
> Who sows on Virtue, shall with glory reap.

The Goddesses gave presents in the Temple of Peace while the three Graces sang about 'Desert, Rewards, and Gratitude/The

[1] J. R. A. Nicoll, *Stuart Masques and the Renaissance Stage*, 1937, p. 19. Nicoll points out that the date of *Four Seasons* is uncertain.
[2] Cf. *The Vision*, ed. Joan Rees, in *A Book of Masques*, Cambridge, 1967, pp. 19–42.

graces of society', then trod a measure in geometrical motions
before dancing with their lords. The whole was introduced and
closed by Iris, messenger of the Gods, who praised Britain as
'the land of civil music and of rest'. This was a stiff formal
entertainment, with no antimasque.

Iris and Juno appeared again in Jonson's much more splendid *Masque of Hymen* (1606) celebrating the marriage of the
fourteen-year-old Robert, Earl of Essex to the thirteen-year-
old Frances, daughter of the Earl of Suffolk.[1] The theme was
'union', the need for order and harmony in private and public
life, the necessary control of Reason over the Humours and
Affections. The masque traced the chief stages of a Roman
wedding, the auspices, the preparation of the bride, the solemnities, the bringing of the bride to her groom, the Epithalamium—all with a great display of classical learning which
doubtless pleased the King. Juno was revealed seated in the
heavens and sending down 'eight of her noblest Powers . . .
That govern nuptial mysteries'. Hymen acted as Presenter.
Jonson tried to deepen the significance of the piece by a setting
of cosmic harmony in which Inigo Jones brilliantly represented
the regions of air and fire, the turning globe which contained
the male masquers, the clouds in which musicians sat figuring
'airy spirits', the rainbow (with Iris), and above it all a statue of
Jupiter. Excerpts are given below to indicate passages most
relevant to *The Tempest* [Text XI].

Before *The Tempest* was written Jonson had written two sea-
masques, which Shakespeare may have seen performed. In *The
Masque of Blackness* (1605/6), by the Queen's request the twelve
masquing ladies were 'at first blackmoors', daughters of Niger,
but, coming to Britain, were 'blanched' by the temperate clime
and royal power. The scene changed from a landscape of
woods and hunting to a seascape, with Tritons (half-men, half-
fish), sea-maids, and Oceanus. In the sequel, *The Masque of
Beauty* (1608/9), Jonson imagined four black Nymphs, yearning
to be white like their sisters, but afflicted by malicious Night,
sea-tossed and landing on a 'floating island'. This approaches

[1] A Quarto appeared in 1606. In this Jonson paid tributes to Jones, to the com-
poser Alphonso Ferrabosco and to the inventor of the dances, Thomas Giles. In the
1616 Folio he omitted the acknowledgments, having quarrelled with Jones. Cf.
Works, ed. C. H. Herford and P. Simpson, vii; D. J. Gordon in *Journal of the
Warburg and Courtauld Institutes*, viii, 1945, 107-45.

Britain and we are shown 'an island floating on a calm water'; on it the Throne of Beauty which 'had a circular motion of its own, imitating that which we call *motum mundi*, from the east to the west, or the right to the left side'. Below were Cupids on steps which 'had a motion contrary, with analogy *ad motum planetarum*, from the west to the east'.

In neither masque did the sea play a dramatic part, but both showed the Court's appreciation of a marine entertainment with 'coloured' participants. Shakespeare may have recalled this when considering an island comedy.

There are a few likenesses between Prospero's betrothal-masque and Jonson's *Hymenaei*. In both (as in Daniel) Juno is queen of the sky, and Iris is present; but these were commonplaces inherent in the mythological conceit. More significant perhaps is the emphasis on chastity. Jonson's Reason insists that passionate love must be restrained and sanctioned by marriage:

> O Juno, Hymen, Hymen, Juno, who
> Can merit with you two?
> Without your presence Venus can do nought
> Save what with shame is bought . . .

After Prospero warns Ferdinand sternly against letting passion overcome him before marriage (IV. 1. 14–56) Iris declares that Venus and Cupid 'thought to have done/Some wanton charm upon this man and maid, Whose vows are, that no bed-right shall be paid/Till Hymen's torch be lighted' (94–7). This is not enough to prove a direct influence of *Hymenaei* on *The Tempest*.

The more general influence of masques has been examined by Miss Enid Welsford.[1] 'In *The Tempest*, as in the masques, music and dancing are closely associated.' Masquers are often supposed to have travelled a long way, to have been hindered by enchantments, and are helped by someone's magic power. Travel and magic are important in the play. 'Only in Shakespeare's play the power who works the magic is no longer a royal spectator, but a character within the drama.' Yet Prospero is somewhat like a masque Presenter as he manipulates both human and spirit characters. As in the masque a moment of transformation is 'marked by the sudden appearance of the

---

[1] E. Welsford, *The Court Masque*, Cambridge, 1927, Ch. XII.

masquers', so in *The Tempest* all leads up to the moment when the victorious Prospero 'discovers Ferdinand and Miranda playing at chess' (V. 1. 171). Undoubtedly there is something in this. Shakespeare had used elements of masque before, but never suffused them, as here, through the stuff of the entire play. The island-setting with its marked antithesis between good and evil, the lofty ideas of Prospero, his didactic strain, and his control of the whole action, may owe something to the masque as well as to the *commedia dell' arte* and the romances. The grotesque behaviour of Caliban and the servants would appeal to lovers of antimasque. And there is much use of costume as well as dance and song. But masque is sublimated into idyllic comedy, whose main features are action, dialogue, and characterization. There is real conflict, not just a statement of principles or attributes. The antimasque figures participate in a plot.

A short survey of the action of the play will serve to show how cunningly Shakespeare fused the several elements in his imaginative conception.

The tempest (I.1) which gives occasion for the story is naturalistically treated (on the lines of Erasmus's celebrated 'Colloquium' [Text XII][1] with the Boatswain cursing like a tough sailor when pestered by landsmen at the height of the storm. Gonzalo shows himself at once a courageous, whimsical old man, whereas Sebastian and Antonio are 'out of patience' and capable of as much bad language as any mariner. In I. 2, Prospero, taking off his magic robe, tells Miranda (and us) that the 'dreadful spectacle of the wreck' was arranged by him and that no one was lost. His long expository speeches explaining it and how they came to the island show a humorous self-consciousness in the dramatist about the awkward nature of the retrospective narrative ('Dost thou attend me?' . . . 'Thou attend'st not!' . . . 'Dost thou hear?' . . .'Hear a little farther'). Prospero brings out the contrast between the Duke neglectful of his office in his pursuit of higher knowledge, and his brother Antonio, whose gradual deterioration when given power is subtly traced (I. 2. 75–109) till he offered to pay homage and tribute to the King of Naples in return for aid in

---

[1] *Familiarium colloquiorum opus* . . ., London, 1571: *Seven Dialogues both pithie and profitable*, trans. W. B[urton], 1606.

removing Prospero. The kindness of Gonzalo (whom we have seen but who has not yet been named) in helping Miranda and her father to survive when set adrift explains how Prospero has been able to educate her and pursue his own studies ('with volumes that/I prize above my dukedom').

He puts her to sleep now in order to speak freely to Ariel, whose obedience and powers are demonstrated in his account of the storm and how he 'flam'd amazement' about the stricken vessel and drove those aboard her out of their minds with fear; yet nobody is hurt, the shipwrecked passengers are dispersed in three groups about the island, and the ship is safely hidden, with 'The mariners all under hatches stow'd' (I. 2. 230). The island must be in the Mediterranean, but the allusion to 'the still-vext Bermoothes' shows that Shakespeare had the recent pamphlets in mind, and intended spectators to draw some parallels.

In supplying Ariel with a past history a vivid contrast is made between the Puck-like liveliness of this 'familiar spirit' and the 'damn'd witch' Sycorax and her 'demi-devil' son Caliban. Ariel, though grateful for being released from the witch's cruel spell, is impatient to be free from service. His ability to change his shape is proved when he appears as 'a nymph of the sea', invisible to all save Prospero and the audience. The dull brutishness of Caliban is at once apparent when he enters, cursing Prospero for taking advantage of his kindness in showing him 'all the qualities o' th' isle/The fresh springs, brine pits, barren place, and fertile'. Prospero reminds him that he tried to violate Miranda, and describes his own efforts to educate the savage.

Meanwhile at his master's bidding Ariel has lured Ferdinand with music to the spot where he meets Miranda. They take each other for gods, and fall in love at once. Prospero is pleased, but must put obstacles in the way, for the best of reasons: 'This swift business/I must uneasy make, lest too light winning/Make the prize light' (447–9). Ferdinand must prove himself; hence he is accused of spying and treated like a prisoner, and Miranda must realize that 'The course of true love never did run smooth.'

II. 1 takes us to the group of nobles round King Alonso of Naples, Prospero's one-time enemy. Several types are portrayed: first, Gonzalo, manfully trying to hearten the King (grieving over the loss of his son), is mocked by Sebastian and

Antonio, who ill-naturedly refuse to agree that the island is agreeable,[1] and go on to regret the marriage of Alonso's daughter Claribel to the King of Tunis. Sebastian indeed openly reproaches his brother for allowing it and so causing their shipwreck (72–3; 124–41). Still trying to amuse his master, Gonzalo describes the Utopia he would set up if he ruled the island—drawing on Florio's Montaigne no doubt, but mindful also of the travellers' tales which both Shakespeare and Montaigne knew.[2] His innocent fancy is ridiculed until he grows angry (183–90).

Ariel, in control of the situation, sends all to sleep save Sebastian and Antonio. When Antonio tempts Sebastian to murder his brother and make himself King of Naples (II. 1. 203–98) the parallel to his former plot against Prospero is drawn (270–92) and his complete lack of conscience displayed. Ariel saves Gonzalo's life, and the King's, by waking the former, and the villains excuse their drawn swords by stories of loud noises (such as were heard in Bermuda (*infra*, p. 280)) while they were guarding the party. They leave in search of Ferdinand.

Attention is now turned (II. 2) to the servants Stephano (a butler) and Trinculo (a jester), whose appearance terrifies Caliban as he carries home wood and curses Prospero for every accident that befalls him. Storms are frequent on this island (as in the Caribbean) and Trinculo, after deciding that the creature cowering there must be 'an islander' struck by a thunderbolt, shelters under his gaberdine, despite his 'very ancient and fish-like smell'.[3]

Stephano, having got ashore on a butt of wine similar to those thrown overboard by the sailors (*infra*, p. 279), is already tipsy, but suspects 'savages and men of Ind' when he sees a monster with four legs, and would like to take it home to Naples. There is much amusing 'business' with the bottle, which convinces Caliban that Stephano is 'a brave god, and bears celestial liquor: I will kneel to him' (II. 2. 114–16). As once he helped Prospero so now he will help Stephano to survive (much

---

[1] So we are reminded of the two opposed views of the New World.
[2] Montaigne got much information from a servant who had spent some years in America (Essay on 'Cannibals').
[3] The allusion 'they will lay out ten [doits] to see a dead Indian' is to the popularity of living specimens brought back by the voyagers and sold to be put on public show, alive or dead (for they rarely survived long).

as the men in Bermuda did). His willingness to be Stephano's servant parallels Antonio's service to Sebastian, and just as Antonio is to be free from tribute (II. 1. 294–5) so Caliban will make no more dams for fish (as the Indians did for the settlers), and like the lazier colonists he'll not 'fetch in firing' (cf. *infra*, p. 298). He goes out drunkenly crying on Freedom.

In immediate contrast III. 1 shows Ferdinand carrying wood (like the nobler settlers, or some fairy-tale hero set an impossible task): 'I must remove/Some thousands of these logs and pile them up.' For love of Miranda he does so gladly, and Prospero approves of their troth-plight, which he has brought to pass; for here the Revenge-convention is broken, since the avenger is glad that his enemy's son is to marry his daughter.

While this tender scene goes on Caliban and the servants are drinking (III. 2) and Trinculo, envious of Stephano's mastery over Caliban, grows quarrelsome and is threatened with the punishment of Bermudan mutineers, hanging from a tree (36–7). Ariel's invisibility enables him to make fun of them, and to overhear their plot to kill Prospero while he is having his siesta, to burn his books, and to give Miranda to Stephano ('She will become thy bed, I warrant/and bring thee forth a brood' (109–10)). The airy Spirit charms them with his pipe and tabor—music for the unsophisticated—and they follow him.

Elsewhere the noblemen are weary with fruitless search for Ferdinand (III. 3), but the plotters Antonio and Sebastian hope to murder the King in the night. Supervising this scene is Prospero, whose Spirits take 'strange Shapes' and offer a banquet. No doubt remembering the feasts sometimes offered to Europeans by friendly Indians, Gonzalo praises the dumb eloquence of these islanders and mentions the strange beings recently made known by travellers' tales (III. 3. 43–9).[1]

He persuades Alonso to eat, but, to the sound of more thunder, Ariel, like a harpy, makes the banquet vanish.[2] This

---

[1] E.g. the mountaineers 'dewlapp'd like bulls', sufferers from goitre found in Switzerland, etc.; and the 'men whose heads stood in their breasts', written of by Raleigh and Keymis, but long before by Mandeville.

[2] The 'harpy' relates the vision to the punishment of Phineus who, because of his cruelty to his children by Cleopatra, daughter of Boreas, was kept in constant alarm by the three Harpies, bird-women sent by Jove to spoil the food on Phineus's tables. Aeneas fought against them in the Photades off Greece (Bk 3, 219–58).

tantalizing piece of masque leads on to the condemnation pronounced by Ariel on the guilty men who injured Prospero and
his daughter. In most romances this would be followed by
death or enchantment; but Prospero's aim is not physical
revenge, for Ariel, as his minister of justice, offers escape from
'lingering perdition' through 'heart-sorrow/And a clear life
ensuing'. The Shapes re-enter to remove the banqueting table
(probably because the 'quaint device' of stage-machinery
could not take away the table with the banquet). Prospero
approves of the way his high charms are working. His enemies
are in his power, and he leaves the leaven of conscience to
work in Alonso. Sebastian and Antonio are defiant. Gonzalo
sees the poison of their guilt beginning 'to bite the spirits'.

While the guilty men's punishment increases, Ferdinand's
testing-time is over (IV. 1), and Prospero gives him his
daughter, with grave warnings against taking advantage of
her innocence before they are married (13–23; 51–4). He proceeds to entertain the happy couple with a masque (60–142)
in which Iris, sent by Juno, brings Ceres to bless the betrothal.
Venus and Cupid have been prevented from seducing them
with 'some wanton charm'. The 'queen of heaven' and her
'bounteous sister' invoke honour, prosperity and increase. Iris
summons Naiads ('temperate nymphs') and Reapers to celebrate in dance the 'contract of true love', but Prospero cuts
short the masque on realizing that Caliban's plot is about to be
attempted. Quickly he dismisses Miranda and Ferdinand, pretending that his 'old brain is troubled', and summons Ariel to
give his report, how (like Puck) he misled his victims through
all sorts of obstacles, and finally left them 'dancing up to the
chins' in a filthy pond.[1] The 'glistering apparel' which Ariel
hangs on a line (IV. 1. 193) distracts the rogues in their

At James I's court the 'disappearing feast' or 'antepast' was an example of Sir
James Hay's 'conspicuous waste', for he 'brought in the vanity of antesuppers . . .
The manner of which was, to have the board covered at the first entrance of the
guests with dishes, as high as a tall man could well reach, filled with the choycest
and dearest viands sea or land could afford. And all this once seen, and having
feasted the eyes of the invited, was in a manner throwne away, and fresh set on to
the same height, having only this advantage of the other, that it was hot.' F.
Osborne, *Secret History of the Court of James I*, 1811 edn, i, 270.
[1] The movements described by Ariel (171–84) recall the dancing of enchanted
persons in the *commedie dell' arte*.

miserable, wet state,[1] despite Caliban's angry protests, and they are loading him with garments to carry away when they are set on by 'divers Spirits, in shape of hounds', and hunted off (255).

Act V begins at six p.m. All Prospero's enemies are in his power. The nobles are pent in the grove near the cell, and melancholy with guilt. The magician's vengeance is complete, and, sending Ariel to release them, he abjures use of magic (33–58). But first he must address his bemused enemies, accusing them, forgiving them, and convincing them of his identity by donning ducal robes 'As I was sometime Milan' (86). He embraces Alonso and loyal Gonzalo and lets Antonio and Sebastian know that he is aware of their treachery. Thus he leads up to the 'discovery' of Ferdinand and Miranda playing chess, the reunion of son and father, and the announcement of the betrothal. Ariel brings the Shipmaster and Boatswain to show their amazement at the safety of their ship and their own liberation; then drives in Caliban, Stephano and Trinculo in their stolen finery to be mocked at. The play is wound up with promise of 'calm seas, auspicious gales' under the care of Ariel, who will then be free to the elements, 'and fare thee well'.

The foregoing survey demonstrates that Shakespeare drew for his plot on the several kinds of narrative and drama already cited. His decision to compress it all into the final day may have been influenced by *commedia dell' arte* practice, or it may have been a reaction against his own method in *Pericles* and *The Winter's Tale*, or even a retort to classicists who accused him of laxity in construction.[2] Shakespeare might well have asserted, with Ben Jonson, 'The laws of time, place, person he observeth',[3] for in this play he is at pains to point out, through

---

[1] Cf. the gods' dresses used by the mariners in *Li Tre Satiri* (*infra*, p. 324). It is possible that Shakespeare was glancing at the Jacobean courtiers' love of expensive, extravagant costume, which James I sometimes tried to curb. (A. Wilson, *History of Great Britain*, 1653, p. 93: 'All the study was, who should be most glorious, and he had the happiest *fancie*, whose inventions could express something *novel*, neat, and unusuall, that others might admire.' He takes Sir James Hay as an example.)

[2] Cf. Jonson's attack on the habit in romantic or history plays 'To make a child, now swaddled, to proceed/Man, and then shoot up, in one beard and weed/ Past three-score years' (*Ev. Man In.*, Prologue).

[3] Prologue to *Volpone*.

Prospero, that the action occupies, not the 'single revolution of the sun' demanded by purists, but only about four hours, i.e. little more than the time taken to play it on the stage.[1] In this, however, he was reverting to his earliest practice in comedy (*A Comedy of Errors*, *The Taming of the Shrew*). And once the expository speeches of Prospero are over, the plot is well-knitted, and flows smoothly, largely of course owing to the banished Duke's function as Presenter and inspirer of it all.

As A. H. Gilbert pointed out,[2] Shakespeare conceived his plot and characters in parallel or antithetical pairs. Two fathers (Prospero and Alonso) who have been enemies, have children (Miranda and Ferdinand) who fall in love. The two brothers Prospero and Antonio are opposed in nature. The island has contained two kinds of supernatural, black (with Sycorax) and white (with Prospero). The children of these two opposed magicians (Caliban and Miranda) are entirely antithetical. The shipwrecked voyagers fall into two parties, the nobles and the clowns. There are two conspiracies, one against Alonso, the other against Prospero, with Antonio and Sebastian in the one, and Stephano and Trinculo in the other. Prospero's two servants, Ariel and Caliban, are continually contrasted with one another both in character and actions, and so on.

With great skill Shakespeare prevented this symmetry from becoming too obvious, and he was helped here by his insistence on ethical rather than merely mechanical plotting. *The Tempest* was built up round a number of moral ideas, some suggested by his sources, others no doubt emerging in the process of composition. So the adventures of the Virginian voyagers suggested both his title and setting and also the essential transformation by which storm and shipwreck give place to life on a happy island, and the turbulent passions of restless and discontented men are allayed under the control of a firm paternal government. Subsidiary topics raised by the travel-books and used in the comedy were the necessity of law and order; the differences between savage and civilized men; the various kinds of human 'nature'; the conditions needed to make an ideal commonwealth; the ideals of service and obedience, of chastity and

[1] Cf. I. 2. 239–41; III. 1. 94–6; V. 1. 3–4.
[2] A. H. Gilbert, '*The Tempest*: Parallelism in Characters and Situations', *JEGP*, xiv, 1915, 63–74.

self-restraint. The basic conflict between good and bad governed his exploration of the manifold ways in which a sad predicament may be faced by the well- and the ill-disposed.

Examples of the way in which Shakespeare adjusted the action and tone to the natures of his characters are to be found in the conspiracies. Within each of them the participants have different motives. Sebastian wishes to be King, Antonio to be free from tribute and to feel his own power; Caliban wants freedom and revenge; the Clowns want booty. The punishments of the two parties also befit their rank and natures. The clowns are tormented physically, the nobles by exposure, 'distractions', and remorse. The idea of servitude is portrayed in two parallel scenes of wood-bearing: Caliban in II. 2 and Ferdinand in III. 1 perform similar tasks but in very different spirit.

The presentation on the island of so much human diversity may well have been suggested by the accounts of Gates's misadventure. As his ship the *Sea-Venture* bore a microcosm of English society, from nobles to layabouts, so Shakespeare's island presents a microcosm of the sublunary world and its hierarchy, from the refined spirit of air and fire, through the several degrees of humanity—Sage, King, Nobles, Sailors, Servants—down to the indigenous savage, Caliban, whose ambiguous birth links him with the base demons of earth and water.

Over all these various beings, Prospero (like Sir Thomas Gates in Bermuda) exercises a mastery which, however apparently harsh at times, is for their ultimate good. But since the play is a romance and not a history, Prospero (more happily than any Governor of Virginia) is able to enforce his will by means of magic. The action is punctuated by a series of supernatural interventions, each occurring at a climax in the testing or punishment of the characters.[1] Thus, Ferdinand is struck motionless when he would resist arrest as a spy (I. 2. 461–83); Ariel draws the clowns after him with music (III. 2) and the courtiers are tantalized by the illusive banquet (III. 3). When Ferdinand has passed the test of obedience and self-discipline his betrothal to Miranda is celebrated by the Masque of

---

[1] Cf. *New Arden*, p. lxxiv, where it is suggested that 'at the climax of each plot there is a spectacular contrivance borrowed from the Masque'.

Ceres (IV. 1).[1] The plot of Caliban and the servants is dissi-
pated when they steal the 'glistering apparel' and are hunted by
spirit hounds (IV. 1), and finally Prospero enchants them all
with spells which bring them together for the 'discovery'.

This use of the supernatural and the masterful aloofness,
the didactic nature of Prospero, have encouraged some critics
to treat the play as an allegory. The whole piece is indeed so
permeated with Christian feeling that it has been interpreted
as a Mystery play in which Prospero, if not the Deity, is 'the
hierophant or initiating priest' in a rite of purification which
the Court party must willy-nilly undergo. Caliban in such a
view becomes the Monster to be overcome, and Miranda Wisdom, the Celestial Bride (like Una in *The Faerie Queene*, Bk I).
This theory touches the nonsensical, yet there can be no doubt
that in *The Tempest*, more than in the other 'romances',
Shakespeare was thinking of human life in a cosmic way and
presenting characters in terms of their approach to or departure from a moral perfection in which reason and the affections
would be united with grace.

Prospero, however, is not Providence, but a Sage with human
weaknesses, whose vengeful promptings have long been schooled
by philosophic meditation. He is given passions, a trace of
humour, and a parental fussiness which prevent his seeming a
bloodless schemer, even a tyrant. He is the instrument of 'The
powers delaying, not forgetting', as Ariel indicates (III. 3.
53–82), and he torments evil-doers because only pain can bring
them to penitence.

Much has been made of the Redemption-theme, but it is
not stressed in this play. The gross and wicked are punished,
but neither the process nor the effect of their repentance is
portrayed in any detail. They are viewed from outside, for the
central figure is always the Good Governor (a sublimated Sir
Thomas Gates) who is a merciful judge. He is satisfied with
verbal expressions of conversion. Even the sullen Antonio,
that 'most wicked sir, whom to call brother/Would even infect
my mouth', is forgiven, but his sins are not forgotten. And
although Gonzalo, amiable and well-meaning to the last,
declares that they have found 'all of us ourselves/When no
man was his own', there is little sign of spiritual regeneration.

[1] A good reason for rejecting the idea that the Masque was inserted later.

In the last resort the play is a 'romance', and the ethical content is not allowed to destroy the sense of wonder, but rather blends with it to evoke pleasure at participating in astonishing events, joy in the miraculous victories of good over evil, and deep satisfaction at the reconciliation of old enemies and the union of young lovers.

I. Source

From
A TRUE REPORTORY OF THE
WRACKE AND REDEMPTION OF
SIR THOMAS GATES, KNIGHT
By William Strachey (1610)[1]

A true reportory of the wracke, and redemption of Sir
Thomas Gates Knight; upon, and from the Ilands of the
Bermudas: his comming to Virginia, and the estate of
that Colonie then, and after, under the government of
the Lord La Warre, July 15. 1610. written by William
Strachy, Esquire.

I

A most dreadfull Tempest (the manifold deaths whereof,
are here to the life described)[2] their wracke on Bermuda,
and the description of those Ilands.

Excellent Lady, know that upon Friday late in the evening, we
brake ground out of the Sound of Plymouth, our whole Fleete then
consisting of seven good Ships, and two Pinnaces, all which from the
said second of June, unto the twenty three of July, kept in friendly
consort together, not a whole watch at any time losing the sight each
of other . . . We were within seven or eight dayes at the most, by
Cap. Newports reckoning of making Cape Henry upon the coast of
Virginia. When on S. James his day, July 24. being Monday (preparing for no lesse all the blacke night before) the cloudes gathering
thicke upon us, and the windes singing, and whistling most unusually
which made us to cast off our Pinnace towing the same untill then
asterne, a dreadfull storme and hideous began to blow from out the
North-east, which swelling, and roaring as it were by fits, some

---

[1] From *Purchas his Pilgrimes*, Pt II, Bk X, 1625. Marginal notes are omitted.
[2] The ensuing narrative mentions no deaths.

houres with more violence then others, at length did beate all light from heaven; which like an hell of darkenesse turned blacke upon us;[1] so much the more fuller of horror, as in such cases horror and feare use to overrunne the troubled, and overmastered sences of all which (taken up with amazement) the eares lay so sensible to the terrible cries, and murmurs of the windes, and distraction of our Company, as who was most armed, and best prepared, was not a little shaken.[2] For surely (Noble Lady) as death comes not so sodaine nor apparant, so he comes not so elvish and painfull (to men especially even then in health and perfect habitudes of body) as at Sea; who comes at no time so welcome, but our frailty (so weake is the hold of hope in miserable demonstrations of danger) it makes guilty of many contrary changes, and conflicts: For indeede death is accompanied at no time, nor place with circumstances every way so uncapable of particularities of goodnesse and inward comforts, as at Sea[3] . . .

For foure and twenty houres the storme in a restlesse tumult, had blowne so exceedingly, as we could not apprehend in our imaginations any possibility of greater violence, yet did wee still finde it, not onely more terrible, but more constant, fury added to fury, and one storme urging a second more outragious then the former; whether it so wrought upon our feares, or indeede met with new forces: Sometimes strikes in our Ship amongst women, and passengers, not used to such hurly and discomforts, made us looke one upon the other with troubled hearts, and panting bosomes: our clamours dround in the windes, and the windes in thunder. Prayers might well be in the heart and lips,[4] but drowned in the outcries of the Officers:[5] nothing heard that could give comfort,[6] nothing seene that might incourage hope. It is impossible for me, had I the voyce of Stentor, and expression of as many tongues, as his throate of voyces, to expresse the outcries and miseries,[7] not languishing, but wasting his spirits, and art constant to his owne principles, but not prevailing. Our sailes wound up lay without their use, and if at any time wee bore but a Hollocke, or halfe forecourse, to guide her before the Sea, six and sometimes eight men were not inough to hold the whipstaffe in the steerage, and the tiller below in the Gunner roome, by which may be imagined the strength of the storme: In which, the Sea swelled above the Clouds, and gave battell unto Heaven. It could not be said to raine, the

[1] I. 2. 3–5.
[2] I. 2. 207–10.
[3] Hence Gonzalo, I. 1. 66–7.
[4] I. 1. 53–6.
[5] Cf. the Boatswain, I. 1. 37–8.
[6] I. 1. 29. Gonzalo whimsically takes comfort from the Bo'sun's gruffness.
[7] I. 2. 8–9.

waters like whole Rivers did flood in the ayre. And this I did still observe, that whereas upon the Land, when a storme hath powred it selfe forth once in drifts of raine, the winde as beaten downe, and vanquished therewith, not long after indureth: here the glut of water (as if throatling the winde ere while) was no sooner a little emptied and qualified, but instantly the windes (as having gotten their mouthes now free, and at liberty) spake more loud, and grew more tumultuous, and malignant.[1] What shall I say? Windes and Seas were as mad, as fury and rage could make them;[2] for mine owne part, I had bin in some stormes before, . . . Yet all that I had ever suffered gathered together, might not hold comparison with this: there was not a moment in which the sodaine splitting, or instant over-setting of the Shippe was not expected.[3]

Howbeit this was not all; It pleased God to bring a greater affliction yet upon us; for in the beginning of the storme we had received likewise a mighty leake . . .

Our Governour, upon the Tuesday morning (at what time, by such who had bin below in the hold, the Leake was first discovered) had caused the whole Company, about one hundred and forty, besides women, to be equally divided into three parts, and opening the Ship in three places (under the forecastle, in the waste, and hard by the Bitacke) appointed each man where to attend; and there-unto every man came duely upon his watch, tooke the Bucket, or Pumpe for one houre, and rested another. Then men might be seene to labour I may well say, for life, and the better sort, even our Governour, and Admirall themselves, not refusing their turne, and to spell each the other, to give example to other.[4] The common sort stripped naked, as men in Gallies, the easier both to hold out, and to shrinke from under the salt water, which continually leapt in among them, kept their eyes waking, and their thoughts and hands working, with tyred bodies, and wasted spirits, three dayes and foure nights destitute of outward comfort, and desperate of any deliverance, testifying how mutually willing they were, yet by labour to keepe each other from drowning, albeit each one drowned whilest he laboured.[5]

Once, so huge a Sea brake upon the poope and quarter, upon us, as it covered our Shippe from stearne to stemme, like a garment or a vast cloude, it filled her brimme full for a while within, from the hatches up to the sparre decke. This source or confluence of water

---

[1] I. 1. 7–8.
[2] I. 2. 206–10.
[3] I. 1. 62–3, 'We split, we split.'
[4] Cf. I. 1. 43–5. Characteristically, Sebastian is unwilling and churlish.
[5] Cf. Stephano in different circumstances, V. 1. 256–8.

was so violent, as it rusht and carried the Helm-man from the Helme, and wrested the Whip-staffe out of his hand, which so flew from side to side, that when he would have ceased the same againe, it so tossed him from Star-boord to Larboord, as it was Gods mercy it had not split him: It so beat him from his hold, and so bruised him, as a fresh man hazarding in by chance fell faire with it, and by maine strength bearing somewhat up, made good his place, and with much clamour incouraged and called upon others; who gave her now up, rent in pieces and absolutely lost.[1] Our Governour was at this time below at the Capstone, both by his speech and authoritie heartening every man unto his labour. It strooke him from the place where hee sate, and groveled him, and all us about him on our faces, beating together with our breaths all thoughts from our bosomes, else, then that wee were now sinking. For my part, I thought her alreadie in the bottome of the Sea; and I have heard him say, wading out of the floud thereof, all his ambition was but to climbe up above hatches to dye in Aperto cœlo, and in the company of his old friends . . . One thing, it is not without his wonder (whether it were the feare of death in so great a storme, or that it pleased God to be gracious unto us) there was not a passenger, gentleman, or other, after hee beganne to stirre and labour, but was able to relieve his fellow, and make good his course: And it is most true, such as in all their life times had never done houres worke before (their mindes now helping their bodies) were able twice fortie eight houres together to toile with the best.

During all this time, the heavens look'd so blacke upon us, that it was not possible the elevation of the Pole might be observed: nor a Starre by night, nor Sunne beame by day was to be seene. Onely upon the Thursday night Sir George Summers being upon the watch, had an apparition of a little round light, like a faint Starre, trembling, and streaming along with a sparkeling blaze, halfe the height upon the Maine Mast, and shooting sometimes from Shroud to Shroud, tempting to settle as it were upon any of the foure Shrouds: and for three or foure hours together, or rather more, halfe the night it kept with us; running sometimes along the Maine-yard to the very end, and then returning.[2] At which, Sir George Summers called divers about him, and shewed them the same, who observed it with much wonder, and carefulnesse: but upon a sodaine, towards the morning watch, they lost the sight of it, and knew not what way it made. The superstitious Sea-men make many constructions of this Sea-fire, which neverthelesse is usuall in stormes: the same (it may be) which the Græcians were wont in the Mediterranean to call

[1] Cf. I. 1. 53, *Enter Mariners, wet.* 'All lost!'
[2] I. 2. 196–203.

Castor and Pollux, of which, if one onely appeared without the other, they tooke it for an evill signe of great tempest. The Italians, and such, who lye open to the Adriatique and Tyrrene Sea, call it (a sacred Body) Corpo sancto: the Spaniards call it Saint Elmo, and have an authentique and miraculous Legend for it. Be it what it will, we laid other foundations of safety or ruine, then in the rising or falling of it, but could it have served us now miraculously to have taken our height by, it might have strucken amazement,[1] and a reverence in our devotions, according to the due of a miracle. But it did not light us any whit the more to our knowne way, who ran now (as doe hoodwinked men) at all adventures, sometimes North, and North-east, then North and by West, and in an instant againe varying two or three points, and sometimes halfe the Compasse. East and by South we steered away as much as we could to beare upright, which was no small carefulnesse nor paine to doe, albeit we much unrigged our Ship, threw over-boord much luggage, many a Trunke and Chest (in which I suffered no meane losse) and staved many a Butt of Beere, Hogsheads of Oyle, Syder, Wine, and Vinegar,[2] and heaved away all our Ordnance on the Starboord side, and had now purposed to have cut downe the Maine Mast, the more to lighten her,[3] for we were much spent, and our men so weary, as their strengths together failed them, with their hearts, having travailed now from Tuesday till Friday morning, day and night, without either sleepe or foode; for the leakeage taking up all the hold, wee could neither come by Beere nor fresh water; fire we could keepe none in the Cookeroome to dresse any meate, and carefulnesse, griefe, and our turne at the Pumpe or Bucket, were sufficient to hold sleepe from our eyes . . . and from Tuesday noone till Friday noone, we bailed and pumped two thousand tunne, and yet doe what we could, when our Ship held least in her, (after Tuesday night second watch) shee bore ten foote deepe, at which stay our extreame working kept her one eight glasses, forbearance whereof had instantly sunke us, and it being now Friday, the fourth morning, it wanted little, but that there had bin a generall determination, to have shut up hatches, and commending our sinfull soules to God, committed the Shippe to the mercy of the Sea: surely, that night we must have done it, and that night had we then perished: but see the goodnesse and sweet introduction of better hope, by our mercifull God given unto us. Sir George Summers, when no man dreamed of such happinesse, had discovered, and cried Land. Indeede the morning now three quarters spent, had wonne a little cleerenesse from the

---

[1] Ariel: 'I flam'd amazement.' I. 2. 198.
[2] Stephano 'escap'd upon a butt of sack'. II. 2. 119. Cf. IV. 1. 252.
[3] I. 1. 35.

dayes before, and it being better surveyed, the very trees were seene to move with the winde upon the shoare side: whereupon our Governour commanded the Helme-man to beare up, the Boate-swaine sounding at the first, found it thirteene fathome, & when we stood a little in seven fatham; and presently heaving his lead the third time, had ground at foure fathome,[1] and by this, we had got her within a mile under the South-east point of the land, where we had somewhat smooth water. But having no hope to save her by comming to an anker in the same, we were inforced to runne her ashoare, as neere the land as we could, which brought us within three quarters of a mile of shoare, and by the mercy of God unto us,[2] making out our Boates, we had ere night brought all our men, women, and children, about the number of one hundred and fifty, safe into the Iland.[3]

We found it to be the dangerous and dreaded Iland, or rather Ilands of the Bermuda: whereof let mee give your Ladyship a briefe description, before I proceed to my narration. And that the rather, because they be so terrible to all that ever touched on them, and such tempests, thunders, and other fearefull objects are seene and heard about them, that they be called commonly, The Devils Ilands, and are feared and avoyded of all sea travellers alive, above any other place in the world. Yet it pleased our mercifull God, to make even this hideous and hated place, both the place of our safetie, and meanes of our deliverance.

And hereby also, I hope to deliver the world from a foule and generall errour: it being counted of most, that they can be no habitation for Men, but rather given over to Devils and wicked Spirits;[4] whereas indeed wee find them now by experience, to bee as habitable and commodious as most Countries of the same climate and situation: insomuch as if the entrance into them were as easie as the place it selfe is contenting, it had long ere this beene inhabited,[5] as well as other Ilands. Thus shall we make it appeare, That Truth is the daughter of Time, and that men ought not to deny every thing which is not subject to their owne sense.

The Bermudas bee broken Ilands, five hundred of them in manner of an Archipelagus (at least if you may call them all Ilands that lie, how little soever into the Sea, and by themselves) of small compasse, some larger yet then other, as time and the Sea hath

---

[1] Hence maybe the 'plummet' in III. 3. 100–2; V. 1. 56.

[2] Cf. Prospero, I. 2. 26–32; Gonzalo, II. 1. 6–7. Jourdain has: 'Our delivery was not more strange in falling so opportunely and happily upon the land, as our feeding and preservation beyond our hopes' (p. 10).

[3] I. 2. 215–19.

[4] Cf. Gonzalo on 'strange shapes' in III. 3. 30–5.

[5] II. 1. 37. 'Uninhabitable, and almost inaccessible.'

wonne from them, and eaten his passage through, and all now lying in the figure of a Croissant, within the circuit of sixe or seven leagues at the most, albeit at first it is said of them that they were thirteene or fourteene leagues; and more in longitude as I have heard. For no greater distance is it from the Northwest Point to Gates his Bay, as by this Map your Ladyship may see, in which Sir George Summers, who coasted in his Boat about them all, tooke great care to expresse the same exactly and full, and made his draught perfect for all good occasions, and the benefit of such, who either in distresse might be brought upon them, or make saile this way.

It should seeme by the testimony of Gonzalus Ferdinandus Oviedus,[1] in his Booke intituled, *The Summary or Abridgement* of his generall *History of the West Indies*, written to the Emperor Charles the Fift, that they have beene indeed of greater compasse (and I easily beleeve it) then they are now, who thus saith: 'In the yeere 1515. when I came first to informe your Majesty of the state of the things in India, and was the yeere following in Flanders, in the time of your most fortunate successe in these your kingdomes of Aragony and Casteel, whereas at that voyage I sayled above the Iland Bermudas, otherwise called Gorza, being the farthest of all the Ilands that are yet found at this day in the world, and arriving there at the depth of eight yards of water, and distant from the Land as farre as the shot of a Peece of Ordnance, I determined to send some of the ship to land, as well to make search of such things as were there, as also to leave in the Iland certaine Hogges for increase, but the time not serving my purpose, by reason of contrary winde I could bring my Ships no neerer: the Iland being twelve leagues in length, and sixteene in breadth, and about thirtie in circuit, lying in the thirtie three degrees of the North side.' Thus farre hee . . .

These Ilands are often afflicted and rent with tempests, great strokes of thunder, lightning and raine in the extreamity of violence:[2] which (and it may well bee) hath so sundred and torne downe the Rockes, and whurried whole quarters of Ilands into the maine Sea (some sixe, some seven leagues, and is like in time to swallow them all) so as even in that distance from the shoare there is no small danger of them and with them, of the stormes continually raging from them, which once in the full and change commonly of every Moone (Winter or Summer) keepe their unchangeable round, and rather thunder then blow from every corner about them, sometimes fortie eight houres together: especially if the circle, which the Philosophers call Halo were (in our being there) seene about the Moone at any season, which bow indeed appeared there often, and

---

[1] Did this suggest the names of Gonzalo and Ferdinand?
[2] Hence Trinculo, II. 2. 18–24; 36–7.

would bee of a mightie compasse and breadth. I have not observed it any where one quarter so great, especially about the twentieth of March, I saw the greatest when followed upon the eves eve of the Annuntiation of our Ladie, the mightiest blast of lightning, and most terrible rap of thunder that ever astonied mortall men, I thinke.[1] In August, September, and untill the end of October, wee had very hot and pleasant weather onely (as I say) thunder, lightning, and many scattering showers of Raine (which would passe swiftly over, and yet fall with such force and darknesse for the time as if it would never bee cleere againe) wee wanted not any; and of raine more in Summer then in Winter, and in the beginning of December wee had great store of hayle (the sharpe windes blowing Northerly)[2] but it continued not, and to say truth, it is wintry or summer weather there, according as those North and North-west windes blow . . .

Well may the Spaniards, and these Biscani Pilots, with all their Traders into the Indies, passe by these Ilands as afraid (either bound out or homewards) of their very Meridian, and leave the fishing for the Pearle (which some say, and I beleeve well is as good there, as in any of their other Indian Ilands, and whereof we had some triall) to such as will adventure for them. The Seas about them are so ful of breaches, as with those dangers, they may wel be said to be the strongest situate in the world. I have often heard Sir George Summers, and Captaine Newport say, how they have not beene by any chance or discovery upon their like. It is impossible without great and perfect knowledge, and search first made of them to bring in a bable Boat, so much as of ten Tun without apparant ruine, albeit within there are many faire harbours for the greatest English Ship: yea, the Argasies of Venice may ride there with water enough, and safe land-lockt.[3] There is one onely side that admits so much as hope of safetie by many a league, on which (as before described) it pleased God to bring us, wee had not come one man of us else a shoare, as the weather was: they have beene ever therefore left desolate and not inhabited.

The soile of the whole Iland is one and the same, the mould, dark, red, sandie, dry, and uncapable I beleeve of any of our commodities or fruits. Sir George Summers. . . . sowed Muske Melons, Pease, Onyons, Raddish, Lettice, and many English seeds, and Kitchen Herbes. All which in some ten daies did appeare above ground, but whether by the small Birds, of which there be many kindes, or by Flies (Wormes I never saw any, nor any venomous thing, as Toade,[4]

[1] II. 2. 106.
[2] Cf. I. 2. 254, 'the sharp wind of the north'.
[3] I. 2. 226–7.
[4] I. 2. 340 suggests otherwise!

or Snake, or any creeping beast hurtfull, onely some Spiders, which as many affirme are signes of great store of Gold: but they were long and slender legge Spiders, and whether venomous or no I know not; I beleeve not, since wee should still find them amongst our linnen in our Chests, and drinking Cans; but we never received any danger from them: A kind of Melontha, or blacke Beetell[1] there was, which bruised, gave a savour like many sweet and strong gums punned together) whether, I say, hindred by these, or by the condition or vice of the soyle they came to no proofe, nor thrived. It is like enough that the commodities of the other Westerne Ilands would prosper there, as Vines, Lemmons, Oranges, and Sugar Canes: Our Governour made triall of the later, and buried some two or three in the Garden mould, which were reserved in the wracke amongst many which wee carried to plant here in Virginia, and they beganne to grow, but the Hogs breaking in, both rooted them up and eate them: there is not through the whole Ilands, either Champion ground, Valleys, or fresh Rivers. They are full of Shawes of goodly Cedar, fairer then ours here of Virginia: the Berries, whereof our men seething, straining, and letting stand some three or foure daies, made a kind of pleasant drinke:[2] these Berries are of the same bignesse, and collour of Corynthes, full of little stones, and verie restringent or hard building . . .

Likewise there grow great store of Palme Trees, not the right Indian Palmes, such as in Saint John Port-Rico are called Cocos, and are there full of small fruites like Almonds (of the bignesse of the graines in Pomgranates) nor of those kind of Palmes which beares Dates, but a kind of Simerons or wild Palmes in growth, fashion, leaves, and branches, resembling those true Palmes: for the Tree is high, and straight, sappy and spongious, unfirme for any use, no branches but in the uppermost part thereof, and in the top grow leaves about the head of it (the most inmost part whereof they call Palmeto, and it is the heart and pith of the same Trunke, so white and thin, as it will peele off into pleates as smooth and delicate as white Sattin into twentie folds, in which a man may write as in paper) where they spread and fall downward about the Tree like an overblowne Rose, or Saffron flower not early gathered; so broad are the leaves, as an Italian Umbrello, a man may well defend his whole body under one of them, from the greatest storme raine that falls. For they being stiffe and smooth, as if so many flagges were knit together, the raine easily slideth off.[3]

Sure it is, that there are no Rivers nor running Springs of fresh water to bee found upon any of them: when wee came first wee

[1] Cf. I. 2. 340.   [2] I. 2. 333–4.
[3] Was Caliban's gaberdine made of these leaves?
*

digged and found certaine gushings and soft bublings,[1] which being
either in bottoms, or on the side of hanging ground, were onely fed
with raine water, which neverthelesse soone sinketh into the earth
and vanisheth away, or emptieth it selfe out of sight into the Sea,
without any channell above or upon the superficies of the earth: for
according as their raines fell, we had our Wels and Pits (which we
digged) either halfe full, or absolute exhausted and dry, howbeit
some low bottoms (which the continuall descent from the Hills filled
full, and in those flats could have no passage away) we found to
continue as fishing Ponds, or standing Pooles, continually Summer
and Winter full of fresh water.

The shoare and Bayes round about, when wee landed first
afforded great store of fish, and that of divers kindes, and good . . .
Wee have taken also from under the broken Rockes, Crevises oftentimes greater then any of our best English Lobsters; and likewise
abundance of Crabbes, Oysters, and Wilkes. True it is, for Fish in
everie Cove and Creeke wee found Snaules, and Skulles in that
abundance, as (I thinke) no Iland in the world may have greater
store or better Fish . . .

Fowle there is great store, small Birds, Sparrowes fat and plumpe
like a Bunting, bigger then ours, Robbins of divers colours greene and
yellow, ordinary and familiar in our Cabbins, and other of lesse sort.
White and gray Hernshawes, Bitters, Teale, Snites, Crowes, and
Hawkes, of which in March wee found divers Ayres, Goshawkes and
Tassells, Oxen-birds, Cormorants, Bald-Cootes, Moore-Hennes,
Owles, and Battes[2] in great store . . . A kinde of webbe-footed Fowle
there is, of the bignesse of an English greene Plover, or Sea-Meawe,[3]
which all the Summer we saw not, and in the darkest nights of
November and December (for in the night they onely feed) they
would come forth, but not flye farre from home, and hovering in the
ayre, and over the Sea, made a strange hollow and harsh howling . . .
Our men found a prettie way to take them, which was by standing
on the Rockes or Sands by the Sea side, and hollowing, laughing,
and making the strangest out-cry that possibly they could: with the
noyse whereof the Birds would come flocking to that place, and settle
upon the very armes and head of him that so cryed, and still creepe
neerer and neerer, answering the noyse themselves: by which our
men would weigh them with their hand, and which weighed heaviest
they tooke for the best and let the others alone, and so our men would
take twentie dozen in two hours of the chiefest of them; and they
were a good and well relished Fowle, fat and full as a Partridge . . .

[1] Contrast the 'springs' in I. 2. 336–8; II. 2. 160; III. 2. 71–2.
[2] Cf. I. 2. 340.
[3] Cf. II. 2. 172. 'Young scamels from the rock' were probably seamews.

Wee had knowledge that there were wilde Hogges upon the Iland, at first by our owne Swine preserved from the wrack and brought to shoare: for they straying into the Woods, an huge wilde Boare followed downe to our quarter, which at night was watched and taken . . . and there bee thousands of them in the Ilands, and at that time of the yeere, in August, September, October, and November, they were well fed with Berries that dropped from the Cedars and the Palmes, and in our quarter wee made styes for them . . .

The Tortoyse is reasonable toothsom (some say) wholsome meate. I am sure our Company liked the meate of them verie well, and one Tortoyse would goe further amongst them, then three Hogs. One Turtle (for so we called them) feasted well a dozen Messes, appointing sixe to every Messe. It is such a kind of meat, as a man can neither absolutely call Fish nor Flesh,[1] keeping most what in the water, and feeding upon Sea-grasse like a Heifer, in the bottome of the Coves and Bayes, and laying their Egges (of which wee should finde five hundred at a time in the opening of a shee Turtle) in the Sand by the shoare side, and so covering them close leave them to the hatching of the Sunne . . . their Egges are as big as Geese Egges, and themselves growne to perfection, bigger then great round Targets.

II

Actions and Occurrents whiles they continued in the Ilands . . .

[The company was split up between two islands, with Sir George Summers leading one, and Sir Thomas Gates ('our Governour') the other.[2] The long boat was sent off to Virginia with messages for Captain Peter Wynne and for the Council in England.]

You may please, excellent Lady, to know the reason which moved our Governour to dispatch this long Boat, was the care which hee tooke for the estate of the Colony in this his inforced absence: for by a long practised experience, foreseeing and fearing what innovation and tumult might happily arise, amongst the younger and ambitious spirits of the new companies to arrive in Virginia, now comming with

---

[1] Prospero calls Caliban 'thou tortoise' (I. 2. 316), and Trinculo asks, is he 'a man or a fish?' (II. 2. 24).
[2] Similarly the shipwrecked people in *The Tempest* are divided into two main parties in different places.

him along in this same Fleet,[1] hee framed his letters to the Colony, and by a particular Commission confirmed Captaine Peter Win his Lieutenant Governour, with an Assistance of sixe Counsellours, writing withall to divers and such Gentlemen of qualitie and knowledge of vertue, and to such lovers of goodnesse in this cause whom hee knew, intreating them by giving examples in themselves of duty and obedience, to assist likewise the said Lieutenant Governour, against such as should attempt the innovating of the person (now named by him) or forme of government, which in some Articles hee did likewise prescribe unto them: and had faire hopes all should goe well, if these his letters might arrive there, untill such time as either some Ship there (which hee fairely beleeved) might bee moved presently to adventure for him: or that it should please the right honourable, the Lordes, and the rest of his Majesties Councell in England, to addresse thither the right honourable the Lord Lawar (one of the more eminencie and worthinesse) as the project was before his comming forth, whilest by their honourable favours, a charitable consideration in like manner might bee taken of our estates to redeeme us from hence.

[Sir George Summers decided to build a boat and got workmen from Gates to help him.]

In the meane space[2] did one Frubbusher (a painefull and well experienced Shipwright, and skilfull workman) labour the building of a little Pinnace: for the furtherance of which, the Governour dispensed with no travaile of his body, nor forbare any care or study of minde, perswading (as much and more, an ill qualified parcell of people, by his owne performance, then by authority, thereby to hold them at their worke, namely to fell, carry, and sawe Cedar, fit for the Carpenters purpose (for what was so meane, whereto he would not himselfe set his hand, being therefore up earely and downe late?) yet neverthelesse were they hardly drawne to it, as the Tortoise to the inchantment, as the Proverbe is, but his owne presence and hand being set to every meane labour, and imployed so readily to every office, made our people at length more diligent, and willing to be called thereunto, where, they should see him before they came.[3] In which, we may observe how much example prevailes above precepts, and how readier men are to be led by eyes, then eares.

And sure it was happy for us, who had now runne this fortune, and

---

[1] Note from here onwards the continual (and well justified) fears of 'innovation', 'tumult', and conspiracy. This strongly influenced Shakespeare's play.
[2] On Gates's island.
[3] This was the lesson Ferdinand had to learn by carrying wood.

were fallen into the bottome of this misery, that we both had our
Governour with us, and one so solicitous and carefull, whose both
example (as I said) and authority, could lay shame, and command
upon our people: else, I am perswaded, we had most of us finished
our dayes there, so willing were the major part of the common sort
(especially when they found such a plenty of victuals) to settle a
foundation of ever inhabiting there; as well appeared by many practises of theirs (and perhaps of some of the better sort). Loe, what are
our affections and passions, if not rightly squared? how irreligious,
and irregular they expresse us? not perhaps so ill as we would be, but
yet as wee are; some dangerous and secret discontents nourished
amongst us, had like to have bin the parents of bloudy issues and
mischiefes,[1] they began first in the Sea-men, who in time had
fastened unto them (by false baits) many of our land-men likewise,
and some of whom (for opinion of their Religion) was carried an
extraordinary and good respect.[2] The Angles wherewith chiefely
they thus hooked in these disquieted Pooles, were, how that in
Virginia, nothing but wretchednesse and labour must be expected,
with many wants, and a churlish intreaty, there being neither that
Fish, Flesh, nor Fowle, which here (without wasting on the one part,
or watching on theirs, or any threatning, and aire of authority) at
ease, and pleasure might be injoyed:[3] and since both in the one, and
the other place, they were (for the time) to loose the fruition both of
their friends and Countrey, as good, and better were it for them, to
repose and seate them where they should have the least outward
wants the while. This, thus preached, and published each to other,
though by such who never had bin more onward towards Virginia,
then (before this Voyage) a Sculler could happily rowe him (and
what hath a more adamantive power to draw unto it the consent and
attraction of the idle, untoward, and wretched number of the many,
then liberty, and fulnesse and sensuality?) begat such a murmur,
and such a discontent, and disunion of hearts and hands from this
labour, and forwarding the meanes of redeeming us from hence, as
each one wrought with his Mate how to divorse him from the
same.

And first (and it was the first of September) a conspiracy was discovered, of which six were found principals, who had promised each
unto the other, not to set their hands to any travaile or endeavour
which might expedite or forward this Pinnace: and each of these had
severally (according to appointment) sought his opportunity to draw

[1] This sentence might well be the text for *The Tempest*.
[2] The leaders of discontent included some Puritans.
[3] Gonzalo too wants 'all men idle, all', II. i. 148–55, but here the idlers are
'knaves', as Antonio will assert (167).

the Smith, and one of our Carpenters, Nicholas Bennit, who made much profession of Scripture, a mutinous and dissembling Imposter; the Captaine, and one of the chiefe perswaders of others, who afterwards brake from the society of the Colony, and like outlawes retired into the Woods, to make a settlement and habitation there, on their party, with whom they purposed to leave our Quarter, and possesse another Iland by themselves: but this happily found out, they were condemned to the same punishment which they would have chosen (but without Smith or Carpenter) and to an Iland farre by it selfe, they were carried, and there left. Their names were John Want, the chiefe of them, an Essex man of Newport by Saffronwalden, both seditious, and a sectary in points of Religion, in his owne prayers much devout and frequent, but hardly drawne to the publique, insomuch as being suspected by our Minister for a Brownist, he was often compelled to the common Liturgie and forme of Prayer. The rest of the confederates were Christopher Carter, Francis Pearepoint, William Brian, William Martin, Richard Knowles: but soone they missed comfort (who were farre removed from our store) besides, the society of their acquaintance had wrought in some of them, if not a loathsomenesse of their offence, yet a sorrow that their complement was not more full, and therefore a wearinesse of their being thus untimely prescribed; insomuch, as many humble petitions were sent unto our Governor, fraught full of their seeming sorrow and repentance, and earnest vowes to redeeme the former trespasse, with example of dueties in them all, to the common cause, and generall businesse; upon which our Governour (not easie to admit any accusation, and hard to remit an offence, but at all times sorry in the punishment of him, in whom may appeare either shame or contrition) was easily content to reacknowledge them againe.

Yet could not this be any warning to others, who more subtilly began to shake the foundation of our quiet safety, and therein did one Stephen Hopkins commence the first act or overture: A fellow who had much knowledge in the Scriptures, and could reason well therein, whom our Minister therefore chose to be his Clarke, to reade the Psalmes, and Chapters upon Sondayes, at the assembly of the Congregation under him: who in January the twenty foure, brake with one Samuel Sharpe and Humfrey Reede (who presently discovered it to the Governour) and alleaged substantiall arguments, both civill and divine (the Scripture falsely quoted) that it was no breach of honesty, conscience, nor Religion, to decline from the obedience of the Governour, or refuse to goe any further, led by his authority (except it so pleased themselves) since the authority ceased when the wracke was committed, and with it, they were all then freed from the government of any man; and for a matter of Con-

science, it was not unknowne to the meanest, how much we were
therein bound each one to provide for himselfe, and his owne family:
for which were two apparant reasons to stay them even in this place;
first, abundance by Gods providence of all manner of good foode:
next, some hope in reasonable time, when they might grow weary of
the place, to build a small Barke, that so [they] might get cleere
from hence at their owne pleasures: when in Virginia, the first
would be assuredly wanting, and they might well feare to be detained
in that Countrie by the authority of the Commander thereof, and
their whole life to serve the turnes of the Adventurers, with their
travailes and labours. This being thus laid, and by such a one, who
had gotten an opinion (as I before remembred) of Religion; when it
was declared by those two accusers, not knowing what further ground
it had or complices, it pleased the Governour to let this his factious
offence to have a publique affront, and contestation by these two
witnesses before the whole Company, who (at the toling of a Bell)
assemble before a Corps du guard, where the Prisoner was brought
forth in manacles,[1] and both accused, and suffered to make at large,
to every particular, his answere; which was onely full of sorrow and
teares, pleading simplicity, and deniall. But hee being onely found,
at this time, both the Captaine, and the follower of this Mutinie, and
generally held worthy to satisfie the punishment of his offence, with
the sacrifice of his life, our Governour passed the sentence of a
Martiall Court upon him, such as belongs to Mutinie and Rebellion.
But so penitent hee was, and made so much moane, alleadging the
ruine of his Wife and Children in this his trespasse, as it wrought in
the hearts of all the better sort of the Company, who therefore with
humble intreaties, and earnest supplications, went unto our
Governor, whom they besought (as likewise did Captaine Newport,
and my selfe) and never left him untill we had got his pardon.

In these dangers and divellish disquiets (whilest the almighty God
wrought for us, and sent us miraculously delivered from the calamities of the Sea, all blessings upon the shoare, to content and binde us
to gratefulnesse) thus inraged amongst our selves, to the destruction
each of other, into what a mischiefe and misery had wee bin given
up, had wee not had a Governour with his authority, to have
suppressed the same?[2] Yet was there a worse practise, faction, and
conjuration a foote, deadly and bloudy, in which the life of our
Governour, with many others were threatned, and could not but
miscarry in his fall.[3] But such is ever the will of God (who in the

---

[1] Ferdinand is threatened with manacles, I. 2. 458. Another mutineer was 'bound
fast to a tree all night'. Cf. III. 2. 37.
[2] Hence the emphasis on Prospero's authority in the play.
[3] Cf. the 'foul conspiracy' against Prospero's life, IV. 1. 139-41.

execution of his judgements, breaketh the firebrands upon the head of him, who first kindleth them) there were, who conceived that our Governour indeede neither durst, nor had authority to put in execution, or passe the act of Justice upon any one, how treacherous or impious so ever; their owne opinions so much deceiving them for the unlawfulnesse of any act, which they would execute: daring to justifie among themselves, that if they should be apprehended, before the performance, they should happily suffer as Martyrs. They persevered therefore not onely to draw unto them such a number, and associates as they could worke in to the abandoning of our Governour, and to the inhabiting of this Iland. They had now purposed to have made a surprise of the Store-house, and to have forced from thence, what was therein either of Meale, Cloath, Cables, Armes, Sailes, Oares or what else it pleased God that we had recovered from the wracke, and was to serve our generall necessity and use, either for the reliefe of us, while wee staied here, or for the carrying of us from this place againe, when our Pinnace should have bin furnished.

But as all giddy and lawlesse attempts, have alwayes something of imperfection, and that as well by the property of the action, which holdeth of disobedience and rebellion (both full of feare) as through the ignorance of the devisers themselves;[1] so in this (besides those defects) there were some of the association, who not strong inough fortified in their owne conceits, brake from the plot it selfe, and (before the time was ripe for the execution thereof) discovered the whole order, and every Agent, and Actor thereof, who neverthelesse were not suddenly apprehended, by reason the confederates were divided and separated in place, some with us, and the chiefe with Sir George Summers in his Iland (and indeede all his whole company) but good watch passed upon them, every man from thenceforth commanded to weare his weapon, without which before, we freely walked from quarter to quarter, and conversed among our selves, and every man advised to stand upon his guard,[2] his owne life not being in safety, whilest his next neighbour was not to be trusted. The Centinels, and nightwarders doubled, the passages of both the quarters were carefully observed, by which meanes nothing was further attempted; untill a Gentleman amongst them, one Henry Paine, the thirteenth of March, full of mischiefe, and every houre preparing something or other, stealing Swords, Adises, Axes, Hatchets, Sawes, Augers, Planes, Mallets, &c. to make good his owne bad end, his watch night comming about, and being called by the Captaine of the same, to be upon the guard, did not onely give his said Commander evill language, but strucke at him, doubled his

---

[1] Like the folly of Stephano and Trinculo.
[2] II. 1. 322–4.

blowes, and when hee was not suffered to close with him, went off the Guard, scoffing at the double diligence and attendance of the Watch, appointed by the Governour for much purpose, as hee said: upon which, the Watch telling him, if the Governour should understand of this his insolency, it might turne him to much blame, and happily be as much as his life were worth. The said Paine replyed with a setled and bitter violence, and in such unreverent tearmes, as I should offend the modest eare too much to expresse it in his owne phrase; but the contents were, how that the Governour had no authoritie of that qualitie, to justifie upon any one (how meane soever in the Colonie) an action of that nature, and therefore let the Governour (said hee) kisse, &c.[1] Which words, being with the omitted additions, brought the next day unto every common and publique discourse, at length they were delivered over to the Governour, who, . . . calling the said Paine before him, and the whole Company, where (being soone convinced both by the witnesse, of the Commander, and many which were upon the watch with him) our Governour, who had now the eyes of the whole Colony fixed upon him, condemned him to be instantly hanged; and the ladder being ready, after he had made many confessions, hee earnestly desired, being a Gentleman, that hee might be shot to death, and towards the evening he had his desire, the Sunne and his life setting together.

But for the other which were with Sir George, upon the Sunday following [they] by a mutuall consent forsooke their labour, and Sir George Summers, and like Out-lawes betooke them to the wild Woods: whether meere rage, and greadinesse after some little Pearle (as it was thought) wherewith they conceived they should for ever inrich themselves, and saw how to obtaine the same easily in this place, or whether, the desire for ever to inhabite heere, or what other secret else moved them thereunto, true it is, they sent an audacious and formall Petition to our Governour, subscribed with all their names and Seales: not only intreating him, that they might stay heere,[2] but (with great art) importuned him, that he would performe other conditions with them, and not wave, nor evade from some of his owne promises, as namely to furnish each of them with two Sutes of Apparell,[3] and contribute Meale rateably for one whole yeere, so much among them, as they had weekly now, which was one pound and an halfe a weeke (for such had beene our proportion for nine moneths). Our Governour answered this their Petition, writing to Sir George Summers to this effect.

[1] Cf. Caliban's abuse of Prospero.
[2] II. 2. 175, 'we will inherit here'.
[3] Ironically this may have suggested the 'glistering garments'.

[That he had indeed promised that if he had to leave some men behind for a time, he would leave them all the necessities of life for a year. This should now be done for the malcontents. Only two of them chose to remain.]

IV

[Strachey relates how when at last they reached Virginia they found the colony at James Town 'full of misery and misgovernment'. A marginal note states that 'Orders were established which continued for their short stay . . . They contained a Preface and 21 Articles for Pietie, Loyaltie, and Politie convenient to the Colonie.']

If I should be examined from whence, and by what occasion, all these disasters, and afflictions descended upon our people, I can only referre you (honoured Ladie) to the Booke, which the Adventurers have sent hither intituled, Advertisements unto the Colony in Virginia: wherein the ground and causes are favourably abridged, from whence these miserable effects have beene produced, not excusing likewise the forme of government of some errour, which was not powerfull enough among so headie a multitude, especially, as those who arrived here in the supply sent the last yeere with us: with whom the better authoritie and government now changed into an absolute command, came along, and had beene as happily established, had it pleased God, that we with them had reached our wished Harbour.

Unto such calamity can sloath, riot and vanity, bring the most setled and plentifull estate. Indeede (right noble Lady) no story can remember unto us, more woes and anguishes, then these people, thus governed, have both suffered and puld upon their owne heads. And yet true it is, some of them, whose voyces and command might not be heard, may easily be absolved from the guilt hereof, as standing untouched, and upright in their innocencies,[1] whilest the privie factionaries shall never find time nor darknesse, to wipe away or cover their ignoble and irreligious practises, who, it may be, lay all the discredits, and imputations the while upon the Countrie.[2] But under pardon, let me speake freely to them: let them remember that if riot and sloth should both meet in any one of their best Families, in

[1] Gonzalo is such a person in the play.
[2] Strachey answers those doubters in England who blame the poverty and climate of Virginia for past failures to settle the region. The fault lies in the people who go there.

a Countrey most stored with abundance and plentie in England, continuall wasting, no Husbandry, the old store still spent on, no order for new provisions, what better could befall unto the Inhabitants, Landlords, and Tenants of that corner, then necessarily following cleannesse of teeth, famine and death? . . .

And with this Idlenesse, when some thing was in store, all wastfull courses exercised to the heigth, and the headlesse multitude, (some neither of qualitie nor Religion) not imployed to the end for which they were sent hither, no not compelled (since in themselves unwilling) to sowe Corne for their owne bellies, nor to put a Roote, Herbe, &c. for their owne particular good in their Gardens or elsewhere: I say in this neglect and sensuall Surfet, all things suffered to runne on, to lie sicke and languish; must it be expected, that health, plentie, and all the goodnesse of a well ordered State, of necessitie for all this to flow in this Countrey?[1] You have a right and noble heart (worthy Lady) bee judge of the truth herein. Then suffer it not bee concluded unto you, nor beleeve, I beseech you, that the wants and wretchednesse which they have indured, ascend out of the povertie and vilenesse of the Countrey, whether bee respected the Land or Rivers . . .

What England may boast of, having the faire hand of husbandry to manure and dresse it, God, and Nature have favourably bestowed upon this Country, and as it hath given unto it, both by situation, height, and soyle, all those (past hopes) assurances which follow our well planted native Countrie, and others, lying under the same influence: if, as ours, the Countrey and soyle might be improved, and drawne forth: so hath it indowed it, as is most certaine, with many more, which England fetcheth farre unto her from elsewhere. For first wee have experience, and even our eyes witnesse (how yong so ever wee are to the Countrie) that no Countrey yeeldeth goodlier Corne, nor more manifold increase: large Fields wee have, as prospects of the same, and not farre from our Pallisado. Besides, wee have thousands of goodly Vines in every hedge, and Boske[2] running along the ground, which yeelde a plentifull Grape in their kinde. Let mee appeale then to knowledge, if these naturall Vines were planted, dressed, and ordered by skilfull Vinearoones, whether wee might not make a perfect Grape, and fruitefull Vintage in short time? And we have made triall of our owne English seedes, kitchen Hearbs, and Rootes, and finde them to prosper as speedily as in England.

Onely let me truely acknowledge, they are not an hundred or two of deboist hands, dropt forth by yeare after yeare, with penury, and leisure, ill provided for before they come, and worse to be governed

---

[1] A crushing retort to Gonzalo's dream of happy anarchy.
[2] Cf. Ceres, 'my bosky acres', IV. 1. 81.

when they are here, men of such distempered bodies, and infected mindes, whom no examples daily before their eyes, either of goodnesse or punishment, can deterre from their habituall impieties, or terrifie from a shamefull death, that must be the Carpenters, and workemen in this so glorious a building . . .

I will acknowledge, deere Lady, I have seene much propensnesse already towards the unity, and generall endeavours: how contentedly doe such as labour with us, goe forth, when men of ranke and quality, assist, and set on their labours? I have seene it, and I protest it, I have heard the inferioor people, with alacrity of spirit professe, that they should never refuse to doe their best in the practise of their sciences and knowledges, when such worthy, and Noble Gentlemen goe in and out before them, and not onely so, but as the occasion shall be offered, no lesse help them with their hand, then defend them with the Sword. And it is to be understood, that such as labour, are not yet so taxed, but that easily they performe the same, and ever by tenne of the clocke have done their Mornings worke: at what time, they have their allowances set out ready for them, and untill it be three of the clocke againe, they take their owne pleasure, and afterwards with the Sunne set, their dayes labour is finished. In all which courses, if the businesse be continued, I doubt nothing, with Gods favour towards us, but to see it in time, a Countrie, an Haven, and a Staple, fitted for such a trade, as shall advance assureder increase, both to the Adventurers, and free Burgers thereof, then any Trade in Christendome.

[Strachey blames the collapse of the settlement on hostile Indians, the improvident greed of the incomers, and the commercial rivalry of shipmasters and pursers. Yet Virginia is 'one of the goodliest Countries under the Sunne'.]

II. Probable Source

From
A TRUE DECLARATION OF THE ESTATE OF THE COLONIE IN VIRGINIA, WITH A CONFUTATION OF SUCH SCANDALOUS REPORTS AS HAVE TENDED TO THE DISGRACE OF SO WORTHY AN ENTERPRISE(1610)[1]

[After discussing the Christian morality of colonizing and trading with primitive tribes overseas, the Council try to minimize the practical difficulties by briefly recounting the recent voyage.]

To returne therefore unto the maine channell of this discourse, and to dispell the clouds of feare, that threaten shipwracks, and sea-dangers: For we are not to extenuate the seas tempestuous violence, nor yet therefore to dispaire of Gods assisting providence. For true it is, that when *Sir Thomas Gates*, *Sir George Summers*, and Captaine Newport, were in the height of 27. and the 24. of July 1609, there arose such a storme, as if *Jonas* had been flying unto *Tarshish*: the heavens were obscured, and made an Egyptian night of three daies perpetuall horror; the woman lamented; the hearts of the passengers failed; the experience of the sea Captaines was amased: the skill of the marriners was confounded: the Ship most violently leaked, and though two thousand tunne of water by pumping from Tuesday noone till Fryday noone was discharged, notwithstanding the Ship was halfe filled with water, and those which laboured to keepe others from drowning were halfe drowned themselves in labouring.

But God that heard *Jonas* crying out of the belly of hell, he pittied the distresses of his servants: For behold, in the last period of necessitie, *Sir George Summers* descryed land, which was by so much the more joyfull, by how much their danger was despairefull. The Islands on which they fell were the *Bermudos*, a place hardly accessable, through the invironing rocks and dangers: notwithstanding they were forced to runne their Ship on shoare, which through Gods providence fell betwixt two rockes, that caused her to stand firme and not immediately to be broken, God continuing his mercie unto them, that with their long Boats they transported to land before

[1] Anon. 'Published by advise and direction of the Council of Virginia.'

night, all their company, men, women, and children, to the number of one hundred and fiftie, they carryed to shoare all the provision of unspent and unspoyled victuals, all their furniture and tackling of the Ship, leaving nothing but bared ribs, as a pray unto the Ocean.

These Islands of the *Bermudos* have ever beene accounted as an inchaunted pile of rockes, and a desert inhabitation for Divels; but all the Fairies of the Rocks were but flocks of birds, and all the Divels that haunted the woods, were but heards of swine. Yea and when *Acosta* in his first booke of the hystories of the *Indies*, averreth, that though in the continent there were diverse beasts, and cattell, yet in the Islands of *Hispaniola*, *Jamaica*, *Marguarita*, and *Dominia*, there was not one hoofe, it increaseth the wonder, how our people in the *Bermudos* found such abundance of Hogs, that for nine moneths space they plentifully sufficed: and yet the number seemed not much diminished.

Again, as in the great famine of *Israell*, God commanded *Elias* to flie to the brooke *Cedron*, and there fed him by Ravens; so God provided for our disconsolate people in the midst of the Sea by foules: but with an admirable difference: unto *Elias* the Ravens brought meat, unto our men the foules brought [themselves] for meate: for when they whisteled, or made any strange noyse, the foules would come and sit on their shoulders, they would suffer themselves to be taken and weighed by our men, who would make choise of the fattest and fairest, and let flie the leane and lightest. An accident, I take it, that cannot be paralleld by any Hystorie, except when God sent abundance of Quayles to feed his *Israel*, in the barren wildernesse. Lastly they found the berries of Cedar, the *Palmeto* tree, the prickle peare, sufficient fish, plentie of Tortoises, and divers other kinds, which sufficed to sustaine nature. They found diversity of woods, which ministred materials for the building of two Pinaces, according to the direction of the three provident Governours.

Consider all these things together. At the instant of neede, they descryed land; halfe an hower more, had buried their memorial in the Sea. If they had fel by night, what expectation of light, from an uninhabited desart? They fell betwixt a laberinth of rockes, which they conceive are mouldred into the Sea, by thunder and lightning. This was not *Ariadnes* threed, but the direct line of Gods providence. If it had not beene so neere land, their companie or provision had perished by water: if they had not found Hogs, and foule, and fish, they had perished by famine: if there had not beene fuell, they had perished by want of fire: if there had not beene timber they could not have transported themselves to *Virginia*, but must have beene forgotten forever. *Nimium timet qui Deo non credit*: he is too impiously fearefull, that will not trust in God so powerfull.

[In Virginia they found a pleasant climate and fertile soil, but much sickness in Jamestown, which was set among fens and marshes, also much dissension among the settlers. Experience showed that the best disciplined of them were the most healthy.]

Adde unto this the discourse of philosophie, when in that Countrie flesh will receive salt, and continue unputrified (which it will not in the West Indies) when the most delicate of all flowers grow there as familiarly as in the fields of *Portingale*, where the woods are replenished with more sweet barks, and odors, then they are in the pleasantest places of *Florida*. How is it possible, that such a virgin and temperat aire, should work such contrarie effects, but because our fort (that lyeth as a semy-Iland) is most part invironed with an ebbing and flowing salt water, the owze of which sendeth forth an unwholsome and contagious vapour? To close up this part with *Sir Thomas Gates* his experiment: he professeth, that in a fortnights space he recovered the health of most of them by moderat labour, whose sickness was bred in them by intemperate idlenes.

If any man shall accuse these reports of partiall falshood, supposing them to be but Utopian, and legendarie fables, because he cannot conceive, that plentie and famine, a temperate climate, and distempered bodies, felicities, and miseries can be reconciled together, let him now reade with judgement, but let him not judge before he hath read.

The ground of all those miseries, was the permissive providence of God, who, in the fore-mentioned violent storme, seperated the head from the bodie, all the vitall powers of regiment being exiled with *Sir Thomas Gates* in those infortunate (yet fortunate) Ilands. The broken remainder of those supplies made a greater shipwrack on the continent of *Virginia*, by the tempest of dissension: every man overvaluing his own worth, would be a Commander: every man underprising an others value, denied to be commanded. [Classical examples of discord are given] . . . when therefore licence, sedition, and furie, are the fruits of a headie, daring, and unruly multitude, it is no wonder that so many in our colony perished: it is a wonder, that all were not devoured. *Omnis inordinatus animus sibi ipsi fit poena*, every inordinate soul becomes his owne punishment.

The next fountaine of woes was secure negligence, and improvidence, when every man sharked for his present bootie, but was altogether carelesse of succeeding penurie . . . An incredible example of their idlenes, is the report of *Sir Thomas Gates*, who affirmed, that after his first comming thither, he hath seen some of them eat their fish raw, rather than they would go a stones cast to fetch wood and dresse it. *Dii laboribus omnia vendunt*, God sels us all things for our labour, when *Adam* himselfe might not live in paradice without dressing the garden. Unto idlenes, you may joyne treasons, wrought by those unhallowed creatures that forsooke the Colony, and exposed their desolate brethren to extreame miserie. You shall know that 28 or 30 of the companie . . . stole away the Ship [called the Swallow], they made a league amongst themselves to be professed pirates, with dreames of mountaines of gold, and happy robberies: thus at one instant, they wronged the hopes, and subverted the cares of the Colony . . .: they created the Indians our implacable enemies by some violence they had offered: . . . they weakned our forces, by subtraction of their armes, and succours. These are that scum of men that sayling in their piracy, that beeing pinched with famine and penurie, after their wilde roving upon the Sea, when all their lawlesse hopes failed, some remained with other pirates, they men upon the Sea, the others resolved to returne for England, bound themselves by mutuall oath, to agree all in one report, to discredit the land, to deplore the famyne, and to protest that this their comming awaie, proceeded from desperate necessitie . . .

Unto Treasons, you may joyne covetousnesse in the Mariners, who for their private lucre partly imbezeled the provisions, partly prevented our trade with the Indians, making the matches in the night, and forestalling our market in the day, whereby the Virginians were glutted with our trifles, and inhaunced the prices of their Corne and Victuall.

The state of the Colony, by these accidents began to find a sensible declyninge. [The Indians began to attack the intruders, and when Gates and Somers arrived the colony was in desperate straits.]

III. Probable Source

From
A TRUE AND SINCERE DECLARATION OF THE PURPOSE AND ENDS OF THE PLANTATION BEGUN IN VIRGINIA (1610)[1]

[Captain Argoll's voyage in the *Discovery* has proved that both the purposes and ways of the Council were 'happy and successful'.]

But from this Ship ariseth a rumour of the necessity and distresse our people were found in, for want of victuall: of which, though the noise have exceeded the truth, yet we doe confesse a great part of it; But can lay aside the cause and fault from the dessigne, truely and home upon the misgovernment of the Commanders, by dissention and ambition among themselves, and upon the Idlenesse and bestiall slouth, of the common sort, who were active in nothing but adhearing to factions and parts, even to their owne ruine, like men almost desperate of all supply, so conscious, and guilty they were to themselves of their owne demerit, and lasinesse. But so soone as Captaine *Argoll* arrived among them, whose presence and example gave new assurance of our cares, and new life to their indeavours, by fishing onely in few days, they were all recovered, growne hearty, able, and ready to undertake every action.

So that, if it bee considered that without industry no land is sufficient to the Inhabitants: and that the trade to which they trusted, betrayed them to loose the opportunity of seed-time, and so to rust and weare out themselves: for the Naturals withdrew from all commerce and trafficke with them, cunningly making a war upon them, which they felt not, who durst no other way appear an enemy: And they beeing at division among themselves, and without warrant from hence, could not resolve to inforce that, which might have preserved them, and which in such a necessity is most lawfull to doe, everything returning from civill Propryety to Naturall, and Primary Community: . . .

[1] Anon. 'Set forth by the authority of the Governors and Councellors established for that Plantation.'

IV. Analogue

From
The first part of
THE MIRROUR OF KNIGHTHOOD,[1]
translated by M. T[yler] (1578)

[The Emperor Trebacio loses his wife Briana, who is carried off in a magic chariot to a ship on the river.]

Beeing thus left on foote, notwithstanding hee dispayred not, but helde on to that place from whence the Chariot was taken, where hee carefully lookt about him to see if peradventure on the one side or the other, hee might trace out a way to follow: so loath was hee to loose the sight of it. But as all this was devised by enchauntment, so lykewise it happened him to see a lyttle Shippe, sayling on the River with great swiftnesse: in the which there satte an olde man with a white beard, by his countenaunce seeming to bee a verie honest man [but really he is the magician Palisteo]. To him the Emperour called with a loude voyce, desiring him to take it towards the shoare. The olde man which had the same thing in charge, incontinently Steered towards him, and asked what hee would have. 'That which I would have, quoth the Emperour, is to bee convayed in thy shippe, to that other ship which rideth beefore us' . . . [The old man agrees.] . . . he guided his ship so neere the shore, that the Emperour leaped up into it, and beeing on the hatches, tourning himselfe to the olde man to give him thancks, the olde man vanished away . . .
    [The ship sails on after the other.] In the fourth day by morning, the ship with the chariot was driven into the great and large Sea called Pontus Euxinus, through the which hee yet sayled within view of the other, until the forward ship arrived in a faire and delectable Iland, where the chariot tooke landing.
    Halfe an houre after, the Emperours shippe rushed on the shoare, with such force that the shippe rent in peeces, and with the violence of the rush threw the Emperour uppon the banck flatlings on his back, where after hee hadde stretched himselfe, he began againe to trevaile on foot that way which he gessed the Chariot had gone. (Ch. 8, f. 14)

[1] *The first Part of the Mirrour of Princely deedes and Knighthood . . . Now newly translated out of Spanish . . . By M. T.*, n.d. (text from 3rd edn, 1590?).

[The Island is described in conventional terms as lovely.]

. . . the ground was beautified with sweet Roses and other fragrant flowers, amongst the beds whereof there ranne by chanells, a very cleere and cristalline water . . . Beesides these, to make up a full messe of disport, there was a sweet and pleasaunt song of Birds, which seemed to rejoyce in the bright and cleere morning, beesides a thousand other pastimes which I let passe, too long to make a tale of . . .

[He comes to a 'good Castle' with a moat too wide for him to cross unaided, but a Gentlewoman ferries him over, and conducts him through the 'terrestriall Paradise' of the garden into the Castle itself, which is of superlative beauty.]

For in comparison of this inchanted castle, either the sumptuous building of Mausolus tombe, or the famous Pyramides of Aegypt, or the maze of Daedalus making, found in Crete, may well be forgotten. [They enter a magnificent chamber.] The Emperour tooke no keepe of the riches of the place, but of the beautie of a number of faire gentlewomen whom hee saw sitting richly apparelled, in every part of the chamber, among these one seemed to bee the principall, stalled in a seate higher then the other, and passing them all so well in beautie as rich apparell: She, as Lady and mistress above them all, held in her hand a Lute, whereon shee played and sung together with such an harmonie, that it was no lesse daungerous unto the poore Emperour, then the aluring song of the mermaides should have beene unto Ulysses company . . . And you must pardon the Emperour if by this hee was wholy possessed with hir love, and forgot his late wife the Princesse Briana. The enterteinment was great, and yet this chaunge proceeded not through the beautie of the enchantresse, for his owne wife was much fairer, but rather by the secret vertue of the place, which was therto devised. (f. 16)

[Twenty years later the young Knight of the Sun, who has been far west across the Atlantic, is carried back in a magic boat through the Mediterranean to the 'broad Euxino' and the Island, which is described much as before. He sounds the horn which hangs by the Castle gate, and fights the giants and horrible beasts which bar his way. Getting into the Castle, he finds the great chamber, and there 'the Emperor Trebacio leaned his head upon the white and delicate breasts of

Lindaraza'. The Knight feels some envy, but his task is to recall
Trebacio to his duty: 'my arrant is for yourselfe, which heere
live unknowen, and have forgotten your wife and Empire'
(f. 145). The enraged Trebacio would attack him, but]

The Knight of the Sunne, knowing that what the Emperour did
was but as done in a dreame, would not strike him to doo him harme,
but onely to save himselfe, and to finde the meanes whereby to
bring Trebacio from that inchauntment.

[He gets the Emperor out of the chamber and they both
rush down the stairs.]

Now hath the Knight of the Sun played the man, for ere they came
fully to the ground, the doores of the inchaunted chamber clapt
together, wherewith, and with the noise thereof, a great parte of the
edifices sanke withall. The Emperour, returned to his former wits,
presently saw that hee thought hee had not staied ther past a daye,
and that which passed beetweene him and Lindaraza, had beene but
a short and pleasaunt dreame. After calling to minde his wife the
faire Princesse Briana, and the great hoast which hee had left before
Belgrade, hee became so sorrowful, that the teeres trickeled downe
his cheekes in great measure. But of this manner and condition are
we mortall men, that for our pleasures we sometimes forget our
spouses, the one halfe of our selves: sometimes neglect our children
. . . and lastly, sometimes we overturne our Countrey, which ought
to bee dearer to us then our selves, neither mindefull to what use we
are created, namely to the benefite of others, neither carefull what
ensueth . . .

When we are at our wittes end, we seeme but as it were now to
begin a fresh. It is like a sweete sleepe, but let us shake off this
drowsie humour, and let us open our sleepie eies. Let us use our
selves so that sometimes wee have recourse to matters of more
importance, and to thinke of heaven, to seperate our selves from the
man of flesh, and willingly to leave him, least hee leaveth us against
our willes (f. 146).

Little shall remaine therof after scores of yeares, and that which
remaineth, shall be shame and griefe, for the life passed, besides
desperate repentance, which is double torment. And much after this
same manner was the valiaunt Emperour, for his long delights with
Lindaraza, now twentie yeare was but a Summers day, and yet
there left him not shame of his fact to fret his conscience, albeit hee
adviseth himselfe the best remedie which I have read of, which is
amendment of life, the safest haven for a wether-beaten penitent.

[Lindaraza's brother Flamides now appears, says that she has died of grief at losing Trebacio, and explains how their father and (later) Trebacio came to the Island.]

My sister Lindaraza and I had both one Father named Palisteo being the second sonne to the King of Phrigia, my father not beeing borne to the kingdome fell rather to seeke his owne delight without envie, then to trouble himselfe with the care of governing. Above all hee studied the Art Magicke, wher by his paines at length he came to the most absolute perfection of all Asia: he was matched with a Lady of high parentage, by whom he had two children, my sister Lindaraza and mee, wee were of young yeares when our mother died in labour of the third child, so there remained none else but our Father alive, and loving to bee solitarie came and dwelled in this Iland, bringing with him my sister and those waiting women which you have seene, by his great skill he builded this castle, heere he lived untill my sister and I were of some discreation to guide our-selves. Heere he drew manie histories of thinges passed in the worlde, and among other, the pictures of manie valyaunt knights, which were then on live, with the rest you were so lively drawen, that it happening my sister to enter one day where the Imagerye was, by the sight of your picture shee was surprised with your love. Our father Palisteo knowing hir disease, devised you should be brought by following your owne wife carried from you . . .

When the wise man our father had done all this, hee declared unto us the secretes of these thinges, and farther told us by his Art, that the time should come when you should be delivered from the inchaunt-ment, although hee knew not when nor in what Manner. (f. 148)

[The Knight of the Sun takes the Emperor in his boat to carry him back to his realm. Lindaraza and Trebacio have had a little daughter, whose adventures begin later in the romance.]

V. Analogue

From
The third part of the First Book of
THE MIRROUR OF KNIGHTHOOD,
translated by R. Parry (1586?)

[The Knight of the Sun is on a ship which, in a great storm, runs near the Island of Artimaga.]

Thus they travailed two daies together with prosperous windes, passing away the time in the best manner hee could, but the third day there arose a great torment in so terrible sort, that the shippe wherein they were was in great perill to bee lost. The windes dyd increase every moment more and more, in such furious sort, that all the cunning of the marriners did not serve for the government of the ship, but were driven of necessitie for to yeeld hir unto the curtesie of the winde and seas, driving wheresoever it pleased them.

In this sort were they tumbled and tossed with that tempest all that day and the night following, without any semblaunce of calmenesse, and looked every minute for to bee cast away, which put greate feare amongst them all, saving unto the knight of the Sun, who seeing the sea troubled, and the mightie waves caused by those terrible windes, fighting one with another, hee was not alonely without all feare, but also did lyke well thereof, and it was agreeable unto his minde, as unto one that was weary of his owne life, but the next day following, at such time as they were without all hope to escape that danger, fortune did so serve them, that the storme beganne to asswage, in such sort, that the Marriners might governe their shippe, but they found that they were put a great way leward from the place where they were determined to goe, and sailing towards on their journey, they discovered afar off an Iland, and out of the middest thereof they might perceive ascend up into the aire at times great flames and sparkes of fire, with a terrible darke and thicke smoake, as though they hadde beene burning of some drie things.

And when they came nigh unto the same Iland, the knights were all desirous to goe there a land, for to ease and refresh themselves for that they were out of quiet with the storme passed, but the Marriners knowing the Iland, haled jackes aboord, and ran of from the land all that ever they could, crying out and saying, they would not goe thether, for that it was the Iland of the divell, called the solitarie

Iland, and how that if they went there they should all die the death.

When the knights of Candia heard these wordes, they were all greatly amazed, for they hadde heard before time verie much of that Iland. But the Knight of the Sun who was inclined by his valiaunt hart to attempt high and mightie things, with great desire for to see what it was that they so greatlie feared, he asked of the Marriners wherfore they called that the Iland of the divell, and why they feared so much the death if they should go thether? And although all the knights that were there present had heard very much of the great perill and daunger of that Iland, yet there was none that could declare the certaintie thereof, but an olde Pilot that came as a passenger in the same shippe, who had heard the whole truth thereof by certaine men which left the said Iland in respect of the great daunger, and he seeing that the Knight of the Sunne had great desire to know the misterie therof, in the presence of all the knights that were there present, began to declare the same as followeth.

You shall understand (gentle Knight) that this Iland was called in times past, the Iland of Artimaga, for that it was governed by a woman so called, who was so abhominable and evill, that never the like was seene nor heard of amongst women, for that after shee came unto the age of fifteene yeeres untill the time of hir death, which was more than thirtie yeeres, she never beleeved in god but in the divell, and there was no day that passed over hir head, but she saw the divell in the figure of a man, and had talke and conversation with him, as though he had bene hir husband, and she did every day twice humble hir selfe unto him and did worship him.

The father and mother of this Artimaga were very evill and perverse, and being Lords and governours of this Iland at their death they left this Artimaga of the age of ten yeeres, little more or lesse, and for that their was no heire male at their decease, she was forthwith accepted for lady and governesse of the whole Iland, who when she saw that she was absolute of hir selfe, and all in hir disposition, she gave hir selfe so much unto all the evils and vices of this world, that for hir abhominable sinnes and wickednesse God did permit that when this Artimaga came unto the age of fifteene yeeres, she was deceived with the divell, and would never consent unto marriage, for that she would not submit hir selfe under the obedience of hir husband, but yet she had more than thirtie gallants at hir commaundement, and had a great delight in chaunge everie yeere so many more, and with the great conversation that shee had continuallie with the divell, shee came to bee so wise and cunning in the art Magicke, that there was none in all hir time, although hee were never so cunning, that might bee compared unto hir. Shee used so many and divers sortes of inchauntments, that all those of the Iland did feare hir very much, and although hir abhominable and horrible life seemed very evill unto them all, yet durst they doe no other thing, but to obey hir for their Ladie and governesse.

It so fell out that this cursed woman was never brought to bedde, nor never was with childe (although in consideration thereof many times shee would not use the companie but onelie of one man) for the which shee received great sorrow and griefe at hir verie heart, in seeing that shee could not have anie issue of hir bodie that might succeede hir in the Lordshippe of that Iland, and many times when she was in companie with the Divell, shee did complaine very much hereof, praying him earnestly with great devotion to doe so much for hir, that shee might have a sonne, with whom she might comfort hir selfe, and put some remedie unto the great sorrow which she received at hir heart, for lacke thereof. Then the deceitfull divell, full of pollicie, and enemie unto all humaine generation, having great desire to bring unto end that evill fortuned woman, the more surer to make his pray upon hir soule, bethought himselfe of a mervailous evill, and said, that unto that time hee would not consent that shee should have any generation, in consideration that she loved him so well, he would not that she should conceive by any humane creature, but onely by him, and that he determined to lye with hir, certifieng that shee should fully perswade hir selfe that the son that should be borne of hir, should be the most strongest that shoulde be found in all the world, and in respect of hir love, that Iland should bee spoken of in all the world.

These words of the divell, caused so great joy and pleasure in Artimaga, that as one from hir selfe she fell downe prostrate at his feete and kissed them, for that great benefit offered unto hir, and with great importunatie shee desired him straight way to put it in ure. Then the divell having no other determination but onely to deceive hir, saide: Thou shalt understand Artimaga, that there is not given to humaine woman, in the forme of a rationall man, but in some other figure and forme of a wilde beast that is furious and wonderfull, the which is onely for to shew the difference that is betwixt our great power, and that of men. And againe, that which shal be begotten by mee, to bee of much more force and strangth.

When that Artimaga heard him say these wordes, with the great joy which she received, shee was voide of all care, and saide unto him, that she should receive great contentment and pleasure therein, although hee came in the most ugliest and fearefullest forme that might bee.

So the divell fell at agreement with hir, that upon a certaine day she should goe into a Parke that was in that Iland, beeing full of mervailous great and thicke trees (whereas shee did many times goe on hunting) and that he would there tarry hir comming. Then the divell for to accomplish and bring to passe that which he had promised, went into the desarts of Affrica, and out from the most highest and afar parts of all the Mount Atlas, he brought foorth a monstrous beast called Fauno, the most terriblest amongst all beasts, and they say that by reason of the great abhomination used in times past by men having copulation with monstrous beasts, did so alter humane nature, that in processe of time it concluded in this so terrible and monstrous beast, the fashion and forme thereof was as I will declare unto you:

His body was as bigge as a great bull, in forme and shape like a Lion, with his feete full of rugged haire, and the clawes of his feete as big as twice a mans finger, and a span long, his breast as big as of a horse, and necked like an Elephant, and from that part upward both head and face like a man, with a long beard of hard and thicke haire, but the head was very bigge, and out of the middest of his forehead came forth an horne as big as a mans arme and as long, whose force was such, as also in his armes, that there was no beast so furious and fierce, that was able to indure beefore him . . .

So the divell finding out this monstrous beast, he entered within him, and brought him unto this Iland, and tarried within the Parke till the comming of Artimaga, at the houre appointed, who with the great desire that she had to conceive by the divell, detracted no time, but kept hir houre, and although she had great astonishment at the fiercenesse and terrible semblance of that monster, yet for all that it did not abate hir courage, beeleeving of a certaintie that it was the divell, and for that the divell was within the monster, hee spake by the mouth of the Fauno all that was requisite.

To conclude, hee deceived Artimaga, and by permission of God, for hir sinnes and abhominable desire, she was conceived by that hellish Fauno, in such sort; that she remained with Child. Then shee returned againe unto hir house, and the divell carried the monster unto the place from whence hee brought him, and in the ende of three moneths shee felt hirselfe with childe, for the which shee received so great joy and contentment as ever shee did in all hir life, beleeving of a certaintie that the sonne that should bee borne of hir, should bee the most strongest and mightiest in all the world, and never ceased giving thanks unto the divell, for that hee was the author and father thereof . . .

So the time was expired and the houre come that Artimaga should bee delivered, and shee was so big, broad, and swelled, that shee could not moove hir selfe from one place to another, in such sort, that all that dyd see hir were greatly amazed, for that shee seemed to bee foure times as big as shee was beefore, and by reason that the fruite of hir cohabitation was deformed, monstrous, and divellish, they had no hope of any naturall birth by ordinarie course, but rent and tore the bellie and entrailes of the Mother, wherewith shee dyed and yeelded hir soule unto him whom shee so much beeleeved and worshipped, and the childe came foorth, the most horriblest and terriblest creature that ever nature formed.

This childe was scarce out of his mothers wombe, when that with a divellish fury hee tore in peeces all that ever were before him, and ran out of the doores and tooke the field, destroying and killing all that ever hee met withall, and never ceased till hee came unto the Parke and wood whereas hee was begotten, and there hee remained certaine daies, and never came foorth till he was growen to a bigger stature, although when hee was borne, hee was as big as [a] reasonable Lyon. Hee had not remained full halfe a yeere in these woods but hee increased so much, that hee seemed to bee as big as an Elephant. His forme and figure was much more horrible than that of his father, although he did resemble him very much, and beesides all this, he had a whole legion of divels within his bodie, who in a figure of armed men, many times came forth at his horrible mouth, and did great harme whereas they went, so that for this occasion he is called the divellish or possessed Fauno.

So afterward when that hee was come unto his ful strength, which was within halfe a yeere, hee left the woods, and went throughout all the Iland, and did so much harme, that hee left none alive where hee beecame, some slaine, and other some hearing the report of his crueltie, fled away, so that the Iland is left desolate, and no inhabitants therein, neither any other living thing. So all those that have any notice of this Iland, doo not onelie refuse to land upon it, but also they dare not come nigh it with their ships, [for the monster wades into the sea and destroys them] . . .

This is the occasion (gentle knight) that this Iland is so much spoken of, and so fearefull unto all saylers that passeth this way, and why it is called the Iland of the divell, and that fire which wee doo see, with that thick smoake that ascendeth into the aire, is all that which proceedeth out of the terrible and horrible mouth of that divellish Fauno, for that it is full of infernal divels.

[The Knight of the Sun was not deterred from going ashore to face the Fauno] as he who for suchlike attempts was created, and did little esteeme the venturing of his life, whereas the honour and glorie of such woorthinesse is put in adventure, and in especiall in that time abhoring himselfe in consideration of his fact: hee was so furious and desperate that hee neither feared nor dreaded the entrie into hell, much lesse the Iland.

[He lands, after telling his two Squires that he has left Constantinople 'for no other intent but to leave the world'. There follows a long, terrific combat with the monster in which the Knight is victorious.]

This monster was not so soone fallen down, but all that infernal crue that were within his bellie beegan to come foorth at his mouth, with so great quantitie of fire, that they seemed all to burne there with. [The sun was darkened] and there appeared unto this good knight many infernall visions, in a horrible manner as might be all full of fire, in such sort, that although it was as darke as night, yet there appeared a mervailous and an innumerable number of them so light as firebrands, that he thought verily that all the divells of hell had ben there joyned together. In this sort they continued a while, and then upon a sodaine he sawe together a mightie legion of divells in ambushment, who brought in the midst amongst them a naked woman, whom they tormented in as cruell sort as might be imagined. Shee gave great and pittifull shrikes, and complained in such sort, that the knight well understood she should bee the wise Artimaga, who was brought thether by those divells whereas hir sonne lay dead . . . So after a while that this endured, it began to lighten and thunder much more then before, in which terrible noise, all this infernall companie began to vanish away, and all those divells that brought Artimaga likewise returned, never ceasing in tormenting hir one minute of an houre.

So when they were all vanished and departed, the day beegan to cleere up, and the Sunne to shine as bright as before, and was nothing seene in all the Iland, but this good knight standing by the Fauno, who was altogether starke dead . . .

[The Knight thanks God for his deliverance.]

Then . . . hee went and vewed all the Iland, and found it to bee solitarie, and not one left in all the whole companie, wheras before it was mervailously replenished with all manner of beastes, and as then not one remaining, for that this infernall Fauno had eaten and destroyed them. Likewise he found that all the edifices and buildings were overthrowen with weather, and broken downe, . . . whereat hee received great griefe, and mooved unto great compassion, to understand that for the sinne of one woman there should come so much harme and damage unto that Iland. He saw likewise that it was replenished with many Trees of full divers sorts of fruit, as well for the Summer as for the Winter, and such as hee might very well sustaine his life, without dying desperately for hunger.

So when that hee had very well perused these things, hee receeved
great contentment, for that the place seemed unto him very neces-
sarie and apparant for him to live out of the world, and ende his
daies, wherefore hee did determine to remaine there, and for the
defence of raine and stormes, he thought it good to make himselfe a
cottage for his continuall habitation, to keepe himself from the furie
thereof, and that farther within the Iland, for that the stinke and evill
savour of the dead Fauno should not trouble him.

VI. Analogue

From
THE FAIR SIDEA
by Jacob Ayrer (1618),[1]
translated by H. H. Furness

[In Act I Duke Ludolff, defeated by Leudegast, Prince of
Wiltau, loses his lands and is banished.]

Enter Ludolff *with* Sidea. *He carries a white silver staff in his hand, and
says:* Alas, how bitter to me are contempt and humiliation . . . I
have lost my Princedom, my kingdom, my wealth, honour and
glory. But although I have no longer any possessions, I shall not
cease to use every wile and guile until Fortune once more shines upon
me and I can be avenged on my foe.

SIDEA   This whole week, sire, I have had a great pain in my heart.
Not for a single hour could I be joyous. My heart foreboded, alas, all
the scoff and scorn of this sorrow. 'Twas no wonder that my heart
burst into a thousand pieces. Formerly I lived in princely rank—now
I have neither land nor people. Formerly I was addressed as Princely
lady—now I am a beggar girl. Formerly my wealth was unbounded
—it needs be that I must now eat grass. Formerly had I many a
suitor—now I shall have to die single, and know not how the end
may be.

LUDOLFF   [*enraged, shaking his staff*]   Hold your peace or may
Jupiter blast you! Have patience with me a minute, while I summon
my Spirit to tell me just what is to happen to us here on earth until
we die.   [*With his staff he draws a circle with certain characters in it.*]

---

[1] *Die Schöne Sidea.* From *Opus Theatricum* by Jacob Ayrer, Nuremberg, 1618. Ayrer
died in 1605. The play is in verse. Excerpts here are from H. H. Furness's version
in *Var.*, 1892, with slight modifications.

SIDEA Alas, if you are going to raise the Spirit, let me go away. He is too fearful to me.

LUDOLFF Be silent, he is harmless. [*He opens the circle and knocks on the opening with his little staff, thereupon the Devil leaps from it, spits out fire, walking around in the circle, and says angrily:*] Ludolff, you're an evil fellow. Owing to you, I can get no rest anywhere. The minute anything occurs to you, you think I must be with you instantly. Now I'd have you know that I have more conjurers than you, and can't hop up to you instantly, however cross you may be about it. So tell me at once what you want of me.[1]

LUDOLFF You rascal, if you are going to be so proud release me from my oath or else answer my questions at once.

RUNCIFAL, THE DEVIL Tell me what you want. If you don't I'll go back to where I came from. You heard me say that I had to go on further.

LUDOLFF Then tell me in one word, whether I can revenge myself on my foe.

RUNCIFAL I can promise you in truth, that:—Before long it will happen that you can capture the son of your foe, and he will long be your servant; and after submitting to misery for a long time, he will be entirely freed from your service, will then return again to his father's house, when you will be restored to honour, and fortune will return to you. More I cannot tell you.   [*Exit.*

LUDOLFF If you hear any huntsmen in this wood let me know at once, and I will take the best of care to catch something myself. If I could only catch that young prince,—if I could only revenge myself on him, he'd have to remain my slave, I promise you; on him I'll wreak all the evil his father did to us. Let us now enter this hut, because just at present we have nothing better.   [*Exeunt.*

[In Act II, after much farcical business between John Molitor and the fathers of the girls he has seduced, Leudegast's son Engelbrecht goes to hunt in the forest.]

Enter Ludolff *with* Sidea, *each with a white staff. He says:* Last night my spirit disclosed to me that the Duke's son, Engelbrecht, would hunt in the forest. He will come to me exactly right, I will track him in the forest, catch him, and so plague him that the like has never before been known.

SIDEA Verily, that is what I'd gladly see. If we can only catch this bird we might fairly hope to gain control, once more, of the whole

---

[1] Ludolff has two servants: the demon Runcifal and the comic Miller, John Molitor.

princely government; and he'd have to pay us a great ransom; and unless he is willing to lose his life he'll have to reinstate us.

LUDOLFF   Be silent, we must be exactly ready; I will shortly revenge myself on him or kill myself and you.   [*Exeunt, sorrowfully.*

Enter Engelbrecht *with his squire. They shout as they enter: Holla, holla, holla, then come forward.*

ENGELBRECHT   We have wandered far from the paths, and no answer is given to our blasts on the horn. Look, look, what people are those just over there? In fact they are running towards us. Therefore be well on your guard.
[*They lay their hands on their rapiers.*

Enter Ludolff, *the Prince, with* Sidea; *he carries in one hand a drawn sword, and in the other a white staff, and says:* Thou young Prince, surrender thyself.

ENGELBRECHT   Such booty thou shalt not gain this day. Squire, run him through with thy sword.
[*They try to draw from the scabbards.* Ludolff *strikes the weapons with his staff.*

SQUIRE   I cannot draw my weapon. I believe it is bewitched.

ENGELBRECHT   Ay truly, it is magic. I am lamed in both hands. I can neither bend nor turn. Therefore since there is no other way, I must be thy prisoner and live according to thy pleasure.[1]

LUDOLFF   Give me at once thy promise of this. And as for you, you saucebox, clear out, or I'll tread you into the dirt, and hack off all your four limbs, so that you'll cease to bother me; and I'll let crows and ravens feed on you.

SQUIRE   Alas, an evil hunt have we. Gracious Prince, in heavy sorrow, at this time I take my leave of you.   [*Exit.*

LUDOLFF   Now thou art my very slave. As thy father unrighteously drove me from home and people, and heaped on me great scoff and scorn, so shalt thou be parted from him and all thy country. Thou shalt carry wood for my daughter, and everything which she tells thee thou must obey and accomplish, or heavy blows shall force thee. And should she complain to me that thou hesitatest at anything, on the spot I'll strike thee dead. [*Beats him to the exit. Strikes him on the back with his staff, as does also the daughter, and exeunt.*

[In Act III Sidea falls in love with Engelbrecht, after illtreating him. They run away together.]

Enter Sidea *with the young prince* Engelbrecht, *who is very meanly clad, and is carrying some logs and an axe, which he lays down.*[2]

[1] Cf. Ferdinand, I. 2. 456–90.   [2] Cf. III. 1. 1–21.

SIDEA (*threatening him with her staff*) Unless you want to get a flogging, you'll split me that wood up pretty quick, you abominable, lazy dog!

ENGELBRECHT (*falling at her feet and imploring with his hands*) Woe's me, I'm utterly sick at heart and cannot go another step in doing this work. I am utterly exhausted, not an atom of strength is left in my body. 'Twere better far to kill me at once than to put on me such daily tasks, such heavy work. I beg you, as sincerely as I can, to kill me outright.

SIDEA (*addressing the audience*) Although his father condemns my father to misery and to need, and I, his princely daughter, have cause enough for vengeance, yet when I think over the whole affair I have to bear in mind that he, too, is of princely birth and has done us no harm; and, sooth to say, ought not to have to pay his father's debt. And, then, he has such a figure that on the score of beauty I cannot hate him. And if I must lead this life for a long time here in the forest, what a joy and happiness it were if he were to prove faithful to me and take me for his wedded wife. I'd like to help him out of all this need and woe. I'll tell him secretly about it. [*She goes up to him.*] My Engelbrecht, what would'st thou do if, on account of thy service, I were to release thee and then take thee in marriage.

ENGELBRECHT (*falling at her feet*) Ah, speak not, or my emotions will kill me. All the living gods in the world could not bring that about, but, if it were possible, my fate were then the best of all. Yes, to thy love I would devote myself, and serve thee body and soul, and make thee a princess.

SIDEA If I could trust thee in this matter, and thou wilt accede and aid me with hand and mouth, I'll speak further with thee.

ENGELBRECHT Ay, you ought to trust me, and you ought also to be my spouse.

SIDEA Art thou then mine? [*They join hands.*]

ENGELBRECHT Yes.

SIDEA Then I am thine. May the gods remain with us! Nothing now but death shall part us. That thou mayst see how earnest I am, I'll follow whithersoever thou leadest. [*They embrace.*

Enter Runcifal *the Devil, and says:* Sidea, this proposal of thine I'll go straight and tell thy father. It's eminently improper that thou shouldst allow thyself to be carried off. [Sidea *takes her staff, strikes him on the mouth. He signifies that he is dumb, and sorrowfully departs.*

SIDEA Now the Spirit cannot harm us by betraying us to my father. Now we can go away from this country. [*Exeunt.*

Enter Prince Ludolff *with* John Molitor; *in a rage he strikes John on the head with his staff, and says:* Where is Sidea? tell me at once.

JOHN   I don't know. If she's not in the forest, she's with Engelbrecht.

LUDOLFF   Art thou not my slave, whose duty 'twas to guard them?

JOHN   Ay, ay, I know that well enough. But, gracious Sir, there
are two of them, and they didn't tell me where they were going.
So I don't know where they are.

LUDOLFF   This shall cost thee thy life. Clear out and find where
they are. And if thou dost not bring them back quickly, I'll cut thy
head off.   [John Molitor *scratches his head and Exit.*

[Engelbrecht loses Sidea, forgets her, and is on the point of
marrying another bride when Sidea arrives with a magic drink
which restores his memory and his love for her. The fathers
are reconciled.]

VII. Source

From
OVID'S METAMORPHOSES
translated by Arthur Golding (1567)

The Seventh Booke, 254–86

The starres alonly faire and bright did in the welkin shine.
To which she lifting up hir handes did thrise hirselfe encline,
And thrice with water of the brooke hir haire besprincled shee:
And gasping thrise she opte hir mouth: and bowing downe hir
    knee
Upon the bare hard ground, she said: O trustie time of night
Most faithfull unto privities, O golden starres whose light
Doth jointly with the Moone succeede the beames that blaze ⎫
    by day   ⎪
And thou three headed *Hecate* who knowest best the way   ⎬ 260
To compasse this our great attempt and art our chiefest stay: ⎭
Ye Charmes and Witchcrafts, and thou Earth which both with
    herbe and weed
Of mightie working furnishest the Wizardes at their neede:
Ye Ayres and windes: ye Elves of Hilles, of Brookes, of Woods
    alone,

Of standing Lakes, and of the Night approche ye everychone.
Through helpe of whom (the crooked bankes much wondring
  at the thing)
I have compelled streames to run cleane backward to their
  spring.
By charmes I make the calme Seas rough, and make the rough
  Seas plaine
And cover all the Skie with Cloudes, and chase them thence
  againe.   270
By charmes I rayse and lay the windes, and burst the Vipers
  jaw,
And from the bowels of the Earth both stones and trees doe
  drawe.
Whole woods and Forestes I remove: I make the Mountaines
  shake,
And even the Earth it selfe to grone and fearfully to quake.
I call up dead men from their graves: and thee O lightsome
  Moone
I darken oft, though beaten brasse abate thy perill soone.
Our Sorcerie dimmes the Morning faire, and darkes the Sun at
  Noone.[1]
The flaming breath of firie Bulles ye quenched for my sake,
And caused there unwieldie neckes the bended yoke to take.
Among the Earthbred brothers you a mortall war did set   280
And brought asleepe the Dragon fell whose eyes were never shet.
By meanes whereof deceiving him that had the golden fleece
In charge to keepe, you sent it thence by *Jason* into *Greece*.
Now have I neede of herbes that can by vertue of their juice
To flowring prime of lustie youth old withred age reduce.
I am assurde ye will it graunt.

---

[1] Prospero, V. 1. 33–50, recalls this passage in Golding and also Ovid's Latin:

> . . . auraeque et venti montesque amnesque lacusque
> dique omnes nemorum, dique omnes noctis adeste,
> quorum ope, cum volui, ripis mirantibus amnes
> in fontes rediere suos, concussaque sisto,
> stantia concutio cantu freta, nubila pello
> nubilaque induco, ventos abigoque vocoque,
> vipereas rumpo verbis et carmine fauces,
> vivaque saxa sua convulsaque robora terra
> et silvas moveo iubeoque tremescere montes
> et mugire solum Manesque exire sepulcris!
> te quoque, Luna, traho, quamvis Temesaea labores
> aera tuos minuant; currus quoque carmine nostro
> pallet avi, pallet nostris Aurora venenis! . . .
>
> (*Met.*, Bk VII, 197–209)

VIII. Analogue

From
A MOST PLEASANT COMEDIE OF MUCEDORUS
Anon. (1598)[1]

[Bremo the Wild Man]
Act II. Sc. 3.

Enter Bremo, a wild man.

BRE. No passengers this morning? what, not one?
A chance that seldome doth befall . . .
Who knowes not Bremoes strength,
Who like a king commandes within these woods?
The beare, the boare, dares not abide my sight,
But hastes away to save themselves by flight . . .
The aged okes at *Bremoes* breath doe bowe,
And all things els are still at my commaund,
Els what would I?
Rent them in peeces and plucke them from the earth,
And each way els I would revenge my selfe . . .

[In Act III. Sc. 3 Amadine enters the forest to meet her exiled lover Mucedorus.]

Enter Bremo looking about, hastily taketh hould of her.

BRE. A hapie pray! now, *Bremo*, feede on flesh,
Dainties, *Bremo*, dainties, thy hungry panch to fill!
Now glut thy greedie guts with luke warme blood!
Come, fight with me, I long to see thee dead . . .
AMA. Yet pittie me and let me live a while.
BRE. No pittie, I, ile feed upon thy flesh,
Ile teare thy bodie peecemeale joynt from joynt.
AMA. Ah, now I want my shephards company.
BRE. Ile crush thy bones betweixt two oken trees.

[1] *A Most pleasant Comedie of Mucedorus the kings sonne of Valentia and Amadine the Kings daughter of Arragon, with the merie conecites of Mouse. Newly set foorth, as it hath bin sundrie times plaide in the honorable Cittie of London. Very delectable and full of mirth.* Printed for William Jones, 1598.

AMA. Hast, shephard, hast, or else thou comst to late.
BRE. Ile sucke the sweetnes from thy marie bones.
AMA. Ah spare, ah spare to shed my guiltlesse blood!
BRE. With this my bat will I beate out thy braines.
Down, down, I say, prostrate thy selfe upon the ground.
AMA. Then, *Mucedorus*, farewel; my hoped joies, farewel.
Yea, farewel life, and welcome present death.

[Shee kneeles.

To thee, O God, I yeeld my dying ghost.

[Struck by her beauty he cannot kill her but takes her to his lair, where he alternates threats and blandishments in an attempt to win her love.]

Act IV. Sc. 3.

BRE. If thou wilt love me thou shalt be my queene:
I wil crowne thee with a chaplet made of ivie,
And make the rose and lilly wait on thee:
Ile rend the burley braunches from the oke,
To shadow thee from burning sunne.
The trees shall spred themselves where thou dost go,
And as they spread, ile trace along with thee.
AMA. You may, for who but you? (*Aside.*)
BRE. Thou shalt be fed with quailes and partridges,
With blacke birds, larkes, thrushes and nightingales.
Thy drinke shall be goates milke and christal water,
Distilled from the fountaines and the clearest springs.
And all the dainties that the woods afforde,
Ile freely give thee to obtaine thy love.
AMA. You may, for who but you? (*Aside.*)...
BRE. When thou art up, the wood lanes shalbe strawed
With violets, cowslips and swete marigolds
For thee to trampel and to trace upon...
And I will teach thee how to kill the deare,
To chase the hart, and how to rowse the roe,
If thou wilt live to love and honour mee.
AMA. You may, for who but you? (*Aside.*)

[Mucedorus comes unarmed and disguised as a hermit. Bremo is about to kill him when Amadine begs that he be allowed to speak.]

BRE. Speake on, but be not over long.
MUCE. In time of yore, when men like brutish beasts

Did lead their lives in loathsom celles and woodes
And wholy gave themselves to witlesse will,
A rude unruly rout, then man to man
Became a present praie, then might prevailed,
The weakest went to walles:
Right was unknowen, for wrong was all in all.
As man thus lived in this great outrage,
Behould one *Orpheus* came, as poets tell,
And them from rudenes unto reason brought,
Who led by reason soone forsooke the woods.
Insteade of caves they built them castles strong;
Citties and townes were founded by them then:
Glad were they, they found such ease,
And in the end they grew to perfect amitie;
Waying their former wickednesse,
They tearmd the time wherein they lived then
A golden age, a goodly golden age.
Now, *Bremo*, for so I heare thee called,
If men which lived tofore as thou dost now,
Wilie in wood, addicted all to spoile,
Returned were by worthy *Orpheus* meanes,
Let me like *Orpheus* cause thee to returne
From murder, bloudshed and like crueltie.
What, should we fight before we have a cause?
No, lets live and love together faithfully.
Ile fight for thee.
　　BRE.　Fight me or die: or fight or else thou diest.

[Amadine persuades Bremo to spare the hermit, whom she does not recognize as her lover, and Mucedorus promises to serve him and her. Soon however, in V. i, he tricks Bremo into letting him have his club, and kills him with it.]

IX. Analogue

From
JOHN A KENT AND JOHN A CUMBER[1]
by Anthony Munday (1594)

GOSSELEN　Content ye good my Lord. No whit too late,
Heere is a lad on whom we doo relye,
For slye conveyaunce of the Ladyes hither.

[1] Text from *MalSoc* edn, 1923.

Full of conceit he is, and deeply seene
In secret artes, to woork for your avayle.
  GRIFFIN Canst thou my freend, from foorth the vaultes beneathe,
Call up the ghostes of those long since deceast?
Or from the upper region of the ayre
Fetch swift wingde spirits to effect thy will?
  JOHN Can you my Lord, and you, and you, and you,
Goe to the venson, for your suppers drest,
And afterward goe laye ye downe to rest?   (102–13)

[John a Kent goes himself in disguise and gets the two maidens Sidanen and Marian away from their bridegrooms, but through the arts of John a Cumber they are taken back to the castle and then sent, escorted by the Countess, Oswen and Amerye, to Chester to be married. John a Kent sends his boy Shrimp to prevent this.]

Actus Quartus, Scena Prima

Enter Shrimp, playing on some instrument, a prettie way before the Countesse, Sydanen, Marian, Oswen, and Amerye.

  OSWEN Madame, this sound is of some instrument;
[Thus] for two houres space it still hath haunted us,
Now heere, now there, on eche syde round about us,
And questionlesse, either we followe it,
Or it guydes us, least we mistake our way.

                 (The boy playes roundabout them.)

  AMERYE It may be that this famous man of Arte,[1]
Doubting least John a Kent should cross our journey,
And seeke revendge for his receiv'de disgrace:
He by this musique dooth direct our course,
More redyly to hit the way to Chester.
  COUNTESSE What ere it be, I would we were at Chester.
My lovely Niece I see is malcontent.
So is my Maryan, but what remedye?
When thinges you see fall out so contrary?
  SYDANEN Ay, poore Sydanen, let no more sweet song
Be made by Poet for Sidanen sake;
Her fine trim day is turn to black cole night,
And she hath lost her sweetest loove delight.

[1] John a Cumber.

SHRIMP (*to her asyde*) But let Sydanen cast away this care,
Comfort is neerer her then shees aware.
    SYDANEN What say you Cossen? did you speak to me?
    MARIAN Not I Sydanen, I with you complayne
On fortunes spight and over deep disdayne.
    SHRIMP But Marian with Sydanen may rejoyse,
For time will let them have their owne harts choyse.
                    (*They look about.*)
    SYDANEN Pray God amen. O Cossen did you heare?
A voyce still buzzeth comfort in mine eare.
    MARIAN And so in mine, but I no shape can see.
Tis John a Cumber mocks both you and me.
    SYDANEN Cursse on his hart for cumber true loove so,
Which else had made full end of all our woe.

        (*Enter Sr. Gosselen, Griffin, Powesse, and Evan.*)

    GOSSELEN How say ye Lordes? now credit John a Kent.
See where they are, and at the selfe same tree,
Where he assurde us all of them would be.
    S. GRIFFIN Sweetest Sydanen, how thy happie sight
Makes me forget all former sorrowe quyte.
    POWESSE The lyke dooth Marians presence yeeld to me,
For all greefes past assurde felicitie.
                    (*Musique chime*)
    EVAN Listen my Lordes, me thinkes I heare the chyme
Which John did promise, ere you should presume
To venture for recoverie of the Ladyes.
             (*A daint*[ie fit] [1] *of music.*)
    GOSSELEN The very same. Stay till the power therof
Have laid the sleepie charge on bothe their eyes,
That should have guyded them from hence to Chester.

(*The boy trips round about Oswen and Amery, sing*[ing to the] *chyme, and
they the one after the other, lay them* [down] *using very sluggish gestures, the
Ladyes amazed* [stare] *about them.*)

Song, to the Musique within

[Sle]ep sweetly: sleep sweetly; sweetly take rest;
[Sha]ll eche goe with her choyse, where she lykes best.
Ladyes cheere up your despayring mindes, for your freendes are
    neere,
That will answere true loove in due kinde; then never more feare.

---

[1] Words in square brackets are speculative.

SHRIMP Lordes, take advauntage, for they bothe are fast.
Bid John a Cumber mend this cunning cast.
GOSSELEN Feare not good Madame, for you must with me,
To ende the joyes these loovers long to see.

(*The chyme playes, and Gosselen with the Countesse goes turning out.*)
[*Exeunt.*

S. GRIFFIN And fayre Sydanen, I dare boldely say,
Rather with me will goe, then heere to stay.

(*The chyme agayne, and they turne out in like manner.*) [*Exeunt.*

POWESSE I not misdoubt, but Marian beares lyke mynde,
This is the way our sweet content to fynd.

(*The chyme agayne, and so they.*) [*Exeunt.*

SHRIMP Sir Evan, follow you the way they take,
For now I must these sleeepie Lordes awake. [*Exit Evan.*
Fye, Gentlemen, what meanes this slothfulnes?

(*They start up.*)

You sleep securely, while the subtill foe,
Hath got your charge, and bred a greater woe.

[Shrimp pretends to be John a Cumber's boy, sent to lead
them after the escaping brides.]

OSWEN Thankes to thy maister, we will followe thee,
To make amends for our fond negligence.
SHRIMP And I will lead ye such a merrie walke,
As you therof shall at more leysure talke.
Come, Gentlemen. [*Exeunt.* (1098–1186)

[Later we see what he has done with them.]

Enter Shrimpe leading Oswen and Amery about the tree.

OSWEN Were ever men thus led about a Tree?
Still circkling it, and never getting thence?
My braynes doo ake, and I am growen so faynt,
That I must needes lye downe on meere constraynt.

(*He lyes down.*)

AMERY This villayn boy is out of doubt some spirit.
Still he cries Follow, but we get no further
Then in a ring to daunce about this tree.

In all my life I never was so wearie.
Follow that list, for I can goe no longer.

(He lyes down.)

SHRIMP   There lye and rest ye, for I think your walke
Hath not beene altogether to your ease.
Now I must hence; I heare my maisters call.
It standes uppon the push of opening all.   (1394–1406)

X. Analogue

From
THE THREE SATYRS, A PASTORAL TALE[1]
Anon. (early seventeenth century),
translated by the editor

Persons: 1. Pantalone. 2. Phillis, a girl. 3. Gratiano. 4. Fausto, a
youth. 5. Coviello. 6. Chloris, a girl. 7. Zanni. 8. Burattino.
9. Magician. Three Satyrs. Shepherds. Cupid.

The Scene represents Arcadia.

Properties: Cupid's dress for Burattino; a half-hoop; a large fat
sausage; two shoes and a riding-boot for a quiver; Mercury's
costume for Zanni; three pork sausages on a spit; two shoes for
wings; Jove's costume for Pantalone; a pestle; a tree; a large
rock made to burst open; a whale; a fountain; a temple; a
donkey's mask; a bull's mask; a wood; macaroni; fire, food;
a suitable book; cords; a woman's dress for Burattino; Greek
pitch; fake cudgels.

Act I.

MAGICIAN [entering] from the grotto, speaks of his wisdom and
power, that Hell serves him, spirits in the shape of wild-men
serve him and do whatever he commands, and that all things
are subject to him; on which
PHILLIS, from A, singing.[2] She talks about the pleasures of hunting.

---

[1] Translated from F. Neri, *Scenari delle Maschere in Arcadia*, 1913. Neri transcribed
scenarii used by B. Locatelli now in Casatense MSS., two volumes entitled, i.
Della Scena de soggetti comici di B.L.R. In Roma. 1618; ii. *Della Scena de soggetti comici
e tragici di B.L.R.* In Roma. 1622. *Li Tre Satiri* is in vol. ii, Scen. 28, fol. 229–36.
[2] The letters A, B, C, D referred to the several entrances to the stage, apart from
the grotto and temple, which are in view throughout.

MAGICIAN tells her to leave the chase and follow Venus, whose pleasures are much sweeter. PHILLIS disdains him. In the end, after much speech, the MAGICIAN, angry with PHILLIS, touches her with his enchanted rod; he must pretend to invoke Pluto; has her transformed into a tree, binding her with a spell so that she cannot be released unless the tree be first touched with iron. He declares that he has punished with his spells many others, shepherds and strangers, who have shown too little respect for his person. He leaves by D.

PANTALONE, from A. He tells of the Shipwreck, of the loss of his companions. He bewails his ill-luck; does not know where he is, or in what country; he is afraid that the wild animals will eat him. He calls out for GRATIANO, ZANNI and BURATTINO, to find out whether they are in those parts. At last, after many (comic) accidents and words there appears

THE SEA, on which large vessels and small boats are seen. PANTALONE calls his companions, but nobody replies. The boats disappear, and now a WHALE appears. PANTALONE shows every sign of fear, and cries out, fearing that the WHALE might eat him. The WHALE opens its mouth and out comes

BURATTINO, from the Whale's mouth. SEA and WHALE disappear. The men remain. Finally, after much 'business' they recognize each other and are amazed. BURATTINO says that he was in a skiff in the WHALE's body; he relates the pranks he played inside there, because of which the WHALE vomited him out. He says that if he had had fire he would have fried all its liver. At last he makes water on a rock; at this

ZANNI, from the rock, which bursts open. He comes out and they all recognize each other and show their joy. He says that he was transformed by an old Necromancer because he would not do what he wanted. Finally they say that they are hungry; they make play with the echo, then, taking the Temple for an inn, they all joyfully enter the Temple.

GRATIANO and COVIELLO, from B. They bewail the loss of their companions, the unknown country, their hunger and ignorance of means to survive. They use words and 'business'. At last they decide to seek news of their fellows and the usual ways of surviving in this country. They discuss how to get a living, and go out by A.

FAUSTO and SHEPHERDS, from C, playing and singing, with presents and eatables to offer to the Gods and to pray for favours. They kneel in front of the Temple and invoke the Gods to be favourable to their prayers. They offer their gifts; on which

PANTALONE, ZANNI and BURATTINO, from the Temple, dressed like

Gods: PANTALONE as Jove, ZANNI as Mercury, BURATTINO as Cupid.[1] At first they mime anger at the SHEPHERDS; finally they accept the gifts and listen to their requests. They say that they will give their answers another time. ZANNI, BURATTINO, with the gifts, re-enter the Temple; the SHEPHERDS go out by C; Fausto remains, discoursing on his love for PHILLIS, who follows Diana and spurns his passion; he laments her cruelty, then speaks of the obligations that bind him to CHLORIS for the many benefits he has had from her; and of her love for him, though he neither loves her nor cares anything for her; on which

CHLORIS, from D. She recalls her love for FAUSTO, begs him to love her, reproaching him with her many kindnesses to him. FAUSTO lacks courage to reply as he would wish; at last, unwilling to listen to her, he pushes her aside and leaves by A. CHLORIS remains, grieving over his cruelty; then she goes out by A.

PANTALONE, ZANNI, and BURATTINO, from the Temple, revelling in the prank they have played on the SHEPHERDS (who thought them gods), and in the presents they gave them. They carry out the eatables and make ready for their meal. They say that they dressed up as Gods in the things they found in the Temple. They praise their own cleverness and say that they will cut off a branch of the Tree to make a club to defend themselves if found out. PANTALONE cuts the Tree into which PHILLIS was transformed; the Tree is released from its enchantment; on which

PHILLIS, from the Tree. They marvel at it, and wish to play tricks on her, inviting her to eat;[2] on which

SATYRS, from the grotto, making a loud noise, beat them all, and they run off in different directions.

Act II.

MAGICIAN from D, talking about his art. He sees that the rock is disenchanted; then the Tree. He wonders at the Fates who so speedily have anticipated everything. He says that he wishes to punish the strangers for the damage they do in the land. He makes incantations, and calls; on which

[1] Miss Lea's valuable note on the Corsini version helps to explain the list of properties: 'Pantalone carries a pestle (for a thunderbolt); Zanni has bound two shoes to his head and two to his ankles for wings; he carries a spit wreathed with sausages for a caduceus; Sardinello (Burattino) has shoes for wings and a half-hoop of sausage-meat (for Cupid's bow)' (*op. cit.*, p. 665n.).

[2] 'In the Corsini version they try to force her, but she escapes with the trick of blindfolding them. Three satyrs find them groping about, and pretend to be the Nymph; the buffoons embrace them' (Lea, *op. cit.*, p. 665).

SATYRS, from the grotto. MAGICIAN orders them to find the strangers and carry them into the cave, so that they may not commit any more excesses. SATYRS go back into the grotto; MAGICIAN leaves by A.

PANTALONE and ZANNI, from C. They talk about their misadventure and their escape from the SATYRS; they say that they have lost BURATTINO. They call him; on which

SATYRS, from the grotto. They carry off PANTALONE and ZANNI, who make a great noise and show terror; all enter the grotto.

PHILLIS, from B. She talks about hunting, and the MAGICIAN's power, and how she is free from his spells. She says that she is tired; speaks evil of love; discourses on the felicity of those who follow Diana. She lies down to sleep by the Fountain; on which

GRATIANO and COVIELLO, from A; desperate through not knowing where they are, and having no news of their fellows; and dying of hunger and the perils they are meeting. They see the Nymph sleeping by the Fountain. They covet her, making mime of enjoying her. They wish to wake her, but do not dare; they talk of annoying her while she is asleep, and make all kinds of gestures; on which

MAGICIAN, from D; suspicious of the strangers who wish to enjoy the Nymph and to harm her. He shouts to them to leave her alone, otherwise they will repent of their presumption. They show contempt for him and say that they are going to do whatever they please. MAGICIAN, enraged, touches the ground with his wand, and fire appears. GRATIANO and COVIELLO, terrified, flee along road A. MAGICIAN remains; says that he means to punish the Nymph, since she is an enemy to love, and make her fall in love with her self, with the reflection she will see in the Fountain. He casts a spell on the Fountain where PHILLIS is sleeping. MAGICIAN leaves; PHILLIS remains; on which

CUPID appears from the heavens, singing, shoots his arrow, and departs. PHILLIS remains, sleeping; on which

BURATTINO, from B; in despair at having lost his companions, and at his various misfortunes. He does not know what to do next. Finally, after some talk and 'business' he sees PHILLIS asleep; he does comic things to her; PHILLIS wakes. BURATTINO hides behind the Fountain. PHILLIS, looking into the water, falls in love with her own face and speaks amorously to her reflection. Finally, after many words, BURATTINO goes through 'business' with PHILLIS; he says that he was in the Fountain; speaks amorously. PHILLIS shows herself amorous of BURATTINO and embraces him; on which

MAGICIAN, from C, hears PHILLIS making love to BURATTINO and marvels at her lack of sense. MAGICIAN is offended. Because she spurns him he makes a spell to change BURATTINO into a woman. He calls; on which

SATYRS, from the grotto, carry away BURATTINO, leaving by D; MAGICIAN also. PHILLIS stays, amazed and terrified, on which

FAUSTO, from B. He reveals his love to PHILLIS; begs her to try to love him. PHILLIS repulses him and will not listen. FAUSTO bewails her cruelty; at which

CHLORIS, from C. She reveals her love to FAUSTO, who will not listen. He spurns her; tells her he loves PHILLIS. PHILLIS says that she follows Diana and does not wish to love him. CHLORIS bewails FAUSTO's cruelty; FAUSTO bewails the cruelty of PHILLIS, who, in order not to hear him, leaves by D. FAUSTO, to avoid listening to CHLORIS, whom he rejects, leaves by D. CHLORIS, grieving at FAUSTO's cruelty and lack of love for her, follows him by D.

PANTALONE and ZANNI, from the grotto, with a book. They say that they have stolen it from the MAGICIAN, and got out of the cave with it. They mime fear of the spirits, and of being beaten, and of the dark place. At length they decide to open the book to learn its power. They open the book; at which

SATYRS, from D. They ask, what commands? The others are surprised that they have come so obediently. PANTALONE commands them to bring a truss; it is brought. ZANNI orders one thing, PANTALONE another. SATYRS bring them, and do whatever they command. Finally they ask for food; require a platter of macaroni. Wishing to eat it they close the book, at which flames of fire appear, playing round the book. They go out, fleeing by A and other exits.

Act III.

MAGICIAN and SATYRS, from C. He learns from the SATYRS how the strangers have forced them to obey their orders by the power of the magic book. MAGICIAN, furious because they have taken his book and left the grotto, orders the SATYRS to go and be vigilant. SATYRS depart into the grotto; MAGICIAN stays. He says that he wants revenge on the strangers and will enchant the Fountain so that all who drink of it will be changed into animals. He performs the spell; then leaves by D.

GRATIANO and COVIELLO, from A. They speak of the misfortunes brought on them by the Nymph; they fear the country they are in; say that they are thirsty. They go to the Fountain and drink, and are changed into animals: GRATIANO into an ass; COVIELLO into a bull. They perform suitable 'business' and bellow; leave by A.

PANTALONE and ZANNI, from C. They tell of the fright they got through the macaroni and how this happened because they closed the book. They express pleasure, saying that the book has power to make them obeyed by the wild men, who will bring them anything they think of asking for. They go through 'business', saying, 'I am going to ask for the city of Bergamo to be brought here' etc.; at which

BURATTINO, from B, in the likeness of a woman, transformed thus by the MAGICIAN. He has much 'business' with PANTALONE and ZANNI, who want to make love to him; but he is unwilling. At the end, after many words and actions, they open the book; at which

SATYRS, from the grotto. They are ordered to carry BURATTINO off. SATYRS do so, leaving by D. ZANNI and PANTALONE remain, laughing over the powers of the book and hoping to make themselves respected by the whole country; on which

FAUSTO, from A. He learns that PANTALONE and ZANNI are now 'bosses' and to be recognized as such. FAUSTO mocks them, laughing. After much talk and action PANTALONE and ZANNI, infuriated, open the book, saying that they mean to punish him; on which

SATYRS, from D. They are ordered to tie up FAUSTO, who is at once bound. SATYRS depart into the grotto; the others remain. FAUSTO, having experienced their power, surrenders completely and begs them to untie him, for he will be very obedient. At length, after much talk and 'business' they release him. FAUSTO thanks them; then begs them to help him get PHILLIS for his wife. He says that they ought to punish the MAGICIAN, who is the cause of all the evil in the land. They promise to do so, and to find the Shepherds; they leave by D.

MAGICIAN, from A. He says that he has foreseen the treachery and plot of the shepherds and strangers against him by means of his magic book. He says that he means to put everything to rights by his magic. He invokes Pluto and draws a circle on the ground with his wand, feigning to make magic. He goes dancing into the grotto.[1]

FAUSTO and PHILLIS, from C. They talk about their mutual love and the bliss of lovers, and show that they are happy. While talking they enter the circle made by the Magician, and both begin to dance, while expressing amazement; on which

---

[1] 'In the Corsini version the spell is that whoever comes to the grotto shall dance himself to death' (Lea, *op. cit.*, ii, p. 669).

CHLORIS and SHEPHERDS, from A. They desire to punish the MAGICIAN for the trouble he causes the people of the place. They enter the circle and they too dance. The astonished victims do not know what to do about it; on which

BURATTINO, PANTALONE, and ZANNI, from B, running, BURATTINO crying out that PANTALONE and ZANNI want to ravish him, thinking him a woman. They enter the circle and also begin to dance; at which

GRATIANO and COVIELLO, from C, making a big noise and bellowing, also enter the circle and dance together with the rest, who are amazed at the animals dancing and their own inability to stop; on which

MAGICIAN, from the grotto, challenges them all for the plot against him. He has foreseen it all and wants his magic book back. Otherwise he will let them die of exhaustion. The dancers all promise to return his book if he will free them. MAGICIAN promises to free them. ZANNI, with suitable 'business', gives him back his book. MAGICIAN makes an incantation and strikes his wand on the ground. They all stop dancing. Then he orders BURATTINO, GRATIANO and COVIELLO to drink from the Fountain so that they may be restored to their former shapes. They drink at the Fountain and are turned back to what they were before. They thank the MAGICIAN and recognize each other, showing delight. Finally GRATIANO recognizes FAUSTO as his son, formerly called Lelio, who was lost while a child. PANTALONE recognizes PHILLIS, previously named Clarice. COVIELLO recognizes CHLORIS, earlier named Lidia, and shows great joy. FAUSTO marries PHILLIS; CHLORIS is promised a son of PANTALONE's. Filled with joy they say that they wish to take ship for Venice at once. So, clearing up the plot, they end the play.

XI. Possible Source

From
HYMENAEI, or THE SOLEMNITIES OF
A MASQUE AND BARRIERS AT A
MARRIAGE
by Ben Jonson (1606)

It is a noble and just advantage, that the things subiected to *understanding* have of those which are obiected to *sense*, that the one sort are but momentarie, and meerely taking; the other impressing, and lasting: Else the glorie of all these *solemnities* had perish'd like a blaze, and gone out, in the *beholders* eyes. So short-liv'd are the *bodies* of all things, in comparison of their *soules*. And, though *bodies* oft-times have the ill luck to be sensually preferr'd, they find afterwards, the good fortune (when *soules* live) to be utterly forgotten.[1] This it is hath made the most royall *Princes* and greatest *persons* (who are commonly the *per-*   10 *sonaters* of these *actions*) not onely studious of riches, and magnificence in the outward celebration, or shew; (which rightly becomes them) but curious after the most high, and heartie *inventions*, to furnish the inward parts: (and those grounded vpon *antiquitie*, and solide *learnings*) which, though their *voyce* be taught to sound to present occasions, their *sense*, or doth, or should alwayes lay hold on more remov'd *mysteries*. And, howsoever some may squemishly crie out, that all endevour of *learning*, and *sharpnesse* in these transitorie *devices* especially, where it steps beyond their little, or (let me not wrong 'hem) no braine   20 at all, is superfluous; I am contented, these fastidious *stomachs* should leave my full tables, and enjoy at home, their cleane empty trenchers, fittest for such airy tastes . . .

[The Masque, performed before the altar of Sacred Union, was introduced by Hymen, who praised Union as represented in the Royal Family. The gentlemen Masquers, representing 'the fowre Humors, and foure Affections', danced in and 'drew all their swords, offered to encompasse the Altar, and dis-

---

[1] This insistence, common in Masques, on the ephemerality of the spectacle, influenced Prospero's remarks in IV. 1. 148–58. Cf. S. Daniel, *Tethys' Festival* (1610): 'we who are the poore inginers for shadowes, and frame onely images of no result'; 'in these things, wherein the onely life consists in show'.

turbe the Ceremonies'. Hymen begged Reason to restrain them. Reason thereat appeared, 'seated in the top of the Globe (as in the braine, or highest part of Man)', and descending, spake:]

REASON

Forbeare your rude attempt; what ignorance
Could yeeld you so prophane, as to advance
One thought in act, against these *mysteries*?
Are Union's *orgies* of so slender price?
She that makes *soules*, with *bodies*, mixe in love,
Contracts the *world* in one, and therein Jove;
Is *spring*, and *end* of all things: yet, most strange!
Her selfe not suffers spring, nor end, nor change.

[To convert them Reason went on to explain the rites of Roman marriage, insisting on the significance of the number five.]

Whence hallow'd Union claymes her blisse,
As being all the summe, that growes
From the united strengths, of those
Which *male* and *female* numbers wee
Doe style, and are first *two*, and *three* . . .

Here, the vpper part of the Scene, *which was all of Clouds, and made artificially to swell, and ride like the Racke, began to open; and, the ayre clearing, in the top thereof was discovered* IUNO, *sitting in a Throne, supported by two beautifull* Peacockes; *her attyre rich, and like a Queene, a white Diademe on her head, from whence descended a Veyle, and that bound with a* Fascia, *of severall-coloured silkes, set with all sorts of jewels, and raysed in the top with Lillies and Roses; in her right hand she held a Scepter, in the other a timbrell, at her golden feete the hide of a lyon was placed: round about her sate the spirites of the ayre, in severall colours, making musique: Above her the region of fire, with a continuall motion, was seene to whirle circularly, and* JUPITER *standing in the toppe (figuring the heaven) brandishing his thunder: Beneath her the* rainebowe, IRIS, *and, on the two sides eight ladies, attired richly, and alike in the most celestiall colours, who represented her powers, as shee is the governesse of marriage, and made the second masque. All which, vpon the discoverie,* REASON *made narration of.*

REASON

And see where JUNO, whose great name
Is UNIO in the anagram,
Displays her glittering *state* and *chair*,
As she enlighten'd all the air!

[The eight lady Masquers, representing Juno's various functions, descended in clouds, danced in twos and then paired off with the men.]

Here, they daunced forth a most neate and curious measure, full of Subtilty
and Device; *which was so excellently performed, as it seemed to take away
that* Spirit *from the* Invention, *which the* Invention *gaue to it: and left it
doubtfull, whether the* Formes *flow'd more perfectly from the* Authors
*braine, or their feete. The straines were all notably different, some of them
formed into* Letters, *very signifying to the name of the* Bridegrome, *and
ended in manner of a chaine, linking hands: To which, this was spoken.*

REASON

Such was the *Golden Chaine* let downe from *Heaven;*
    And not those linkes more even,
Then these: so sweetly temper'd, so combin'd
    By UNION, and refin'd.
Here no *contention, envy, griefe, deceit,*
    Feare, jealousie have weight;
But all is *peace,* and *love,* and *faith,* and *blisse:*
    What *harmony* like this?
The gall, behinde the *altar* quite is throwne;
    This *sacrifice* hath none.
Now no *affections* rage, nor *humors* swell;
    But all composed dwell.   330
O JUNO, HYMEN, HYMEN, JUNO! who
    Can merit with you two?
Without your presence, VENUS can doe nought,
    Save what with shame is bought;
No father can himselfe a *parent* show,
Nor any *house* with prosp'rous issue grow.
    O then! What *deities* will dare
With HYMEN, or with JUNO to compare?

[After other dances Hymen and the Auspices led the bride
'as to the nuptial bower'. Jonson had written a charming

Epithalamium of fourteen stanzas, but only one stanza was sung, apparently to his regret, for he printed it all, commenting, 'and do heartily forgive their ignorance whom it chanceth not to please'.]

Hitherto extended the first nights *Solemnitie*, whose grace in the execution, left not where to adde unto it, with wishing: I meane, (nor doe I court them) in those, that sustain'd the *nobler* parts. Such was the exquisit performance, as (beside the *pompe, splendor,* or what we may call *apparelling* of such *Presentments*) that alone (had all else beene absent) was of power to surprize with 570 delight, and steale away the *spectators* from themselves. Nor was there wanting whatsoever might give to the *furniture,* or *complement;* eyther in *riches,* or strangenesse of the *habites,* delicacie of *daunces,* magnificence of the *scene,* or divine rapture of *musique.* Onely the envie was, that it lasted not still, or (now it is past) cannot by imagination, much lesse description, be recovered to a part of that *spirit* it had in the gliding by.

Yet, That I may not utterly defraud the *Reader* of his hope, 580 I am drawne to give it those briefe touches, which may leave behind some shadow of what it was: And first of the *Attyres.*

[The costumes were certainly gorgeous, with many 'glistering garments'.]

No lesse to be admir'd, for the grace, and greatnesse, was the whole *Machine* of the *Spectacle,* from whence they came: the first part of which was a ΜΙΚΡΟΚΟΣΜΟΣ, or *Globe,* fill'd with *Countreys,* and those gilded; where the *Sea* was exprest, heightned with silver waves. This stood, or rather hung (for no *Axell* was seene to support it) and turning softly, discovered the first *Masque* (as wee have before, but too runningly declared) which was of the *men,* sitting in faire *composition,* within a *mine* of severall metalls: To which, the lights were so placed, as no one was seene; but 640 seemed, as if onely REASON, with the splendor of her crowne, illumin'd the whole Grot.

On the sides of this (which began the other part) were placed two great *Statues,* fayned of gold, one of ATLAS, the other of HERCULES, in varied postures, bearing up the Clouds, which were of *Releve,* embossed, and tralucent, as Naturalls: To these, a cortine of painted clouds joyned, which reach'd to the upmost roofe of the Hall; and sodainely opening, reveal'd the three *Regions of Ayre:* In the highest of which, sate JUNO, in a 650 glorious throne of gold, circled with *Comets*, and fierie *Meteors*, engendred in that hot and drie *Region;* her feet reaching to the lowest: where, was made a *Rainebow*, and within it, *Musicians* seated, figuring *airie* spirits, their habits various, and resembling the severall colours, caused in that part of the *aire* by reflexion. The midst was all of darke and condensed clouds, as being the proper place, where *Raine, Haile,* and other watrie *Meteors* are made; out of which, two concave clouds, from the rest, thrust forth themselves (in nature of those *Nimbi*, wherein, by *Homer*, 660 *Virgil*, &c. the *gods* are fain'd to descend) and these carried the eight *Ladies*, over the heads of the two *Termes;* who (as the engine mov'd) seem'd also to bow themselues (by vertue of their shadowes) and discharge their shoulders of their glorious burden: when, having set them on the earth, both they and the clouds gathered themselues up againe, with some rapture of the *beholders*.

But that, which (as above in place, so in the beautie) was most taking in the *Spectacle*, was the *sphere* of *fire*, in the top of all, en-compassing the *ayre*, and imitated with such art and industrie, 670 as the *spectators* might discerne the Motion (all the time the *Shewes* lasted) without any Moover; and that so swift, as no eye could distinguish any colour of the light, but might forme to it selfe five hundred severall hiewes, out of the tralucent bodie of the *ayre*, objected betwixt it, and them.[1]

And this was crown'd with a statue of JUPITER, the *Thunderer*.

[1] The public theatre could hardly vie with such splendour, but the cosmic idea may have influenced Shakespeare.

XII. Possible Source

From
COLLOQUIA: THE SHIPWRECK
by Desiderius Erasmus
translated by W. B[urton] (1606)

[Seven Dialogues both pithie and profitable. By W.B. Printed for Nicholas Ling. 1606]

Naufragium. A pittiful, yet pleasant Dialogue of a Shipwracke, shewing what comfort Popery affoordeth in time of daunger.

The speakers names. Antonius. Adolphus.

ANT.   You tell me horrible things, *Adolphus*, of your sea voyage; is this to be a Mariner? God keepe me from going to sea.

ADOL.   Yea, that I have told you hitherto, is meere sport to those things you shal now heare.

ANT.   I have heard of evills more then enow, I trembled all the time you were reciting them, as if my selfe had beene in danger with you.

ADOL.   But to me my labours past were pleasing enough. But that night there happened a certaine thing, which for a great part of the night, tooke away all hope of life from the Maister of the ship.

ANT.   What, I pray you?

ADOL.   The night was somewhat light, and in the top of the maste stoode one of the mariners in the basket (for so I thinke they cal it) looking about to see if he could spie any land: fast by this man beganne to stand a certaine round thing like a bal of fire,[1] which (when it appeareth alone) is to the shipmen a most feareful signe of hard successe, but when two of them doe appeare together, that is a signe of a prosperous voyage. These apparitions were called in old time *Castor* and *Pollux*.

ANT.   What had they to doe with sea-men, being one of them a Horseman, the other a Champion, or stowt warrior?

ADOL.   So the Poets did feigne. The Pilot of the ship, sitting at the sterne, said to him that was aloft, Fellow (for so doe the ship-men call one another) doost thou not see what a companion stands by thy side? I see it (said the other) and I pray God it be for good: By and

---

[1] Cf. Ariel, I. 2. 196–201.

by the fiery globe sliding downe by the ropes, tumbled it selfe until it came to the Maister of the ship.

ANT. Did he not die with feare?[1]

ADOL. No, Mariners are accustomed to monsters. It having stayed there a while, it roled it selfe along the brimmes of the ship, and falling from thence downe into the middle roomes, it vanished away. About mid-night the tempest beganne to increase more and more. Did you ever see the Alpes?

ANT. Yes, I have seene them.

ADOL. Those mountains are but hillockes in comparison of the waves of the sea: so often as we were heaved up with them, we might have touched the Moone with our fingers; so often as wee went downe againe, it seemed unto us as though the earth had opened, and we had beene going directly to hell.

ANT. O madmen that commit themselves to the sea!

ADOL. The mariners striving with the tempest, but all in vaine, at length the Maister of the ship came unto us very pale.

ANT. That palenesse doth presage some great evil.

ADOL. My friends (quoth he) I can be no longer Maister of my ship, the windes have gotten the upper hand; it remaineth now, that we commit our selves unto God, and every man to prepare himselfe for extreamity.[2]

ANT. O right Scythian sermon!

ADOL. But first (quoth hee) the ship must be disburdened. Necessity hath no law, a sore weapon it is, there is no remeady; better it is to save our lives, with the losse of our goods, than to lose both goods and life together. The truth prevailed, many vessels were throwne over into the sea, ful of rich marchandise.[3]

ANT. This was indeede to suffer wracke.

ADOL. There was a certaine Italian in the ship, who had gone Ambassador to the King of Scots; he had a chest ful of plate, gold rings, cloth, and silke apparel.

ANT. He would not bestow them upon the sea.

ADOL. No, but desired either to perish with his beloved riches, or to be saved with them. Therefore he was somewhat wilful, and stoode against the rest.

ANT. What said the ship-maister?

ADOL. We could be wel content (quoth he) that thou, and that thou hast, should perish together: but it is not fit that all we should be in danger for the saving of thy chest: if you wil not be ruled, we

[1] I. 2. 208–12.
[2] Cf. Mariners, I. 1. 53.
[3] Stephano 'escaped upon a butt of sack, which the sailors heaved overboard'. II. 2. 118–19.

will throw both you and your chest hed-long together into the sea.

ANT. A right mariners oration!

ADOL. So the Italian lost his goods, wishing all evil both to the heavens and the hells, for that hee had committed his life to so barbarous an element.

ANT. I know that is the manner of Italians.

ADOL. A little while after, when we saw that the windes raged more and more, and we had done what we could, they cut the ropes, and cast the sailes over-boord.

ANT. O miserable calamity!

ADOL. Then the Maister came to us againe. Friends (quoth he) the time doth exhorte every man to commend himselfe to God, and to prepare himselfe for to die. He was asked of certaine, who were not altogether ignorant of seafaring, for how many houres he thought the ship might defend it selfe. He said that he could promise nothing, but above three houres hee said it was not possible.

ANT. This speech was yet harder then the rest.

ADOL. When he had so said, he commanded al the ropes to be cut, and the maine-maste[1] to be sawen downe close by the boxe wherein it stood, and together with the saile-yardes to be cast over boord into the sea.

ANT. Why did he so?

ADOL. Because (the saile being gone or torne) it served to no use, but to burthen the ship: all their hope was in the sterne or rudder.

ANT. What did the passengers and shipmen in the mean time?

ADOL. There you should have seene a miserable face of things, the mariners singing *Salve regina*; they cried to the Virgine *Mary* for help, they called her the Star of the Sea, the Queene of Heaven, the Lady of the World, the Haven of Helth, flattering her with many other titles which the holy Scriptures never gave her.

ANT. What had she to doe with the sea, that I thinke never went to sea in all her life?

ADOL. *Venus* had sometimes the charge of mariners, because she was thought to be borne of the sea: and because she gave over her cure, the Virgin mother was substituted in her steed, which was a mother, but no virgin.

ANT. Now you jest.

ADOL. Many falling flat upon the boordes, did worship the sea, crying, O most gentle Sea, O most noble Sea, O most rich Sea, be quiet, save us: and thus they cried to the deafe sea.

ANT. O ridiculous superstition! What did others?

ADOL. Some did nothing but vomite, and some made vowes.

[1] I. i. 35, 'Down with the topmast!'

There was a certaine Englishman, who promised golden mountaines to his Lady of *Walsingham*, if ever he came safe to land. Others promised many things to a woodden crosse that stood at such a place: and others to another that stoode in another place . . .

[Erasmus illustrates the folly of praying to Saints instead of to God Himself.]

. . . Within a little while after, the Master tolde us that he had spied a holy Tower, or a Church, wishing us to call for helpe unto that Saint that was patrone of that Church. All fell downe and prayed unto an unknowne Saint.

ANT. If you had called him by his name, he would have heard you.

ADOL. No man knew his name. In the meane time the Pilot, as much as lay in him, did guide the ship that way, which was now torne and rent, and leaking on every side, and had fallen all to peeces, if it had not beene bound togither with Cables.

ANT. Things were now at a hard passe.

ADOL. We were driven so neare, that the inhabitants of that place might see us, and in what daunger we were. They came running out by heapes unto the shoare, and holding up their cloakes, and their hats upon poles, did invite us to come unto them. And casting up their armes towards heaven, did thereby signifie how much they did bewaile our hard fortune.

ANT. I listen for an end, to heare what successe you had.

ADOL. By this time the ship was full of water, and we were no safer in the ship then in the sea. The Mariners emptied the ship boate of water, and put it out to the sea: into that boate all endeavoured to goe, all the Marriners crying out with great tumulte, that the boate was not able to holde such a multitude. Let every man (said they) get what hee can, and swimme out. There was no time to take long counsell; one tooke an oare, another a quant,[1] another the bottome of the shippe, one gat a basket, another a table, and every man with such as hee could get, committed themselves to the waves.

ANT. What became in the meane time of that same woman that was so quiet?

ADOL. She was the first that came to the shoare: for we had put her upon a broade table, and had made her so fast unto it, that shee could not easily fall off, and we put a little boord into her hand, which she might use in steade of an oare, and so bidding her farewell,

[1] A boat-pole.

wee thrust her off with a quant, that shee might be free from the shippe, where was all the daunger.

ANT. O couragious woman!

ADOL. When nothing was now left, one plucked downe a woodden image that was there of the virgine *Marie*, that was rotten, and eaten hollow with rattes, and having gotten that in his armes, he began to swimme.

ANT. The boate came safe to shoare, did it not?

ADOL. That was the first that was drowned, with thirtie persons in it: for before it could get free from the great ship, with the waving and wallowing of the shippe, it was overthrowne.

ANT. O hard hap, what then?

ADOL. While I gave counsell to others, I had like to have perished myselfe, for there was nothing left that was good for swimming.

ANT. There corke would have done good service, if one had had it.

ADOL. In such a straite, I had rather had a peece of vile corke, than a golden candlesticke: while I was looking about for a thing to swimme upon, at the last I remembered the lower end of the maste. And because I could not pull it up alone, I tooke another unto me. We lying both upon that, committed our selves to the sea, so as I held by the right horne, and he by the left. While we were thus tossed, and putting off from the shippe, that same masse Priest that preached to the Mariners threw himselfe in the middest upon our shoulders. And hee was not very light, for hee had a bigge body. We cryed out, Who is that third? He will cast us all away: but he aunswered us somewhat cheerefully, Be of good cheere, heere is rowme inough for us, God will be with us . . . While wee were tossed and tumbled hither and thither by the shippe side, the Rudder of the ship chaunced to hit him that held by the left corner of the Maste, and brake his thigh, so hee let goe his holde and fell off. The priest praying God to send him eternall rest, tooke his place, exhorting mee with great courage to hold fast my corner and to stirre my feete lustily. In the meane time wee drunke in a great deale of salt water; but the priest taught me a remedie against it.

ANT. What was that, I pray you?

ADOL. So often as any wave came toward us, hee would turn his noddle against it with his mouth close.

ANT. A strong olde man!

ADOL. When wee had by swimming in this manner gone some way, the Priest being a wonderfull tall man, saide unto me, Be of a good cheere man, I feele the bottome. But I durst not hope for so great happinesse. We are further (quoth I) from the land than to hope for any bottome. Nay (quoth he) I feele the ground with my feete. Peradventure it is (said I) some chest that the sea hath rolled hither. Nay (said he) I doe plainely feele the ground with my fingers. When we had swumme a little longer, and hee againe had felt the bottome, Doe you (quoth he) what you thinke best to be done; I give you all the maste, and I will betake my selfe wholy to the ground: and withall, when he sawe the billow go from him, he ran after it as fast as ever he could. And when the billowe came againe, he clasping both his hands together about both his knees, he strove with all his might against the waves, hiding himselfe under them as Cormorants and duckes[1] use to doe when they dive under the water. And when the billowe was past him againe, he set forward and ranne. I (seeing him to speede so well) followed him. There stoode on the shoare some strong men, and used to the sea, which with long poales did strengthen themselves against the waves, so as the hindermost of them could reach his pole unto him that could swimme, and so by that means divers were drawen to shore, and saved.

ANT. How many?

ADOL. Seaven, but of them twoo died so soone as they came to the fire: there were in the shippe 58. But when wee came to land there, we had experience of the countrey mens kindenesse, which indeede was incredible, who with wonderfull speede and cheerfulnesse, provided for us lodging, fire, meate, apparrell, and all necessaries for our journey.

ANT. What country was that?

ADOL. It was *Holland*.

ANT. There is no nation in the world more kinde and full of humanitie then they be, and yet they are compassed about with cruell and barbarous nations. But I beleeve you will not go to sea againe in haste.

ADOL. I doe not meane it, unlesse God shall deprive me of my wittes.

ANT. And I had rather heare such tales, than make triall of them: but thankes be to God that hath preserved you, and I hope you will be the better for this to him-ward while you live.

ADOL. God graunt I may.

---

[1] Trinculo 'Swam ashore . . . like a duck', II. 2. 126.

GENERAL CONCLUSION

Let us now praise famous men, and others not so famous, whose labours have made the study of Shakespeare's sources possible and fruitful. Many early critics and editors from Langbaine and Dennis onwards pointed out particular points of his indebtedness to classical and Renaissance authors. Mrs Charlotte Lennox thought that Shakespeare spoiled much that he borrowed, and Richard Farmer in his celebrated *Essay* (1767) put an end to the long controversy about Shakespeare's learning, though not, as he hoped, to the 'rage for parallellisms', and he was the first to insist on the importance of minor Tudor writers for the elucidation of the text.[1] Charles Knight summed up the major developments in source-study until the Victorian period as follows:[2]

> Rowe, Pope, Theobald, Hanmer, Johnson, belong to the school which did not seek any very exact acquaintance with our early literature . . . A new school arose, whose acquaintance with what has been called 'black letter literature' was extensive enough to produce a decided revolution in Shakespearean commentary. Capell, Steevens, Malone, Reed, Douce, are the representatives of the later school. The first school contained the most brilliant men; the second, the most painstaking commentators.

After the work of Steevens (who printed twenty 'Shakespeare Quartos' in 1766, and added much in his edition of the plays), and Malone (in the supplements to the *Variorum* editions of 1813 and 1821), most of the main sources (as we regard them today) had been noted, but there was ample room for analogues and parallel passages, for allusions to contemporary

---

[1] 'Nothing but an intimate acquaintance with the writers of the time, who are frequently of no other value, can point out his allusions, and ascertain his phraseology.'
[2] Charles Knight, 'History of Opinion on the Writings of Shakespeare' in vol. xii of his *Cabinet* edition, Edinburgh, 1856.

history, beliefs, and social life. Hence the vogue of 'Illustrations', exemplified in the work of Francis Douce (1807), Joseph Hunter (1845), J. O. Halliwell and other avid collectors of detail, or writers of essays on specific topics such as fairies or clowns. J. P. Collier's large collection of sources in *Shakespeare's Library* (2 vols), 1843, augmented by W. C. Hazlitt in six volumes (1874–6), made available much that had hitherto been difficult of access, and the forty-eight numbers of Shakespeare Society papers (1841–53) contained much of value.

Meanwhile in Germany the widespread interest in folktales associated with the brothers Grimm and their school bore fruit in Karl Simrock's *Remarks on the Plots of Shakespeare's Plays* (1831) which Halliwell translated, with emendations, in 1850. Other scholars entered the field: Albert Cohn's *Shakespeare in Germany* (1865) raised the spectre of the *Ur-Hamlet* and incited inquiries into the origins of other pieces performed by the 'English Comedians' in seventeenth-century Germany. Gregor Sarrazin and E. Koeppel among others inquired into the historical or literary background of the plays, and the literary history of some of the major heroes was traced, e.g. Richard III by G. B. Churchill (1900) and King Lear by W. Perrett (1904). Editions of the chronicles of E. Hall (1809), R. Holinshed (1807–8), and J. Hardyng (1812) led to the closer examination of the English Histories, and later to the excerpts from Holinshed by W. G. Boswell-Stone (1896, 1907) and the briefer extracts by A. and J. A. Nicoll (1927).

Unfortunately the cult of the Ph.D. thesis first in Germany and then in Anglo-Saxon countries led to exaggerated claims for obscure and doubtful analogies; and the tendency to imagine that once a 'source' had been unearthed and its parallels noted all that was necessary had been done, brought discredit on research. Source-hunting was regarded in the early part of the present century as a form of truancy from the proper study of the plays, an occupation only suitable for pedants, outside the scope of true criticism. No doubt there was a good deal of indolence behind this dismissal of evidence about the materials used by Shakespeare in making his plays, but the source-hunters were to blame for not realizing that their pursuit should be the first stage in an investigation of Shakespeare's methods of composition. Hence, although good work

was done by editors of individual plays who presented or discussed source-material (e.g. H. H. Furness in his Philadelphia
Variorum, and some of the first *Arden* editors), the study of
Shakespeare's literary origins fell into disrepute, and the
'gentlemanly' critics of the early twentieth century confined
themselves to the moods, structure, characterization, and
staging of the plays themselves.

Sir Arthur Quiller-Couch was impatient of preliminary
spadework, and Sir Walter Raleigh, while acknowledging the
breadth of Shakespeare's reading and the richness of his
memory, saw little value in comparing the plays with alleged
sources or contemporary drama:[1]

> The careful study of Shakespeare's sources, though it throws some
> light on his dramatic methods, does not bring us much nearer the
> heart of the matter. Its results are mainly negative . . . What he
> added to the story was himself; and a comparison of what he
> found with what he left forces us to the conclusion that his choice
> of books was largely accidental.

Plutarch was an exception, however.

T. S. Eliot was more perceptive. Although his own critical
method owed little to extraneous considerations, he thought
that there might be value in Shakespeare's laundry-bills if
they were discovered, and that the study of his reading was well
worth while:[2]

> There are plots and there are characters; the question of sources
> has its rights, and we must, if we go into the matter at all, inform
> ourselves of the exact proportion of invention, borrowing, and
> adaptation in the plot.

Benedetto Croce's theory of critical immediacy was an influence in the right direction when he declared that it was the
critic's task, by entering into the imagination of the poet, so to
recreate the moment of vision and the process of composition
as to apprehend the work of art in its totality. This is far from
being an endorsement of the doctrine of some recent 'new

---

[1] W. Raleigh, *Shakespeare*, 1907, pp. 76–7; cf. Mark Van Doren, *Shakespeare*, New
York, 1939, p. 2. 'Shakespeare does not seem to call for explanations beyond those
which a whole heart and a free mind abundantly supply.'
[2] Introduction to G. W. Knight, *The Wheel of Fire*, 1930, p. xvii.

critics' who have taught that the words on the page and one's immediate reaction to them are all that matters, and that the artist's biography, background, and beliefs are irrelevant. Croce rightly called attention to the imaginative intuitions in the work of art itself, but he assumed that the critic would have assimilated the results of scholarship, wide reading and knowledge of the period, and would bring this to bear upon the poem or play.[1]

Modern study of Shakespeare sources has been increasingly aware of its twofold obligations: first, to investigate the ambience of story, drama, ideas, beliefs, and current events which affected the dramatist from time to time; second, and even more important, to consider how he used this material as a poet and craftsman in the theatre so as to produce plays which were not only 'for an age' but also 'for all time'. To list the works which have contributed most to our understanding of source-relationships would be to repeat many names from my Bibliographies. Their claims are often modest. Thus in one of the best short essays on the subject yet written, Professor V. K. Whitaker wrote that the comparison between a play and its source gave 'perhaps the best single clue to his artistic methods', concluding, 'the study of Shakespeare's sources is no infallible guide to an understanding of his plays, but it does afford an insight into his mind and habits'.[2] He has since applied his method with great erudition to trace the relationship between the ideas of the time and Shakespeare's ethical and religious development.[3] In several massive volumes Professor T. W. Baldwin has shown the influence of Shakespeare's (probable) early education and knowledge of the classics, e.g. in his use of the Terentian five-act structure.[4] Professor Kenneth Muir has taken the comedies and tragedies one by one and discussed in a most judicious manner Shakespeare's use of his varied materials, leaving the Histories aside, 'since there is so much disagreement about the materials on which Shakespeare worked'. He concludes mildly, that 'the sources throw rela-

[1] Hardin Craig, 'The Trend of Shakespeare Scholarship', *Sh Survey* 2, 1949, 111.
[2] V. K. Whitaker, 'Shakespeare's Use of his Sources', *PhilQ*, xx, 1941, 377–88.
[3] V. K. Whitaker, *Shakespeare's Use of Learning*, San Marino, 1953.
[4] T. W. Baldwin, *William Shakspere's Petty School*, 1943; *William Shakspere's Small Latine and Lesse Greeke*, 1942; *Shakspere's Five-Act Structure*, 1947; *The Literary Genetics of Shakspere's Poems and Sonnets*, 1950.

tively little light on the finished plays' although they may help resolve disputed interpretations, and deviations from known sources 'will cause us to ask questions which may lead us to a true interpretation of the play', and help us to appreciate Shakespeare's craftsmanship or methods of composition.[1]

I would go much further than this and would particularly wish to develop Muir's last suggestion. Of course the plays can be enjoyed at many different levels either in the theatre or through reading them. They appeal to simple intelligences such as Partridge in *Tom Jones*, and children acting *Julius Caesar* in the classroom can get as much enjoyment out of it as, say, Polonius who was killed in the Capitol. For centuries audiences in many countries have delighted in them despite ignorance of Elizabethan life and thought; even the difficulties of language have been transcended by the dramatic urgency and general sense of the scenes. Sophisticated spectators and readers have nevertheless gained much by the devoted work of countless editors, commentators, and educators, and by the analysis of dramatic techniques undertaken by critics and producers. All this without departing from the play as it has come down to us in somewhat doubtful texts.

Scholars such as those named above, and (I hope) the present series of volumes, have thrown light not only on obscurities in the text but also on Shakespeare's immediate literary milieu, the pressures both external and internal which affected the substance of his plays by causing him to incorporate allusions, attitudes, and ideas which he might otherwise have omitted (e.g. the Porter Scene in *Macbeth*, the madness in *Lear*). More important still, the study of Shakespeare's sources and probable reading enables us to enter somewhat into his mind during the process of composition, lets us see the difficulties he must have overcome when writing history plays based on Hall and Holinshed; the opportunities afforded him for dramatic scenes by Plutarch, Lodge, or Cinthio; the skill with which he avoided the weaknesses of previous plays on the same subjects; the manner in which he interwove materials taken from different authorities (as in *Lear*); and how he changed the tone and purport of a story (as in *As You Like It* and *Othello*).

[1] K. Muir, *Shakespeare's Sources I. Comedies and Tragedies*, 1957.

Above all, the comparative study of sources with the finished plays often lets us glimpse the creative process in action as he took over, remade, rejected, adapted, or added to chosen or given materials. Indeed, I would claim that this is the best, and often the only, way open to us of watching Shakespeare the craftsman in his workshop—not indeed of 'explaining' the mystery of his artistic genius, but at least of perceiving his constructive powers in operation, of seeing the ingenious collocations and associative energies which underlie the dynamic balance of the plays and which fuse plot, character, dialogue, and imagery into a poetic unity.

In the present work, first roughly sketched out during the last war, I have limited my scope to narrative and dramatic sources of some degree of probability, and have also printed analogues which may suggest how Shakespeare's contemporaries and predecessors approached similar topics, and also how individual or traditional his treatment was.

In this concluding essay I wish to bring together various common topics which have emerged while considering individual plays, and to discuss briefly their relationship to Shakespeare's handling of his material, i.e. (1) factors affecting his choice of subjects and sources; (2) some technical devices; (3) structural use of source-material; (4) characters taken over, developed, or invented; (5) thematic approach; (6) folk-material and ethical development; (7) the developing hero in tragedy; (8) the 'Romances' and the gods; (9) imagery and the narrative and dramatic sources of some plays.

(1)

Shakespeare was not academically learned; he was no specialist, but vastly well informed. He remembered the popular lore of his country upbringing with regard to flowers, birds, animals, medicine, and superstitions. He knew enough about sea-faring terms, warfare, and the law to astonish modern inquirers into these subjects; he knew and could apply the terms of rhetoric seriously and with humour; he developed an interest in the ethical psychology of his day which profoundly affected his work; he knew the Bible, Prayer Book, and Homilies well. All these and other fields he drew from to vitalize his dialogue and imagery. He seems to have forgotten nothing that he read or heard, or rather, his powers of associative memory were such that if he required a parallel or contrast for plot and incident or a poetic image, something relevant and vivid floated up from his unconscious.

This does not mean that there was no conscious search for suitable ancillary material. As we have seen, he was rarely content with one narrative or dramatic source alone. We cannot tell how much he read about English history before Richard II's reign, but for the English Histories he read not only Hall and Holinshed but also some Grafton, Fabyan, Stow and Foxe. Later, for *King Lear* and *Macbeth*, he read the general introductory material in Holinshed. Greek and Roman history he took from Plutarch, Livy and Tacitus; classical myths he knew mainly from Ovid; the Greek tragic themes from Seneca. He knew Latin fairly well, although he preferred to use translations. He also knew some French and Italian, enough to follow Macon's version of Boccaccio and Cinthio's story of the Moor. It is possible that he knew a few plays in Italian, such as *Gl'Ingannati* (for *Twelfth Night*), and *Epitia* (for *Measure for Measure*). He may have seen some *commedie dell' arte* performed. From English poetry he made use of Chaucer, Gower, Lydgate, Spenser, Daniel and the *Mirror for Magistrates*. He knew many collections of short stories translated from Italian and French, as well as native imitations of them. He probably perused versions of longer romances such as *The Mirrour of Knighthood*, the *Diana Ennamorada* of Montemayor, Ariosto's *Orlando Furioso*, and Caxton's *Recueil*, and he enjoyed the prose works of Greene and Lodge, and especially Sidney's *Arcadia*. As a man of the theatre he must have seen a great many plays performed besides those in which he acted. He knew about the Mystery and Morality plays, and must have rummaged in the bookkeeper's chest for manuscript pieces. He almost certainly made good use of unpublished pieces such as *The Jew* and the older Hamlet play, and he not only drew suggestions from published dramas but rewrote several, including *King John*, *The Famous Victories*, and *King Leir*. One concludes that Shakespeare added a specialized professional interest in drama to the pleasure he shared in the leisure-time reading of his educated contemporaries.

Shakespeare's choice of sources may sometimes, as Raleigh supposed, have been accidental, but the genesis of many plays was obviously affected by various pressures. As a playwright in a particular company he was doubtless sometimes asked to provide a play on some theme of immediate interest to the public. It is difficult to believe that early in his career he would have chosen the tangled reign of Henry VI for a trilogy but for a specific request, maybe because it had not yet been done, and in the first instance because English soldiers were once more fighting in France in 1588–91 in support of Henry of Navarre. A play about a Jewish usurer would have an appeal in the mid-nineties when the Jew Lopez had allegedly attempted the Queen's life, and when the morality of interest was being discussed. Recent events were frequently glanced at, as in *Coriolanus* and *The Tempest*. A special occasion such as a wedding may have elicited *A Midsummer Night's Dream*, and *Henry VIII* was probably written to celebrate the marriage of Princess Elizabeth to the Elector Palatine in 1613. This play illustrates another reason for choosing a particular topic, namely, rivalry between theatre-companies, for *Henry VIII* may well have been a riposte to Samuel Rowley's *When You See Me*. Similarly *Troilus and Cressida* may have been a response to Dekker and Chettle's tragedy on the same themes, appealing, however, not so much to a popular audience at the Globe as to the gentlemen lawyers at the Inns of Court, who would appreciate its up-to-date disillusionment and its debunking of the heroic mood of Chapman's recent *Seven Books* of Homer's *Iliad*.

The influence of a particular audience is not easy to gauge. Most of the plays were intended for performance in public theatres. *The Comedy of Errors* would be especially liked by spectators who perceived its embroidery on Plautine originals, but although it was performed at Gray's Inn during the Christmas festivities of 1594, it was written some time before. Maybe the acquisition in 1609 of the private Blackfriars Theatre, with its evening performances and higher prices, brought an audience of higher class who liked music, masque, and dramatic effects of a graceful kind; and this may have affected Shakespeare's 'Romances'. But his change to these could be explained otherwise, and *Pericles* had anticipated them. There can be little doubt, however, that after the Lord Chamberlain's Company became the King's Men in 1603 and Shakespeare wore the King's livery as a Groom of the Chamber in Ordinary (without fee), his work was affected by the prospect of performance before the King and Queen, and that he frequently thought of the royal interests when choosing and writing his plays, e.g. the King's views about justice and the duties of magistrates (in *Measure for Measure*), James's interest in witches, abnormal psychology and his own ancestry (in *Macbeth*), and the Queen's love of music, dance, spectacle, the Masque (in the Romances).

There have always been fashions in plays as well as in dress. One thinks of the popularity in the 1930s of historical biographies such as *Clive of India*, *Viceroy Sarah*, and of comedies concerning three generations (*Dear Octopus*, *The Matriarch*); in the 1960s of the drama of cruelty and the absurd. If Shakespeare helped to start a fashion of dramatic chronicle, he certainly continued in it for many years. He followed the romantic manner in comedy in the 1590s. As Bernard Shaw asserted, titles like *As You Like It*, *What You Will*, *All's Well that Ends Well* may have mocked gently at the taste they catered for, but there is every evidence that Shakespeare enjoyed indulging it. He then adapted his talent for romance to the new vogue of comedies with realistic features and social satire (e.g. *Measure for Measure* and *Troilus*); wrote revenge plays (*Hamlet*, *Othello*) when these were popular; and excelled Henslowe's dramatists in plays based on pre-Conquest themes (*Lear*, *Cymbeline*). *Pericles* was rewritten, either as a first shot in the campaign to bring back the episodic romance, or else as part of that revival, to which *Cymbeline* also contributed. Few critics today would argue that Shakespeare's genius was smothered or debased through theatrical needs, playing down to the groundlings, and desire for quick profit. His dramatic genius fed on the circumstances in which he had to work. Intensely aware of shifting currents in thought, feeling, and literary expression, he gave the public what it wanted and more than it could ever have expected. He never hesitated to take hints from other dramatists of the time, Marlowe, Kyd, Lyly, Greene, Jonson, and lesser men, and whatever he took he infused with his own poetic and theatrical characteristics.

The effects on Shakespeare's choice and handling of his materials of his knowledge that the plays would be acted by certain players were doubtless considerable but are difficult to assess. The fact that Burbage, a most versatile actor, would play Hamlet, Othello and Lear,[1] would encourage him to try differing kinds of tragic hero and to introduce subtleties which he might otherwise have avoided.

Changes in the company's comedians were reflected in the changing nature of Shakespeare's clowns. Launce and Speed in *Two Gentlemen of Verona* had nothing to do with the source-material, but are clowns of traditional kind with comic *lazzi* such as the scene of Launce with his dog (II. 3) and his word-twisting with Speed. William Kempe (until 1600) and Thomas Pope (until 1603)[2] probably did most of the clowning parts for the Chamberlain's Company, with plenty of 'business', 'merriment', and low comedy. Kempe was regarded as Tarleton's successor, and was famous for his jigs with their dancing and horseplay.[3] Pope was blamed by Samuel Rowlands for speaking 'so boorish'. Shakespeare deplored the tendency for clowns to intrude with extraneous nonsense and 'ad libbing' (*Hamlet* III. 2); so he wrote them into the action of the play. In *A Midsummer Night's Dream* a special plot and a burlesque tragedy were written for the clowns; in *Much Ado* Dogberry (played by Kempe) and Verges hold back the dénouement by their comic stupidity. Whether Kempe or Pope played Falstaff (I favour Pope), certain it is that the potentialities of both the character and the actor who must play him led the dramatist to go far beyond the usual functions of the comedians in a history play.

It has been argued that the coming of Robert Armin in 1599, himself a writer of some ability who had reflected upon the art of clowning, led Shakespeare to create his later more sensitive fools, Touchstone, Feste, and the fool in *Lear*, court jesters who are more than witty scapegraces or knockabout comedians, and have important parts which involve sophistication, subtlety and even pathos. Such figures not only affect the handling of

---

[1] Cf. *ElSt*, ii, p. 309, the *Elegy on Burbadge*.
[2] Both had played in Denmark (1586–7) and could tell Shakespeare about the customs of that country when he was writing *Hamlet*.
[3] For the Fools see *ElSt*, ii, Ch. XV.

major plot-sources but also, by their wisdom or ironic comments, affect the mood of the entire play.

In *Hamlet* the source-material allows the hero to play the fool for most of the play, but a special scene is inserted for two clowns as Gravediggers. In *Othello* Iago and Roderigo take over some of the clown's functions. In *Macbeth* the clown's part is diminished to the Devil-Porter scene, but in *Lear* the fool becomes a major character, the King's companion and bitter shadow. Obviously Shakespeare had become increasingly impatient with the fool's set piece, with the clown who thrust himself head and shoulders into a play. Whenever possible he was assimilated into the action and made to enforce the mood of the play by parallel, contrast, or ironic comment.

The nature of his company may have affected Shakespeare's composition in other ways.[1] Thus he had to write parts for the boys who played women; hence maybe the several scenes of lamenting ladies in *Richard III* as well as the wooing of Anne. Here as elsewhere Shakespeare used necessity as an opportunity for dramatic master-strokes. The availability of boys of contrasting build and type would help the creation of Helena (tall) and Hermia (short), Portia and Nerissa, Beatrice and Hero, and foster Shakespeare's liking for double love-plots. Maybe because the actor John Sincklo was very thin the Apothecary in *Romeo and Juliet* was 'meagre' in looks ('Sharp misery had worn him to the bones') and Dr Pinch in *The Comedy of Errors* was 'a hungry lean-fac'd villain,/A mere anatomy'. Such details prove that Shakespeare kept his actors' looks and powers in mind when adapting his source-material.

(2)

Shakespeare was an adapter of other men's tales and plays; he liked to build a new construction on something given, not to make up an entirely new plot. So he would follow the outline of a story as closely as his idea of its implications would

---

[1] Cf. T. W. Baldwin, *The Organisation and Personnel of the Shakespearean Company*, Princeton, 1927; M. M. Reese, *Shakespeare, his World and his Work*, 1953, pp. 234–70.

allow, and this has been shown in considering his Histories, Roman plays, and most other pieces for which sources are now extant. Whatever he took over, however, his creative instinct was alert to alter if he thought fit, and in his later works, especially in the 'great' tragedies, his concentration on ethical problems and the analytic presentation of character in conflict led him to transform and make new combinations of his original material.

The early Histories afforded a valuable training in compressing lengthy actions, selecting episodes, grouping characters, and discovering patterns of likeness and contrast, different sorts of climax. So the tetralogy made from the apparently unmanageable detail in Hall's chronicle proved his powers of construction, suspense, and overall tone. Indeed, these plays and the first comedies suggest that Shakespeare's dramatic technique developed before his poetic genius. In the early Histories he was already skilled in direct, workmanlike statement and in rhetorical flights owing something to Seneca and Marlowe. About the time of writing *Venus and Adonis, Lucrece* (and some of the Sonnets), a remarkable awakening to lyricism and witty ambiguity, a self-conscious use of rhetorical and psychological terms seems to have occurred, which affected the choice and handling of material in *Titus Andronicus, Richard II, Love's Labour's Lost, Romeo and Juliet, A Midsummer Night's Dream,* in which the stylistic formulae become the expression of fancy, thought, and passion. Out of this gradually developed the varied styles characteristic of the mature work and Shakespeare's ability to reshape the source-material in terms of a pervasive ethical and poetic conception, as we find in plays from *The Merchant of Venice* onwards.

If the historical material of the first tetralogy necessitated tragic treatment, that of the second group lent itself to a mingling of serious chronicle with comedy, for a comic handling was encouraged by the tradition of Prince Hal's exploits embodied in *The Famous Victories* and by the somewhat lightweight nature of Henry IV's opponents, Glendower, Hotspur, and Northumberland. Hence Shakespeare was led to experiment in a new kind of chronicle play in which comedy was at least as important as history, culminating in the happy epic of *Henry V.*

Much has been written about Shakespeare's dramatic technique and here I can touch only briefly on some aspects. As Professor V. K. Whitaker has written, 'Any deviation from [the sources] was likely to be deliberate and to reflect Shakespeare's methods as a dramatic artist or his aims in writing a particular play.'[1] But in turning a story into drama he took over devices from others or evolved them for himself: in either case he usually produced something entirely new in effect. He was drawn to stories or chronicle-matter which fell naturally into clear-cut episodes, with some dialogue, easily made into scenes for the theatre. Hence the lasting attraction of Plutarch, Hall and Holinshed; hence no doubt his choice of Lodge's *Rosalynde* and Greene's *Pandosto*, as well as Cinthio's Moor story with its well-marked stages, and Bandello's tale of Timbreo and Fenicia.

The plays began usually not at the outset of a tale but at some early crisis which excited expectation and tension and interest enough for the dramatist to look back on what had gone before. So *A Midsummer Night's Dream* begins with the stern father's threat to Hermia; *Romeo and Juliet* with a brawl which illustrates the feud; *Julius Caesar* with evidence that Rome is divided for and against Caesar; and *Macbeth* with the Witches awaiting the hero. But Shakespeare had no fixed ideas about the exposition. Often he at once introduces some major figures to set the atmosphere and general situation (e.g. *1 Henry IV*). In *Richard III* the villain proclaims his nature and purpose directly to the audience. In *As You Like It* and *King Lear* we are plunged at once into the central situation. In *A Midsummer Night's Dream* three plots get under way in three successive scenes. Antony and Imogen enter after some lines outlining the situation, but Coriolanus only after 160 lines of mainly general discussion. In *Twelfth Night* Viola is kept offstage until Orsino has sketched the sentimental mood which she is to disturb; and in *Hamlet* and *Othello* the heroes do not come on until the atmosphere (of foreboding in the one and scurrilous enmity in the other) has been well prepared.

By his early manipulation of chronicle-material Shakespeare taught himself how to telescope time and compress

[1] V. K. Whitaker, 'Shakespeare's Use of his Sources', 382. I am indebted to his admirable summary.

events widely separated in his sources. Thus *1 Henry VI* includes events between 1419 and 1453; *Macbeth*'s ten years of good rule are omitted and Banquo is murdered immediately after news comes that Duncan's sons have found refuge. In *Julius Caesar* the dramatist assumes that the audience knows something of the wars between Caesar and Pompey and that the conspirators may justly fear Caesar's ambition. Our attention is directed towards personal relationships, and generations of playgoers have enjoyed the play despite its lack of political background. We may be thankful that, unlike Jonson in his Roman tragedies, Shakespeare did not try to be scrupulously full and accurate in his expositions. However, in *Richard II*, owing to the lack of preliminary explanation 'the opening triangle, involving Richard, Mowbray and Bolingbroke, is almost unintelligible'.[1] So it is, unless the audience has read Hall or seen *Woodstock*. Yet the enmity between Mowbray and Bolingbroke and the arbitrariness characteristic of Richard are clear enough. The audience accepts what it sees and is told during a performance without inquiring into what lies behind, unless the playwright suggests it. But it was a mistake to suggest in *Macbeth* I. 7 that the hero and his wife had previously planned to murder Duncan, since it makes us wonder when that was, and seems inconsistent with Macbeth's state of mind when he first met the Witches.

Shakespeare often altered the end of his sources. A perfectly good play with a happy end could have been made out of the Hamlet story, ending with his triumphant vengeance on his uncle and acceptance as king. The old *King Leir* was a tragicomedy. But Shakespeare knew that both Hamlet and Cordelia died unhappily, though some time after the action he meant to present, and this knowledge helped to make him conceive both plays as tragedies. He altered the dénouement which he found in *Promos and Cassandra*, and entirely remodelled the ends of Cinthio's Moor and Ensign.

Love's Labour's Lost and *Two Gentlemen of Verona* conclude somewhat hastily, but usually Shakespeare liked both a complicated imbroglio and a leisurely 'discovery' scene, especially in comedies, where he piled surprise on surprise for the people in the play and pleased the audience by fulfilling their expecta-

[1] Whitaker, 'Shakespeare's Use of his Sources', 382.

tions, but often in a slightly unexpected manner.[1] Final scenes
of this kind occur in *Much Ado*, *Twelfth Night*, *Cymbeline*, and
The Winter's Tale. In *All's Well* and *Measure for Measure* the
elaborate disclosure of identity or deception is accompanied
by a moral discovery, the exposure of misconduct and the
repentance of a sinner.

The puritan Shaw complained about the low moral tone of
Shakespeare's dialogue, declaring that it was often saved only
because 'however poor, coarse, cheap and obvious the thought
may be, the mood is charming and the music of the words expresses the mood' (*ibid.*). In fact Shakespeare often elevated the
tone of his originals and purified their incidents. Thus in the
sub-plot of *The Taming of the Shrew* he rejected the initial situation of Gascoigne's heroine Polynesta who is pregnant after
loving Erostrato secretly for two years (*supra*, I, pp. 112–14) and
in *Twelfth Night*, unlike her prototype in Riche's story (*supra*, II,
pp. 353–4), Olivia is not pregnant before marriage. Isabella
does not sleep with Angelo. As Coleridge wrote, Shakespeare
keeps[2]

> at all times on the high-road of life. Shakespeare has no innocent
> adulteries, no interesting incests, no virtuous vice . . . Shake-
> speare's fathers are roused by ingratitude, his husbands stung by
> unfaithfulness; in him, in short, the affections are wounded in those
> points in which all may, nay, must, feel.

A word should be said about Shakespeare's repetitions of
incidents, situations, types of personages, etc.

Some of these are the inevitable results of the stories he chose.
Thus, he often used plots involving missing children who are
finally identified, as in *CE*, and all the romances (*Per*, *Cym*,
WT, *Tem*). The twins of *CE* are repeated very differently in
TN, and in both plays brother and sibling find each other. Sex

[1] Writing after Ibsen, Bernard Shaw anticipated some recent playwrights in his
contempt for 'surprises that no longer surprise anybody'. 'Plot', he wrote, 'has
always been the curse of serious drama . . . It is so out of place there that Shakespeare never could invent one. Unfortunately, instead of taking Nature's hint and
discarding plots, he borrowed them all over the place and got into trouble through
having to unravel them in the last act, especially in *Two Gentlemen of Verona* and
Cymbeline' (*Shaw on Shakespeare*, ed. E. Wilson, New York, 1961, p. 64). But Shaw
himself borrowed plots and few readers regard his version of *Cymbeline* as an im-
provement.
[2] 'Lectures on Shakespeare, 1818' in *Shakespeare Criticism*, ed. D. Nicol Smith,
1916, p. 269.

disguise was a valuable device when boys had to play girls' parts and Shakespeare obtained great piquancy from it (e.g. Julia in *TGV*, Portia in *MV*, Viola in *TN*, Rosalind and Celia in *AYL*, Imogen in *Cym*). In *TGV* and *TN* the disguised girl must woo another woman for the man she loves and serves. In *AYL* Rosalind, as Ganymede, is wooed in fun by Orlando who loves her as Rosalind. In most of these plays a highborn lady takes refuge in the greenwood or other wild place— Imogen in the Welsh mountains. Perdita is brought up as a shepherd's daughter.

Storms and shipwrecks, as in Greek romances, are frequent in the plots as means of separating people (*CE*, *TN*, *Per*, *Tem*). Antonio is nearly ruined by losses at sea (*MV*). Magic is used freakishly but benevolently in *MND* and *Tem*, malevolently in *2H6* and *Mac*. Ghosts appear in several tragedies (*R3*, *JC*, *Ham*, *Mac*). Outside the Histories swordplay (in which some of the actors were well trained) occurred quite often (*TGV*, *RJ*, *TN*, *TrC*, *Cym*, *Ham*, *Lear*). There were riots in *2H6*, *RJ*, *JC*, *Cor*.

Parallelism and contrast are features both of Shakespeare's plotting and of his characterization. So we are shown the differences between brothers in *R3*, *AYL*, *Lear*, *Tem*; between two male friends and also two ladies in *TGV*. Ladies are contrasted in *TSh*, *MND* and *LLL* (but slightly), *Ado*, *AYL*, *Ham*, *Lear*.

Repetition of situation is used for different effects: thus in *LLL* we have the effects of love on three lords, and the reactions of three ladies; and the theme is repeated among the retainers. The three Casket scenes in *MV* are used to delineate three different suitors. We watch magic affecting the lovers, Titania and Bottom, in *MND*, and influencing the Lords, Sailors, Caliban, and Ferdinand in *Tem*. Eavesdropping is an important device in *LLL*, *Ado*, *TN*, *TrC*, *Ham*. In *Ado* the same trick is played on Benedick and on Beatrice.

Shakespeare lacks the classical *liaison des scènes*, but his apparently accidental or purely chronological sequences are often linked by association of situation or theme, in likeness or difference. Thus in *2H6* the Duchess of Gloucester's raising of an evil spirit for treasonous purposes (I. 4) is closely followed by her noble husband's exposure of the false miracle of Simpcox (II. 1). Jessica's disobedience of her father (II. 5–6) is immediately followed by the proof that Portia is carrying out her father's strange will in the first Casket scene (I. 7). The three Casket scenes, however, are separated by intermediate scenes, in order to give variety. The contrast in attitudes to honour between Hotspur, Hal and Falstaff is presented in neighbouring scenes in *1 Henry IV*, Acts IV and V. The sentimentality of Orsino in *Twelfth Night* I. 1 is immediately contrasted with the true grief of Viola mourning for her brother. The murder of Cinna the Poet by the Roman mob is followed by the proscription scene with the Triumvirate (*Julius Caesar*, III. 3; IV. 1). 'It is an epiphany of Rome in forty lines.'[1]

Scene-linkage is often associated with irony. In *Romeo and Juliet* the hero's lovesick unwillingness to go to the Capulet feast is contrasted with Mercutio's frivolous gaiety, and almost at once becomes passionate love at first sight for Juliet (I. 4, 5). In *Much Ado* Benedick, after marvelling that Claudio 'after he hath laughed at such shallow follies in others, [will] become the argument of his own scorn by falling in love', hears that Beatrice is in love with him, and at once turns round: 'Love me! Why, it must be requited.' All this in one long scene. Othello's welcome to his wife in Cyprus (II. 1. 180–97) and hope for lasting joy and harmony is almost at once followed by the opening of Iago's campaign against him. In *Richard III* Hastings's confidence in Richard's friendship (III. 2) very shortly precedes the scene in which he is condemned to death. Similarly Falstaff is expecting honours at the coronation of Henry V but receives his dismissal instead. At the level of speech the Gravedigger in *Hamlet* says things with implications far beyond those he intends; the same is true of the Porter in *Macbeth*. Lady Macbeth's 'A little water clears us of this deed' is already seen as doubtful by the audience—and Macbeth—and this leads much later to the sleepwalking scene. *Macbeth*, as we have seen, is entirely based on the diabolical irony of the Witches' promises; irony runs through *Othello* as the deluded Moor trusts the villain who is determined to destroy him. And the end of *Lear* brings an ironic questioning of the goodness of the cosmos. But this is to go far beyond the liaison of scenes.

---

[1] N. Coghill, *Shakespeare's Professional Skills*, Cambridge, 1964, p. 62. He gives several of the examples cited above.

(3)

In planning a play Shakespeare had to consider structural problems such as its length, climaxes, catastrophe, or discovery, preservation of suspense, contrast in tone, mingling of light comedy with more serious matter. He shared the common Elizabethan liking for manifold incident and variety of scenes and characters. Indeed, he so packed his plays with incidents that he required far more material than more classical dramatists to occupy the two-hour (or more) traffic of the stage. Hence not only was he inventive in expanding his main sources, but he commonly drew on other sources as well, and soon learned to follow the practice of Lyly and Greene in running two plots together side by side in parallel or contrast. The early comedies supply a series of experiments in various ways of play-building.

In *The Comedy of Errors*, where the substance of Plautus' *Menaechmi* was too thin for the Elizabethan stage, he tried to double the fun and increase the imbroglio by having twin servants as well as twin masters, and by pairing off one of the latter with his brother's unmarried sister-in-law (thus also providing two major young women's parts for his actors). He also took an episode from another Plautine play to complicate the predicament of the married Antipholus. Further to enrich the piece by adding more characters and a more serious predicament, he placed the main action in a frame, making Aegeon's life depend on discovering his missing son, and ending with his discovery not only of one but of two sons, and of his long-lost wife as well.

The idea of a frame round an inset play pleased Shakespeare so much that he used it at least twice more. In *The Taming of the Shrew* he substituted for the misadventures of two identical twin brothers the contrasted wooing of two very unlike sisters, and differentiated between them by interweaving strikingly different plots from separate sources. Moreover, he treated this double action as a comedy presented before the tinker Sly, whose manners and temporary transformation provide additional contrast and gaiety.

In *A Midsummer Night's Dream* diverse actions derived from many sources are set within the framework of Theseus's marriage, which is announced at the start and celebrated in

Act V. The adventures of the young lovers, the fairies, and the 'mechanicals' are interwoven in a delightful phantasmagoria, and the wedding feast itself is capped by a performance of the burlesque *Pyramus and Thisbe*.

After this Shakespeare did not use the frame as a major structural device, but he recurred frequently to the play within the play, the courtly entertainment and the inset masque, as in *Love's Labour's Lost, Romeo and Juliet, Much Ado, Hamlet, The Winter's Tale* and *The Tempest*, each time with a different significance for plot and atmosphere.

In the later comedies the structure was usually built up in one of two ways: either by the movement in echelon of two plots involving different characters who are connected with one another at various points in the action, or by the linear or serial movement of one stream of plot with a number of smaller tributaries which flow in and are assimilated by it. A good example of the first kind is *Love's Labour's Lost*, where the action alternates between the witty posturings and love-affairs of the lords, and the pedantry and love-affairs of the underlings. The resultant effect is one of formal symmetry and dance-like sophistication. So in I. 1 both plots get started, when the impossible new law against ladies has to be broken by the King, and Dull has caught Costard with Jaquenetta. In I. 2 it appears that Armado too wants Jaquenetta and in III. 1 the lords fall in love with the ladies. Henceforth in alternate scenes the love-fancies of the nobles are parodied unconsciously by the rhetorical verbalism of their retainers. In V. 2 the masque of Russians is paralleled by the entertainment of the Nine Worthies.

In *Much Ado* the tragi-comic story of Claudio's love for Hero and his rejection of her is set alongside the merry war between Beatrice and Benedick and their coming together— two contrasted plots which touch one another at few points.

The Merchant of Venice provides the finest example of the other method of construction. Here Shakespeare took the basic theme of Antonio's friendship for Bassanio and traced its course and effects, plaiting together the bond-story and Bassanio's winning of Portia and taking in the Casket-story, Jessica's elopement, and Shylock's determination to have his pound of flesh as they emerged, placing the Casket-scene at the very centre of the play as that to which everything before leads up and from which everything afterwards springs, including the resolution of the imbroglio by Portia. To these Shakespeare adds the ring-story as a charming device to bring about the 'Discovery' of Portia and Nerissa as the lawyer and his clerk.[1] The marvellous skill with which Shakespeare introduces all these elements and makes them flow into the main stream of his plot makes this play one of the most perfect examples of his craftsmanship. He may have found the bond and the caskets in the older play *The Jew*, but what other Elizabethan dramatist could have used them with such ingenuity and balance of mood, incident and character?

The intertwining of two strands in a single story is found in *As You Like It* and *All's Well*. In *As You Like It* first Orlando's and then Rosalind's situation is expounded and then they are got into the greenwood, where a third element is introduced, the life of the exiled court in the greenwood, by which the various levels of rustic naturalness and pastoral artificiality are contrasted, and also, in their freedom and generosity, set over against the cruelties of Duke Frederick and Oliver. The discussions of Corin, Touchstone, and Jaques form a backcloth for the several love-affairs, and all are brought together when Rosalind is revealed in her true person. *All's Well* provides another example of the linear method applied to the story of two persons who are brought together, and separated in a series of forkings and confluences. In the first two acts we see Helena following Bertram to Paris, where she is married to him, then sent home. In the remainder of the play the action alternates between them. At the wars Bertram is made to realize the unworthiness of Parolles, and we watch his attempted seduction of Diana. Parallel to this is Helena's second pursuit of him, to Florence, where she observes him and then deceives him with the bed-trick—so that their two stories are brought close together in Acts III and IV, then separate again as we learn of Bertram's return home and see Helena on her way to Marseilles before the final Discovery-scene unites them in Roussillon where it all began.

Compare with this the structure of *Measure for Measure*, in

---

[1] See the admirable analysis of the play in R. G. Moulton, *Shakespeare as a Dramatic Artist*, Oxford, 1885, Ch. II.

which Shakespeare took over from Whetstone two plots, that of Promos and Cassandra, and the other of the low-life scenes where the injustice of Promos is paralleled by that of his lawyer, the venal Phallax ('Money, or faire women, workes him as waxe'), among whores, conny-catchers and honest victims. In Shakespeare's play this second plot is less prominent and there is no second unjust judge. The story of Mistress Overdone and Pompey is confined to five scenes (I. 2; II. 1; III. 2; IV. 2; and IV. 3) and is used both to show the need for moral reform, the incorrigible nature of the human heart, and also for grotesque comedy. The contrast between the vices of such characters and the comparative peccadillo of Claudio is made apparent and there is little contact otherwise between the two plots, except that Lucio appears in both.

An examination of these and other plays shows that Shakespeare chose subsidiary source-material for several purposes, e.g. (i) to illustrate or expand the principal source, as by the introduction of a scene from Plautus's *Amphitryon* into *The Comedy of Errors*; the exposure by Gloucester of the fraudulent Simpcox (taken from Foxe's *Book of Martyrs*) in *2 Henry VI*, and the Hay episode from Holinshed's *Chronicle of Scotland* introduced for topical compliment and to fill out the battle scenes in *Cymbeline*; (ii) to replace morally or dramatically unsatisfactory incidents, e.g. the story of the caskets in *The Merchant of Venice*, substituted for the bedroom scenes in *Il Pecorone* (but we cannot safely attribute this to Shakespeare, since it may have been done in *The Jew*, which represented 'the greediness of worldly choosers'); the substitution of Imogen's adventures in the Welsh mountains for those of Frederyke of Jennen in Egypt; the method of Desdemona's murder and her momentary revival, suggested maybe by Bandello's tale of the Albanian captain; (iii) to provide a parallel movement, contrast, or parody, as in the Bianca plot in *The Shrew*, the Beatrice–Benedick plot in *Much Ado*, the Gloucester plot in *Lear*, and the *Pyramus and Thisbe* playlet in *A Midsummer Night's Dream*.

(4)

In adapting to his own use the personages in his sources Shakespeare displayed great flexibility, preserving where possible the main outlines of a character as sketched in a short story or play, but inventing new twists of situation and motivation to bring out qualities only faintly suggested in the original. Whereas most romantic dramatists of his time made little attempt at relating story to character, Shakespeare seems to have asked himself, 'What conceivable kind of person would fit in with such a situation or perform such an action, however unlikely?' Much of his artistic skill was directed to making improbable actions plausible by inventing the right people to perform them. Given the incidents reported in the chronicles, what sort of a man must Richard III or Richard II or Henry IV be, to fit in with them, to preserve the audience's interest, and to support the political and moral lessons which the history plays were intended to inculcate?

Once the basic traits of a character were firm in his mind Shakespeare would if necessary alter the source-material slightly to make it clear to all, and would invent appropriate new scenes and dialogue. So the wooing of Anne was invented to illustrate the conception of Richard III as a fascinating devil with a most persuasive tongue; the weak vanity of Richard II was developed in passages of posturing self-pity; Henry IV the usurper became the anxious monarch troubled by rebellions and Hal's apparent worthlessness. Always, however, Shakespeare went to some pains to adapt the personalities of his major figures to their behaviour in his sources. Thus Claudio, whose conduct in the source of *Much Ado* is incredibly rash and brutal, becomes a very young officer, with little experience of life and somewhat credulous by nature, and an incident is invented which shows him as willing to let his C.O. do his wooing for him, yet easily made suspicious of Don Pedro's kindness. In this way his facile conviction of Hero's unchastity is prepared for.

Shakespeare's skill in varying the depth of his characterization to fit the requirements of the dramatic action has often been noted. He was always quick to make use of an anecdote delineating a minor personage such as Iras, Charmian, or Eros in Plutarch,[1] or Talbot and his son or young Siward in Holinshed.[2] He also brought out the potentialities of unusual personalities such as the garrulous Nurse with her idiosyn-

---

[1] *Supra*, V, pp. 309–16.
[2] *Supra*, III, p. 73; cf. *1H6* IV. 6; *supra*, VII, pp. 507–8; cf. *Mac* V. 8. 68–82.

cratic speech in Brooke's *Romeus and Julietta*,[1] Coridon in Lodge's *Rosalynde*.[2]

Some major characters grew from slight hints in the sources. Prince Hal was such a one, and his madcap pranks necessitated the presentation of boon companions. The *Famous Victories* sketched some, including Sir John Oldcastle; but Falstaff and his crew were really new creations whose parts grew out of all proportion to their basic functions in the two *Henry IV* plays. In Arthur Brooke's poem there was little to suggest the personality of Mercutio except that Romeus's friend was 'pleasant of devise', a lion among the ladies and had perpetually cold hands[3]—which might be taken to imply hostility to love and to foreshadow premature death. Shakespeare used him at an important moment in the action (the duel with Tybalt) but he was chiefly valuable as a contrast in temperament. Autolycus was probably suggested by the episode in which Sabie's hero disguised himself as a lame beggar (*supra*, pp. 210–11).

Among the host of persons 'augmented' or wholly invented by Shakespeare is a particular class of 'normal' men who serve as confidants, foils or commentators to the major figures. Such a man is Mercutio with his wit and ability to combine realism with fancy, who tries to keep Romeo's enthusiasms within bounds and dies through trying to stop the feud. Horatio is another, sceptical about the Ghost until he sees it, to some extent Hamlet's confidant, in his reasonableness a great contrast to the hero, as Hamlet himself acknowledges (III.2.63–74). Kent, Lear's faithful retainer, an offshoot of Perillus in the old play, is another 'normal' man, warning the King (and the audience) of his folly, his undying loyalty set beside the treachery of Oswald and Cornwall, and an example of sanity in the madness of the storm. Menenius in *Coriolanus* preaches good government and balance between the classes. He advises plebeians, aristocrats, and the rash, unpolitic hero. Domitius Enobarbus, built up on the scantiest of allusions in Plutarch,[4] is a commentator on the conduct of Antony, whom he criticizes,

---

[1] *Supra*, I, pp. 302–4, 309, 345 etc.; cf. *RJ* II. 4. 5; III. 2. 3; III. 5.
[2] *Supra*, II, pp. 183–9; cf. *AYL* II. 4; III. 2.
[3] *Supra*, I, pp. 292–3.
[4] *Supra*, V, pp. 291, 298. Plutarch also wrote that once in Parthia when Antony had to obtain a truce and retreat, he was ashamed to tell his soldiers, so got Domitius to do it.

not for loving Cleopatra but for letting his love interfere with his 'absolute soldiership'. He admires Cleopatra greatly but he knows Antony's weakness, and gives both of them good advice on occasion, which neither takes. Enobarbus's common sense is at war with his loyalty, and when he deserts it is not because he is 'corrupted' by Antony's misfortunes, as the latter declares, but because the general has made 'his will/Lord of his reason'. Enobarbus's blunt common sense illuminates for the audience both Antony's fatal weakness and his natural splendour which becomes tarnished but is never quite lost.

(5)

We have already touched on another important aspect of Shakespeare's approach to his sources, namely, his 'thematic' apprehension of his material. Some remarks of C. S. Lewis will clarify what is meant by this. Writing about the causes of delight in stories, Lewis asserted that although excitement, 'the alternate tension and appeasement of imagined anxiety', is an important ingredient, 'it is the *quality* of unexpectedness, not the *fact*, that delights us'.[1] Plot is important, but so is theme, and 'the real theme may be . . . something other than a process, and something more like a state or quality. Giantship, otherness, the desolation of space, are examples that have crossed our path . . . I suggest that this internal tension in the heart of every story between the theme and the plot constitutes after all, its chief resemblance to life.'

From the beginning of his career Shakespeare was aware of the tension between theme and plot, and in shaping his plays he was increasingly influenced by some topic concerned with human relationships which he found implicit in his major sources and sought for in, or imposed upon, his secondary source-material. There are links between plays, not only those due, as in the Histories, *Troilus* and *Lear*, to participation in a common range of political ideas such as Order, Disorder, and Degree, but others suggested in the first instance by a particular source and not completely worked out on that occasion, but engaging the dramatist's mind for some time, and affecting his choice and handling of later subject-matter.

[1] C. S. Lewis, 'On Stories', in *Of Other Worlds*, 1966, pp. 17–20.

In a television interview[1] the British painter Keith Vaughan, when asked about the development of his work, replied: 'One painting grows out of the one that went before . . . it always grows out of previous painting.' Drama cannot be as 'pure' as painting, since many external factors are involved in bringing a play to birth, but broadly speaking we can observe in the sequence of Shakespeare's plays a linkage of topics, repeated elements not confined to the recurrence of technical devices and incidents of plot such as the sex-disguise, mistaken identities, eavesdropping, villainous intrigues, etc.[2] Assuming that the chronology suggested in these volumes is approximately correct, we can trace certain continuities of theme within groups of plays, and a gradual deepening of ethical content through the years.[3]

Thus in Plautus' *Menaechmi* the dramatist found a faint adumbration of family relationships between the brothers Menaechmi and the shrewish wife of one of them. This he greatly augmented by introducing not only the father and mother, but also Adriana's gentle sister Luciana with her conventional defence of female submissiveness. In this way, while increasing the complications and adding sex-interest, Shakespeare gave his comedy more emotional depth. In *The Taming of the Shrew* the problem of mastery in marriage became more prominent, and the contrast between the realistic 'fabliau' and the romantic attitudes to love and marriage governed the choice of Gascoigne's *Supposes* for the sub-plot.

To marital relations the question of a daughter's obedience to her father was added (and with a more liberal view) in *A Midsummer Night's Dream*, *Romeo and Juliet*, and *The Merchant of Venice*, for all imply that in certain romantic circumstances parents' wills may be defied.

Other links between the early plays are also apparent, notably the widening of the canvas to represent not just a few personages essential to the plot, but the picture of a whole society with a range of classes from servants to noblemen or royalty, all operating according to their ranks and functions.

[1] London, 6 November 1966.
[2] Cf. P. V. Kreider, *Repetition in Shakespeare's Plays*, Princeton, 1941.
[3] I have sketched this development with special regard to his interest in the operations of the mind in *Mirror of Minds*, London and Toronto, 1962, Ch. 2.

The desire to allow a varied company of actors to show their special gifts must have had something to do with this enduring practice, but Shakespeare probably transferred the idea of a play as a little commonwealth from his early Histories to his work in comedy and tragedy, and he obviously took great pleasure in presenting the interaction of persons high and low with their different backgrounds, manners, and speech, going far beyond his usual sources in this respect.

A common feature arising from this lasting habit is the presence of a prince who takes some part in the action but generally stands apart, judging the other characters. The successful introduction of Duke Solinus to threaten Aegeon at the opening of *The Comedy of Errors* and to clear matters up at the end probably led Shakespeare to introduce the Haroun-al-Rashid motif into *The Shrew*, then to make Duke Theseus's wedding the setting for *A Midsummer Night's Dream*, and to make the most of Arthur Brooke's 'prudent prince' who tried in vain to quench the feud in Verona. Later, in *All's Well* we find the King as a kindly adviser and judge, in *Measure for Measure* the Duke as austere investigator and benevolent plotter. The chief function of these noble observers was to invoke law, reason, and mercy. In the Romances the conception of the story as evolving under the eyes of a wise governor is fortified or replaced by source-material suggesting that a god or Providence is directing the whole; of this more later. In *The Tempest* the wise Duke becomes the main instigator of the action.

Common also to the early comedies are suggestions of magic, trickery, dream, illusion or madness. Ephesus in *The Comedy of Errors*, like Plautus' Epidamnum, is a place of tricksters and conjurers. The Traveller thinks that he has fallen among witches or lunatics, and his brother is treated as a madman. Enchantment, dream and madness are touched on in the Sly scenes of *The Shrew*. In *The Dream* fairies, spells, illusions are all-important. Apparently for a time Shakespeare regarded comedy as a play of fancy evoking a sense of wonder, magic, irrationality and dream, even if he did not altogether agree with Theseus's strictures on 'the lunatic, the lover and the poet'.

Along with this went the dramatist's awareness that his work was indeed a *play*, performed by actors, counterfeit men, 'but shadows', and ephemeral by its very nature. So the attempt to make the source-plot plausible by the infusion of realistic personages was occasionally crossed by a recognition that the drama was after all only a fiction and the world of the play illusory; and this easily passed into the notion, expressed finally by Prospero (IV. 1. 148–58), that life itself is but a dream.[1]

(6)

As we have seen in these volumes it is not difficult to find analogues to the basic situations in many of Shakespeare's plays. What is surprising, and significant, is that so much of his source-material contains strong folk-elements which anthropologists have traced in oral story and legend. Among these we may note: 'the long-lost child and/or wife' motif (*CE, Per, Cym, WT*); 'the wife-taming' (*TSh*); 'the faithless friend' (*TGV, Oth*); 'the pound of flesh bond', 'the wife as judge saving her husband', and 'the triple choice' (*MV*); 'the cruel brother' and 'the brother dispossessed and restored' (*AYL, Lear, Tem*); 'the calumniated wife' (*Ado, Oth, Cym, WT*); 'the reluctant husband' and 'the impossible task' (*AWW*); 'the monstrous bargain' (*MM*); 'the disguised ruler observing his subjects' (*H5, MM*); 'the savage infidel' (*TA, MV, Oth*); 'the pretended simpleton or madman' (*Ham, Lear*); 'the delayed revenge' (*Ham*); 'the incestuous parent' (*Ham, Per*); 'the love-test' and 'Cinderella theme' (*Lear*); 'the prince and the shepherdess' (*WT*).[2]

In a brilliant paper Professor Northrop Frye, considering the nature of comedy in relation to Christian belief, has argued that Shakespearian comedy goes back, not to the Mysteries and Morality plays, but to the ritual folk-drama of the mummers and the St George play: 'We may call this the drama of the green world, and its theme is . . . the triumph of life over the waste land, the death and revival of the year impersonated by

---

[1] Cf. Anne Righter, *Shakespeare and the Idea of the Play*, 1962; H. Fisch, 'Shakespeare and the Theatre of the World', in *The Morality of Art*, 1969.
[2] Examples of most of these are listed in Stith Thompson, *Motif-Index of Folk Literature*, 6 vols, Copenhagen, 1955–8, and *The Types of Folk-Tale*, 1964. Cf. Grimm, J. and W., *Kinder- und Hausmärchen*, 1812–57; J. Bolte, *Anmerkungen zu den Kinder- und Hausmärchen des Brudern Grimm*, 5 vols, 1913–31; H. Coote Lake, 'Some Folk-lore Incidents in Shakespeare', *Folk-Lore*, 39, 1928, 307–28; M. R. Cox, *Cinderella*, 1892; J. Spens, *Shakespeare's Relation to Tradition*, Oxford, 1916.

figures still human, and once divine as well.'[1] He identifies th e
'greenwood' in *Two Gentlemen of Verona, A Midsummer Night's
Dream, As You Like It, Cymbeline* and *The Winter's Tale* with
this 'green world'. Somewhat sweeping, no doubt, but Dr
Frye is surely right in pointing to Shakespeare's preference for
a comedy which 'begins in a world represented as a normal
world, moves into the green world, goes into a metamorphosis
there in which the comic resolution is achieved, and returns to
the normal world'. 'In *The Tempest*, the entire action takes
place in the green world.'

Shakespeare's treatment of the 'greenwood' differs from that
of his contemporaries who wrote Robin Hood plays and
pastorals. It is a place where things go oddly, magic can play
pranks, erotic idylls are conducted, and conversions from bad to
good occur with unsurprising suddenness. There human nature
exercises itself more simply, more joyously and more benevolently than in the normal world of everyday life. It is a place
of wish-fulfilment, and undoubtedly Shakespeare revelled in it
because he could set its natural pleasures and temporary freedom from the ordinary world against the cares and intrigues of
court and city, producing romantic comedy at its most refined,
indeed 'the triumph of life over the waste land'.

As Professor R. B. Heilman writes, 'His poetry has fed on
myth, but he has also been engaged in mythopoeic activity.'[2]
This does not, however, mean that Shakespeare, like Shelley
and Keats, was in the habit of creating personages out of
natural and ethical forces, or that he saw his plays as concerned
with 'the death and revival of the year'. He was not an ancient
myth-maker but a projector of modern stories in sophisticated
form. Yet by some instinctive drive within him, and perhaps
also through habit learned in his boyhood at Stratford, he was
attracted more than most poets of his time to those 'patterns of
imagination that haunt, create wonder in, human minds, for
generation after generation'.[3] As the list above shows, the
greenwood itself was only one of many such patterns.

Shakespeare's interest in moral questions and the explora-

---

[1] 'The Argument of Comedy', *Eng. Inst. Essays, 1948*, New York, 1949, 67.
[2] R. B. Heilman, 'The Lear World', in *Eng. Inst. Essays, 1948*, New York, 1949,
30–8.
[3] N. N. Holland, *The Shakespearean Imagination*, 1968, p. 285.

tion of men's motives, already keen in the early Histories, affected his comic vision and his handling of his chosen themes. Whether the sources suggested the themes or whether certain stories were selected because of their themes is not always clear, but the concatenation of plays and the recurrence of the ideas in them proves that the choice of sources was not, as Raleigh thought, accidental.

From *Love's Labour's Lost* onwards we also see Shakespeare realizing the importance, in presenting his characters, of the traditional psychology of the medical and ethical textbooks. This gave him a new instrument of analysis. In *Love's Labour's Lost* there is a delighted discovery of psychological principles and their significance for the anatomy of passion. Henceforward delineation of moods, discrimination between types of personality and between individuals, help to base the plots firmly in character, and often play round the source-material with shrewd observation and poetic fancy. One thinks of the first and last scenes of *The Merchant of Venice* with their representation of mood. This comedy also initiated a portrayal of national types (I. 2, etc.) which strongly affected the characterization in *Henry IV* and *Henry V*. Shakespeare used the theory of 'humours' in depicting the gay young Venetians and the melancholy Antonio, Jaques and Hamlet. Ajax is a chaotic mixture of humours; Brutus (Antony asserts) had 'the elements/So mixed in him' that he was all that a man should be. But almost as if in reaction against Ben Jonson's rigid application of the theory, Shakespeare created characters of very mixed, even almost incompatible, qualities, paradoxical beings like Achilles and Caesar, Hamlet, Othello, Coriolanus. And as his view of life darkened, as his interest in the springs of human behaviour deepened, the fascination of love and adventure was equalled by that of evil and its temptations, so that he chose subject-matter involving moral dilemmas, problems of justice, loyalty, honour, the war of passions against reason. Inevitably this must result in some difficulty in preserving dramatic and ethical balance. This was bound up with the increasing depth of characterization in the 'dark comedies' and tragedies.

In the farcical *Comedy of Errors* the more like each other, the less individualized the two brothers and the two servants are, the more acceptable are their adventures and misunderstandings; and in the fanciful *A Midsummer Night's Dream* it is a great advantage to have the young lovers very lightly sketched. The major comedies of 1597–1600 have plots which call for more substantial characters, and in *As You Like It* and *Twelfth Night* there is almost perfect adaptation of personages to plot. But already in *The Merchant of Venice* and *Henry IV* there was a surplusage of character-drawing in Shylock and Falstaff. By humanizing the cruel Jew of western folk-lore, by giving Shylock abundant reason for resentment and also a strong natural sense of family and race, Shakespeare ran the risk of raising questions about the Christians' conduct which might lessen the sympathy with Antonio of any audience less anti-semitic than the Elizabethan. As it is, Shylock's conduct is so vengeful that though we understand him we do not condone. Falstaff, however, is made far too big and important a personality and is given too much scope in too many scenes for his function in the History of Henry IV and of the King's relations with his heir. Because he is so richly humorous and delights us more than any of the historical characters it is arguable that he mars the artistic unity of the two plays, and his dismissal, inevitable though it be, detracts from the joy of Prince Hal's coronation. There can be no doubt that, in *2 Henry IV* especially, faced with unexciting historical material, Shakespeare's inventive genius was greater than his political judgment.

The contrast between the 'dark comedies' and those immediately preceding them shocked many Victorians, not only by the sexual nature of the dilemmas forced upon Helena and Isabella but also by their resolute and 'unwomanly' behaviour. Some modern critics accuse Shakespeare of putting new wine into old bottles, so that there is in *Measure for Measure* a fundamental antipathy between Shakespeare's new learning and his old plot situations, 'an incongruity between the Christian framework of the characters and the folk-materials of the plot'.[1]

While accepting entirely that the play is based more closely on Christian doctrines than any previous play, I must reject the assumption that folk-stories were merely 'fairy-tales' in the sense of being incredible, fantastic toys of fancy. Rather they were ways of expressing fundamental and recurring dilemmas and difficult situations inherent in human nature. The 'mon-

[1] V. K. Whitaker, *Shakespeare's Use of Learning*, p. 221.

strous bargain' is a folk-tale motif, which presents in extreme
form a kind of sexual blackmail which is not infrequent in life,
and the choice before the heroine is always terrible. For
Shakespeare to develop the characters of Isabella and Angelo
as he does is not to destroy the credibility of the situation but to
expose its full implications.

The dilemma is resolved by means of another folk-lore
device, the bed-trick already used in *All's Well*. E. C. Pettet
comments, 'barely has life been breathed into Angelo when he
has to be distorted to the necessities of a romantic story'.[1]
Again the assumption is wrong. For spectators bred up on
fabliaux and *novelle*, for whom 'the act of shame' was best done
in darkness, substitution in bed was not incredible or 'romantic'.
Angelo is not 'distorted'; he plays his part according to his own
nature, and the trick is given plausibility by the plight of
Mariana and the benevolent authority of the 'friar'. Conventional it is, but in order that Isabella may escape Angelo the
audience willingly accepts the device, which neatly turns the
tables on a corrupt, deceitful man (measure for measure), and
is intimately related to the moral themes of the play, justice,
rigour, and mercy. For Shakespeare and his contemporaries
the world of folk-lore coexisted with the world of everyday.

There is no need to postulate any sudden awakening or conversion of Shakespeare round about 1600 to a moralistic
approach in his art. He had treated the Wars of the Roses in
the light of the Anglican Homilies, and most of his English
kings in the light of generally accepted Christian principles
and ideas of good government. In the mature comedies he
increasingly used ethical topics as a dramatic instrument for
unifying the plays—e.g. legality, justice, and mercy in *The
Merchant of Venice* and *Measure for Measure*, the nature of honour
and nobility in *Henry IV* and *Henry V*, *All's Well* and *Troilus*,
deception and/or self-deception in *Much Ado*, *Twelfth Night*,
As You Like It, *Julius Caesar*—and throughout we find the
contrast in human conduct between truth and falsehood,
loyalty and treachery, appearance and reality. The presence
of such congenial topics in his sources helps to explain why he
chose certain main plots and characters rather than others,

[1] E. C. Pettet, *Shakespeare and the Romance Tradition*, 1949, cited by Whitaker, *Shakespeare's Use of Learning*, p. 221.

and also why he picked on particular subsidiary material. External factors may have operated too, but there can be no doubt that the psychology of inordinate passions, the 'mystery of iniquity', and the persistence of goodness in a naughty world affected the choice and handling of material for the major tragedies. All this without overt didactic intention, for Shakespeare worked from an innate sense of propriety and goodness rather than from a wish to propagate any sectarian gospel.

The exploration of complex passions was not enough for Shakespeare, with his pleasure in the social setting of his plots. His tragic characters must be involved in state affairs and subsidiary interests, and connected with a wide range of minor figures. So in *Hamlet*, whatever the immediate sources may have been, Shakespeare created an entire society, with court, international relations, private domestic life, theatrical affairs, the education of young people, and a fickle multitude, all throwing into relief the many-sidedness of the hero and his attitudes towards his terrible task. The play is not only about revenge, and the Prince, but about Denmark too. The thematic enrichment of a primary source is especially well illustrated by *Othello*, in which Cinthio's sordid story is elevated out of domestic tragedy to become a 'historical' tragedy in which the recent Turkish menace gives added significance to the noble hero's conflict between honour, love and jealousy. In *Lear*, where the legendary background is left indefinite, the themes of parental folly and moral blindness punished excessively by filial ingratitude are deepened by combining the story of Lear with the analogous one of the blind Paphlagonian king, until the fusion of ancient tale with modern fiction evokes questioning of man's very nature and his place in an ambiguous universe.

(7)

One important novelty affecting the use of sources in some of the great tragedies was in the portrayal of moral and mental disintegration. Changes in affection, loyalty, attitudes to life and mankind are of course the very stuff of drama, and Shakespeare from the outset had drawn characters whose behaviour was inconsistent or changeable; hence Proteus (who lived up to his name), and the royal circle in *Love's Labour's*

Lost. Such characters do not alter fundamentally; they merely express themselves in new ways, change the directions of their wills. Similarly Richard II remains the same man throughout the play, but is made to reveal different sides of himself before and after his fall. Does Prince Hal's nature suffer any great sea-change in *1* and *2 Henry IV*? Does he not rather carry out in each play the programme which he announced in Part 1, Act I? Certainly he is more mature in *Henry V*, as the sources necessitated, but we cannot watch the alteration taking place. Perhaps Romeo and Juliet grow up a little in the course of their tragedy, but the dramatist does not call our attention to it.

In the main Shakespeare in his early work explores magnificently the varied moods and emotions which his plots afford without tracing any deep psychological processes in character. Sudden twists and turns abound. We watch Proteus turning traitor to Valentine and Julia, Romeo falling out of one love into another; but the convention of love at first sight makes much analysis unnecessary. There are other rapid conversions when comedy requires a happy ending: Oliver, Claudio, Bertram. Less perfunctory and less due to source-material, maybe, are the transformations of Benedick and Troilus—the one from misogyny to love, the other from love to misogyny; but the essential nature of each is unchanged. Nor is that of Brutus, either by the need to murder his friend or by its baleful consequences. His character remains as static as in Plutarch, and although he tells us that:

> Between the acting of a dreadful thing
> And the first motion, all the interim is
> Like a phantasma, or a hideous dream

we are not taken into his experience to share his horror. In *Hamlet*, however, we share the hero's agonies, for the play is conceived in part as a psychological study of a mind thrown into confusion. How far this depends on the *Ur-Hamlet* we cannot tell, but the moral shock and vehemence adumbrated by Belleforest and the incoherent fragmentation of Hieronimo in *The Spanish Tragedy* are worked up into the brilliant analysis and representation of a noble and witty imagination whose profound disturbance and essential sanity are displayed in occasions which, however much they 'conspire' against his task, evoke our sympathy. We see Hamlet in three phases: in Act I as the prince whose grief and resentment come to a shocking climax with the Ghost's revelations; in Acts II to IV as heartsick, brooding, indulging now in distractions, now in self-accusations; from Act IV, Sc. 6 onwards as cool, reconciled to Providence and expectant of the end. Hamlet does not degenerate morally; his aberrations arise 'Out of his weakness and his melancholy', and he recovers from them. The transitions between the three phases—occurring while he is absent from the stage—are not shown or explained, and his character remains mysterious, perhaps for lack of one or two explicit pointers. I suspect that in composing *Hamlet* Shakespeare was on the verge of a great discovery, namely, the developing hero, to be shown in the process of gradual change; but that by keeping to his episodic sources, and by introducing so much topical material, he let slip the opportunity.

That discovery Shakespeare made in *Othello*, in which he traced the history of a soul's degeneration; and this was adumbrated in Cinthio's tale, in which the Moor was shown as gradually, over a considerable period of time, driven deeper and deeper away from his initial nobility and tranquillity into suspicion and jealousy. So he moved from anger at his wife's partiality for the Corporal to considering how he could kill them both while avoiding all suspicion; and his wife saw that he had entirely changed his nature. Furthermore, the sordid and cruel murder in Cinthio demonstrates the result of this transformation, which was caused by the step-by-step opportunism of the wicked Ensign. Shakespeare's characterization of Othello was vitally affected by this decline, and for the first time he produced a tragedy based not, as in *Richard III*, on the many-sided villainy of a completely bad man, or on the pathos of virtuous lovers trapped by adverse circumstances, as in *Romeo and Juliet*, or on the errors of judgment of a good man as in *Julius Caesar*, but on the disintegration of a noble soul gradually destroyed by evil machinations working on its passionate gnorance and misplaced trust. And we watch it all happen.

Once having struck out this new conception of tragic process, Shakespeare applied it in *King Lear* and *Macbeth* to source-material in which such a process was not inherent. So he reshaped the stories of Lear and the Paphlagonian king into twin portraits of two old men broken down by external evil and their own blind arrogance to extreme suffering only alleviated by the 'kindness' of other sufferers. The tragedy consists not merely in the sad end but in the whole process (only faintly suggested in the sources) by which their agony is consummated.

Similarly in *Macbeth* where the chronicle-material about Macbeth and his wife was scanty and contained a gap of ten years between his murder of Duncan and his lapse into tyranny, Shakespeare interfused other matter from Holinshed and elsewhere to create the portrait of a soul swiftly rushing down from initial temptation to mental and moral destruction. Again the tragic interest includes the psychological stages in the process of degeneration. In both plays the source-material is transcended in a complex dramatic creation whose impulse derives mainly from the poet's vision of dynamic evil and its operation in society and within the human mind.

In *Antony and Cleopatra*, finally, this growing interest in the activities of passion found in Plutarch's narrative ample evidence of Antony's decline under the influence of Cleopatra's irresponsible fascination. Here the dramatist had to invent less, but used his poetic and theatrical skills to keep a balance between implied reproof and admiration, so that the sense of waste is mitigated by sympathy with the unequalled pair.

In all these later tragedies the protagonists make a good end and revive in us the admiration which has waned during their decline into irrationality. *Timon* and *Coriolanus*, no doubt owing to the nature of their basic material, are exceptions to the practice of 'gradualness'. Timon swings between the extremes of excessive generosity and excessive hatred of his fellow-men, being quite suddenly converted from one to the other, after which we are shown various instances of his insane bitterness. His end shows no recovery, but its miserable isolation is the logical result of his sudden and complete descent to misanthropy. Coriolanus does not change. His fall is caused by his consistency, for he behaves to the plebeians and their tribunes, and then to Rome itself, with the violent irascibility which he uses against the Volscians. In exile he is still self-centredly arrogant when he makes war on Rome, and although his love for his mother overcomes his hatred enough to make him withdraw, this does not indicate any change in his nature, and his hot temper finally brings about his death. Herein Shakespeare remained faithful to his sources. Both plays are cautionary tales and in neither are we wholeheartedly implicated in the conduct of the hero and his psychological processes, as we are in, say, *Macbeth.*

It is evident that Shakespeare did not restrict himself to one rigid conception of tragedy, but experimented with different kinds of action and motivation, and with different degrees of audience involvement. Every play was a new start, but there was an overriding preoccupation with the ethical and political implications of passion in individuals, and at different periods of his career he emphasized one tragic effect rather than another, so that it is possible to trace some common tendency in the plays of each phase, and some links between them. The treatment of the sources varies according to the particular themes Shakespeare saw in each and to his desire to intensify and augment them.

(8)

From *The Merchant of Venice* onwards Shakespeare frequently experimented in the kind of drama described by Daniel in *Hymen's Triumph* (1614) as

> No merry tale, my boy, nor yet too sad,
> But mixed like the tragic comedies. (IV. 3)

The tragi-comic form had achieved some popularity before Fletcher (though with little immediate relevance) defined it in the manner of Guarini in his Dedication of *The Faithfull Shepherdess* (*c.* 1610):

> A tragicomedy is not so called in respect of mirth and killing, but in respect it wants deaths, which is enough to make it no tragedy, yet brings some near it, which is enough to make it no comedy, which must be a representation of familiar people, with such kind of trouble as no life be questioned; so that a god is as lawful in this as in a tragedy, and mean people as in a comedy.

Shakespeare certainly never held the classical ideas about the limited range of tragedy and comedy implied here, but *All's Well* and *Measure for Measure* were tragi-comedies in the seriousness of their stories, and the latter play brought some characters near to death. In his last comedies Shakespeare returned to this kind of play, but with important differences. As we have seen, the change from tragedy to romance may have been helped by the acquisition of the Blackfriars Theatre in late 1609, a private theatre allowing artificial lighting effects, music, and scenic display, for a slightly more sophisticated audience than that of the Globe—where, however, the Company continued to play. *Pericles*, written 'To glad your ear, and please your eyes', was composed before the King's Men got possession of their new home, but may have been planned with the Blackfriars in mind.

This play initiated a tendency for Shakespeare to use episodic stories of the kind found in Greek romances rather than the more tightly knit Italian *novella* material. *Pericles* indeed 'sounds the keynote of the group with themes and incidents repeated later'.[1] The separation and reunion of parents and children (already found often from *Comedy of Errors* to *Lear*) is involved with pseudo-historical affairs of state and court life, journeys by sea or land, almost incredible adventures, a supernatural vision and a great Discovery scene. This set the pattern for *Cymbeline* and *The Winter's Tale*, which have most of these features. The main sources of *Cymbeline* had no vision, but one was inserted for spectacle and to add a flavour of Greek romance. Wanderings in Wales were substituted for Frederyke's adventures. *Pandosto* had similar ingredients, with an oracle instead of a vision (to which the dramatist added the spectacular 'miracle' of Hermione's statue), and a long stretch of pastoral life which Shakespeare (remembering *As You Like It*) adapted, maybe to demonstrate a better way of dramatizing pastoral than Fletcher's unsuccessful *Faithfull Shepherdess*. The same ingredients are traceable in *The Tempest*, though somewhat obscured by the classical structure, which necessitates much retrospective narrative. This structure may have been caused, not only by a reaction against the episodic romance technique, but also by a desire to make the most of the play's topicality by starting with a spectacular storm and shipwreck on an island.

[1] F. Pyle, in *The Winter's Tale, A Commentary on the Structure*, 1969, shows how closely the plays were linked, and the implications of the Blackfriars Theatre.

Another common element in the last plays, due no doubt to the supernatural suggestions in the material but also indicating Shakespeare's gracious benignity of mood, is the intermittent impression of divine guidance. Although at the end of *The Comedy of Errors* Shakespeare had introduced, from Gower's story of *Apollonius of Tyre*, the revelation that the 'abbess' of the 'priory' at Ephesus was Aegeon's long-lost wife, no religious feeling was involved. Following Gower more closely in *Pericles*, he took over the vision of the Goddess Diana who told the hero to go to Ephesus (V. I. 220–53). This divine intervention comes late in the play, which has hitherto given little sign that the gods cared at all for the disconsolate wanderer. But it lends to the Discovery an atmosphere of mystery, wonder, and reassurance. Posthumus's dream of his parents and discovery of the Oracle come too late in *Cymbeline* to affect the issue greatly (V. 4. 29–122). They provide only a tardy proof of divine interest, but serve mainly to indicate Posthumus's noble birth and to provide a riddle for the Soothsayer to solve, though they also show that 'The fingers of the pow'rs above do tone/The harmony of this peace'. So the play can end with attractive rituals in the Temple of Jove.

Since the Oracle taken from *Pandosto* into *The Winter's Tale* is appealed to in II. I, and made known in III. 2, there is more suspense about its meaning and fulfilment, and the death of Mamillius is taken by Leontes to mean that 'Apollo's angry; and the heavens themselves/Do strike at my injustice'. The 'death' of Hermione completes the king's conversion, giving proof that the 'higher pow'rs' demand a lifetime of suffering and repentance. Here there is definitely an attempt to interpret the gods of old romance in terms of Christian feeling; but the return of Hermione is treated as a work of magic rather than as a 'resurrection' in any religious sense. Yet the visions and oracles in these plays seem to have been used to suggest, as against *King Lear*, that the universe is ultimately benevolent towards the innocent, the long-suffering, and the penitent.

That is surely a necessary condition for romantic comedy, but Shakespeare manipulates his materials with a more than usual delight in sheer goodness and its triumph over evil. In *The Tempest* magic is associated with the wisdom born of suffering, isolation, and philosophic contemplation. The 'higher pow'rs' are implied, but the providence of the island is the human sage, Prospero, protector and agent of truth, beauty and goodness, enforcing harmony and peace—as may be done in a drama of wish-fulfilment, even though the antitheses in men's natures must not be ignored.

(9)

Recent studies of Shakespeare's imagery have revealed the complexity of its origins and usage. Here we are concerned with its relation to narrative and dramatic sources only, and in those plays therefore of which direct sources of these kinds are extant. We must omit plays such as *Love's Labour's Lost*, *The Merchant of Venice* and *Hamlet*. There remains a formidable body of work, too much to be adequately treated in a short summary. It suggests that Shakespeare's imagery was evoked in several ways. It might be taken over from or directly suggested by the language of a major source and either confined to a few details or repeated with variations through one or more scenes. An image or statement in the original might even be expanded and objectified into a whole scene. Sometimes, where there was more than one source, imagery derived from one of them was assimilated into the material taken from another. Frequently Shakespeare's imagery was not taken from the wording of a particular source but was created out of his meditation upon the themes, ideas, or implications of his source-material and his resultant apprehension of incidents and characters. Such new imagery might refer to only one or two scenes, or it might form part of a recurrent pattern of images as Shakespeare remoulded his source-material into his own unity. As Wolfgang Clemen has written, 'Only little by little did Shakespeare discover the possibilities which imagery affords the dramatist,' and achieve a technique which in J. D. Wilson's words, 'conveyed the intentions of its creator through a series of impressions, each fleeting as the phrases of a musical symphony'.[1]

Arising from the transformation of sources and Shakespeare's occasional revulsion against their drift or tone, images some-

---

[1] Clemen, *The Development of Shakespeare's Imagery*, 1951, p. 5. He cites *What Happens in Hamlet*, p. 230.

times arose which, while derived from the sources, seem deliberately to reject their purport and to suggest a very different interpretation of character and action. Examples of these usages, which frequently occur in conjunction, will be pointed out in the following short survey.[1]

(*a*) In the early Histories and *Titus Andronicus* the imagery was often a stylistic device applied to the surface of the dialogue rather than an inevitable expression of characters in specific situations. Thus *Henry VI* and *Richard III*, while drawing their matter mainly from Hall and the *Mirror for Magistrates*, were conceived stylistically in terms of Senecan and Marlowesque tragedy, but not consistently so. For his imagery of curse and abuse, doom-laden prophecy and warlike declamation, the dramatist took advantage of the generic Senecan rant and Marlowe's 'high astounding terms'. Certain scenes were little more than exercises in formal rhetoric, e.g. *Richard III*, IV. 4, where, in an invented incident, Queen Margaret, Queen Elizabeth and Richard's mother turn from mutual recrimination to cursing the usurper. Elsewhere imagery of a different type from that found in the sources is imposed upon a situation. Thus in *1 Henry VI*, I. 6. 4–31 Hall's naturalistic account of French rejoicings after the capture of Orleans (*supra*, III, pp. 58–9) is replaced by a Marlowesque paean, with allusions to Astraea, Adonis, the pyramis of Rhodope or Memphis, etc. The crude horror-story behind *Titus Andronicus* was transformed into a slow-moving pageant of cruelty and misery by mingling Senecan display of passions with pictorial lyricism in the manner of Ovid.[2] The resulting tension between two forms of stylization produced a remarkable *tour de force*. Here again the patterns of imagery suggest that Shakespeare was experimenting with different kinds of sententious speeches, emotional outbursts, set orations, and that his rhetorical schemes were more important than naturalistic dialogue.

[1] The illustrations are arranged in the following sequence: (*a*) imposed 'rhetorical' imagery and imagery from the sources (*H6, R3*); (*b*) imagery based on the conception of a character (*R2, H5*); (*c*) poetic use of one particular source (*RJ*); (*d*) augmentation of slight material (*Tim*); (*e*) tonal transformation of a major source (*AYL*); (*f*) transference between sources (*Lear*); (*g*) fusion of sources (*Mac, WT*); (*h*) imagery from discarded source-material (*Cym*).

[2] See *supra*, VI, pp. 26–32, and the detailed examples cited in *New Arden TA*, 1953; also P. Simpson, *Studies in Elizabethan Drama*, Oxford, 1955, pp. 49–54; and E. M. Waith, 'The Metamorphosis of Violence in *TA*', *Sh Survey 10*, 1957, 39–40.

General Conclusion 381

Yet some of the imagery in *1 Henry VI* was due to Hall. Thus the English abuse of Joan of Arc came from Hall's account of her as 'a shepherd's daughter', 'chamberlein in an hostrie, and a beggers brat', 'an enchauntresse, and orgayne of the devil' etc. (*supra*, III, p. 60). The three suns seen by Richard (*supra*, III, p. 179) are used in *3 Henry VI* to encourage Richard and Edward and suggest their union with Clarence to 'o'er-shine the earth' (II. 1. 25–40; 91–3). The sun image reappears in II. 3. 7. There are other similar instances. More striking is Shakespeare's ability to develop a simple statement or image into a vivid incident. Thus Hall's assertion that at Towton, 'hope of life was set on side on every parte, and takyng of prisoners was proclaymed as a great offence, by which every man determined, either to conquere or to dye in the fielde' (*supra*, III, p. 182) was worked up into the dialogue in which Warwick vows on his knees never to pause 'Till either death hath clos'd these eyes of mine/Or fortune given me measure of revenge' (*3H6*, II. 3).

Similarly the king's vision at II. 5. 55–122 was built on Hall's brief comment, 'This conflict was a maner unnaturall, for in it the sonne fought against the father, the brother against the brother' (*supra*, III, p. 183).

Noting that the commonest floating images in these early Histories referred to plants and flowers, their growth and decay, Professor Spurgeon suggested that they might arise 'simply from the badges of York and Lancaster, together with the meaning of the name Plantagenet'[1](sprig of broom). Hall does not mention the roses of Lancaster and York, and the red rose was an emblem of the Tudors originally, not of Lancaster, though the Lancastrians appropriated it, and Shakespeare's scene in the Temple Garden (*1H6*, II. 4) symbolized well for his audience the rivalry between the two houses. Shakespeare the country-man was not the first poet to draw imagery from the life of trees, crops, fruits, and flowers, and it suited his organic view of existence.

The idea of the state as a garden was not novel when Queen Margaret in *2 Henry VI*, III. 1. 31 used the metaphor of weeds which 'o'ergrow the garden/And choke the herbs for want of

Shakespeare's Imagery, p. 216.

husbandry'.[1] In *The True Tragedy of Richard III* Richmond promised to reclaim the state

> Which now lies like a savage shultred grove
> Where brambles, briars, and thornes, o'ergrow these sprigs.
>
> (*supra*, III, p. 334)

And the early Tudor ballad, 'The Rose of England' (*supra*, III, p. 346), not only played on the garden image but introduced the gardeners whom Shakespeare used for a striking 'mirror' scene in *Richard II*, III. 4:

> But now this garden fflourishes ffreshly and gay,
> With ffragrant fflowers comely of hew
> An gardners it doth maintaine
> I hope they will prove just and true.

The ballad also makes play with the heraldic symbols of combatants in the great Wars: Richard III is the white boar, Stanley the eagle, Richmond the rose. The boar and other animal images occurred frequently in the *Mirror for Magistrates*. Baldwin's Clarence (1559) declares, 'My brother Richard was the Bore/Whose tuskes should teare my brothers boyes and me', and Baldwin, while condemning most heraldic prophecies, approved of likening men to beasts for their moral qualities:

> Truth is no Harold nor no Sophist sure:
> She noteth not mens names, their shildes nor creastes,
> Though she compare them unto birdes and beastes.
>
> (*supra*, III, pp. 302–3)

There was ample precedent for the diverse animal references to the usurper in *Richard III* besides the fatal rhyme of Collingbourne in Hall (*supra*, III, p. 286). So Richard becomes a 'rooting hog', and Stanley dreams that 'the boar razed off his helm' (III. 2. 11). Richard is 'a bottled spider', 'a poisonous bunchback'd toad', 'a dog' (I. 3. 228–48) and Queen Margaret's invective is later recalled by Queen Elizabeth (IV. 4. 80–1). Henceforth Shakespeare often used animal imagery to denote human behaviour. This was natural enough in a poet who believed in the traditional scale of being.

Richard III contains a few verbal reminiscences of Hall, e.g.

[1] See P. Ure, *New Arden R2*, App.

when Dr Shaa preached that Edward IV's sons were bastards, the people 'stood as they had been turned into stones' (*supra*, III, p. 273). Shakespeare has 'like dumb statues or breathing stones' (III. 6. 25). More interesting is his manipulation of Hall's details, as when out of Buckingham's saying, 'Woe to that realm whose king is a child' (*supra*, III, p. 274) he creates a scene (II. 3) between three Citizens who foresee 'a troublous world'.

Hall vividly described the tortured restlessness of Richard's conscience (*supra*, III, pp. 279–80). From this came not only Queen Anne's allusion to his disturbed nights and 'timorous dreams' (IV. 1. 84) but also the Duchess of York's wish that 'the little souls of Edward's children/Whisper the spirits of thine enemies' (IV. 4. 191–8), as they do indeed to Richmond in the night before Bosworth Field. The visitation of his victims to Richard in that scene (V. 3) probably owes more to the King's soliloquy in *The True Tragedy* (*supra*, III, pp. 338–9) which Shakespeare made Hamlet recall when he cried, 'The croaking raven doth bellow for revenge' (*Ham* III. 2. 257) misquoting the line 'The screeching Raven sits croking for revenge' (line 1892).

(*b*) *Richard II* provides little imagery taken directly from the chronicles, but much (in the second half of the play) derived from a conception of the King which probably owes much to Daniel's *Civil Wars* and the play *Woodstock*. Richard's self-conscious pathos, his posturings and sense of himself as an actor, his delight in words, help make up a portrait of a self-indulgent man who neglects action for fancy, and substitutes talk about kingly rights for thought about kingly duties. The teeming imagery of this tragedy is invented to set forth Richard's peculiar nature and predicament, and there is a striking contrast between his figurative manner of thought and that of his cool enemy, Bolingbroke. An instance of Shakespeare's adaptation and objectifying of an image already used elsewhere occurs in the abdication scene. In *Richard III* that cunning trickster, delighted to have won Lady Anne, jestingly declares:

> I do mistake my person all this while:
> Upon my life, she finds, although I cannot,
> Myself to be a marvellous proper man.

> I'll be at charges for a looking-glass
> And entertain a score or two of tailors
> To study fashions to adorn my body . . . (I. 2. 254–9)

Richard II, faced with dethronement and told to read the record of his offences, calls for a mirror

> That it may show me what a face I have,
> Since it is bankrupt of his majesty,

and so that he may see 'the very book indeed/Where all my sins are write, and that's myself'. He uses the mirror to lament his downfall (recalling Faustus's 'Was this the face . . . ?') and breaks the glass to symbolize the brittleness of glory (IV. 1. 264–88).

Henry V provides another example of a play composed round a conception of the central figure derived from the source-material (and in this case, tradition); but in the historical comedy a more consistent and complex view of character and setting produces more varied styles and imagery. Professor Spurgeon noted many images concerned with flight, swift and soaring movement, speed of action.[1] No doubt this dynamic impression was to some extent due to the dramatist's desire to capture the energy of epic, mindful of Daniel's wish for a modern heroic poet able to portray

> that magnanimous King
> Mirror of vertue, miracle of worth,
> Whose mightie Actions with wise managing
> Forst prouder bosting climes to serve the North.
>
> (*supra*, IV, pp. 422–4)

Aware of the inadequacy of the stage to do this, Shakespeare filled his Choruses with appeals to the audience: 'On your imaginary forces work', 'make imaginary puissance', 'For 'tis your thought that now must deck our kings,/Carry them here and there, jumping o'er times' (Prologue). The Chorus to Act III continues the idea: 'Thus with imagin'd wing our swift scene flies/In motion of no less celerity/Than that of thought', and so on.

---

[1] Spurgeon, *op. cit.*, p. 243.

Within the play the suggestion of great speed and energy comes not only from this epic intent but from Henry V's qualities in the sources, his vigour, nimbleness in wrestling, leaping and running; 'at everie alarum he first in armor, and formost in ordering' (*supra*, IV, pp. 406–7). Both Holinshed and *Famous Victories* emphasize the speed of his preparations to invade France, and this is reflected in the play (I. 2. 300–8). In *Famous Victories* (*supra*, IV, p. 327) the French court is surprised by news of his landing. Shakespeare's French King tardily orders his defences to be repaired, 'For England his approaches makes as fierce/As waters to the sucking of a gulf' (II. 4). Henry's refusal to dally before Harfleur (*supra*, IV, p. 388) is transformed into the stirring exhortation to his troops (III. 1) with its ferocious imagery, quickly relieved by the comedy of Fluellen driving the reluctant Bardolph, Nym and Pistol, 'Up to the breach you dogs!' but soon followed by Henry's awful threats to the citizens of Harfleur (III. 3). Imagery of action rises to a climax at Agincourt and is used to develop the merest hints in the sources to illustrate the contrast between French and English attitudes, the King's piety, sense of responsibility, modesty, eloquence, righteous anger and humour.

The King's light-hearted gaiety and ability to talk with common men refer back no doubt to Prince Hal's *bonhomie* in the two previous plays, but his conversation with the soldiers may in part have been suggested by a sentence in Holinshed: 'Everie honest person was permitted to come to him, sitting at meale, where either secretlie or openlie to declare his mind' (*supra*, IV, p. 407).[1] The contrast in styles in IV. 1 indicates the difference between Henry as a man among men and as a monarch in private meditation. The wooing of Princess Katherine takes its bluffness from *Famous Victories*, where Henry says, 'I cannot do as these Countries do,/That spend halfe their time in woing' (1375–6). The hero whose understatement thrilled us in IV. 3 ('We are but warriors for the working day') now appears as the 'plain soldier', the blunt Englishman, with little French and no 'cunning in protesta-

[1] See *supra*, IV, pp. 362–3 for other possible sources. The style and imagery of this conversation, as of the others between common soldiers, are Shakespeare's own invention.

tion' but eloquent enough about essentials—'A speaker is but a prater: a rhyme is but a ballad . . . But a good heart, Kate, is the sun and the moon', etc.

Henry V, therefore, is not merely an epic drama. For Shakespeare Henry was not simply a hero in war, but a responsible ruler, an honest man and lover, the friend of his people. After *Henry IV* the common folk could not be omitted from an English history-play, and the new king's victories were not just personal triumphs but the work of many men from all parts of the British Isles. Hence the many-sidedness of the King and his environment made Shakespeare build on scattered hints in the sources and out of his own delighted inventiveness a great variety of styles, from the rhetorical–heroic to the most colloquial, dialectal and broken English. The total effect is inevitably less homogeneous than, say, that in *Romeo and Juliet*, but 'unity in diversity' is achieved by the suffusion of the whole play by auguries of success and involvement in the national struggle.

(c) *Romeo and Juliet* is an especially valuable illustration of Shakespeare's flexible use of one particular source. Brooke's pedestrian narrative-poem (*supra*, I, pp. 284–363) gave the main impulse, but the rich texture of the tragedy expresses Shakespeare's insight into all that the story could imply in passion and language. The imagery of the 1560s was replaced by that of the ornate 1590s, and the diversity of mood and figuration was given emotional unity by Shakespeare's sense of the joys and perils of young love in a hostile world ('These violent delights have violent ends'). The impression made on us is like 'an almost blinding flash of light, suddenly ignited, and as swiftly quenched'.[1] That Shakespeare imagined the story thus was doubtless because so much of the action in *Romeus and Julietta* takes place at night, and because Brooke scattered images of fire and light over his poem, e.g. in describing the family feud ('a kyndled sparke of grudge in flames flashed out theyr yre' (35–6)), the torches at the feast ('But brighter then the sunne, the waxen torches shone' (173)), Romeus's love ('this sodain kindled fyre' by which 'In Lethies floud his wonted flames were quenched and drenched deepe' (209, 214)), the candle in the tomb (2707, 2794). He wanders nightly by

[1] Spurgeon, *op. cit.*, p. 312. Cf. Clemen, *op. cit.*, Ch. VIII.

Juliet's house until 'anon the Moone did shine so bright/That she espyde her love' (468–9). Out of such poor soil sprang Shakespeare's rich poetry with its sun, moon, stars, lamps, torches, jewels and other founts of brightness in the gloom.

Brooke's frequent allusions to Fortune as controlling the lovers' lives doubtless influenced the treatment of accident in the plot, but Shakespeare almost ignored the dreary, fickle deity, emphasizing rather the few astrological references in the source,[1] so that the fated pair became 'star-cross'd lovers' with premonitions of misfortune.[2]

That *Romeo and Juliet* affords more instances than usual, outside the Histories, of Shakespeare's close reading of a source, R. A. Law has proved by a long list of lines or phrases echoing or approximating to *Romeus and Julietta*.[3] Such are: Friar to Romeus, 'Art thou (quoth he) a man? Thy shape saith so thou art' (1353; cf. III. 3. 108); the Apothecary, of his poison, 'This is the speeding gear' (2585; cf. Romeo, 'such soon-speeding gear', V. 1. 60). Often the dramatist condensed a thought to make it more concrete and telling (e.g. Juliet on prayer, 2325–30; cf. IV. 3. 2–5); or he would intensify the emotion by appropriate images (e.g. Juliet's fear of the tomb, 2363–400; cf. IV. 3. 31–59). There are also instances of expansion by the introduction of specific detail, as in the description of the Apothecary's shop (2567–70; cf. V. 1. 37–48) and Friar Lawrence's meditation on 'herbs, plants, stones, and their true qualities' (II. 3), which grew out of *Romeus* (565–74, 2108–11).

An unusual example of expansion occurs in IV. 5. 31ff. where Capulet, mourning his daughter's supposed death, emulates the father in Brooke (who 'ne had the powre his daughter to bewepe,/Ne yet to speake' (2453–4)) when he declares, 'Death . . . Ties up my tongue, and will not let me speak'; yet immediately, on the entrance of Paris and the Friar, he leads them in a formalized lament.

It seems likely that the holding of hands in Brooke (258–68),

---

[1] E.g. Romeo when banished: 'The time and place of byrth he fiersly did reprove,/He cryed out (with open mouth) against the starres above,/On Fortune else he raylde' (1327–44). Cf. III. 3. 118, 'Why rail'st thou on thy birth, the heaven, and earth?' But in Shakespeare Romeo has not really done this.

[2] Romeo at I. 4. 107–14, Juliet at II. 2. 116–22; III. 5. 54–7; IV. 3. 14–16.

[3] R. A. Law, 'On Shakespeare's Changes of his Source Material in *Romeo and Juliet*', *U. of Texas Studies in English*, no. 9, 1929, Austin, 86–102.

when Mercutio seized one of Juliet's hands in his own icy one and she took Romeo's 'tender palme' in her own 'tender hand' gave rise to the 'palmer-palm' conceits with which the lovers play (I. 5. 96ff.). More important, not only was the Nurse's character developed out of the wily creature in Brooke's poem, but also the special quality of her garrulity, and the idiom in which she expresses her nursery reminiscences, were found there in the germ:

A pretty babe (quod she), it was when it was yong,
Lord how it could full pretely have prated with it tong.
A thousand times and more I laid her on my lappe,
And clapt her on the buttocke soft and kist where I did clappe . . .
(653–6)

All this demonstrates how Shakespeare made the most of his material, however commonplace in expression, and used it as a springboard for his imagination. He did not need any poetic imagery in his source to give him an initial impetus. The story, a few characters, an ethical or sentimental motif, comic, piquant or tragic, was enough. This is true of *Twelfth Night* and *Much Ado*. But his voracious fancy fed on any little details of significance in the source; and what he could do with very little to start him off is illustrated by *Timon of Athens*.

(*d*) The primary images of *Timon* are based on three ethical motifs: misanthropy, profligate generosity, and ingratitude. The first was derived from the portrait-sketch in Plutarch with its brief anecdotes of Timon's rudeness, hatred of his fellows, and general misery. The images of generosity and ingratitude originated in Lucian's dialogue (or some derivative from it) in which Mercury asserts that Timon was ruined by 'his bounty, humanity, and compassion towards all in want . . . not realizing that he was giving his property to ravens and wolves', and that his false friends would quickly abandon him. Shakespeare's imagery, however, owes little verbally to Lucian. There are indeed few images in Timon's brief early speeches, for he is modest and impatient of ceremony (I. 2. 15–20). His clients, however, extol him in colourful terms: 'he outgoes/The very heart of kindness.' 'He pours it out.' 'Plutus the god of gold/ Is but his steward' (I. 1. 281–8).

Against the benevolent Timon is set the malevolent Apemantus, whose sour comments may owe something to Lyly's
Diogenes and to the depiction of cynic philosophers in other
dialogues of Lucian:[1] 'The strain of man's bred out/Into
baboon and monkey' (I. 1. 258–9); 'It grieves me to see so
many dip their meat/In one man's blood, and all the madness
is/He cheers them up too' (I. 2. 41–3). The 'dog' image, frequently used when he is about, is naturally associated with the
cynic (Greek, κύων, κυνὸς: dog) but it is also connected to images
of flattery and subservience, of tongues licking sweetness of
blood, as in many other plays (e.g. IV. 3. 201–28; 251–60;
528–31).

Once Timon understands how thoroughly he has been betrayed he takes over and intensifies the scurrilous language of
Apemantus, which was to some extent anticipated by Thersites
in *Troilus*. Timon also owes much to Lear in his rage and
despair. Lucian here gave little except the mood. Perhaps the
most striking instance of Shakespeare's expansion of a single
image from a source occurs in his repeated variations on
Timon's dying curse in Plutarch's first epitaph: 'a plague
consume you wicked wretches left!' (*supra*, VI, p. 252).

Plague combines with Lear-like imagery in the first com-
mination against Athens (IV. 1): 'Obedience fail in children . . .
Bankrupts hold fast! . . . Bound servants, steal! . . . Maid, to
thy master's bed; Thy mistress is o' the brothel! Son of sixteen/
Pluck the lin'd crutch from thy old limping sire,/With it beat
out his brains! . . . Plagues incident to men,/Your potent and
infectious fevers heap/On Athens, ripe for stroke . . . Itches,
blains,/Sow all the Athenian bosoms, and their crop/Be general
leprosy . . .'.

Apemantus also distorts Lear's storm-imagery when, mocking at Timon's self-exile ('A madman so long, now a fool'),
he accuses him of having enjoyed the flattery of poorer men:
'Call the creatures/Whose naked natures live in all the spite/

---

[1] Cf. the dialogue 'Philosophies going cheap', in which Diogenes describes his
way of life: 'You must cultivate a hideous accent, and speak in a grating voice,
just like a dog snarling . . . To hell with all modesty, decency and sense of
proportion. Be barefaced and completely unblushing. Pick out the most crowded
place you can find to be a recluse in, and refuse to have anything to do with either
friends or strangers' (*Satirical Sketches*, trans. P. Turner (Penguin), 1961, pp. 152–
3).

Of wreakful heaven, whose bare unhoused trunks/To the conflicting elements expos'd,/Answer mere nature; bid them flatter thee!' (IV. 3. 228–32).

In four great curses in IV. 3 Timon develops the 'plague' idea. First he calls on the sun to 'infect the air' and change the order of nature and society, and on the gold to make 'Wrong right, base noble, old young, coward valiant' (1–35). Next he elaborates on Plutarch's story that he affected Alcibiades because 'he shall do great mischiefe to the Athenians', urging the warrior, 'Be as a planetary plague . . . Make large confusion' (106–29). Then, addressing the courtesans, he sends them off to spread disease: 'Be whores still;/And he whose pious breath seeks to convert you,/Be strong in whore, allure him, burn him up . . . Consumptions sow/In hollow bones of man . . . plague all,/That your activity may defeat and quell/The source of all erection' (140–66). Finally he invokes the 'common mother', earth: 'Ensear thy fertile and conceptious womb,/Let it no more bring out ingrateful man!/ . . . Teem with new monsters . . .' (178–93).

In this scene of passionate invective two meanings of 'plague', as disease and as torment, are interwoven so as to call up images of universal disruption, the very elements infected, and a total collapse of human life through social disorder, moral breakdown, war and venereal disease, until nature herself is perverted and the race of man is destroyed. Incomplete as it is, *Timon* shows Shakespeare's ability to intensify the mood of his sources and to develop out of the smallest *données* a vast web of powerful imagery.

So far we have considered mainly plays in which Shakespeare accepted the plots and moods of his sources however much he modified them in detail. Sometimes, however, whether for theatrical, moral or other reasons, he rejected important aspects of major sources, and his changes vitally affected his poetic imagery (e.g. *Othello*, *Measure for Measure*). Two contrasting examples of the effects on imagery of a divergence from sources are provided by *As You Like It* and *King Lear*.

(e) In *As You Like It* the dramatist followed the plot of *Rosalynde* yet did not accept the highfalutin' pastoralism of Lodge but differentiated substantially between the characters he found in the romance, and added new ones so as to imply comment on different attitudes to country life popular at the time.[1]

Much of the play is an exercise in deflation, for the poet mocks at all these pastoral modes, gently and with appreciation of their several styles and imagery. He eschews Lodge's long-winded euphuism, reshaping the dialogue, eliminating the obvious antitheses and absurd similes, and increasing the humour with wit nearer to Castiglione than to Lyly. Always he treats the romance with delicate irony and pulls it down from airy flights to language such as men might use. The song 'Under the greenwood tree' is at once countered by Jaques's 'Here shall he see/Gross fools as he'. The impossible eloquence of Adam Spencer's speech when faint with hunger (*supra*, II, pp. 194–5) is cut down to three lines (II. 6. 1–3); and for the first meeting of Rosader and Rosalynd after the former has marred trees with his poems (II. 200) Shakespeare substitutes a lively exchange of wit in which Rosalind treats Orlando 'like a saucy lackey' and a love-doctor, replacing the banal classical references and unnatural natural history by a torrent of clever mockery ending with a rustic promise: 'and this way will I take upon me to wash your liver as clean as a sound sheep's heart, that there shall not be one spot of love in't' (III. 2. 298ff.). The sophisticated vein is thus crossed by a streak of dramatic fitness as if Rosalind were indeed a rural youth.

Moreover Shakespeare gives to the group created round Corin (Lodge's Coridon) naturalistic motives and speech flavoured with country-imagery found little in Lodge, whose old shepherd has naught but praise for the life of the fields: 'Oh, Mistresse, did you but live a while in their content, you would saye the Court were rather a place of sorrowe, than of solace.' He describes their humble happiness, 'and Mistres, I have so much Latin: *Satis est quod sufficit*' (*supra*, II, 188–9).

Shakespeare's Corin is contented, too, but he has no exaggerated ideas about the sweetness of the shepherd's lot, and he is no Latin scholar. He tells the facts about country life and toil, with down-to-earth imagery, in his oft-quoted conversation with Touchstone (II. 2), in which he says that shepherds' hands are greasy with 'handling our ewes', and 'often tarred

[1] See *supra*, II, pp. 150–7; K. Muir, *Shakespeare's Sources*, 1957, pp. 62–6.

over with the surgery of our sheep'. And Touchstone, while
pretending to damn Corin for ignorance of Court ways, mocks
at the courtiers' pretensions to refinement: 'Why, do not your
courtier's hands sweat? and is not the grease of a mutton as
wholesome as the sweat of a man? . . . civet is of a baser birth
than tar, the very uncleanly flux of a cat' (III. 2. 53–66).
Touchstone's casual wooing of Audrey, which shows him to be
'a material fool', continues the admixture of ordinary life and
language with those of romance, and he burlesques the euphuis-
tic similes in country style: 'As the ox hath his bow, sir, the
horse his curb, and the falcon her bells, so man hath his desires;
and as pigeons bill, so wedlock would be nibbling' (III. 4. 77–
80).

The contrast with the dismal wooing of Phoebe by Silvius
(Montanus) is highly effective; and whereas Lodge spins out
the Italianate pastoral game at great length (*supra*, II, pp.
180–91, 238–45), Shakespeare reduces its length and artificiality. Phoebe is made into a pert minx rather than a votary
of Diana, and she becomes a real person in her coy pretence
of not loving Ganymede after Rosalind has tried to bring her
down to earth by ridiculing her pretensions in plain business-
like terms:

> I see no more in you than in the ordinary
> Of nature's salework . . .
> You foolish shepherd, wherefore do you follow her
> Like foggy south puffing with wind and rain?
>   . . . 'Tis such fools as you
> That make the world full of ill-favour'd children . . .
> But, mistress, know yourself: down on your knees,
> And thank heaven, fasting, for a good man's love:
> For I must tell you friendly in your ear,
> Sell when you can: you are not for all markets. (III. 5. 35–62)

Later she tries again to cure Silvius by insisting on Phoebe's
ordinariness:

> I saw her hand: she has a leathern hand,
> A freestone-colour'd hand; I verily did think
> That her old gloves were on, but 'twas her hands:
> She has a housewife's hand. (IV. 3. 24–7)

Phoebe is no goddess, but suited to be a farmer's bride. The shepherds of Arden are not to be confused with Tasso's Silvia and Aminta.

(*f*) In *Lear*, as we have seen (*supra*, VII, pp. 277–308), Shakespeare used the older play as a starting-point for a very different handling of the Lear-story, turning sentimental tragi-comedy into darkest tragedy, changing not only the mood but also important features of the plot, and combining his principal story with material taken from the *Arcadia*. The play contains some imagery suggested by *King Leir*, but vastly more that is new, and also a considerable amount based on Sidney's tale of the blind King of Paphlagonia and his two sons, including some which is transferred from one plot to the other, proving how thoroughly the two main sources were fused in Shakespeare's imagination to produce a unified effect.

In recasting the old play Shakespeare remodelled most of the imagery, discarding obsolescent 'classical' passages and many laborious similes. He cut out the anachronistic references to Christian institutions such as Cordella's church-going, and her suitability to be 'a Parson's wife' or a nun. Yet, although he tried more than his predecessor to preserve the pagan setting of the chronicle-story, the atmosphere in court and castle is medieval (e.g. Edgar's challenge to Edmund), the discussions about astrology and providence echo those current in Elizabethan times, and the moral assumptions frequently invoked are entirely Christian.

Shakespeare takes over and develops the contrast between 'nature's sacred law', 'the course of nature's power' (which operates in Cordella's love for her father), and the unnatural conduct of Leir and his other two daughters. This is one of the most important sources of imagery.[1] Also assimilated are the ideas behind the daughters' contempt for his senility: 'His old doting, doltish, withered wit' (*Leir*, 784), 'old fool' (788), 'a child with age' (2598), etc.; so Goneril reminds him of his age (I. 4. 250), and Regan says, 'I pray you father, being weak, seem so!' (II. 4. 201). But though Lear soon pities himself as 'a

---

[1] *Supra*, VII, pp. 302–4. Maybe it was Gonorill's boast that for her father she would gladly 'leap into the Sea', or 'leap headlong to the ground' from 'the highest turret in all Brittany' (*Leir*, 240–7) which first reminded Shakespeare of Sidney's suicidal Paphlagonian king when seeking to strengthen his plot.

poor old man' (*ibid.*, 273), he is not 'the myrrour of mild patience' (*Leir*, 755) until Cordelia has rescued him. The pelican-image in *Leir*: 'I am as kind as is the Pelican/That kills itself, to save her young ones' lives' (513) is reversed when Lear raves about his 'pelican daughters' (III. 4. 72–3). The 'viperous' nature of the daughters in *Leir* may have suggested the serpent images of I. 4. 288; II. 4. 160, etc. but Shakespeare always shows a fertility in invective lacking in his source. Leir's hope that Ragan 'would be kinder [than Gonorill] and treat me fayre' (920) becomes 'Who, I am sure, is kind and comfortable: /When she shall hear this of thee, with her nails/She'll flay thy wolvish visage' (I. 5. 305–7), and this 'nails' image probably comes from *Leir* (1906), where Ragan, accusing Cordella of ill-treating her father, says that she would like to go to France 'And with these nayles scratch out her hatefull eyes'.

In both plays there is much emphasis on deprivation of clothing. The French King and Mumford go to Britain as poor pilgrims: Cordella, banished, will put off her 'costly robes' (614), and (soon) wear palmer's garb like her lover (697–701); later she would go barefoot and in sackcloth to regain her father's love (1080–3); Leir and Perillus exchange clothes with the seamen. This motif is even more important in *King Lear*, when Edgar becomes the half-naked Poor Tom and the King casts off his clothes; and the imagery associated with these actions is infinitely more violent, passionate, and morally symbolic.

Similarly, as has already been demonstrated, the repeated thunder-claps in *Leir*, Sc. 19 doubtless suggested Shakespeare's storm-imagery, used, not to show Heaven's disapproval of 'heinous acts', but to symbolize universal disruption and objectify the tempest in Lear's mind. Shakespeare makes no use of the dream in which Leir imagines himself stabbed by the bad daughters and then healed by Cordella 'with a boxe of Balsome in her hand' (1488–1500), but this may have suggested the medical passage in IV. 7, and Cordelia's 'Restoration, hang/Thy medicine on my lips . . .' (26–9).

The contrast between Perillus's protest against Jehovah for allowing murder and parricide 'without just revenge' and Leir's submissive trust in God's goodness (1649–58) was the germ of the overwhelming ironies of the last scenes in *King*

Lear. Shakespeare rejects the rhetoric by which (aided by the thunder) the two old men move the heart of the Messenger to fear of 'the hotest hole of hell' till he shows 'some sparke of grace' and spares their lives. Albany's outburst against evil in IV. 2. 39–67 is more fierce and foreboding; the atheist Edmund's last-minute goodwill is a futile whim; and although it seems as true of Cordelia as it was of Cordella that 'No worldly gifts, but grace from God on hye/Doth nourish vertue and true charity' (*Leir*, 1772–3), and although imagery of grace and forgiveness flows through the great reconciliation scene (IV. 7) and reappears briefly in V. 3, yet the presence of benevolent gods is not indicated in the final actions and imagery, whose agony and bitterness owe nothing to the older play.

The importance of the Edmund–Gloucester story from the *Arcadia* in intensifying the Lear story and darkening the tragedy has already been noted.[1] But as R. B. Heilman writes, 'In addition to carrying out its function in the plot and in the system of symbols, it also serves to focus a considerable body of language concerned with sight and blindness.'[2] Shakespeare was attracted to Sidney's story not only by the parallels in incident and character, but also because it gave an opportunity to interweave with the moral blindness of Lear an instance of moral blindness which became physical also. The horror of blinding, invoked years before in *King John*, IV. 1, but there avoided through the kindness of de Burgh, is in *Lear* III. 7 made an atrocious spectacle. As P. V. Kreider pointed out,[3] it casts its shadow before on to the companion-plot, so that images of eyes, seeing, blindness are frequent: 'this scene made such an impression on Shakespeare that it determined many of the most striking passages and many of the most striking figures of speech in the whole play'. A few instances of this transference may be given: Goneril protests that she loves her father 'Dearer than eyesight' (I. 1. 56). Lear bids Cordelia, 'Avoid my sight!' (124), and Kent, 'Out of my sight!' (157); to which Kent retorts, 'See better, Lear; and let me still

[1] *Supra*, VII, p. 284; F. Pyle, '*Twelfth Night, King Lear*, and *Arcadia*', MLR, xliii, 1948, pp. 449–55.
[2] R. B. Heilman, *This Great Stage: Image and Structure in King Lear*, 1948, p. 24.
[3] *Repetition in Shakespeare's Plays*, 1941, Ch. X, p. 205.

remain/The true blank of thine eye' (157–60). Cordelia lacks 'A still-soliciting eye' (232). At Goneril's court the rejected king cannot believe his senses: 'Where are his eyes? Either his notion weakens, his discernings/Are lethargied . . .' (I. 4. 225–8); and soon he is crying, unwittingly anticipating Gloucester's torture: 'Old fond eyes,/Beweep this cause again, I'll pluck ye out/And cast you with the waters that you lose/ To temper clay' (301–4). An anticipation of Regan's savage jest, 'Let him smell his way to Dover!' (III. 7. 93–4) occurs when the Fool declares that the nose is placed 'to keep one's eyes on either side's nose, that what a man cannot smell out, he may spy into' (I. 5. 23–25). He takes up the association of eyes and smell again in II. 4. 68–71: 'All that follow their noses are led by their eyes but blind men; and there's not a nose among twenty but can smell him that's stinking.' And he has just commented: 'Fathers that wear rags/Do make their children blind' (II. 4. 47–8). In III. 1. 8 Lear is suffering the 'eyeless rage' of the storm-winds, and the 'mad' Edgar raves about the 'foul fiend's' eyes, as does Lear: 'Look where he stands and glares! Wantest thou eyes at trial, madam?' (III. 6. 24–5).

Gloucester suggests the manner of his own blinding when he ascribes the desire of it to Regan, 'I would not see thy cruel nails/Pluck out his poor old eyes' (III. 7. 56–7). We need not pursue the imagery after the event through Gloucester's wanderings and Edgar's use of pretended observation to save his blind father from suicide, Lear's distressful jests upon the Earl's lack of sight, and the end when Lear dies, trying to see what is not there, a breath of life in his beloved daughter.

The eyesight imagery does not operate alone, but blends with imagery from the other senses, and it expands so as to refer to moral and mental vision, to uncertain knowledge of others and of oneself, to the politician's blindness and pretences, to the royal 'stare', the devil's glare, and the blind indifference of nature. In these and other ways Sidney's account of the blind Paphlagonian king and his sons affected the tone, characterization and poetic texture of the entire play.

(g) In *Macbeth* much of the recurrent imagery was the result of the dramatic fusion of several stories found in one major source—Holinshed's *Chronicles of Scotland*—with ancillary

material from other histories and Senecan tragedies (*supra*, VII).
The imagery is not verbally close to Holinshed's prose, but
springs naturally from his accounts of three murders and their
effects: Donwald's slaying of King Duff, Kenneth's of his
nephew, and Macbeth's of Duncan.

Preponderant themes in these stories were cruelty, ambition,
bloodshed and remorse. Macbeth's cruelty is stressed by most
authorities (*supra*, VII, p. 488ff.); Donwald was equally ruth-
less; and this pervades the atmosphere and imagery of the
play, from the Sergeant's grim recital of Macbeth's deeds as
'Bellona's bridegroom', and Lady Macbeth's prayer to be
filled 'top-full/Of direst cruelty' onwards.

The imagery of blood is naturally connected with the murders in the sources, and especially with that of King Duff,
his throat being cut, his bed 'all beraied with bloud' so that
next morning Donwald found 'cakes of bloud in the bed and on
the floore about the sides of it'. 'Beray' meant 'defile', 'sprinkle',
'bespatter'. Hence, maybe, the frequency with which blood in
the play is smeared, dripping, reeking.[1]

The imagery of darkness which plays so big a part was also
suggested by incidents in the sources. King Duff's witches
were raided 'about the middest of the night', and he was
murdered in the night as he slept; Kenneth heard the minatory
voice 'in the night-time'; Macbeth's witches appeared in the
day-time, but 'the same night after supper' Banquo's jest set
Macbeth thinking about ways of gaining the crown; Banquo
was killed at night and Fleance escaped 'by the benefite of the
darke night'. After Duff's murder six months passed without
sun, in gloom and tempests which ceased after his body was
found. Shakespeare developed this symbolism from the moment when Macbeth exclaimed, 'Stars, hide your fires!/Let not
light see my black and deep desires' (I. 4. 51–2), and set most
of the great scenes in the night: the murders of Duncan and
Banquo, the banquet, the visit to the Witches, the sleepwalking, and the final advance on the castle (V. 6, 7).

Images of sleep and restlessness derive ultimately from

---

[1] E.g. 'steel . . . smok'd with bloody execution' (I. 2. 18); 'reeking wounds' (40);
'make thick my blood' (I. 5. 43); 'smear/The sleepy grooms with blood' (II. 2.
50–1); 'on thy blade and dudgeon gouts of blood' (II. 1. 46); 'Steep'd in the
colours of their trade', etc. (II. 3. 116–17).

Kenneth's uneasy life after killing Malcolm, and from the
'prick of conscience' which afflicted Kenneth with fear of discovery, and Macbeth 'lest he should be served with the same
cup, as he had ministered to his predecessor'.[1] But how much
more Shakespeare made of these ideas!

Other frequent images in *Macbeth* relate to fertility (trees,
seeds, babes), clothes and horses. H. N. Paul's argument that
the fertility images were fostered by Leslie's genealogical tree
has already been mentioned (*supra*, VII, pp. 441, 517). The
origins of the 'babe' images no doubt include Macbeth's
childlessness, for Holinshed's first witch prophesied 'neither
shall he leave anie issue behind him to succeed in his place';
hence Macbeth's 'barren sceptre' and Macduff's 'He has no
children' (IV. 3. 216). Shakespeare's knowledge that Lady
Macbeth had a son by a former marriage is used to indicate
her Medea-like cruelty when she exclaims, 'I have given suck',
etc. (I. 7. 54–9). Macbeth's fear that

> Pity, like a naked new-born babe,
> Striding the blast, or heav'ns cherubin, hors'd
> Upon the sightless couriers of the air,
> Shall blow the horrid deed in every eye,
> That tears shall drown the wind. (I. 7. 21–5)

recognizes the existence in others of an emotion he scarcely
feels himself, as he makes the most defenceless creature the
messenger of retribution.[2] His lack of pity is shown in the
murder of Lady Macduff and her little boy.

The images of the baby and the cherubin in the clouds
probably come from Renaissance pictorial art and the Bible.[3]
It is possible, however, that Shakespeare was influenced in his
'babe' images and others by Marcus Gheeraerts's illustrations
in the 1577 edition of Holinshed (*supra*, VII, pp. 489, 491, 494,

---

[1] *Supra*, VII, pp. 439, 485, 498.

[2] Cf. Cleanth Brooks, 'The Naked Babe and the Cloak of Manliness', in *The Well-
Wrought Urn*, 1949. He wonders whether pity or fear of retribution was meant to
be uppermost in Macbeth's mind (pp. 27–8).

[3] Putti, with or without wings, were common in paintings, either as Cupids (often
with bows) or as cherubs. In Dürer's *Virgin adoring the Child* (1496) cherubs
swing censers and carry her crown. Parmigiano's *Adoration of the Shepherds* (1524–5)
has a winged baby flying over. Quarles, *Emblems* (1635), III. 12 has Justice (a
young girl) with fiery darts flying down from clouds against the sinful soul which
tries in vain to hide. The cherubim in *Ezekiel* i, are terrifying spirits, with wheels.

497). One of these shows Makdowald's children lying dead in the foreground while he is stabbing himself. The pitiless nature of Macbeth is mentioned on the same page of the chronicle.

If Shakespeare was indeed interested in the 1577 cuts, his use of horses and riding imagery may have been encouraged by the fact that Macbeth and Banquo are shown on horseback, watching the hanging of rebels, and meeting the 'weird sisters'. Also on the page where Banquo is first mentioned is a cut showing a man struck down from his horse by three others who are striking at him with their swords as he falls to the ground. This picture probably referred to the attack on the king's official at Lochaber, but it could easily be transferred to Banquo himself, and might explain why Shakespeare introduced a Third Murderer in III. 3. It is, moreover, noteworthy that in these illustrations Macbeth on horseback is depicted as a small, meagre man against a much larger Banquo. In the cut of the Coronation, used also for Malcolm's, there are ample, flowing robes. It is not impossible that the frequent clothes-imagery in Macbeth (with its implications of uneasy fit (I. 3. 144–6), 'borrow'd robes' (I. 3. 109), and the later 'now does he feel his title/Hang loose about him, like a giant's robe/Upon a dwarfish thief' (V. 2. 20–2)) owed something to the woodcuts, for Shakespeare was quick to take hints from anything he read or saw.

Much of the imagery in *The Winter's Tale*, like the incidents and characters, was developed out of the themes and feelings implicit in the sources. Here there is not, as in *Lear*, much transference of images from one source to material derived from another; rather sources containing similar motifs were so combined that the imagery derived from *Pandosto* led naturally at the climax into imagery proper to the Pygmalion-story.

As Professor Spurgeon pointed out[1] one major set of images is concerned with diseases and their cure. This springs, of course, from Pandosto's jealousy and lust, especially the former, which is briefly described in its growth (*supra*, pp. 158 ff) and effects ('choler', 'rage', 'fury') before the moment when realizing his 'brutish cruelty' he exclaims, 'Ah, jealousy! a hell to the mind, and a horror to the conscience, suppressing reason, and inciting rage; a worse passion than frenzy, a greater plague

[1] C. Spurgeon, *op. cit.*, Ch. XIV, p. 306; Clemen, *op. cit.*, pp. 196–8.

than madness' (*supra*, p. 172). Later, desiring Fawnia, he, 'contrary to his aged years', is 'pestered . . . with fresh affections and unfit fancies' (*supra*, p. 193). With his previous experience in analysing jealousy and lust, Shakespeare scarcely required these passages to make him regard them as diseases of mind and soul.

Disease-images are related to other groups connecting with what is natural and unnatural. Childhood is another main theme and source of imagery,[1] and this is associated with the likeness between friends and between children and parents. So Polixenes and Leontes enjoy reminiscences of their boyhood friendship (I. 2. 62–75) and delight in their own children's resemblance to them (I. 2. 154–65).[2] Mamillius's likeness to his father is not in Greene, but Shakespeare invents it to make Leontes's folly the more apparent when the boy's 'varying childishness' fails to 'cure in me/Thoughts that would thick my blood'. Paulina asserts the newborn baby's likeness, but in vain (II. 3. 95–107):

> And thou, good goddess Nature, which hast made it
> So like to him that got it, if thou hast
> The ordering of the mind too, 'mongst all colours
> No yellow in't.

Years later Leontes recognizes Florizel's likeness to Polixenes (V. 1. 123–8). The 'likeness-imagery' supports the pervasive notion of 'good goddess Nature' as breeding true, keeping the stock pure—an idea implicit in *Pandosto*, where Fawnia, reared as a poor shepherdess, is worthy of a prince since 'her natural disposition did bewray that she was born of some high parentage'. Perdita's revulsion against grafting and 'nature's bastards' in the symbolic conversation on gardening (IV. 3. 87–97) is beautifully expressed and true to her character, but cannot destroy the truth of Polixenes's reconciliation of art and nature in the power man 'shares/With great creating nature' to 'make conceive a bark of baser kind/By bud of nobler race', and this 'itself is nature'.

Thus Shakespeare, in reflecting on Greene's story, moved

[1] G. W. Knight, *The Crown of Life*, 1947, pp. 77–8.
[2] N. N. Holland, *The Shakespearean Imagination*, 1968, notes images of likeness, pp. 287–9.

away from simple romance and modulated from theme to theme within various natural relationships, from Nature keeping true to kind in human beings to Nature in plants and seasons, and man's power over Nature in agriculture and art. The pastoral occupations in the middle section of *Pandosto* inspired the poet's preoccupation (alongside his plot) with the cycle of growth and decay, so that the imagery teems with fertility, and although the play is not 'a ritual mystery' about Demeter and Persephone, its winter's tale of old folk parted and reconciled and young ones united proceeds for a time in an idyllic atmosphere of sunshine and fulfilment.

The frequent allusions to dress and clothing found in *Pandosto* are remodelled and augmented by Shakespeare to project this festive joy. Greene's Fawnia, shepherding her flock, defended her face from the sun 'with a garland made of boughs and flowers, which attire became her so gallantly as she seemed to be the goddess Flora herself' (*supra*, p. 176). This description is objectified in IV. 3, where Perdita appears 'most goddess-like prank'd up', and Florizel calls her 'no shepherdess, but Flora/Peering in April's front'. Her garlands appear again later. After she has given out her flowers Perdita modestly apologizes for her forwardness:

> Methinks I play as I have seen them do
> In Whitsun pastorals: sure this robe of mine
> Does change my disposition. (IV. 3. 133–5)

Referring to her singing and dancing, Florizel replies that everything she does

> Crowns what you are doing in the present deed,
> That all your acts are queens. (*ibid.*, 145–6)

Clearly Shakespeare for the moment was thinking of Perdita as a Summer Queen in the village folk-festivals held all over Britain in May or June until Puritan opposition diminished them.[1]

[1] See E. K. Chambers, *The Medieval Stage*, 1903, Ch. 8, for 'summer kings and queens' and May games. Whitsun processions with elaborate floral displays are still common in the north of England. At Tissington in Derbyshire the wells are dressed with flowers for Ascension Day.

On the other hand, Florizel, like Dorastus and Sabie's hero, must become a shepherd in order to woo the maid. Sabie's hero buys a farm; Dorastus disguises himself and fears that he is demeaning himself and keeping 'a right decorum—base desires and homely attires' (*supra*, p. 184). When he implies that he has stooped to become a shepherd Fawnia tells him flatly: 'this attire hath not made Dorastus a shepherd, but to seem like a shepherd' and she is very conscious of her 'base birth' and his 'high dignities'. Shakespeare omits any doubts Florizel may have overcome, but makes Perdita say:

> Your high self,
> The gracious mark o' the land, you have obscur'd
> With a swain's wearing. (IV. 3. 7–8)

And she fears the King:

> How would he look, to see his work, so noble,
> Vilely bound up? (*ibid.*, 21–2)

This leads Florizel (like Dorastus) to remind her of the many transformations of the gods. Polixenes's wrath soon brings home to them the difference between pretence and reality, but in the end the Summer Queen will become royal in fact, not only by marriage but as a princess in her own right. Shakespeare plays with great delicacy round the ironies of the situation.

Images relating to the power of man over nature through art and to the ideas of likeness and disguise are brought together in the dénouement when Hermione's 'statue' is described and brought to life by Paulina's 'magic'. Its likeness to her inspires such images as 'the life as lively mock'd as ever/Still sleep mock'd death' (V. 3. 19–20); 'O thus she stood . . . warm life/As now it coldly stands' (V. 3. 34–6). Many of these images closely resemble those in Ovid's story (*supra*, p. 233), especially the play on ideas of cold stone and warm flesh, stillness and movement, the eyes, lips, and blood.[1] It may well be that,

---

[1] Cf. Ovid: 'such a one as that yee would beleeve had lyfe, and that/Would moved bee . . ./So artificiall was the work' (269–71): (*WT* V. 2. 103–5; V. 3. 18–20); 'feeling if the woork that he had made/Were verie flesh or Ivorye still' (273–6); 'he felt her pulses beating' (316): (*WT* V. 3. 64–5); 'In her body streght a warmenesse seem'd to spred./He put his mouth againe to hers and on her brest did lay his hand' (306–8): (*WT* V. 3. 65–6).

having decided to replace Greene's ending by the Pygmalion-
story, the poet deliberately accentuated the art–nature relationships already implied in *Pandosto*. If so, here is another example
of a secondary source affecting the ideas and imagery educed
from the primary source.

(*h*) My last illustration of the influence of sources upon
imagery is *Cymbeline*, where many of the images are suggested
by an aspect of the source-material which the dramatist did
not otherwise use. Caroline Spurgeon noted 'the theme of
buying and selling, value and exchange, every kind of payment, debts, bills, and wages'.[1] She thought it possible that 'the
two central motives of the plot, the wager and the Roman
claim for tribute' might have suggested such images, but this
did not seem an adequate explanation; hence she surmised
that Shakespeare had the subject of money on his mind, as he
seems to have had house-building when writing *2 Henry IV*. We
need not postulate that, however, since a sufficient basis for
the unusual amount of commercial imagery in *Cymbeline* is to be
found in Boccaccio's *novella* and *Frederyke of Jennen*, in both of
which the prototype of Posthumus is a merchant.

In Boccaccio (*supra*, p. 51) Bernabò is one of several important Italian merchants staying in Paris on business; his tor-
mentor Ambrogiuolo is also a merchant. Bernabò boasts that
his wife is as good at writing and accountancy 'as if she were a
merchant herself'. When Ambrogiuolo theorizes about women's
frailty Bernabò says, 'I am not a philosopher but a merchant.'
The wager is made with articles signed in due form.

The second part of the tale also has a commercial setting,
for, at the trade fair in Acre, Zenovra (Sicurano) is sent to
guard the many 'Christian and Turkish merchants' gathered
there. Ambrogiuolo has come with a great stock of goods, and
seeing them on display Zenovra learns how he tricked her
husband and stole her purse, gown, ring, and girdle. She
persuades him to open a shop in Alexandria and advances him
money, then gets some Genoese merchants to bring her poverty-
stricken husband to Egypt, where the dénouement takes place.

In *Frederyke of Jennen* the word 'merchant' occurs about a
score of times in the first three pages (*supra*, pp. 63–5), and there
are many new details. The merchants order a splendid feast,

[1] *Op. cit.*, p. 296.

promising to repay the Host's outlay, and he buys 'the best
meat that he could get for money'. They sleep in a chamber
'rychly hanged with costly curtaynes', and they talk of the
money they give their wives. Then comes the wager, with the
Host as stake-holder, and Johan's desire to win the money is
mentioned more than once. He plays on the greed of the old
woman before offering her a big reward to get the chest into
Ambrosius's house. We are told the value of the purse, girdle,
and ring stolen by Johan. He takes his merchandise to Cairo
where Frederyke promises to buy the three tokens and gives
him 'livery for two or three men every day'. She gets Ambrosius
to Egypt by offering him 'a grete profyt'; and so on to the end
when Ambrosius and his wife are given 'many grete gyfts'.

The mercantile nature of both sources is obvious. In Shakespeare, imagery of this kind centres on scenes concerned with
Posthumus and Imogen, and with Iachimo, but is not confined to them. A few examples should suffice. At I. 1. 25
the 1st Gentleman praises Posthumus as if he were a folded
piece of silk in a mercer's shop:

> I do extend him, sir, within himself,
> Crush him together rather than unfold
> His measure duly.

The Queen says of Cymbeline: 'I never do him wrong,/But he
does buy my injuries to be friends,/Pays dear for my offences'
(I. 1. 104–6).

As Miss Spurgeon saw, 'The idea of the relative value of the
two lovers themselves is constantly in the minds of both', e.g.
Posthumus: 'As I my poor self did exchange for you,/To your
so infinite loss, so in our trifles/I still win of you' (I. 1. 118–20).
There are many metaphors 'of estimating (including measuring
and weighing), of equivalence and non-equivalence, of
jewellery, of debts, contracts and exchange'.[1] Posthumus,
declares Iachimo, 'must be weighed rather by her value than
his own' (I. 4. 15–16) and Guiderius loves Imogen (Fidelio):
'How much the quantity, the weight as much,/As I do love
my father' (IV. 2. 17–18). Cloten believes, ' 'Tis gold/Which
buys admittance' to a lady (II. 3. 68–77), but Imogen tells

[1] A. A. Stephenson, 'The Significance of *Cymbeline*', *Scrutiny*, x, 1942, 329–38.

him, 'You lay out too much pains/For purchasing but trouble' (89–90).

The wager is led up to by a long series of mercantile images when Posthumus and Iachimo compare Imogen to the diamond (I. 4. 72–103), and the wager itself is concluded in similar terms: 'if I come off' (says Iachimo) 'she your jewel, this your jewel, and my gold are yours' (153–8). Imogen, like her diamond ring, is priceless, 'unparagon'd', 'chaffless'. Posthumus boasts of her perfection but does not really understand it until he has lost her. Finally Iachimo calls her 'a shop of all the qualities that man/Loves woman for' (V. 5. 167–8).

In the repentance soliloquy in prison (V. 4. 13–28) imagery of debts and debtors—coinage (correct and lightweight), audit, cancelling bonds—is all-important. The gaoler, grim and gay at once, carries it on, calling death 'a heavy reckoning', bringing 'discharge' and 'acquittance' (V. 4. 157ff.).

It is significant that when the scene moves from court to the Welsh mountains the imagery shifts from financial dealings to creatures of the open air, birds, trees, and flowers. These have no place in Boccaccio or *Frederyke*, but enforce the contrast between country simplicities and the material preoccupations of the great world.

One concludes that, while changing the period and place of his main action and in making Posthumus the son of a famous warrior and Iachimo an Italian gentleman, Shakespeare's imagination was still immersed in the bourgeois commercial associations of his source-stories. Accordingly he treated not only the wager and its results but also the relations between his hero and heroine with a wealth of mercantile imagery which some modern readers might regard as more suited to middle-class comedy than to romance. But to Shakespeare commercial transactions were no despicable part of life, and imagery from finance and commerce could be evoked by the most delicate emotions (as in Sonnet 30). In *Cymbeline* he manipulates it, in context with other images, to give his romance of ancient Britain a footing in the modern world, and in such a way as not to diminish the 'value' of his heroine and her love-story, but rather to suggest the high worth, even by worldly standards, of spotless chastity, courage, repentance, and fidelity.

BIBLIOGRAPHY

I. General Critical Works
(This list includes some essays on particular plays which are relevant to the Conclusion of this volume)

BENTLEY, G. E. 'Shakespeare and the Blackfriars Theatre', *Sh Survey 1*, 1948, 38–50.

BISWAS, D. C. *Shakespeare's Treatment of his Sources in the Comedies*, Jadavpur, India, 1971.

BLACK, M. 'Repeated Situations in Shakespeare's Plays', in *Essays . . . in Honor of H. Craig*, ed. R. Hosley, 1963, pp. 247–59.

BRADBROOK, M. C. *The Growth and Structure of Elizabethan Comedy*, 1955.

BROCKBANK, J. P. 'Shakespeare and the Fashion of these Times', *Sh Survey 16*, 1963, 30–41.

BROOKS, H. F. 'Themes and Structure in *The Comedy of Errors*', in *Early Shakespeare*, 1961, pp. 55–71.

BROWN, J. R. *Shakespeare and his Comedies*, 1957.

CLEMEN, W. *The Development of Shakespeare's Imagery*, 1951.

CLEMEN, W. *Schein und Sein bei Shakespeare*, Munich, 1959.

COGHILL, N. *Shakespeare's Professional Skills*, 1964.

DAICHES, D. 'Image and Meaning in *Antony and Cleopatra*', *E. Studies*, xliii, 1962, 343–58.

DRAPER, J. W. *The Tempo-Patterns of Shakespeare's Plays*, Heidelberg, 1957.

DUNLOP, J. C. *The History of Fiction*, 3 vols, 1814, 1816; 1 vol., 1845.

EDWARDS, P. 'Shakespeare's Romances, 1910–57', *Sh Survey 11*, 1958, 1–18.

EDWARDS, P. *Shakespeare and the Confines of Art*, 1968.

EVANS, B. *Shakespeare's Comedies*, 1960.

EWBANK, I.-S. 'More Pregnant than Words', *Sh Survey 24*, 1971, 13–18.

FISCH, H. *Hamlet and the Word*, New York, 1971.

FROST, W. 'Shakespeare's Rituals and the Opening of *King Lear*', *Hudson Rev.*, x, 1958, 577–85.

FRYE, N. *A Natural Perspective: The Development of Shakespearean Comedy and Romance*, New York, 1965.

FRYE, R. M. *Shakespeare and Christian Doctrine*, Princeton, 1963.

GESNER, C. *Shakespeare and Greek Romance*, 1970.

HENN, T. R. *The Harvest of Tragedy*, 1956.

HOLLAND, N. N. *The Shakespearean Imagination*, Bloomington, 1968.

HOLLOWAY, J. *The Story of the Night*, 1961.

JACQUOT, J. ed. *Les Fêtes de la Renaissance*, 2 vols, Paris, 1956.

JENKINS, H. *The Catastrophe in Shakespearian Tragedy*, Edinburgh, 1969.

KANTAK, V. Y. 'The Actor Image in *Macbeth*', *Sh Survey 16*, 1963, 42–52.

KNIGHT, G. W. *The Crown of Life*, 1947.

KNIGHTS, L. C. *Some Shakespearean Themes*, 1959.

KREIDER, P. V. *Repetition in Shakespeare's Plays*, Princeton, 1941.

LANGBAUM, R. 'Character *versus* Action in Shakespeare', *ShQ*, viii, 1957, 57–69.

LEECH, C. 'The Structure of the Last Plays', *Sh Survey 11*, 1958, 19–30.

LERNER, L. *Shakespeare's Comedies: An Anthology of Modern Criticism*, 1967.

MCCLOSKEY, J. C. 'The Emotive Use of Animal Imagery in *King Lear*', *ShQ*, xiii, 1962, 321–5.

MACLEAN, H. 'Disguise in *King Lear*', *ShQ*, xi, 1960, 49–54.

MILWARD, P. *Shakespeare's Religious Background*, 1973.

MINCOFF, M. 'What Shakespeare did to *Rosalynd*', *ShJb*, xcvi, 1960, 34–46.

MUIR, K. 'Shakespeare and the Tragic Pattern', *Proc. Brit. Acad.*, 1959.

MUIR, K. *Last Periods of Shakespeare, Racine, Ibsen*, Detroit, 1961.

MUIR, K. 'Shakespeare the Professional', *Sh Survey 24*, 1971, 37–46.

O'BRIEN, G. W. *Renaissance Poetics and the Problem of Power*, Chicago, 1956.

PETTET, E. C. *Shakespeare and the Romance Tradition*, 1949.

PRICE, H. T. *Construction in Shakespeare*, Michigan, 1951.

PROUTY, C. T. 'Observations on Shakespeare's Sources', *ShJb*, xcvi, 1960, 64–77.

RIGHTER, A. *Shakespeare and the Idea of the Play*, 1962.

RISTINE, H. *English Tragicomedy*, 1910.

SEHRT, E. T. *Der dramatische Auftakt in der elisabethanischen Tragödie*, Göttingen, 1960.

SIEGEL, P. N. *Shakespeare in His Time and Ours*, Notre Dame, 1968.

SIMPSON, P. *Studies in Elizabethan Drama*, 1955.

SPURGEON, C. F. E. *Shakespeare's Imagery and What it Tells us*, Cambridge, 1935.

STAMM, R. 'Elizabethan Stage-Production and the Transmutation of Source-Material', *Sh Survey 12*, 1959, 64–70.

STAUFFER, D. F. *Shakespeare's World of Images*, New York, 1949.

STYAN, J. L. *Shakespeare's Stagecraft*, Cambridge, 1967.

THORNDIKE, A. H. *The Influence of Beaumont and Fletcher on Shakespeare*, New York, 1901.

TILLYARD, E. M. W. *Shakespeare's Last Plays*, 1938.

VICKERS, B. *The Artistry of Shakespeare's Prose*, 1968.

VYVYAN, J. *Shakespeare and Platonic Beauty*, 1961.

WELSFORD, E. *The Court Masque*, Cambridge, 1927.

WEST, R. H. *The Invisible World*, Athens, Ga., 1939.

WHITAKER, V. K. 'Shakespeare's Use of his Sources', *PhilQ*, xx, 1941, 377–88.

WHITAKER, V. K. *Shakespeare's Use of Learning*, San Marino, 1953.

WHITER, W. *A Specimen of a Commentary on Shakespeare*, ed. A. Over and M. Bell, 1967.

WICKHAM, G. 'From Tragedy to Tragi-Comedy: *King Lear* as Prologue', *Sh Survey 26*, 1973, 33–48.

WILSON, F. P. *Elizabethan and Jacobean*, 1945.

WOLFF, S. L. *The Greek Romances in Elizabethan Prose Fiction*, New York, 1912.

II. Editions and Criticism of Individual Plays

Cymbeline

1. Editions of the Play

F 1. 1623. Modern edns: C. M. Ingelby, 1866; A. J. Wyatt, *Warwick*, 1897; E. Dowden, *Arden*, 1903; H. H. Furness, *Var.*, 1913; S. B. Hemingway, *Yale*, 1924; J. M. Nosworthy, *New Arden*, 1955; J. C. Maxwell, *Camb.*, 1960.

2. Sources and Analogues
(a) *Editions*

[Anon.] *A most pleasant Comedie of Mucedorus . . .*, 1598, 1610, 1611, 1613. Modern edns: J. P. Collier, 1824; N. Delius, 1874; *Dodsley's Old Plays*, ed. W. C. Hazlitt, 1874–6, vol. vii; K. Warnke and L. Proescholdt, Halle, 1878; C. F. T. Brooke, *Sh. Apocrypha*, 1908.

[Anon.] *Frederyke of Jennen*, Antwerp, 1518? Eng. trans. 1518, 1560. Modern edns: J. Raith, Leipzig, 1936; J. M. Nosworthy, *New Arden*, App. A.

[Anon.] *The Rare Triumphes of Love and Fortune*, 1589. Modern edns: J. P. Collier, in *Five Old Plays*, 1851; Hazlitt's *Dodsley*, 1874, vi; W. W. Greg, *MalSoc*, 1930.

BOCCACCIO, G. *Il Decamerone* [Venice], 1471, etc. French trans. L. du Premierfaict, Paris, 1521; A. le Macon, Paris, 1545, etc. Eng. trans. [J. Florio] 1620, 2 vols. Modern edn: E. Hutton (*Tudor Translations*), 4 vols, 1909.

FENTON, G. *Certaine Tragicall Discourses of Bandello*, 1567. Modern edn: R. L. Douglas, 1898, 1924.

FORDE, E. *Parismus, The Renowmed Prince of Bohemia*, 2 vols, 1598–9, 1608–9, etc.

HOLINSHED, R. *The first volume of Chronicles*, 1587 edn. Modern edns: 1808; W. G. Boswell-Stone, *Sh's Holinshed*, 1896, 1907; A. and J. A. Nicoll, 1927; R. Hosley, New York, 1968.

RUEDA, L. DE. *Las Primeras dos elegantes . . . Comedias . . .*, ed. Juan Timoneda, Valencia, 1567. Modern edn: *Obras*, Madrid, 1908.

SIDNEY, SIR P. *The Countesse of Pembrokes Arcadia*, 1590. Modern edns: Facsimile, O. Sommer, 1891; A. Feuillerat, 1922.

TASSO, T. *Gerusalemme Liberata*, Parma, 1581, 1584, etc. Trans. Edward Fairfax, 1600, 1624, etc. Modern edns: S. W. Singer, 1818, 1853; R. Weiss, 1962.

(b) *Critical studies of sources, etc.*

BARKER, H. G. *Prefaces to Shakespeare*, Ser. 2, 1929.

BOODLE, R. W. 'The Original of *Cymbeline*', *N&Q*, 19 Nov. 1887.

BOODLE, R. W. 'Die Quellen zu *Cymbeline* und eventuell zum *Sturm*', *ShJb*, xxiii, 1888, 344–7.

BRIE, F. 'Eine neue Quelle zum *Cymbeline*', *ShJb*, xliv, 1908, 167–70.

BROCKBANK, J. P. 'History and Histrionics in *Cymbeline*', *Sh Survey 11*, 1958, 42–9.

CAMDEN, C. 'The Elizabethan Imogen', *Rice Inst. Pamph.*, 38, 1951.

ELZE, K. 'Last Notes on *Mucedorus*', *EngStud*, vi, 1883.

HOENIGER, F. D. 'Two Notes on *Cymbeline*', *ShQ*, viii, 1957, 132–3.

KOENIG, V. F. 'A New Perspective on the Wager Cycle', *MPhil*, xliv, 1946/7, 76–83.

LAWRENCE, W. W. 'The Wager in *Cymbeline*', *PMLA*, xxxv, 1920, 391–431.

LEONHARDT, B. 'Über die Quellen *Cymbelines*', *Anglia*, vi, 1883, 1–45.

LEVY, S. 'Eine neue Quelle zu *Cymbeline*', *Anglia*, vii, 1884, 120–7; 1885, 197–200.

MEYERSTEIN, E. H. W. 'The Vision in *Cymbeline*', *TLS*, 15 June 1922, 396.

MOFFET, R. '*Cymbeline* and the Nativity', *ShQ*, xiii, 1962, 207–18.

MONMERQUÉ, L. L. N. and MICHEL, F. *Théâtre français au moyen âge*, Paris, 1842.

OHLE, R. *Shakespeares Cymbeline und seine romanischen Vorläufer*, Leipzig, 1890.

PARIS, G. *La Littérature française au moyen âge*, Paris, 1888.

PEROTT, J. DE. 'Der Prinzenraub aus Rache', *ShJb*, liii, 1917.

RAITH, J. *Die Historie von den vier Kaufleuten*, Leipzig, 1936.

REICH, H. 'Zur Quelle des *Cymbeline*', *ShJb*, xli, 1905, 177–81.

SHAW, G. B. *Cymbeline Refinished*, 1938.

SIMROCK, K. *Die Quellen des Shakespeare*, 1831, trans. 1850.

STEPHENSON, A. A. 'The Significance of *Cymbeline*', *Scrutiny*, x, 1942, 329–38.

THRALL, W. F. '*Cymbeline*, Boccaccio and the Wager Story in England', *SPhil*, xxviii, 1931, 639–51.

WILSON, H. S. '*Philaster* and *Cymbeline*', in *Eng. Inst. Essays, 1951*, New York, 1952.

The Winter's Tale

1. Editions of the Play

F 1. 1623. Modern edns: H. H. Furness, *Var.*, Philadelphia, 1898; F. W. Moorman, *Arden*, 1912; F. E. Pierce, *Yale*, 1918; A. T. Quiller-Couch and J. D. Wilson, *Camb*, 1931; J. H. P. Pafford, *New Arden*, 1963; E. Schanzer, *New Penguin*, 1969.

2. Sources and Analogues

[Anon.] *A most pleasant Comedie of Mucedorus* . . . *as it was acted before the king's Majestie at Whitehall on Shrove-Sunday night*, 1598, 1610 [1611], 1613. Modern edns: See under *Cymbeline*, 2.

[Anon.] *The History of the Tryall of Chevalry* . . . 1605. Modern edns: A. H. Bullen, in *Old English Plays*, iii, 1884; *TFT*, ed. J. S. Farmer, 1912.

[Anon.] *The Thracian Wonder*, 1661. Modern edns: C. W. Dilke, 1815; collections of Webster, e.g. A. Dyce, 1830; W. B. Hazlitt, 1857; A. H. Bullen, 1881.

CINTHIO, G.-B. GIRALDI. *Selene*, Venice, 1583; in *Le Tragedie*, 1583.

DAY, J. *Humour out of Breath*, 1608. Modern edns: J. O. Halliwell, 1860; A. Symons, 1881.

[FORDE, EMMANUEL]. *Parismenos. The Second Part of the* . . . *pleasant Hystorie of Parismus, the renowmed Prince of Bohemia*, 1599, 1609, etc.

GREENE, R. *Pandosto. The Triumph of Time*, 1588, 1592, 1595, 1607. Modern edns: *Works*, ed. A. B. Grosart, 1881–6; Collier-Hazlitt, 1875; P. G. Thomas, 1907; in *New Arden*, ed. J. H. P. Pafford, 1963.

GREENE, R. *The Second and last Part of Conny-catching . . . by R.G.*, 1592; *The Third Part of Conny-catching* . . . 1592. Modern edns: *Works*, ed. A. B. Grosart, 1881–6; G. B. Harrison, 1923.

LONGUS. *Daphnis and Chloe*. French trans. J. Amyot, 1559; Eng. trans.

Angell Day, 1587 (modern edn: H. Jacobs, 1890); P. Turner, 1956.

MARGUERITE OF NAVARRE. *Heptameron*, 1558. Trans. R. Codrington, 1654; W. H. Kelly, 1846; A. Machen, 1886; J. S. Chartres, 1894.

OVIDIUS NASO, P. *Metamorphoses*, 1472, etc. Eng. trans. A. Golding, 1567, etc. Modern edn: W. H. D. Rouse, *Shakespeare's Ovid*, 1904, 1961.

PETTIE, G. *A Petite Pallace of Pettie his Pleasures*, 1576, 1608, etc. Modern edns: Sir I. Gollancz, 2 vols, 1908; H. Miles, 4 vols, 1930.

SABIE, F. *The Fisherman's Tale*, 1595; *Flora's Fortune*, 1595.

SIDNEY, SIR P. *The Countesse of Pembrokes Arcadia*, 1590. Modern edns: Facs. O. Sommer, 1891; A. Feuillerat, 1922.

SILVA, F. DE. *Amadis de Gaule*, Bk x, 1532, etc. French trans. *Le neufiesme Livre d'Amadis de Gaule, auquel sont continuez les gestes de Dom Florisel de Niquée . . . par C. Colet Champenois*, Paris, 1563; Lyon, 1577.

SILVA, F. DE. *Amadis*, Bk vii: *Lisuarte de Grecia*, 1542.

3. Critical Studies

BARBER, C. L. '*The Winter's Tale* and Jacobean Society', in *Shakespeare in a Changing World*, ed. A. Kettle, 1964.

BETHELL, S. L. *The Winter's Tale: A Study*, 1947.

BIGGINS, D. 'Exit Pursued by a Beare', *ShQ*, xiii, 1962, 3–14.

BONJOUR, A. 'The Final Scene of *The Winter's Tale*', *E Studies*, xxxiii, 1952.

BRYANT, J. H. '*The Winter's Tale* and the Pastoral Tradition', *ShQ*, xiv, 1963, 411–17.

COGHILL, N. 'Six Points of Stagecraft in *The Winter's Tale*', *Sh Survey* 2, 1958, 31–41.

DUNCAN-JONES, E. E. 'Hermione in Ovid and Shakespeare', *N&Q*, n.s. 13, 1966, 138–9.

ELZE, K. *Essays on Shakespeare*, 1874, pp. 284–9.

HARTWIG, J. 'The tragicomic Perspective of *The Winter's Tale*', *ELH*, xxxvii, 1970, 12–36.

HASTINGS, W. T. 'The Ancestry of Autolycus', *Sh. Ass. Bull.*, xv, 1940.

HATCHER, O. L. 'Sources and Authorship of *The Thracian Wonder*', *MLN*, xxiii, 1908.

HOENIGER, F. D. 'The Meaning of *The Winter's Tale*', *Toronto U.Q.* xx, 1950, 21–6.

HONIGMANN, E. A. J. 'Secondary Sources of *The Winter's Tale*', *PhilQ*, xxxiv, 1955, 27–38.

412   *Bibliography*

HOSLEY, R. ed. Jonson's *Oberon* in *A Book of Masques*, ed. T. J. B. Spencer, Cambridge, 1967.

KNIGHT, G. W. *Myth and Miracle*, 1929.

KOEPPEL, E. 'Ein Vorbild für Shakespeares Statue der Hermione', *Archiv*, 97, 1896, 329–32.

LANCASTER, H. C. 'Hermione's Statue', *SPhil*, xxix, 1932.

LAWLOR, J. L. '*Pandosto* and the Nature of Dramatic Romance', *PhilQ*, xli, 1962, 96–113.

MUIR, K. ed. *The Winter's Tale: A Casebook*, 1968.

PEROTT, J. DE. 'Die Hirtendichtung des Feliciano de Silva und Shakespeares Wintermärchen', *Archiv*, 30, 1913, 53–6.

PYLE, FITZROY. *The Winter's Tale: A Commentary on the Structure*, 1969.

SCHANZER, E. 'The Structural Pattern of The Winter's Tale', *Review of English Literature*, April 1964.

SCHARF, SIR G. *Notes on the Authentic Portraits of Mary, Queen of Scots*, ed. L. Cust, 1903.

STUDTING, R. 'Spectacle and Masque in *The Winter's Tale*', *English Misc.*, xxi, 1970, 55–80.

TAYLOR, G. C. 'Hermione's Statue Again', *Sh. Ass. Bull.*, xiii, 1938.

THOMAS, SIR H. *Shakespeare and Spain*, Oxford, 1922.

THOMAS, SIR H. *Spanish and Portuguese Romances of Chivalry*, Cambridge, 1920.

VASARI, G. *Le Vite de' più eccellenti . . . pittori et scultori italiani*, 3 pts, Firenze, 1550, 1568, etc. Trans. Mrs J. Foster, 6 vols, 1850–2; A. B. Hinds, 1900, 1927; G. du C. de Vere, 10 vols, 1912–15.

WHINNEY, M. *Sculpture in England, 1530–1830*, 1964.

WICKHAM, G. 'Shakespeare's Investiture Play', *TLS*, 18 Dec. 1969, 1456.

WICKHAM, G. *Shakespeare's Dramatic Heritage*, 1969, pp. 249–65.

WILSON, E. C. *Prince Henry and English Literature*, Ithaca, New York, 1946.

The Tempest

1. Editions of the Play

F 1. 1623. Modern edns: H. H. Furness, *Var.*, 1892; F. S. Boas, *Warwick*, 1897; M. Luce, *Arden*, 1902, 1926; C. B. Tinker, *Yale*, 1918; A. T. Quiller-Couch and J. D. Wilson, *Camb*, 1921; F. Kermode, *New Arden*, 1954, 1961; A. Righter, *New Penguin*, 1968.

2. Sources and Analogues

(a) *Travel books*

[Anon.] *A True and Sincere Declaration of the purpose and ends of the Plantation begun in Virginia*, 1610.

[Anon.] *A true Declaration of the estate of the Colonie in Virginia*, ... 1610. Modern edn in *Tracts and Pamphlets*, ed. P. Force, vol. iii, Washington, 1844.

[Anon.] *Virginia's Verger*, 1625.

EDEN, R. trans. *A treatyse of the newe India*, 1553.

EDEN, R. *Decades of the new worlde, by Pietro Martirio*, 1555. Modern edn: E. Arber, *The First Three English Books on America*, Birmingham, 1895.

EDEN, R. *The History of the Travayle in the West and East Indies*, 1577.

HAKLUYT, R. *The Principal Navigations, Voyages, Traffiques, and Discoveries of the English Nation*, 3 vols, 1598–1600. Modern edns: E. Golsmid, 16 vols, Edinburgh, 1885–90; Hakluyt Soc. edn, 12 vols, Glasgow, 1903–5; Everyman's Lib., 8 vols, 1907; J. Masefield, 10 vols, 1927.

HARIOT, T. *A briefe and true report of the new found land of Virginia*, 1588, 1590. In Hakluyt (1598), vol. iii; 1927 edn vol. vi. Facs. (1588), R. G. Adams, Ann Arbor, 1931; Facs. (1590), Quaritch, 1893.

JOURDAIN, S. *A Discovery of the Bermudas, otherwise called the Ile of Divels*, 1610. In Hakluyt (1610) and modern edns. Facs. J. Q. Adams, New York, 1940.

PIGAFETTA, A. *The First Voyage round the World by Magellan.* Trans. Lord Stanley of Alderley, Hakluyt Soc., 52, 1874.

RALEIGH, SIR W. *The Discoverie of Guiana, 1596*. In Hakluyt (1598), vol. iii. Modern edns: R. H. Schomburgk, Hakluyt Soc. 3, 1848; W. H. D. Rouse, n.d.; Hakluyt, 1927 edn vol. vii.

SMITH, J. *A True Relation of such Occurrences . . . as hath passed in Virginia since the first planting of that Colony*, 1608. Modern edn: C. Deane, Boston, Mass., 1866.

SMITH, J. *The Generall Historie of Virginia, New England, and the Summer Isles*, 1624. Modern edn: Book III ed. W. H. D. Rouse, 1904.

SMITH, J. *Works (1608–31)*, ed. E. Arber, 1878, includes both of the above.

STRACHEY, W. *A True Reportory of the Wracke and Redemption of Sir Thomas Gates, Knight*, in *Purchas his Pilgrimes*, 1625, Pt II, Bk x. Modern edn: *Purchas*, Glasgow, 1906, xix, 5–72.

(b) *Romances*

ESLAVA, A. *Noches de Invierno*, 1609. Modern edn: A. Gonzalez Palencia, Madrid, 1942.

LONGUS. *Daphnis and Chloe* (2nd–3rd cent. A.D.). See under *Winter's Tale*.

ORTUÑEZ DE CALAHORRA. *Espejo de Principes y Caballeros*, 1562, 1583, etc. English trans.: *The first part of the Mirrour of Knighthood*, by M. T[yler], 1578, 1583, etc. *The third part of the First Book*, by R. P[arry], 1586?, 1599.

WATSON, H. trans. *Valentine and Orson*, ed. A. Dickson, *EETS*, orig. ser. 204, 1937.

(c) *Plays, poems, etc.*

[Anon.] *A Most pleasant Comedie of Mucedorus*, 1598, 1610 ('Amplified'), 1613, etc. Modern edns: J. P. Collier, 1824, 1878; N. Delius, 1874; Hazlitt's *Dodsley*, vii, 1874; Warnke-Proescholdt, Halle, 1878; C. F. T. Brooke, Oxford, 1908.

[Anon.] *The Rare Triumphes of Love and Fortune, c.* 1582. Modern edns: J. P. Collier, *Five Old Plays*, 1851; Hazlitt's *Dodsley*, vi, 1875; W. W. Greg, *MalSoc*, 1930.

AYRER, J. *Die Schöne Sidea* in his *Opus Theatricum*, 1618. Modern edn and Eng. trans. in A. Cohn, *Shakespeare in Germany*, 1865. Trans. in *Var.*, 1892.

DANIEL, S. *The Vision of the Twelve Goddesses*, 1604. Modern edn: J. Rees in *A Book of Masques*, ed. T. J. B. Spencer, Cambridge, 1967.

ERASMUS, D. *Familiarium colloquiorum opus*, 1516, 1571. Trans., W. B[urton], *Seven Dialogues both pithie and profitable*, 1606; R. L'Estrange, 1689.

GREENE, R. *Friar Bacon and Friar Bungay*, 1594. Modern edns: A. Dyce, *Dramatic Works*, 1831, 1861; A. B. Grosart, *Complete Works*, 1881–6; J. C. Collins, *Plays and Poems*, 1905; T. H. Dickinson, 1909; W. W. Greg, *MalSoc*, 1926; J. A. Lavin, 1969.

JONSON, B. *Workes*, 1616. Modern edn: C. H. Herford and P. Simpson, 11 vols, Oxford, 1925–52. Masques in vol. vii.

MONTAIGNE, M. DE. *Essais*, Bordeaux, 1580; 5th edn Paris, 1588. Eng. trans. J. Florio, *The Essayes or Morall, Politike, and Militarie Discourses* . . . 1603. Modern edns: G. Saintsbury, 3 vols, 1892; A. R. Waller, 6 vols, 1897, 1910; G. B. Ives, 3 vols, Cambridge, Mass., 1902–4; C. Whibley, 1905, etc.

MUNDAY, A. *John a Kent and John a Cumber*, 1594. Edns: J. P. Collier, 1851; J. S. Farmer, *TFT*, 1912; M. St C. Byrne, *MalSoc*, 1923.

NERI, F. *Scenari delle Maschere in Arcadia*, 1913.

OVID. *The XV Bookes of P. Ovidius Naso, entytuled Metamorphosis translated oute of Latin into English meeter, by Arthur Golding*, 1567, etc. Modern edn: W. H. D. Rouse, *Shakespeare's Ovid*, 1904, 1961.

SPENSER, E. *The Faerie Queene*, 1596. Modern edn: J. C. Smith, 2 vols, Oxford, 1909, 1961.

Bibliography

3. Historical Background
BROWN, A. *The Genesis of the United States of America*, 1890.
DOYLE, J. A. *The English in America*, 1881–2.
HOTSON, L. *I, William Shakespeare*, 1937.
OSBORNE, F. *The Secret History of the Court of James I* [1658] Modern edn: 1811.
ROWSE, A. L. *Shakespeare's Southampton, Patron of Virginia*, 1965.
SMITH, BRADFORD. *Captain John Smith, His Life and Legend*, 1953.
STITH, W. *The History of the First Discovery and Settlement of Virginia*, Williamsburg, 1747, 1865.
STOPES, C. C. *The Life of Henry, Third Earl of Southampton*, Cambridge, 1922.
THOMAS, W. *The History of Italy*, 1549. Modern edn: Ithaca, New York, 1963.
WILKINSON, H. C. *The Adventurers of Bermuda*, 1933.
WILSON, A. *The History of Great Britain*, 1653.

4. Critical Studies of Sources, etc.
BECKER, G. 'Zur Quellenfrage von Shakespeares *Sturm*', *ShJb*, xliii, 1907, 155–68 (includes trans. from Eslava).
BERNHEIMER, R. *Wild Men in the Middle Ages*, Harvard, 1952.
BOODLE, R. W. 'The Original of *Cymbeline*, and possibly of *The Tempest*', *N&Q*, 19 Nov. 1887.
BROCKBANK, P. 'The Tempest: Conventions of Art and Empire', in *Later Shakespeare*, Stratford Studies, 8, 1966.
CARO, J. 'Die historischen Elemente in Shakespeares *Sturm* und *Wintermärchen*', *EngStud*, ii, 1879, 141–85.
CAWLEY, R. R. 'Shakspere's Use of the Voyagers', *PMLA*, xli, 1926, 688–726.
CAWLEY, R. R. *The Voyagers and Elizabethan Drama*, 1938.
CAWLEY, R. R. *Unpathed Waters*, Princeton U.P., 1940.
CHAMBERS, E. K. 'The Integrity of *The Tempest*', *RES*, i, 1925, 129–50; reprinted in *Shakespearean Gleanings*, 1944.
CROCIONI, G. 'P. M. Scandora', *La Bibliofilia*, Nov. 1909–Feb. 1910.
CURRY, W. C. *Shakespeare's Philosophical Patterns*, Baton Rouge, 1937.
DAVIDSON, F. 'The Tempest: An Interpretation', *JEGP*, lxii, 1963, 501–17.
FOUQUET, K. *Jakob Ayrers 'Sidea', Shakespeares 'Tempest' und das Märchen*, Marburg, 1929.
GAYLEY, C. M. *Shakespeare and the Founders of Liberty in America*, New York, 1917.
GESNER, C. '*The Tempest* as Pastoral Romance', *ShQ*, x, 1959, 531–9.
GILBERT, A. H. '*The Tempest*: Parallelism in Characters and Situations', *JEGP*, xiv, 1915, 63–74.

416 *Bibliography*

GOLDSMITH, R. H. 'The Wild Man on the English Stage', *MLR*, liii, 1958, 481–91.

GRAY, H. D. 'The Sources of *The Tempest*', *MLN*, 35, 1920, 321–30.

GRAY, H. D. 'Some Indications that *The Tempest* was revised', *SPhil*, xxviii, 1921, 129–40.

GRÉGOIRE, H. 'The Bulgarian Origins of *The Tempest*', *SPhil*, xxxvii, 1940, 236–56.

HANKINS, J. E. 'Caliban the Bestial Man', *PMLA*, lxii, 1947, 793–801.

HODGEN, M. T. 'Montaigne and Shakespeare Again', *Huntington Lib. Q.*, xvi, 1952, 23–42.

JAMES, D. G. *The Dream of Prospero*, Oxford, 1967.

JOHNSON, W. S. 'The Genesis of Ariel', *ShQ*, ii, 1951, 205–10.

KNIGHT, G. W. *The Shakespearean Tempest*, 1932.

KNOX, B. '*The Tempest* and the Ancient Comic Tradition', *Eng. Inst. Essays, 1954*, 1955.

KOSZUL, A. 'Ariel', *E Studies*, xix, 1937, 200–4.

KUHL, E. P. 'Shakespeare and the Founders of America: *The Tempest*', *PhilQ*, xli, 1962, 133–46.

LAWRENCE, W. J. 'The Masque in *The Tempest*', *Fortnightly Review*, June 1920.

LAWRENCE, W. J. 'Shakespeare avrebbe tratto . . . *La Tempestà* da scenari italiani', *Le Lettere*, 1923, ii, 3.

LEA, K. M. *Italian Popular Comedy*, 2 vols, Oxford, 1934 (vol. II includes translations of scenarii).

LEE, SIR S. 'Caliban's Visits to England', *Cornhill*, n.s. 34, 1913, 333–45.

LONGWORTH-CHAMBRUN, C. 'Influences françaises dans *La Tempête* de Shakespeare', *Rev. de Lit. Comp.*, 1925, 37–59.

MCPEEK, J. A. S. 'The Genesis of Caliban', *PhilQ*, xxv, 1946, 378–81.

NEWELL, W. W. 'Sources of Shakespeare's *Tempest*', *Journ. of Amer. Folk-lore*, Boston, xvi, 1913, 234–57.

NICOLL, J. R. A. *Stuart Masques and the Renaissance Stage*, 1937.

NOSWORTHY, J. M. 'The Narrative Sources of *The Tempest*', *RES*, xxiv, 1948, 281–4.

NUTTALL, A. D. *Two Concepts of Allegory*, 1967.

PEROTT, J. DE 'The Probable Source of the Plot of Shakespeare's Tempest', *Clark U. Lib. Pubns*, Worcester, Mass., vol. i, 8, Oct. 1905.

PEROTT, J. DE. 'Die Magalonen- und die Sturmfabel', *ShJb*, xlvii, 1911, 128–31.

REA, J. D. 'A Source for the Storm in *The Tempest*', *MPhil*, xvii, 1919, 279–86.

REED, T. T. 'The Probable Origin of Ariel', *ShQ*, xi, 1960, 61–8.

SARRAZIN, G. 'Neue italienische Skizzen zu Shakespeare', *ShJb*, xlii, 1906, 179–86.

SISSON, C. J. 'The Magic of Prospero', *Sh Survey 11*, 1958, 70–7.

STILL, C. *Shakespeare's Mystery Play*, 1921.

STILL, C. *The Timeless Theme*, 1936.

THALER, A. 'Caliban and Spenser', *Sh. Ass. Bull.*, x, 1935, 203.

THOMAS, SIR H. *Spanish and Portuguese Romances of Chivalry*, 1920.

WARD, SIR A. W. 'Shakespeare and the Makers of Virginia', *Proc. Brit. Acad.*, 1919.

WEST, R. 'Ceremonial Magic in *The Tempest*', in *Shakespeare and the Outer Mystery*, U. of Kentucky, Lexington, 1968.

ZIMBARDO, R. 'Form and Disorder in *The Tempest*', *ShQ*, xiv, 1963, 49–56.

INDEX TO INTRODUCTIONS
AND CONCLUSION